Ain't Gonna
Let Nobody
Turn Me
Round

RICHARD A. COUTO

Ain't Gonna Let Nobody Turn Me Round

The Pursuit of
Racial Justice
in the Rural
South

Temple University Press   Philadelphia

Temple University Press, Philadelphia 19122
Copyright © 1991 by Temple University.
All rights reserved. Published 1991
Printed in the United States of America

The paper used in this publication meets the minimum
requirements of American National Standard for
Information Sciences—Permanence of Paper for Printed
Library Materials, ANSI Z39.48-1984 ⊗

Library of Congress Cataloging-in-Publication Data
Couto, Richard A., 1941–
Ain't gonna let nobody turn me round : the pursuit of racial justice in the
rural South / Richard A. Couto.
p.   cm.
Includes bibliographical references.
ISBN 0-87722-806-X
1. Afro-Americans—Civil rights—Southern States.   2. Afro-Americans—
Southern States—Economic conditions.   3. Afro-Americans—Southern
States—Social conditions.   4. Southern States—Race relations.
5. Southern States—Rural conditions.   6. Afro-Americans—Southern
States—Interviews.   I. Title.
E185.92.C68   1991
976'.00496073–dc20   90-20645

For Square

*This is largely the story of the pursuit of justice
of his generation that will pass too soon.*

For Barbara

*I hope that her generation finds in these words
and events a starting point for their
own pursuit of justice.*

Contents

Acknowledgments

Among the motivations that kept me going through the long and often lonely effort of writing this book was the indebtedness I felt to the many people who helped me and the anticipation of saying "Thank you."

First and foremost, it is obvious that there would be no book without the interviews. I thank the many people I interviewed for their time, patience, and trust. I never worked on this book without the words of Bill Saunders echoing in my mind. "I believe that whites do a good job at documenting what they cover about blacks. I have problems with how they interpret what they've documented."

His gentle chiding was itself an echo of the sentiments of Thomas Hall. Hall, born in slavery in Orange County, North Carolina, angrily recounted for a white interviewer of the Federal Writers' Project in the 1930s the lack of planning for the freedpeople and their transition from slaves to wage laborers. Finally, he directed that anger at his interviewer.

> You are going around to get a story of slavery conditions and the persecutions of negroes before the civil war and the economic conditions concerned them since that war. You should have known before this late day all about that. Are you going to help us? No! You are only helping yourself. You say that my story may be put into a book, that you are from the Federal Writers' Project. Well, the negro will not get anything out of it, no matter where you are from. . . . No matter where you are from I don't want you to write my story cause the white folks have been and are now and always will be against the negro.[1]

I am grateful for the willingness of the narrators to set aside sentiments such as Thomas Hall's, which I came to understand and appreciate more and more. The people I interviewed not only shared their experiences and views with me but explained their significance and patiently filled in the gaps in my information, knowledge, and understanding. They illuminated my biases, gently, and helped me to deal with some of them. I hope the book adequately re-presents the important lessons they provided me.

The people I interviewed placed a great deal of trust in me. Tom Ishmael even interrupted his interview with me to ask: "We've got friends but we also got enemies who are still working against us. Do you have anything to show you are who you say?" I had no conclusive proof of my intention, but he agreed to continue anyway. There was risk of reprisal just as there was risk of misinterpretation and misrepresentation, and the narrators assumed them for my benefit. I am very grateful for that trust.

The people I interviewed provided me an example as well as information. I have worked hard to see that this book measures up to the standard they set for me in their lives and efforts. I am particularly indebted to Square Mormon, a resident, organizer, and leader in Fayette County, Tennessee. Square provided my first insight into the extraordinary dimensions of the human experiences of rural southern black people. This book is dedicated to him.

Several research assistants helped me greatly during the course of this work. Steven Downey, Terry Meng, Karen Baker, and John Baker, especially, helped me gather interviews. James Richmond and Edgar Halphen helped me with the research for Part II. Jonathon Simon provided me with invaluable assistance. From problems with computer software to problems with conceptualization and clarity, Jon dedicated himself to this work as if it were his own. I am grateful also to the staff of the various archives and libraries that I mention in the references.

Several foundations and agencies provided me with financial assistance for this work. The Werner-Gren Foundation for Anthropological Research and the Commonwealth Fund provided me support very early, which encouraged me to undertake this task in earnest. They have been patient with me as the project grew larger but no closer to completion. The Ford Foundation provided support as I was completing the project, and I am grateful to Alice O'Connor, Charles V. Hamilton, and Leslie Dunbar for their assistance. The Lyndhurst Foundation, Dean Russell Hamilton of the University Research Council, and Vice Chancellor Roscoe R. Robinson also provided me with financial support.

I benefited from extraordinary help of several scholars. Peter New and Thomas May, in particular, provided me the interviews they conducted with staff members of the Office of Health Affairs. I use the interviews in Chapter 8, and I know of few instances of such generosity among researchers. Patricia Sullivan offered me encouragement by her careful reading of the manuscript in its late stages and suggestions that sharpened the book's analysis considerably. Theodore and Dale Rosengarten gave me encouragement along the way and hard-headed and sound advice at the end. Jacquelyn Hall also gave me criticism and encouragement. Herbert Aptheker, Lewis Baldwin, Dan Blumenthal, M.D., Phil Brown, David Colby, Bruce Cooperstein, John Egerton, Jimmie Franklin, Jan Fritz, David Garrow, Dewey Grantham, Colin Greer, Erwin Hargrove, David Montgomery, Edward O'Neil, Julie Saville, Steve Suitts, Shinobu Uesugi, and Quentin Young, M.D., all encouraged and assisted me at different points along the way.

Kelen Taylor processed and edited the interviews and most of the manuscript. Her dedication and efficiency are remembered kindly. Timothy Hillhouse, Denise Overton, Marjorie Seward, and JoAnne Egbunine also processed the manuscript in its later stages with great dedication. Stanley H. Rice provided photographs of the Farm Security Administration taken in Haywood County. The Institute for Southern Studies graciously granted permission to use material from an article in *Southern Exposure* in Chapter 1. The editors at Temple University Press, Michael Ames and Richard Gilbertie, as well as Barbara Reitt, assisted me greatly when my themes and syntax wandered.

My wife, Took, displayed extraordinary patience, understanding, and forgiveness as I permitted this book to make extraordinary demands on me and us. I am very grateful.

I am pleased to share with these people, and many others who are not named, credit for all that is good and accurate in this book. Errors of fact and interpretation, as well as the book's limits, are mine, solely.

Prologue

Blessed are they who hunger and thirst for justice,

for they shall be satisfied.

Matthew 3:6

Introduction

For a century the conditions of African Americans in the rural South measured the extremes of economic inequality and political repression in America. In the 1960s the federal government moved to catch up with the civil rights movement to reduce these extremes. The legislation and programs of the Great Society expressed in specific but partial terms the grand vision of democratic equality and human dignity that the civil rights movement inspired. Some people merged the movement into services and dared to make programs from dreams. This book is about such people in four separate rural, southern, poor, predominantly African American communities. They conducted voter-registration efforts, integrated schools, conducted economic boycotts, and lived with fear of violent reprisals during the civil rights movement. When the federal government offered assistance, they extended their movement work into the development of community health centers. Their health centers, no less than their civil rights efforts, gained national and international acclaim. The centers addressed health needs in the context of poverty and new equality. They provided a range of services, including nutrition, home repair, and improved water quality, that redefined health care. Several evaluations demonstrate the centers' success as health reforms.[1] The emphasis here is on the health centers as an extension of the movement to acquire civil rights and on the people who linked them.

The people in this book also continued a century-long succession of efforts to redress the economic deprivation and political repression of African Americans that was an antecedent of the civil rights movement. They represent the ordinary people who carry out large social movements of change and who bear the burdens of oppressive economic and political arrangements. The names of the people in this book will be unfamiliar to most readers. They are men and women, young and old, white and black, articulate and hesitant to talk, charismatic and unassuming, and native and "brought on," who are largely indistinguishable by appearance and position

3

from the other men and women in each of their communities. What distinguishes them is that they lived at a time of profound change in their nation and communities and took extraordinary steps, sometimes at great risk to themselves, to introduce change where they lived. These people, like people before them whose names are largely unrecorded, dealt personally and as effectively as possible with the intractable problems of poverty and racial inequality in America. If the American political body has a soul, these people express it.

Despite the need, importance, and success of these health centers, the decade of the 1980s saw one of them close for several years and all of their services reduced. The reaction of the Reagan administration to social programs of the 1960s and 1970s went beyond cutbacks in services. Who controlled the remaining and reduced programs was also important. Three of the four centers still operate only because control has passed from the people who started them to others who invest less political significance in them. In this regard also, the health centers, as reforms, had antecedents. They resemble previous federal efforts of Reconstruction and the New Deal that started with a breadth of vision imparted by preceding social movements but then moved from reform, to retreat, and then to reaction.

These earlier federal efforts and social movements nurtured the origins of the civil rights movement, including the development of health centers, in each of these four counties. This book shows how. It is about a set of model federal programs, their relation to social movements for democratic equality and human dignity, the people who conducted both the programs and movement locally, and the impact of previous programs and movements on them.

The Plan of the Book

The three sections of the book examine related change efforts in distinct ways. Part I recounts events in each of four communities in the words of the local leaders. Part II portrays four elements of race relations over the course of a century that are the origins and the context of the narratives of Part I. Finally, Part III offers generalizations about change from the material of the first two sections.

Each chapter of Part I deals with one of the four communities, the movement for civil rights there and the establishment and conduct of its health center. The chapters begin with events and conditions in the 1930s when the oldest of the narrators were young men and women. Chapter 1 deals with Haywood County, Tennessee, and traces the voter-registration effort, school desegregation efforts, and the health center back to the Resettlement Administration's program in that county during the New Deal. Chapter 2 recounts events in Lowndes County, Alabama, with special emphasis on the Selma-to-Montgomery march, political organizations, and political change in the county, and the changing role of the federal government in its support of the health services. New Deal programs and labor organizing efforts in the 1930s were important here as well. The development of the Lee County Co-operative Clinic in Marianna, Arkansas, as Chapter 3 explains, stimulated a great deal of political and economic change that occurred in a short period of time. The center was the most controversial War on Poverty program in Arkansas and among the most controversial health centers of the Office of Health Affairs. Chapter 4 deals with the Sea Island Comprehensive Health Care Corporation. Johns Island, where the main operation was located, was a cradle of leadership for Reconstruction and the civil rights movement.

Three of the communities played prominent roles in the civil rights movement. Citizenship Schools, developed on Johns Island, spread throughout the South from 1956 to 1964 and provided training for tens of thousands of African American southerners who had been stymied in their efforts to vote by literacy tests. Haywood County residents conducted one of the first major efforts to register African American voters in the rural South, incurred particularly severe reprisals, and presented the Kennedy administration its first civil rights problem. Local leaders in Lowndes County, Alabama, organized an independent political party in the aftermath of the Selma March in 1965. Their success and their party's symbol, the black panther, inspired other African Americans to organize their resources and use them to promote change. The community health center in Lee County became a contested and celebrated model of the War on Poverty precisely because it was a source of the political and economic changes that had occurred earlier in the other communities.[2]

These chapters depend almost exclusively on interviews that I conducted in each community. They are edited and organized to resemble a conversation among several people, whom I interviewed separately. Their conversation narrates local events and conditions. These narratives explain that the community health centers were needed; how they came about; who opposed them; what they did for the people who served in them and the people whom they served; the relationship of local leaders with federal officials; and the backgrounds and motivating experiences of the narrators. These narratives take us beyond the health centers as health care reform to issues of democratic equality and human dignity.

In this way the health centers resemble previous efforts to address these same basic issues, as Part II, the Elusion of Emancipation, suggests. The neglect of health care was only one way in which the nation eluded the promise of emancipation. Poverty, inadequate education, and the repression of civil liberties were others. The chapters of Part II develop these elements of race relations and the efforts to improve them. Specific events, taken from scholarship, archives, or the memory of residents, ground these elements in the four counties. These struggles to deal with these elements of racial inequality in each county locates the movement for civil rights, and other national change efforts, in local struggles. Indeed, these chapters suggest how national organizations learned and benefited from local struggles for change.

The result is a political archeology rather than a history. I have stood in four different places in the rural South on the site of community health centers and excavated down in time. There were strata that I searched for at each site: the civil rights movement, the New Deal, and Reconstruction. In between these major strata and uniting them, at one or several of the sites, I found, unexpectedly, evidence of schools, land-acquisition efforts, and labor organizing. In each place, at different times, I found three agents of change: local leaders, assisting organizations, and federal agencies. What makes this study a political archeology is the effort to relate these strata and change efforts as foundations on which later change agents built. Those readers seeking a broad history of the civil rights movement or of Reconstruction should look to a number of excellent works. What they will find here are the local efforts, events, and conditions that constituted the broader movement that these other studies discuss.[3]

The order of Parts I and II assume that history is connected to the lives of individuals who have a firm grasp of their proximate situation but a limited, though basically accurate, understanding of the historical forces before their lifetime. These forces shaped their conditions and their abilities to change them. I begin with specific human experiences of Jim Crow, the civil rights movement, health center development, and the voice of the people who lived them. Part II explains the context of the narrators' experiences and actions. This is the order in which we learn most lessons, from individual experience to the experience of others, from matters that we think are unique to matters that we learn are common. This is certainly how the matters in this book unfolded for me. Some readers, however, may find it easier to begin with Part II and then take up Part I.

Part III, A Politics of Hope, generalizes from the material of the first two sections about how we have made change in these communities and the nature of that change. Chapter 9 discusses three common actors in political change in each community over time: the community of memory, redemptive organizations, and heroic bureaucracies. Chapter 10 assesses the change in race relations in these communities on the basis of the views of people involved in the most significant change efforts in these communities in the past three decades. It interprets the community health centers as social capital investments, like the programs of Reconstruction and the New Deal that they resemble and to which they are connected.

Methods, Narrative, and Truth

This study began with my work with residents in Fayette and Haywood counties in west Tennessee on health care issues in 1975. Very early, Square Mormon instructed me in the civil rights movement in Fayette County and its relation to health care.

> The black didn't want to run Fayette County; they wanted to be part of Fayette County. They wanted to send their children to the best schools and they wanted to be part of the citizenship in Fayette County. Whatever the system of the federal government was, they wanted to be equal in it. . . . For a long time we went through a lot of suffering before we could demonstrate to the whites that these things were right. So we put the pressure on them through '59 up through the '60s up to '70.
>
> So these are the things that we thought were wrong. The people in Fayette County, when their eyes came open, they had really got sick for justice and they were willing to pay any kind of price to be paid to be heard.

His instruction guided me as I learned the histories of the struggles in other counties; the relationship of those efforts to landownership, including land reform measures of the New Deal; and to the development of health services, in which I was engaged. I began to trace the history of some other community health centers back to New Deal land reform efforts and found other antecedents to later change efforts.

Eventually, I chose four centers to examine in detail. I hoped that four centers would provide patterns and safer generalizations. Each center had to be in the rural South and in a predominantly African American community. I was also interested in centers with comprehensive services. Other studies had shown that community-sponsored health centers generally had more political and economic development activities that accompanied their health programs. So I eliminated church and medical school–sponsored efforts. The number of resulting centers is small, about twelve.[4] I chose centers in different states and far enough apart so that events in one place would not spill over to another through ordinary contacts and interaction. Finally, I sought out centers that were less known in public health circles and that other studies had not already reported extensively. Lee County Cooperative Health Center is probably the best known center. Having selected the centers to study, I began inquiring of people in the community who were the people key to the formation of the health program. In a short time it became obvious that the names of twelve to fifteen people kept recurring. Most of these people appear as narrators in Part I. The centers I chose are not a random sample, nor are the people. The centers are representative of outstanding and exceptional federal and local partnerships to address racial inequality in the rural South. The people in this book made these partnerships possible. The Poor Peoples Health Center in Fayette County, Tennessee, the Beaufort-Jasper Comprehensive Health Center in South Carolina, and other centers like them would be just as illustrative of the themes of this book as the centers I used.[5]

Each of the communities has the poverty we associate with rural African American communities in the South. When the health centers began, African Americans made up one-half to three-fourths of each community's population. The communities were overwhelmingly rural areas with grave problems. At least 40 percent of the housing in each county was substandard, and between 50 and 65 percent of African Americans in the communities had incomes at or below the poverty level. The communities had one-third to one-fifth the number of physicians for the population as the national average.[6] These statistics are serious, but the emphasis of this book is on what local leaders did to improve them.

Parts I and II attempt to save the record of ordinary people as change agents. This is difficult because, as W. E. B. Du Bois lamented, little effort has been made to preserve the records of African Americans' speeches, actions, work and wages, homes, and families. When they are reported in the historical record, they are often caricatured or disparaged. In contrast, Du Bois noted, "We have the record of kings and gentlemen ad nauseum and in stupid detail."[7]

The narratives of Part I tell the story of change in the words of those who made it. They differ substantially from other excellent oral histories. I made little effort to reproduce the dialects of the people I interviewed. I concentrated more on what was said than on how people said it, though I have made every effort to maintain the powerful metaphors that struck my imagination as well as my ears. I have edited the interviews thoroughly. I eliminated the repetition within an individual's remarks and among the segments of the interviews I included. I also reordered the sequence of comments of some people in order to integrate them into the combined narrative. My intention has been to simulate a conversation among local leaders.

After editing, I reviewed the manuscripts on each county with the people I interviewed. This procedure proved invaluable. They corrected errors in names, dates, and similar matters. They endorsed their edited statements or requested revisions to express themselves better. I generally acceded to such requests. They also most often requested that I present their words in the most grammatically correct manner possible.[8]

Narrative is central to this book's methodology. The methodology assumes that human beings acquire and impart truth by stories. The people in this book are presented as narrators of stories about the truth of their conditions and their efforts. Our idea of truth, including the truth that stories impart, depends on a tradition of values that stories also convey. These stories, traditions, and values are the history of a group that holds them together and separates them from others. The more marginal and powerless a group is, the more important is its own history as self-definition. The group's self-constituted history provides its members an alternative understanding of their conditions that preserves self-esteem and worth. That self-constituted history also refutes the interpretations about their marginal status, which privileged people promulgate, that assume the shortcomings and inferiority of members of a subordinate group.[9] Part I conveys the stories and traditions that sustained this group of people in their efforts to end their subordination. Part II develops their traditions further.

In all traditions and stories truth exceeds its factual basis. Marybelle Howe, one of the narrators in Chapter 4, illustrated this when she explained how Esau Jenkins would introduce people to the conditions of poverty on Johns Island.

> He brought everybody he could and he would take people by and show them the conditions of people's homes. Well, it's real hard to get from one place to another down there because you've got so many winding roads and things. So, they would sometimes pass this road and sometimes another. But he always had a story he told. He moved the story to fit whatever road they were on. When they passed a house, he would say, "I hate to pass that house. I hate to pass it.

"You know, a mother was home the other day with a little child nursing at her breast. She was sitting up in a rocking chair nursing the child. When the other children came home from school, the mother was dead. She'd been dead. Malnutrition."

That is a true story. A woman did die of malnutrition nursing her child. He moved the houses. But that is a true story.[10]

A Value-Ladened Study

Because values and stories establish fact, a narrative methodology is necessarily value ladened. It assumes that history is "enacted narrative," something of which we are part. As characters within our own narrative, we never start from the beginning but in the middle of things, and we assemble our pasts differently to interpret our present. Different narrative sequences offer various meanings of human acts, practices, and institutions. These differences are an argument, sometimes public and sometimes private, over our traditions, the people we should choose to extol, the nature and order of human virtues, and the allocation of the opportunities for a full human life to different members of society.[11]

Different social purposes are part of the traditions that influence narrative and establish different contexts or prejudices for what we know. They also explain why different facts are selected at different times or why the same facts may lead to different conclusions at different times. What we "know" about a problem is related to what we want to do about it. What we knew about Reconstruction for most of this century, for example, was related to the defense of Jim Crow segregation. What we know about Reconstruction now is part of our attempt to dismantle Jim Crow.[12] Not surprisingly, then, we have studies today that argue that less needs to be done to address human need at a time when the federal government is doing less in social programs. We can "know" enough about a problem to do something or to do nothing about it.[13]

The Carnegie Corporation sought to break this circular pattern of knowledge and action and to acquire a new look at American race relations in the 1930s. They sought someone who "knew" little about them, someone uninfluenced by the traditions of our enacted narratives and relatively innocent of the social purposes that our prejudices served. They selected Gunnar Myrdal, a Swedish economist and eventually a Nobel laureate. Myrdal undertook a comprehensive study of American race relations in the summer of 1938. In 1944, after seven years of study of American race relations and the conditions of African Americans, Myrdal and his many associates published a two-volume, 1,440 page study of "the negro problem and modern democracy." The exhaustive work detailed the condition of African Americans and concluded that it contrasted plainly and painfully with American democratic principles. Their condition represented a "dilemma" for a nation that purported to be founded on and directed by democratic principles of equality. Myrdal observed, "America believes in and aspires to something much higher than its plane of actual life."[14] American social sciences were also caught up in this dilemma. They purported an objectivity and value neutrality that Myrdal found a delusion. Social scientists could only be fair, and the first principle of fairness is to make clear one's assumptions and values.

Myrdal expounded a set of values that this book shares. These ideals—the "American Creed"—have a few, profound tenets: "the essential dignity of the individual human being . . . the fundamental equality of all men [*sic*], and . . . certain inalienable rights to freedom, justice and a fair opportunity."[15] In day-by-day practice, this creed holds:

There is nothing wrong with economic inequality by itself.

No American population group should be allowed to fall under a certain minimum level of living.

Negroes shall be awarded equal opportunity.[16]

Myrdal maintained that the "American creed" was so strong that most African Americans shared with white Americans faith in it despite their lower socioeconomic status and its agonizingly slow improvement.[17] Indeed, many of the people in this book not only pledged allegiance to this creed but were surprised when people threatened them for acting on what they thought were values everyone shared.

These threats suggest that Myrdal offered his American audience a too generous account of their creed. The unequal status of African Americans when Myrdal studied it, and today, represents a dilemma for only some Americans, not all. Some of us have found the means to either ignore or to reconcile with ideals of the "American Creed" the existence of ill-fed, ill-housed, and ill-clothed Americans of all races, ages, and both genders. Although we believe in some minimum social guarantee, we disagree on its nature and to whom it should be provided. The creed, we reason, extends to opportunity, not results. We assume that sufficient opportunity of employment exists or is on the way through educational opportunities to provide every American the means to redress need through individual effort. Those who are in need, we conclude, have not made sufficient effort to avail themselves of the available opportunities and thus deserve their condition. From the time of Booker T. Washington to present-day opinion polls, individual improvement through education and accumulated achievement are extolled as the most feasible political course of action to redress the inequalities of African Americans, and we can add other low-income minorities, including now the homeless. There are numerous instances of successful individual efforts to escape conditions of acute deprivation, and these indicate for us, like a flickering, fragile flame of candlelight in the dark, the presence of opportunity to match individual effort.[18]

This reconciliation of ideals of equality and evidence of acute need suggests a fundamental paradox of American politics, not a dilemma. American political culture eschews politics, public response to public problems. The strong ethos of individualism and the premise of abundant and adequate opportunity for the willing individual to attain economic success negate the public nature of poverty and inequality. In terms of redress, we ordinarily prefer private and individual action, not public, collective action.

Myrdal was aware of this paradox. He understood the American proclivity to avoid politics and to substitute individual interpretations of poverty and inequality for public ones. This substitution obfuscates the moral nature of public problems by treating them as individual decisions rather than social relations. He offered a set of propositions about racial inequality that helps identify it as an issue of social relations. The propositions also serve to distinguish the social interpretations of racial inequality from individual interpretations just as well today as they did when Myrdal formulated them. They are premises for this study.

> The Negro problem is an integral part of, or a special phase of, the whole complex of problems in the larger American civilization;
>
> The white majority . . . determines the Negro's "place";
>
> The moral struggle goes on within people [black and white] and not only between them;
>
> There [is] . . . a mesh of struggling inclinations, interests, and ideals, some held conscious and some suppressed for long intervals but all active in bending behavior in their direction;
>
> American Negroes . . . have eagerly imbibed the American Creed;
>
> [The] starting point [for the study of race relations is] in the ordinary man's [*sic*] own ideas, doctrines, theories and mental constructs;

The interrelations between the material facts and people's valuations of and beliefs about these facts are precisely what make the Negro a social problem.[19]

One finds among the narrators people who worked all their lives for the improvement of their political and economic conditions and those of people like them. Their stories contradict stereotypes of the passivity and incompetence of African Americans in the rural South that are part of the American mental construct that Myrdal found was part of our American dilemma. James Agee, in his account of sharecroppers in the Depression, judged that the most effective anesthesia of middle-class morality about the needs and deprivation of the poor is the rationalization that they are "used" to their condition.[20] Any semblance of acceptance of the condition of poverty and repression among the narrators was imposed by the difficulty, including violent retaliation, of doing something about them. When the opportunity came for collective action on their conditions, the narrators of this book seized the opportunity. As one of them explains, "It happened so fast. When the opportunity came, why it just moved us."

As Myrdal began his study, W. E. B. Du Bois was concluding his study of Reconstruction. Du Bois also reflected on the bias hidden in what Americans "knew" about race relations. All historians had the same facts Du Bois had when he undertook his 1935 study of Reconstruction, but they differed in their prejudices. Du Bois informed his readers of his "prejudice": "The Negro in America and in general is an average and ordinary human being, who under given environment develops like other human beings." He went on to tell his story of Reconstruction "as though Negroes were ordinary human beings."[21] He understood that these assumptions would curtail his audience and that his study was unlikely to persuade others who held different assumptions. He also explained, twenty years before a significant number of historians began to share the same belief, that the dominant history of Reconstruction was ideological support for the racial segregation and subordination of Jim Crow.[22]

Because the narrators and I share Du Bois's "prejudice," this book is ladened with the values of democratic equality. This term has several distinct meanings. It clearly does not mean that everyone has equal ability or should have the same amount of wealth. It does mean that the human dignity of every individual entitles him or her to a minimum standard of housing, health care, income, education, and nutrition higher than we have now. It also means that excesses of wealth should be reduced as long as there are excesses of need. Finally, democratic equality understands the public provision of services as the social means for people to develop their abilities in order to contribute to their own and society's welfare. Obviously, we cannot cheat in the provision of these services to any group without cheating everyone eventually.

Unfortunately, the largest portion of this country's history includes the denigration of programs of democratic equality that we attempt upon occasion. The negative terms applied to such programs in this study include: *radical* and *mischief* (1865–1876), *nuisance* and *folly* (1880–1920), *un-American* (1920 to the present), and *communistic* (1920–1970). In the 1960s and 1970s we reverted to *radical,* and most recently and surprisingly, we have adopted *liberal* to disparage policies and programs of democratic equality and enhanced human dignity. These terms hinder our understanding and acceptance of the public nature of social problems.

Without that understanding, our imagination of public solutions to public problems is stifled. Awareness of the problems of American life invites us, as it did Myrdal and the narrators of this book, to envision new forms of politics and democratic possibilities. Myrdal observed that his examination of race relations made him familiar with all that was right as well as all that was wrong in America.[23] From what was wrong Myrdal fashioned a vision of leadership and education combined with mass participation for social and economic change that would benefit the entire nation. It would

> realize in the highest degree the age-old ideal of a vitalized democracy. It would result, not only in a decrease in the immense class differences in America, but more fundamentally, it would effect a higher degree of integration in society of the many millions of anonymous and atomized individuals; a strengthening of the ties of loyalty running through the entire social fabric; a more efficient and uncorrupted performance of all public functions; and a more intense and secure feeling on the part of the common citizen of his belongingness to, responsibility for, and participation in the commonwealth as a great cooperative human endeavor.[24]

Myrdal saw in the New Deal a nascent form of this vitalized democracy.

Du Bois also found hope amidst the injustices that marked the relations of white and black Americans. He affirmed a faith in the "self-resurrection" of American democracy. He found in the New Deal hope that the American political system had acknowledged that redistributive policies are a legitimate and essential function of the state. He understood that such policies were beyond the abilities of the policy makers of Reconstruction to embrace but hoped that with the New Deal's beginnings, "long before the end of the twentieth century, the deliberate distribution of property and income by the state on an equitable and logical basis will be looked upon as the state's prime function."[25]

The civil rights movement ushered in a new round of redistributive federal policies. How they did that in four different places and the people who brought our practices more in line with our highest aspirations as a society is the story of this book.

PART I

The Pursuit of Justice

The narrators' biographies offered in these chapters entwine local and national events of the civil rights movement with local conditions of need and repression and with previous struggles to change them. The older narrators were teachers, share-croppers, and, in two cases, employees of programs of the New Deal. Their memories stretch to a time when people, like their parents or grandparents, were property, slaves. Their experiences and conditions in the 1930s influenced profoundly their attitudes and actions in the 1960s. Other narrators were children in the 1930s and 1940s. They attended schools that separately and unequally influenced their chances in life. Still other narrators were not even born until later. They inherited a set of conditions that they and others would change. Whatever their age, the narrators continued local traditions of virtue and of heroism.

The map below provides the location of each of the communities.

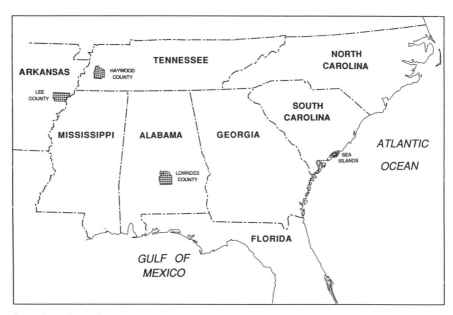

Location of the Sea Islands and Haywood, Lee, and Lowndes counties.—*Courtesy of the University of Kentucky Cartography Laboratory*

CHAPTER 1

We Lost the Idea of Being Afraid

Haywood County, Tennessee

The Place

Located some fifty miles from Memphis, Haywood County is one of two counties in Tennessee with a majority African American population.[1] Fayette County, which adjoins Haywood, is the other. In the mid-1970s, when the organization of the Douglas Community Health Center began, Haywood County had a population of 19,000 people, 55 percent of whom were African Americans. Seventy-four percent of its population lived in rural areas in 1970, and about half of the county's residents still do. Brownsville, the county seat, is the largest town and has a population of 9,300. Other towns, like Stanton where the health center was located, are much smaller and have populations of a few hundred people.

When the health center began, the median income of African American families in the county was $2,789, or 29 percent of the national median and 62 percent of the county's overall median. About 40 percent of the county's housing was substandard. There were eight physicians in the county, all of whom were white. All of them maintained separate waiting rooms for white and black patients. Haywood County remains poor. In 1980 the median per capita income of African Americans was $2,555, or 27 percent of the national median. There has been a slight population increase since 1970.[2] The health center's origins are in a New Deal program that preceded it by almost forty years and that supported the county's civil right movement in the years between.

The People

Dr. Currie Porter (C. P.) Boyd began the Haywood County Civic and Welfare League with the help of many others in 1959. He taught school, like his mother, in numerous cities and counties and eventually acquired his Ph.D.

from the University of Tennessee in educational administration and supervision. He taught at Jackson (Tennessee) Community College for several years before his recent retirement. He served four terms on the Haywood County Commission.

Jesse Cannon, Sr., lives in the house to which he moved when he joined the Haywood County Farms Project of the Farm Security Administration (FSA) in 1939. He assumed responsibility for his family at the age of thirteen when his father died. He raised eight children of his own. He was an original member of the community group that introduced health services and the clinic. Like many other small farmers, he began working in nearby factories when income from the farm was inadequate. He is now retired.

Jesse Cannon, Jr., M.D., was born and raised in the Douglas community. Upon completing his medical training in 1979, he fulfilled an obligation to serve in a medically underserved area by coming to Stanton, Tennessee, and the Douglas Community Health Clinic. He served as the first physician for the clinic. Dr. Cannon is presently in private practice in neighboring Tipton County.

Jean Thomas Carney was the first director of the Douglas Community Health Clinic and served in that role from 1979 until 1983. She is a native of Haywood County but moved to New York City, where she lived for a time. After her return to Haywood County she studied public administration, worked as a child advocate, and directed the development efforts of the Douglas Community Health and Recreation Council that sponsored the clinic. In 1987 she was elected to the county commission and thereby became the first African American woman ever elected to public office in Haywood County.

Betty Douglas is a lifelong resident of the Stanton community and participated in the FSA project, the voter registration drive of 1960, and the development of the clinic in the mid-1970s. She presently farms and drives a school bus.

Earl Rice was the first president of the Douglas Health and Recreation Council. He is head of the Science Department and vice principal at Haywood County High School, a school he could not attend as a boy because of segregation. In addition, he has been a Democratic national committeeman several times. He owns and farms land that earlier belonged to his father.

Tom Rice was another of the original members of the Haywood County FSA project. He lived in the same house that he purchased as a member of "The Project" and ran a small store near his home until his death in 1985. He was the father of thirteen children, the youngest of whom is Earl Rice.

Tom Sanderlin arrived at "The Project" within two years of its beginning. He lived in the project house into which he moved until his death in 1985. "Mister Tom" was renowned for his cooking both at the August 8th celebrations and at the camp that was conducted for the New Farmers of America, the segregated counterpart of the all-white Future Farmers of America. He was a charter member of the NAACP in Haywood County and widely recognized for his quiet determination to pursue civil and political rights for African Americans in Haywood County. He served on the first board of directors of the health center and played an active role in establishing health services in and around Stanton.

You're a White Man and I'm a Negro

Jesse Cannon, Sr.: Back in the early days I was trying to do better all the time, but it was hard. In 1936 I moved from Tipton County to Haywood County, and I was a sharecropper. I improved myself a bit, and I went to renting.

I had a situation concerning the rental check that the government was paying people not to plant crops. I made the first crop, and by the spring she, the landlord, requested of us to give her the check for reducing that crop. So I went to the officials and asked them about it. They said, "It's your check. When it comes, it's yours." They said, "You're entitled to it." This landlord didn't want me to have the rental check, but the government official said I was entitled to it.

So I got a card one evening, when I come out of the field, telling me to come to Brownsville to pick up the check. So I took the card up to the landlady, gave it to her, showed her, told her what happened, how I got the notice, and I wanted her to go with me over there so they could tell her who the check belonged to. I said, "If it's your check, I want you to have it. If it's mine, I want it." She said, "It's my check. It's my land, it's my check. You don't have no land and you don't have no check comin'." I said, "Well, I'd like for us to go and let them explain it." She wouldn't go. So, me and the other fellow that lived on the place, we went over to Brownsville and picked up the checks.

Somehow or another she got the word we went. I guess they called her and told her we picked the checks up. She left word at our house to come up there to her house. Well, it was about night when we got home, so we wouldn't go to her house because we knew she was hot because she didn't

Jesse Cannon, Sr.

think enough of us to go over to Brownsville with us to let them explain to her about the checks. So then the next morning, we decided we would go up there. We went up there and she set out at us. She called me a Nicodemus. I went out by cover of night. She called him a Judas, he betrayed her. He was her right hand man; he would carry [drive] her places and so on. She called the other man a Judas. Well, she wanted us to give up the checks, but we wouldn't give them up. We went back home and talked it over, me and my wife. And I decided since they told me it's mine, I was going to keep it.

Soon after, her nephew came by the house and asked, "Jesse, you decided to give that money up?" I told him, "No, the government said it's mine; I want it." "Well, I tell you one thing," he said, "if you keep it, it's gonna' cost you a hell of a lot." He asked me if I knew the boundaries of my place. Well, I didn't know how the lines went. He said to me, "Well, if you don't, you better get somebody to show it to you." I was under the impression he was talking about messing with me if I stepped on his property.

I lived near a lawman, a sheriff. We were neighbors; I mean, I borrowed from him, he borrowed from me. I went over to him and told him what the gentleman said and that he might come over to try to beat me. I told him, if he does I'll give you a holler and I want you to come and protect me. We were neighbors. And he told me, he said, "Now Jack," (he called me Jack), he said, "I'll tell you what to do. They ain't comin' over there. They ain't coming over there to mess with you. But if they do, you do like a rabbit. Come out the back door, come on down to my house. And I'll take care of you."

Then I had to think for myself, and I said, "I can see he ain't going to help me. When those folks are around the house trying to get me to hang me, I'm going to run out of the house and right into the hanging." I said, "I'm going to die in this house. I'm going to shoot as long as I can." I just disregarded what he said. I thought, you were supposed to get help from the law when you're in trouble. With what he's telling me, I'd be killed before I even got out of the yard. I'm going to run out to those folks!? Didn't make no sense to me.

So I just slept with a rifle next to my bed. Said, "I'm going to die trying. I'm going to take care of myself. I hadn't bothered nobody. I had done what was right, and they didn't want me to do it."

Well, I had to go up in her yard to get water in that old well, and after a couple of days I got to considering things in the proper place, and I said, "I'm going up there in her yard getting water and they could say I insulted her some kind of way. She is an old maid, and there were three or four sisters there, and a nephew." I started to leave the crop, started to just move by night, but I said, "To do that would be a bad mark against me in years to come. I might want to farm again and it would hurt my children." So we, my wife and I, decided to give the check up, make that crop, and leave the next year.

After I gave it up, a month or better, she come by the house one day, and she was telling us, "Jesse, before you got my check, I passed the road and looked at my crop and said, 'It was so pretty.' But when you had my money and wouldn't give it to me, I passed the road and looked at it and said, 'I wished there was some way I could burn it up.'" She was happy then, after she had the money.

When she left, I went on back in the house and I told my wife, "You know we were in danger when I had that money." I related what the landlord told me. I said, "She could have come here and set us afire overnight. The old house ain't no count, no how. It'd burn us up."

Then the landlord, she told me, in August, "I'm going to have a lawyer come up here, and we're going to fix up some papers so we won't have any trouble next year about the check." She told me one day, "Jesse," she said, "I got the papers fixed up. I want you to go to Stanton to Mr. Willis Douglas' office and sign those papers before him." So I went on down there. Mr. Douglas wasn't there, but finally he came about 7:30 that night. So I told him what I come down for. "I do not want to sign this paper," I said, "but I'm living there with that lady. I have to go up in the yard to get water every day, and I'm afraid not to sign!" "Well," he said, "I don't have anything to do with it, no more than witness that you did sign it." I signed it, and I went over to Brownsville to the ASCS [Area Soil Conservation Service] chairman, Mr. Tom Freeman, and I told him what had happened. I told him I didn't want to sign it but she requested it. So he told me, "Say, that won't work. That will never happen. That's just like highway robbery."

So the following spring [1938] I was on another man's farm, and I got a notice one day to come to Stanton to the bank and pick up my check for reducing that previous crop. When I got there to get the check, they told me my old landlord had my check. I said, "Got my check?" They said, "Yes." I said, "What's she doin' with my check?" They said, "You signed a paper for her to get that check. Said she loaned you some money to make that crop. Stated on that paper she was entitled to get that check."

I left the bank and took the bus or train to Brownsville and went to Mr. Freeman. I said, "The thing you said couldn't happen, done happened." "What thing?" he said. And I explained about the paper and how she had my check. He said he would have the whole ASCS committee meet and straighten it out.

So we met. There were five white men, Mr. Douglas, he was one, and me. Mr. Douglas said, "I don't remember your saying anything about not wanting to sign the paper." Now, they were five white men, so I looked down a while, and then I looked at him straight in the eyes and I said, "Mr. Douglas, you're a white man and I'm a Negro and I can't call you a liar and I'm not trying to do that but don't you remember how I come to you in August at 7:30 in the evening. You were late and I said that I did not want to sign the paper but I was afraid because I live on her land and had to go up to the house for water." I was looking him in the eyes. Then the old man looked away and said, soft as can be, "I reckon I do."

The chairman sent them out and told me I could get the check back. I said, "Will you get it back?" He said, "No, but I'll tell you what to do." So he told me, write to Mr. Wallace, secretary of agriculture, and tell him what happened. So I wrote, and sure enough about two weeks later I got a letter saying to come to Brownsville again for a meeting with the old lady, me and the other man who was still renting from her. Well, me and him got there first, and she came with her nephew and said, "The thieves beat us here." She called us thieves.

They told all of us we were meeting to settle the matter of the check and if we didn't do it, it would have to go to Washington. Now the other man, whose check she had, he was willing to give her a third for peace sake. They asked me how much I was willing to give and I told them, "Not a dime. It's mine and I want it." Well, we talked some more and then we took a break and the other man said he was willing to give half. Now that weakened my position and made me seem uncooperative and I was afraid if we didn't settle it, I would have to go to Washington—I wouldn't have had to but I thought I did—and I didn't have money for that, so I agreed to give her a third.

But that only made me more determined to get my own place, and when "The Project" started, I went down to sign up. I had a chance to own my own place and I jumped at it.

The Lord blessed me and my family and saw us through this. We got the check back and got our own place. This whole area of "The Project" was Mr. Willis Douglas's place, you know, the man who drew up the papers to take my check away. In fact, when we came on "The Project," our house was the one they had made out of Mr. Douglas's old house.

We Didn't Have Bosses Then

Tom Rice: "The Project" got started during that mighty Depression. It was like we couldn't get work to do, and couldn't get fair price for our farm projects. Cotton was four and five cents a pound, hogs and cows were four and five cents a pound, corn was thirty-five cents a bushel. Before I moved on "The Project," I stayed on three different farms. I stayed with Dr. Surrell in 1938, and I stayed with Ms. Hattie Taylor in 1937, and I stayed with Jerry H. Chandler. I was successful, pretty good. I done fair in those times.

Master Stanley H. Rice was the supervisor over "The Project"; we didn't have bosses then. The first year, our supervisor had a meeting, called us together in a meeting, and he told us we had forty years to pay for one of these units, but he said, "My advice to you is to pay all you can. The government is not going to push you for no certain amount of money. The government is going to let you live. But we want you not to throw your money away. We want you to put it to good use." He told us, "If you can't pay way ahead on it, then I advise you to pay three years ahead of schedule, and if you have a bad year, why, you still won't be in no cramp. You won't have to pay anything those years because the payments have already been paid."

So I had taken in his advice and I started to buy here in 1944, and by 1947 I had it paid for. I made three payments on it and paid it out. But I had a stream of luck. When I started to buying, cotton was five cents and when I got set to sell, cotton jumped from five cents to thirty cents, and from thirty to forty cents, and I was making good crops all the way from twenty

Fredonia Lodge Fife and Drum Band at the 8th of August celebration, about 1940.
—Courtesy of Stanley Rice

Officials and local staff of the Farm Security Administration at the 8th of August
celebration in Haywood County, about 1940.*—Courtesy of Stanley Rice*

FSA administrator with Haywood County Farms Project participant, circa 1940.

Program of the 8th of August celebration on the stage of the Douglas School auditorium, about 1940.—*Courtesy of Stanley Rice*

to twenty-five bales of cotton and all the hay and corn the barn could hold and I put it all to good use. I gave the money to them as I made it.

Tom Sanderlin: An old lady organized an 8th of August celebration to mark when we come over to "The Project" and got the place. Everybody would give so much and then we would all have a celebration. We would make a big stew. Everybody came by, you know, and furnished the tomatoes, green beans, chicken, and stuff to go in for the making of it. Then after we got it made, in a thirty-gallon pot, we would take it and give everybody what they wanted. We would give all the people all the stew they wanted to eat.

Tom Rice: We'd have music to entertain the people, the Fredonia Band and the Miller Brothers' Band, and sometimes we would have music machines [jukeboxes] to entertain the people. And everything to eat or drink was free.

Jesse Cannon, Sr.: Different families would bring different kinds of foods. We would have a program. We would have representatives from various parts of the country—even as far as Washington—attending our meeting. They would lecture to us and after the meeting we would spread the food and sit down and eat like one big family. And then, we would go home. We enjoyed that tremendously. We looked forward to that affair every year.

We did other things together, too. We used to work together cleaning off the roads and whatnot. We formulated a group that worked together. If something needed to be done down at the school, we would go to school and clean up the campus grounds there. And that was just lovely—that men could get together and work and beautify the place. We did that, and I enjoyed every year that I've been here.

I was happy and am still happy that I went ahead and was able to purchase. It puts some responsibility on a person, whereas if I was still sharecropping, I'd be looking to the "man" for whatever is necessary. But now, I have to look to myself to figure it out for myself.

Tom Sanderlin: We were special. The first paved roads in a black area, we had them. We had electricity long before other black people. I remember visiting my cousin who had kerosene lamps, and I would walk in the house and start saying, "It's dark in here. I can hardly see. Why is it so dark in here? Somebody strike a match." Of course, I had the light [electricity] by that time, and he didn't.

Tom Rice: I started the store in October 1947, that's when this building was built. I started a theater here in 1949; I ran it about two years. We had Floyd

Nelson from [radio station] WDIA and B. B. King played here off and on for two years until he left and got famous.

Earl Rice: Johnny Ace played the piano with B. B. King's band at the time. I remember Johnny Ace very vividly. I was very small at the time, but I remember him. Other people came through. Muddy Waters played there on weekends. It was just a total thing for the people in the community to come on weekends and let out some of the frustrations of the work that they had been striving with during the week—just kind of let it all hang out and get it out of their systems. I think that was one of the things that was very important.

Like We Were in Our Own Little World

Jesse Cannon, Jr.: Douglas Community at that time was totally a farming community. You had, up until I was in about the sixth grade, split sessions where school was geared around your farming activities. You were out during the summer months to tend the cotton, you went back to school for the month of August and part of September, and then you were out again a couple of months to pick cotton. It was like we were in our own little world; we had a lot of food because we were farmers. We didn't have any money, and we worked like dogs and we felt that was the way it ought to be. We were satisfied. That was pretty much the way it was. It was like we were sheltered from a lot of things that went on in the outside world. Because all the houses looked alike, everybody farmed, everybody had a hundred- or hundred-fifty-acre farm for the most part. Initially, they were using mules and horses, but then, I guess from the late fifties on, most of the people started getting small tractors. But just about everything was done manually otherwise.

Tom Rice: People kept their kids in school. They wouldn't keep the kids out for anything. There was always good attendance. The school brought this community up 100 percent. Sometimes we had programs inside the school. We had a few that were just exercises for the young children to speak and to sing or like that. I think they raised a pretty good little sum of money at those programs.

I really can't explain how important it was to own the land, also. It meant a whole lot to me. First, I could keep my children in school and train them the best I knew how to train them. When I was working other land, I didn't have time to train them, and I didn't have money enough to send them to school. It meant a lot to me in many ways.

C. P. Boyd: I taught at Douglas Junior High for one year. I guess it was natural that I would teach. I enjoyed my own schooling. We went to school for three months in the winter and two months in the summer. My mother taught, and she encouraged me a lot.

My mother taught for forty-four years, and for the greater part of those years, she had a salary of $25 to $30 a month; a month, not a week. I remember the time that she was making $30 a month and white teachers in Dancyville with fewer students were making $80 a month. My mother started teaching when she was in the seventh grade. She continued her education and eventually she went to Lane College.

My mother was a good teacher. She was a strict disciplinarian. You would need Perry Mason with you if you got in trouble with her. She had to be strict, she had so many students. One summer, we had one hundred students, which she taught. She had the eighth-grade kids get together and teach the kids in the lower grades. I learned more in the one-room school than any other place, including the University of Tennessee and Iowa State.

I did real well in grammar school and went to high school, where I ran upon a social problem when I went to the city. It was like a racial problem. This was an all-black high school in Brownsville, but the city kids had the same prejudice against us country kids that you would find between blacks and whites. We couldn't get into the plays. We couldn't get into the cliques. We were on the outside looking in. It was tough. As a result, I made low grades. I got Cs and maybe even a D and just one B. Teachers thought we were loafers, but we weren't. We had to walk a mile to get a bus. We had trouble getting to school. My father's Chevrolet would break down. The bus would break down. I came to school late one day, and I didn't know some things. I tried to explain to the teacher, but she kept saying, "Shut up, shut up." I never will forget that day. I talked with momma about that later, and she said, "Well, do you want to change?" I said, "Well, I really think I should." I finished my school in Jackson, and there I had the highest grades of any boy in the class. Right now I am president of the alumni association.

Jesse Cannon, Jr.: Let me tell you a little bit about Douglas Junior High School and what that was like. Of course, it was an all-black school. One that had as teachers people who lived in the community for the most part; some were from Brownsville. They were an extremely proud group of teachers, kids, and parents, and it was one of those schools where the PTA had the community behind it. The community would get together and have picnics and something like this to raise money for the school. The entire community was always behind those type things, anything that would raise funds for the school, because a lot of the things such as books and even equipment was not given to them simply because the funds were channeled in another direction. They always got the used books, the second-hand books, and quite often teachers would request new books and not get them. So the community would put on some type of function to get those kinds of things because they knew they needed them.

Invariably, when kids from Douglas Junior High School went to high school—at that time they went to the all-black school in Brownsville—they were the class leaders. It was really uncanny how it happened, so that I think it all started there.

Earl Rice: The original Douglas School building was torn down in 1977 but stood from 1939 up until then. The federal government built it as part of "The Project" and turned it over to the county. At one time the school was grades one through ten, and we had an enrollment here at one time of about 600 to 700 students. I can remember this as being probably some of the best days of my life.

After the tenth grade I had to be bused. Every day we got on the bus about 6:30 in the morning and went twenty-two to twenty-three miles to school. Back during that time it was not a problem to bus, no one fussed and argued about busing because only black people were being bused at that time. It was okay to bus us twenty or twenty-five miles past the white school to the all-black Carver High School in Brownsville, Tennessee. Many of my friends found it extremely hard, and many of them did not complete high school because of the fact that they had to get up early in the morning and be bused from home, and they dropped out. But I was determined to continue on, so I entered Carver High School and finished my last two years at Carver High School, grades eleven and twelve.

Betty Douglas: We lost a lot when we lost that school. We had a chance to see our kids go there and learn and develop. Kids today, you can't tell them anything. I see them every day when I drive the bus. I tell them, "Child, get your learning because you ain't going to go as far as I did. You need more of it than I had." But they don't listen. They tell me, "You don't know what's happenin', woman." But I do know what's happening, on that bus. They complain about my being strict, but I tell them, "If I don't control this bus, you will."

But there's always something left though. The school is closed, but the county still owns the land and we're trying to buy it to start a community center.

We Went to Start How We Could Be a Better Citizen

Tom Rice: We started the Haywood County Voters League in 1957. In part, we got started because we got to reading different books and reading Dr. Martin Luther King, and he had explained to us what it takes to make a citizen and what a citizen ought to have, what he ought to be to be a citizen, and without that we wasn't a citizen. And so we went to start how we could be a citizen and better citizen. Spent a smart amount of our personal cash money because we didn't know how to go at it. When we went to them, they gave us the run-around and gave us some of that for a year or more, and we couldn't get anywhere, and then we had to take further steps.

C. P. Boyd: I spent a whole year working on civil rights. I worked in Decatur County after teaching in Douglas. I worked there eight years and enjoyed them immensely. I experienced my first voting in Decatur County. The politicians sort of got to me there. I got a leave of absence and studied for my master's degree at Iowa State for one year. Iowa State was very different. Black and white worked together, and especially in the church. I experienced a lack of discrimination and prejudice.

The next year I came back to Decatur County, and they put pressure on me to buy a Chevrolet. I refused to buy a Chevrolet because the chairman of the board was selling them and he sort of decreed, under the table, that the teachers should buy one. I suddenly got a taste for Fords and I bought a Ford. Teaching in those days was a little bit like sharecropping; you just had verbal agreements. If the superintendent said, "You go to that school," you went to that school. They wouldn't renew my contract with my Ford, and so I left and finished my master's at Iowa State. I finished at Iowa State in 1957 in vocational agriculture. I came back to Haywood County then.

When I came back to Haywood, I went down to change my registration. I just had to change my registration from Decatur to Haywood; then I could start to vote. That was my position.

I went down, looking innocent, wearing a pair of jeans, a tee-shirt, and ball cap. I went into the registrar and told her I had moved back and I wanted to change my registration. The lady looked all bothered. She said, "You can ask the sheriff or talk to Mr. Moore, the county court clerk." He's a great guy. I knew him very well. I went to him and said, "Mr. Moore, the lady told me to bring this to you." I showed him the form and explained to him that I had moved back and I wanted to change my registration. He looked at the form and looked at me and said, "You'll have to take this to Decatur County. We are not allowed to register them here." He meant negroes. I said, "Why? I live here."

I wrote to Washington before I went and asked them, "What shall I do in order to register to vote in the August 7th primary?" After they turned me down, I wrote another letter. It was sizzling. I was as hot as a six-shooter; a little bit indignant. I had no trouble at all to register in Decatur County. They sent two FBI men out later.

They had a presidential civil rights commission that sent a man down here. Our sheriff, at the time, hit the man—hit the commissioner. The commission didn't have much teeth in it. It was more or less kind of a figurehead thing; it was better than nothing. The local paper had a big write-up. They were going to buy the sheriff a suit for his brave deed. The Ku Klux Klan was pretty active in the county, and the White Citizens Council. Among them, I'm sure it would have been a nice suit.

There were two major events in those two counties that really spurred black folk toward working for independence or some equality. In Fayette County it was the Burton Dodson trial. Burton was a distant relative of mine. He killed a white man who had attempted to kill him or his girlfriend. Anyway, he left, and he was gone for many years. I think eighteen years. They found him and brought him back to Somerville to trial in 1959. Attorney Estes, a black man, pleaded his case. This was a major event for black folk. They just didn't think it could happen. It was a great inspiration to see him, a black man, argue with witnesses, white men, and to plead the case in Fayette County. That was new hope.

Betty Douglas: We all went up there and was talking to Attorney Estes. He was asking the question, were we registered to vote in Haywood County? We told him, "No." He said, "Why not? Y'all have a right to register and vote." Attorney Estes was a wonderful man. I just love to hear that man talk. That was a God-sent man. You know, they always said that it has to come from the heart to reach the heart. When that man started talking, something just went all over you.

And we started from there. We all talked to Attorney Estes, and he told us what to do. We went to Memphis to his office, and he said, "If y'all want to register to vote, we'll draw you up a charter. See how it can get started."

Betty Douglas

Of course, when we went to pick up the charter, they beat the man who went, and our charter at the courthouse had blood on it, really.

C. P. Boyd: That was the only bloodshed that we know of, but people thought back to Elbert Williams. That was on their minds all the time. I was fifteen or sixteen in 1940 when Elbert Williams was lynched. It was like a horror story. Williams attempted to establish a chapter of the NAACP in this county. The story is that the sheriff, Tip Hunter, led the mob that took him, along with several business men. Ollie Bonds was kind of the brains behind the NAACP movement. They were going to kill him but let him leave town. His daughter is now a high official in New York with the NAACP. The Davis men, Elisha, Casher, and Thomas, were involved and forced to leave the county. The reaction to Elbert Williams's lynching was mass fear. After that, the desire to vote subsided. They scared everyone off.

Haywood County was a terrible place for blacks. You could get a beating because a policeman didn't like you. It was hard to imagine. It was awesome; you could be beaten for nothing. The police force was always selected from the most sadistic, brutal, ignorant men that they could find, racist types, to frighten and intimidate black folk. We had a curfew at night. They blew the whistle then; you had to leave town by 10:00 P.M. Nothing happened in particular, just curfew.

I was jailed for improper brakes. I never heard of that before nor after.

What happened is, I had a load of food and clothing going over to a community not far from here, Good Hope, to take to some people who had been evicted from their farms. A highway patrolman was waiting on me. I made sure that I stopped for a good 10 or 15 seconds at each stop sign, so they couldn't say I ran a stop sign. Twelve o'clock in the day, sun shining, he pulled me over. He said, "Let me see your driver's license!" I let him see it. It was proper. He walked in front. "Turn on your headlights! Dim them!" They worked.

He went behind the car. "Step on your brakes!" The brake lights worked. "Turn signals!" They worked.

He came back in front. "Windshield wipers!" Wipers worked. He couldn't find anything.

He came to the side of the car. "Step on your brakes!" The brakes went down to about two inches off the floor. That's the normal distance. He went to writing. Wrote me out a ticket.

I went to trial. They charged me $36.75 for improper brakes. They gave me one phone call, which I made, but I didn't have anybody there in five minutes and I didn't have the money, so they took me to jail. They charged me $3.75 for the ride from the courthouse to the jailhouse, about two blocks.

I was threatened by some white farmers, some local boys. I bluffed them out of carrying out their threat. I told the lady who came to me to ask me to leave town for a while to let things cool off. I said, "No m'am, I haven't done anything wrong. I don't want anyone saying I quit on my own." I really had a feeling that I was going to be killed. But I wanted to know what it was for, if it did happen. I said to that woman, "You tell them, they might throw me in the river but I bet they will be surrounded by the FBI men in less than five minutes."

They were foolish enough to believe that. I had been away from home, you see, and they didn't know what connections I had. I had a CB radio with a 102 hook on the back of my car. I always drove through town with my head up and my shoulders back. Looking with what I thought was an important look. I tried to look as important as possible. They would say, "That joker must have something. He wouldn't do that. He's supposed to be runnin', duckin' and hidin'. He doesn't even look at us or look scared." I was looking, but with my peripheral vision. I was watching everything.

The second major event had the same effect as Dodson's trial. The sheriff was killed by a black man in Haywood County, in 1960. The sheriff was a very bulldozing type of person, and his whole family had been sheriffs in this county for years—the Hunters, the Hunter family. Jack Hunter was killed by Willie Jones in a self-defense situation. Of course, Willie was not killed on the spot, which was a marvelous thing to the rest of us.

Jesse Cannon, Sr.: I didn't hear the man say it, but they told me the sheriff, the high sheriff, Jack Hunter, made the expression, "The first negro" (he didn't say "negro") "stick his head in the courthouse to register, will have his head blown off."

Somehow the Lord suffered that he got killed before anybody went up there. He went to a man's house, Willie Jones, looking for another man, Willie Jones. This man and another man he was looking for were named the same thing. And he went to this man's house who hadn't done anything. He and his wife were out on the front porch cutting okra. The sheriff pulled in, out of uniform and in an unmarked car and, as usual, he started cursing and raising hell, calling names, whatever he wanted to call him.

So the man said, "I hadn't done anything." The man and his wife tried to plead with the sheriff, and he just wouldn't pay attention to him and told him to come on and get in the car. So the man got up and went into the house. Shut the door. So the sheriff went around the back of the house and assured him, he'd kill him when he came out of the back of the house. The man got his gun, and when the sheriff pulled the back door open, he blew him up. He let him have it.

I didn't see it. I don't even know the man who did it. Said this man went to church, was minding his own business, wasn't bothering nobody. They took him on down to another county. They put him up for safety. They gave this man a trial. We knew that something had changed then. We knew something had changed when a black man killed a white policeman and he wasn't lynched.

I understand that they gave him only one year, but he didn't spend a day in prison. He worked for the man who kept the jail. But he worked for him in the kitchen. And he just died a year or two ago.

I was aware of one particular lynching in Tipton County. I lived not too far from him [Albert Gooden]. He had a brother named Tony Gooden who was an undertaker down there. They lynched him in the 1930s, 1936 or 1937. This man was running a place of business, and this sheriff, as usual, just came in and did like he wanted. He shot a man and killed him, but he died from a wound that someone shot him. And they told me that actually it was not the man that was running the business who shot him, but since he was running a business, that's who they took it out on. That's the way I heard it.

C. P. Boyd: But like I said, the thing that really gave black folk a little strength and heart was when Jack Hunter was killed. If he was killed by a

Dr. Currie Porter Boyd

black, who got away without being lynched, then maybe, you know, some legitimate things could be done. I think it was also a big thing for the white community to find out that bullets don't have eyes to pick out black folk.

After these two catalytic events for black involvement into civic affairs, we organized, through the assistance of Attorney Estes, these civic leagues. They were fashioned after the federal government.

We had a club with officers in each civil district in the county. From them, the presidents made up the executive council. It was this group that discussed the problems and made the decisions. Of course, we were autonomous. We fought and cussed over a situation. Once we settled it, that was it. This again gave black folk a new feeling of worth and dignity.

However, the fear still remained. The landowners and business men made such statements as, "Well, you can go vote if you want to. But, we've been friends all this time, and you know I've always tried to help you. Now, stay away from that thing. You're free to go. But, if I were you, I wouldn't fool with that mess. All it would do will cause trouble." You know, it was kind of hard for a fellow to get over that. So they kept a lot of people back through some subtle kinds of intimidation activities.

Tom Sanderlin: The time when we went to register and vote, the white people called it a "thing." "Ya'll niggers got that 'thing' goin' on out there. Ya'll tryin' to take the county over." That wasn't it at all; we were just trying to get registered and vote. They called it a "thing."

I thought that some of the white friends I had were my best friends in the world, but when I got my name on that charter, I'd speak to them, and they'd ask me what could they do *to* me, not what could they do *for* me.

Earl Rice: Because of the fact that my father was one of the cofounders, it brought on a lot of problems. The grocery store was thriving at the time, and during the crisis situation that arose after that, my father's business was totally cut off. He was boycotted. He was refused service by the Coca-Cola Company here in Brownsville and the wholesale houses here in Brownsville, which used to deliver groceries to him. His credit was cut off at the bank.

Betty Douglas: Doctors got to where they didn't want to wait on you. They would tell you, "Go to your black doctors because I don't want nothin' to do with you."

It was so funny. My baby was five or six when she had her first operation. And it wasn't any more than six months when she had the other one. The doctor teased her all the time, "Girl, I'm going to have to put a zipper in there. You come back here one more time, instead of sewin' you up, I'm going to put a zipper in there." He just kidded and carried on with so much foolishness. And then to change like that, he wouldn't see her because my name was on the charter of the League. I didn't get angry with the doctor, but when you lose the confidence you have in a person, especially someone who operated on your baby, you lose everything.

Jesse Cannon, Sr.: The way I understood it, those that were denied were those whose name was on the charter. Then they would have spies in cars taking names of people who were in line to register. Then they would encourage merchants not to let those people in line buy anything in the store.

C. P. Boyd: The first registration, it took a whole afternoon to register four people in the court square; all afternoon for four people. They had a lot of good delaying tactics. The literacy test was still in force in a deceptive sort of way. I didn't get registered that day. I was too far down the line. There were thirty of us, and they registered four. But that was a beginning.

It was summer. We lined up in the square, in the hot sun, with policemen around us with dirty looks on their faces. Someone put battery acid on the steps, and one of the guys sat in it and it ate the back of his pants. They really did some terrible things.

Jesse Cannon, Sr.: It took me weeks to register. I was in line four or five days. In the summer when it was hot. We'd stand there from morning till noon, from noon to the time it was dark, and come back the next day. They just wouldn't let us through. We'd have seven or eight one day, one the next day. They just wouldn't let us through. They wouldn't even let us stand on the grass or in the shade. But I made it. I guess we all was determined to get registered.

Tom Sanderlin: If they just had opened up and said, "All ya'll niggers come on up here, register and vote," it wouldn't been a bit of problem because they wouldn't have went. But when we found out that they were trying to keep the vote from us, then we went to getting the folks to register and vote. We knowed it was important. I knew by reading, reading the best reading I could, at night sometime. I knew what registering and voting meant in the county, but a lot of them didn't even pay it no attention.

C. P. Boyd: When the black folk began to go to register to vote, nine times out of ten, the white landlord sent them a registered letter evicting them from the farm, and they had to go.

What our organization did was to solicit aid from outside forces to help the people forced off their farms. Among them were SNCC [Student Non-violent Coordinating Committee] and CORE [Congress of Racial Equality]. The California CORE was our greatest supplier of food and clothing and everything, survival material.

Jesse Cannon, Sr.: Many a family that was living on the other man's place had to move, but we, having our own place, we weren't threatened about moving whatsoever because we didn't have to worry about that, and it gave us consolation to know that we could set still and still we could fight for our rights, and that's what we did.

Jesse Cannon, Jr.: The largest group of blacks at that time who were leading the movement were people from this particular community. They were the ones who provided homes for various civil rights workers or other legal people to have a place to stay during that particular struggle. They provided homes for them, and they knew that they could provide those homes without fear that some one was going to kick them out of their home because they were doing that. Not only that, they organized rallies and provided transportation. They did the legwork, and they organized the first massive groups to descend upon the courthouse here in Brownsville, the county seat, and they were the ones who stood there in lines for weeks to get registered. They could do this because they had their own farms. They weren't tenant farmers who, if they weren't out there in the fields, they were going to get kicked off the farms. This was something that they were doing, and they could farm at their own pace, so to speak. So they were the only ones who had the luxuries, so to speak, for doing that, and they stepped up and did it.

During those years I remember my parents being very edgy all the time. I know they took turns sitting up at night while sort of standing guard, particularly after there had been some bombing incidents in some of the other communities. I remember that they organized a community-type guard system, and they would take turns watching for any strangers coming through the community. Fortunately, this community is made like a horse shoe so what you could do was guard two points at night, and you didn't have to worry about anybody getting in. That's about all I remember about that struggle because that was in the late 1950s. I was only about seven or eight years old.

C. P. Boyd: After we got organized, I went back to Washington. John Doar, who I knew personally, was about second or third in command. I twisted the truth a little bit, but I told him, "Folks have rusty pistols and shotguns. They're raring to go. It's all I can do to hold them together. I'm trying to hold them down. But you just keep putting off this, and it's going to be catastrophic in Haywood County, Tennessee."

They picked up their ears, and in two weeks' time John Doar was down here. Because we had an organization, we could get our fingertips on people pretty easily. I helped them to meet at local churches at night with Justice Department people. John Doar came down, and he took the depositions.

I wanted action. I asked him, "Had these people in Haywood County been breaking the law by not letting us register to vote for two years?" And he said, "They have." I said, "All right, if I was caught with 10 gallons of white whiskey, would I be breaking the federal law?" He said, "Yes, you would." I said, "What would you do to me?" He said, "We'd put you in jail." I said, "Well, why then in the blankety-blank can't you put these men in jail?" I was pretty angry. They were breaking the law.

He kind of went around and said, "Well, you see, when you make a criminal charge, a man is entitled to trial by jury." I said, "So?" And, I'll never forget, he kind of knocked me back on my heels, and I've never forgotten that. I said, "So what?" And he said, "Well, say if we have a trial by jury, who's the jurors going to be in Haywood County?" I said, "White citizens." And he asked, "And what is the verdict going to be?" And I said, "Not guilty." He said, "You can't try a person for the same charge twice."

And then I calmed down pretty quick. I started thinking, "What are we going to get here, then?" He said, "We're going to try to get it tried before a federal judge or panel of three judges and get an injunction." I said, "What good is that going to do?" And he said, "Well, if we get an injunction and they violate that injunction, we can send them straight into prison." I said, "Oh, let's get an injunction, then!"

They called in twenty-eight of the local power structure into federal court in Memphis. Betty Douglas was one of our chief witnesses at the federal trial in Memphis.

Betty Douglas: John Doar and I went to Memphis, and we testified. I was nervous. Being with Mr. Doar, he really lifted me up. He told me not to be afraid of nothing, and I wasn't. He told me just to tell the truth. And when you tell the truth, that's all that counts. I could just go through those matters like nobody's business.

C. P. Boyd: Judge Boyd, I wanted to change my name after that, ruled in favor of the landlords. That was ridiculous! Of course, they appealed and took it to the Sixth Circuit Court in Cincinnati, and we got an injunction. That was the beginning of the end of the freeze on black votes. When we started voting, they had the federal government breathing down their collars. We had a straight line to the Justice Department. If I called there, they would accept the calls.

Jesse Cannon, Sr.: Somehow or another we lost the idea of being afraid of anybody when we realized that it was right for us to have our rights to vote like anybody else. We decided we were going, even if we die. So we went on into it. One of the officials there, he had some of we fellas that was interested in it to come to his house and talk. He was trying to tell us not to register. We told him that they register dogs, they register old cars, trucks, why couldn't we be registered? He said it was too early. And we knew a hundred years wasn't early. He told us, "Well, it just ain't time. I don't want you to be too hasty." But we realized that we had waited too long then, and we were just determined to go on.

Earl Rice: I remember my involvement well. For example, I was about sixteen years old, and we were trying to integrate the swimming pool so we could cool out in the summer and have a good place to swim. We were going into Brownsville on Saturday morning; just as we passed the red light and turned on Boyd Avenue, we passed by the National Guard Armory. The troops were there that morning for a drill, or something I suppose, and as we passed the National Guard Armory going to the swimming pool there were some rocks thrown at us by the National Guard. We felt at that point that we would be somewhat protected by the National Guard, but we found

Douglass chapter of the New Farmers of America. Tom Sanderlin, second row left. Earl Rice, seventh from the left, second row.—*Photo Courtesy of Earl Rice*

on that particular morning, they were the ones throwing rocks. They closed the swimming pool down for two years to keep from integrating the pool.

Jesse Cannon, Jr.: The first year there was freedom of choice, I had the choice of starting as a freshman as a member of the first integrated class at Haywood High School here. I opted to do that with the encouragement of my eighth-grade instructor, and that was how it all started as far as the integration was concerned. I was a member of the first integrated class, and my class was the first to have gone through four years of integrated situation. There were only fifteen blacks that first year, and the total enrollment was about 800 students.

That experience was one that taught me a lot. It was an atmosphere of hatred. It was almost as if you were living in two different worlds or two different planets, to go to school there. You got on the bus, rode there, you were put off, you went to school for six to eight hours, and you got back on the same bus and went back into your own little world. It was a type of experience that was very traumatic for some of the children, and they had some long-lasting emotional damage because of it.

Somehow I survived, and I think there were some things that I was able to do and a lot of other kids were eventually able to do, too, that sort of gave them some peace of mind and made them fit. From an academic standpoint, I had had good preparation here at Douglas and things just kind of fell in place. It was pretty obvious to some of my peers, even though they might not have liked me, that, hey, maybe this guy has something to offer. So I started participating in various activities such as the band, and we got into sports, my brother and I; it was not a bad experience by the fourth year. One that I think made me a different person. A lot of things changed because of us, and a lot of people probably changed because of us, and I'm sure we did, too.

C. P. Boyd: We've come a long way, and we've made some progress. We have blacks in the sheriff's department, in the police department, and folks get together fine. Like I told them in the beginning. They thought if the blacks got the right to vote, it would be a mass coup and that kind of thing. It was foolish. I think I'm truthful in saying that black folk don't hate white folk as much as white folk hate black folk. We are more forgiving and this sort of thing.

Now, Ralph Abernathy said something about the problem of race. The problem of blacks and whites, that's the real race problem we have. He said, "We hate each other because we fear each other. We fear each other because we don't know each other. We don't know each other because we won't sit together." That's one of the most true statements I have ever heard.

You know, when you don't know someone, you can have all kinds of fears. I'm not fighting the United States. I love it. My philosophy could be summed up in two beliefs. I believe in Christian principles and the democratic ideal. The democratic ideal involves liberty and justice and the ideal of equality. That summarizes my whole philosophy and attitude.

I Really Wonder What the People Were Doing Before

Jesse Cannon, Sr.: Sometime in the early 1970s, some students from Vanderbilt and Meharry came down, and they were talking to us about a clinic that was being established in Fayette County and telling us how what a grand job they were doing. They were trying to get the idea in us whether or not that we would like to have one in this community. Finally, they come down and set up a health fair here; I believe it lasted about two weeks. People could go in to be examined, treated, and different things. They even carried some to the hospital and directed them to doctors for certain complaints. They had a dentist there; he pulled teeth. And they helped the people out so much until we just admired it, admired the effort.

Later on they asked the question, "What do we feel that we need the worst down in this community?" It was suggested that we needed a recreation center, and later on it was suggested that we needed a clinic. Mr. Laymon Johnson, I believe, brought up the idea that if we want a clinic, money was available; we could get help.

The next step we took was to try to rent a place in Stanton and saw a fellow that had a building there; he let us have one there. We had to renovate it. It was a whole store, and we had to get money to have it renovated. We are thankful that we were able to get the money and a good job renovating it. Then we had a place that the doctor and dentist could come to. During this procedure we were getting these people lined up so, when they got the building completed, the doctor, my son, was ready to come.

Jesse Cannon, Jr.: My becoming a doctor was strictly an initial impulse. I graduated from high school in 1969. I had already received a scholarship in engineering at UT-Knoxville. Three days after my graduation, my mother suddenly died unexpectedly. My response was not one so much as remorse but of anger. I felt that there had been some foul play. My initial impulse was to find out what it was, and I figured the only way I would ever find out was for me to be a physician. So I promptly called my guidance counselor and told her that I was going to change my major in college, and that's how it all started. Of course, as time went on I started to train, and obviously I gained other reasons to be a physician. And later on I found out what did happen and that there was no foul play; just one of those things. I had no burning desire to be a physician, however.

When I was finishing up, I was looking for some source of funds. I had scholarships and grants in medical school, but I also got married and couldn't raise a family on those. A single person could have done well. I needed extra money, so I sold my soul to the National Health Services Corps, and that's honest.

Then when it came my time to be assigned, this site was becoming available. I started working with the site about six months before I finished my residency, trying to get it organized along with the community members here because my father was on the board and I knew all the people who were working with it. So I just started coming out every so often, giving them some pointers about things I thought should be included in the project, and

Jean Thomas Carney

then I asked the regional office if I could be assigned to it. They said, "Fine." So there I was.

Jean Thomas Carney: Thirty years ago I finished high school and I wanted to get away from Haywood County and never come back. When I left Haywood County, I said I would never, never come back. I did come back, not because I wanted but because there was illness in my family and I had to come back. But after I got back here, I saw a need, and I saw some things that I wanted to do here at home, and I felt that I couldn't get these things done living someplace else. The only way to get them done was to stay here and work with the people to make these changes.

My grandmother fell and hurt her hip. I came home to take care of her. I took her to the doctor one day, and we waited hours to see him. He saw all his white patients and came to my grandmother, after being there all day, and said, "Sorry, I've seen all my Medicare patients for today. Y'all will have to come back tomorrow." I said to myself, "We'll just see about this!"

I really wonder what the people were doing before. For instance, you have people coming in here to the health center that you wonder, how did they live with some of the problems that they have? They've had hypertension for years, and it's been five or six years since they had been to the doctor, and they are living with it, you know, and the physician looks at them and says, "Wow! This blood pressure is so high I don't understand why you didn't have a stroke." Or even people coming in with diseases that they have had for a long time, and the physician can tell that it's gone into a second stage or different stage.

They should have had care a long time ago, but they couldn't receive the care for a number of reasons. They just didn't have the money for the care, or they had Medicaid/Medicare cards and the physicians are so overbooked in the areas that they take a certain number of Medicare patients and no more. Well, then that leaves these people having to travel long distance for care or to find someone who would accept the Medicare/Medicaid card, and if they haven't got the transportation, they still can't go, and if they hire someone to carry them, it's going to cost them. I guess we see that in this area there is a lack of income. This is a poverty area, and by the clinic being here, there's no question about the need here and what the clinic is doing for that need.

A Dream Come True

Jesse Cannon, Sr.: I'm proud of his (my son's) way of dealing with people, I mean his attitude toward people. He has a nice attitude and personality. We raised him up to be like that, and he seems to be following it. In meeting people, he seems to recognize all people as equal and not have some he recognizes and some he doesn't, and that is what I like for him to do. I told him when he got started, I said, "Now, son, you do all you can for everybody." I believe he is doing it.

I believe and I hope that by the clinic being in here that it will inspire some other young people to try to prepare themselves to do a greater job than what is being done now, realizing that my son was farm boy just like a lot of other people. He was brought up a poor boy, a hard-working boy, and if he can do it, I hope it will inspire some others that they can do the same thing.

Tom Rice: I feel wonderful about my son being president of the health council. I feel like he took my teaching in. The teaching I gave him when he was a little boy. He started out when he finished Carver High there in Brownsville, which is kind of a training school. He finished that, and he started out with a band that was no investment. I told him then that the band wasn't all of it, he'd better finish his education, and I told him I believe he would be more happy with his education than he would with the band. He said he didn't have the money to go to college with. I said, "I ain't got it, enough to put you through. But I got enough to start you, and I'll keep you in there if I have

Earl Rice and Tom Rice in a scene from video production, "Generations of Health."

to work by the moonlight." And I had to work by the moonlight. I finally got him through. I feel good over it. I reckon there is many a hard day's work that I put in to get him through it.

Earl Rice: The clinic was working probably as well as I've seen any integration measure. Our staff was fully integrated. Dr. Cannon was the black physician. We had a white nurse practitioner. We had a dental assistant; the head dentist was white. So the entire staff was fully integrated, with the front office being black and white. Each time I went into the clinic, I could see the chemistry working and coming together so great and the people were working together. This is a thing fifteen years ago that I would not have believed. If someone had told me this would be going on in Stanton, Tennessee, I would not have believed it. But it was working. We not only had an integrated staff but the patient load was fully integrated. We saw large numbers of white patients, and that, too, I think, was a tremendous advancement over the last fifteen years.

One of the greatest things about the clinic was that I was a part of it; that I have been able to help and to work as hard as I possibly can to help the people within the community to make this a reality. I think putting these things all together, the clinic, as a whole, was a dream come true, and I'm proud of it and the fact that I had a part in it.

It was a tremendous difference. I was bused past one school to get to another, and now when you think of working together side by side, having the head people within the clinic's position, Dr. Cannon being black and head of the medical staff, Jean Thomas Carney, who is black and the director of the clinic, who took care of the administration of the clinic—with whites working under her—and working side by side, hand in hand. It was a thing that really was a dream come true. Besides, as I said earlier, I wouldn't have believed it fifteen years ago.

It Was All Unreal to Me, Like in a Dream

Jean Thomas Carney: I saw a complete turn-around relative to primary health care services. It was just the opposite of what it originally started out to be. When the Democrats were in, they were more liberal in terms of meeting indicators or, let me just say, the indicators were just in the experimental stage. They were there, and you completed the BCRR [Bureau of Community Health's Common Report Requirement] report. But nobody really put a lot of emphasis on the BCRR report because they knew as long as you were in a county with 50 percent of the people living below the poverty guidelines, your statistics showed a high infant mortality rate, the elderly population was 14 percent and above, there were problems with transportation in the general area, and the physician-patient ratio was high, then they knew you were needed and you would be refunded.

The BCRRs just became fearsome in the Republican administration. When Reagan came in, the attention was turned to the clinic indicators instead of the poverty guidelines, the elderly, unemployment, the infant mortality rate. It turned from those to indicators: productivity, taking in money, generating charges, and that kind of thing. They said that we are going to look at how long you were opened and whether you have met your objectives and what efforts you have made to meet those objectives. And take a closer look at those indicators. Charges must be 98 percent of your reimbursable costs. Your collections must be 80 percent of the billing. Your physician must see a minimum of 4,200 encounters per year. Your administrative cost can be no more than 16 percent of the overall cost of operating the center.

It got nasty, it really did. There was just one pressure after another. Then they started sending the auditor. He came in January [1983]. He came back

Author with resident of Haywood County in front of the Douglas Community Health Center in Stanton, which had suspended operation. —*Courtesy of Patricia Couto*

six months later. The mayor was on TV talking about alleged misappropriation and misuse of funds. They said the administrator would not talk to the reporter when their reporter got there. It just went around and around.

My thing was, I am innocent until proven guilty. But it never got down to that. I was not successful in getting anybody to take a good look at what was happening, that I was getting railroaded. At one point I had a lawyer looking into it, and he was finding a pattern with the clinics. Prior to coming to the Douglas Clinic in January 1983, they had gone to Chattanooga and stirred up a big mess and got rid of an administrator down there, a black guy. In Alabama they were instrumental in getting the black person out of there.

So they came up with a group headed by the judge of the county to look into the possibility of finding a new grant. And after that they decided that if the present board would reorganize they would work with them. There were no clear-cut guidelines; no right or no wrong to the situation. It was whatever Atlanta decided, day to day. You might wake up in the morning and they would say red is the color of the day and the day before the color was blue. You just never knew from day to day.

It got to the point where they convinced the board chairman, Mr. Giles, that it was to their best interest to get me out. He had to come to me and said, "I am going to have to ask for your resignation because everybody is telling me that is the best thing to do."

It just got to be too much. So I helped them get the new board together, and the new board met in November 1983 for the first time. At that time and at that meeting I gave them my resignation. There were thirteen people present and eight voted to accept my resignation and five, the old board members, did not.

It was all unreal to me. It was like in a dream.

Betty Douglas: You know about the clinic now. They had it open a few days a week, but it wasn't the same. The hospital in Somerville ran it as a satellite. But that's the way, you know. You get something good going, and they won't let you have it. They take it away.[3]

CHAPTER 2

The Value of Improved Self-Worth

Lee County, Arkansas

The Place

Lee County is delta land bordering the Mississippi River. It is sixty miles southwest of Memphis and due east of Little Rock. In 1970, when the health center, the Lee County Cooperative Clinic, was starting, the county had 18,884 residents, of whom 10,868, or 57 percent, were African American. The poverty of Lee and four surrounding counties attracted a unique VISTA (Volunteers in Service to America) project staffed by fifty specially trained volunteers, including VISTA's first physician-volunteer, Dan Blumenthal. About half of the county's residents had poverty-level incomes or less when the health organizing work began. African American families had a median income of $2,589, or 27 percent of the national median and 64 percent of the county's median for all families. Forty-four percent of their housing was substandard, and there were six white physicians in the county. These physicians acquired a regional and national reputation because of their rigid opposition to the efforts to introduce new health services to the county.[1] The county remains very poor. The economy is row-crop agriculture, predominantly. Marianna, the county seat, has a population of about 6,220. In 1980 Lee County's per capita income for African Americans was $1,923, or 20 percent of the national per capita income. In 1986 Lee County had the fifth lowest per capita figure of all counties in the Southeast. The population of the county continues to decline and is now about 15,000.[2]

The People

Dan Blumenthal, M.D., is presently professor and chairman of the Department of Community Medicine at Morehouse Medical School in Atlanta, Georgia. Blumenthal's comments are taken from an article he wrote that appeared in *Southern Exposure*.[3] He and his wife, Janet, worked as VISTA volunteers in Lee County after completing their training as physician and child psychologist, respectively. They were key actors in beginning the health center. He was its first physician.

Pitson Brady is the center of much that happens in the African American community of Marianna. His small auto repair shop is a clapboard structure with a cement floor; it accommodates one car at a time. It adjoins one of Marianna's two cafes. Between the men who lounge about his shop and the customers in the cafe, Brady is always part of a conversation. He is in his sixties, a quiet man and especially reluctant to talk to strangers or in interviews. He was on the first board of the health center.

Thomas Ishmael moved much more slowly when I met him than when he was a young man and a mover and shaker in events in the African American community in Lee County. His large hands overlapped each other as they rested on the top of his cane, which he needed to walk. His carriage and deportment conveyed a stature of authority that exceeded his physical size. His failing eyesight imposed unaccustomed limitations on him in his seventh decade of life. He died in 1988. His wife, *Lucille Ishmael,* was a VISTA worker with the clinic in the first years of its operation. I talked with him and his wife in the shade provided by his garage. As we talked, *Andrew Williams,* farmer, carpenter, and preacher in his fifties, worked on repairs to the front porch of the Ishmael's home.

Olly Neal, Jr., is a tall man in his early forties who served as the health center's first administrator. He speaks with a great deal of energy if he feels comfortable with a person and a great deal of reluctance if he does not. His exceptional articulateness and clarity may have been acquired from his father, who was a preacher. We spoke in Neal's law office, which is in the Neal Building on the square in downtown Marianna. Our conversation was interrupted by the business of conducting a law practice, phone calls, proofreading briefs and correspondence, and the like. After any interruption Neal resumed without hesitation the narrative of the Lee County Cooperative Clinic or his answers to my questions.

Theressa Ramey lives in a small frame house outside of Marianna, where she was born. Her house is completely surrounded by fields of crops. She is a neat woman in her sixties. She shuns conflict and separates the clinic from other actions that took place about the time of the clinic's start.

Sara Sauls served for three decades as a midwife in Lee County. She is in her seventies, and since her husband "passed," she has lived alone in a small two-room house in Aubrey ten miles outside of Marianna. Her quiet dignity is offset by her Ford pickup truck by the front porch. She swears by Fords and recounts with nostalgia the faithful service her several Ford pickups have provided her. However, she also remembers when occasionally someone would have to transport her on a large tractor through mud to reach a woman giving birth.

Trenton Trice is semi-retired from farming at present and lives on his farm in Moro. His voice is large and contrasts with his small size. His diction is as precise as that of a teacher of English. It is as if his body has special parts to project his voice and fine tune his diction. His expressions, eyes, and gesticulations express a friendly but teasing and mischievous manner. The fingers of his left hand are missing beyond the first knuckles because of a farming accident in about 1970.

Other people in this chapter are staff members of the clinic. They are *Mildred Broadway, Cleola Bursey, Eliza Dobbins, Frances Fields, Annie Green, Alice Morganfield, Lillie Mouton, Gloria New,* and *(Big) John Wilson.* The background and accomplishments of each of these people is important and integral to the success that the Lee County Cooperative Clinic represents. They introduce themselves and their accomplishments in their narratives below.

A Real Milestone and Opportunity

Olly Neal, Jr.: I had aggressive parents and grandparents. My daddy was not aggressive in the sense of always challenging white folks. His aggressiveness was to try and always do what he thought was best for his children. My daddy had come out of the Army around 1920 or 1921, and when he came out he had about $500 to $600. Through his first marriage and through the Depression years, he was able to hold on to this money, and he bought forty acres of land in 1938. Later he sold this forty acres and bought the eighty acres. I think it was easier for blacks to get land back then than it is now. He was particularly committed to doing whatever was necessary to see that we made it through high school and on to college.

Daddy got to the sixth grade, or maybe only to the third, but he had as much desire that we go to school as Momma did. My Momma started teaching school with just a high school diploma. She started college in the 1940s and got her bachelor's degree in 1959. My mother came from a family whose people were independently employed. Her father was a gin manager, ran a post office, and he taught school.

By the time I was in the third grade, they had sons in the fifth, sixth, and ninth grade. The schools in the Moro District were not as good as those in Marianna, so Daddy borrowed $300 or $400 and used half of it to buy a lot in Marianna, and the other half to build a house, a little three-room house. There was a high school in Marianna that had a fairly good reputation.

After three years Daddy had to sell the farm in Moro, twelve miles from Marianna, because we just didn't have the money for the house in Marianna and the farm. He used part of that money he got for the farm to buy another farm, larger and with timber, in the extreme southwest corner of Lee County. It was two hours' travel time from Marianna because you couldn't come straight out there. There were no roads yet. The water would rise, and Daddy would be caught back there, three and four weeks at a time, sometimes. We would come within about a mile and a holler. I used to have the loudest voice, and he would holler back. We would know he was all right, and we'd go back to Marianna.

We lived with Momma in Marianna, and Daddy was back in the woods trying to keep his farm and family together. That was substantial and significant, I guess. First, he built a new house in Marianna; second, he stayed back there in the woods while his kids went to school. So my parents' emphasis upon education was one factor that influenced me.

Another was my mother's attitude that neither she nor any one of us was of lesser status because we were black. She didn't like the fact that when she was teaching back in the 1940s, that she was getting $40 a month and the white teachers were getting at least $100 a month, and she let us know this. Or she would complain when in 1947 or 1948 the white kids were riding buses to school while we were walking two or three miles to school. She would never announce it because she was against fighting in principle. But you could tell that she gave her approval that if a white boy ever called us "nigger" we could whip his tail.

I became involved with the clinic for three or four reasons. First, Momma died in 1969, and I came back home from Chicago to be with Daddy. Second, I had been trying to come back south since I had left the Army in 1966. However, I did not want to come back and be at the mercy of the white plantation owners and landowners. If I was going to work, I wanted to work for someone black and not some white boy who might decide, because I was talking too much, that I wasn't going to work next week and not get any money. Third, I met Dan and Janet Blumenthal, Jan Wrede, and Coreen Cass, and what they were talking about was exciting to me because they talked about community organizing.

I had had a vision of community organization grow in me throughout the 1960s, and this was why my stay in Memphis, at college, during the 1960s was so frustrating. We never could convince a lot of black folks in Memphis of how important it was to unite in order to force others to share with us the use of the city's resources. Other places had started with the restaurants, but in Memphis we wanted to integrate the public library, the zoo, and the museums.

I remember specifically two or three other boys, and myself, had decided that we were going to the library come hell or high water. We were all in a chemistry class at LeMoyne College in Memphis, and the only way we could get books for the class was to ask the teacher to send someone down to the public library to get the book for us. We were getting mad as hell about that. I was eighteen at the time, and I thought this was insane. I just couldn't understand it. But a lot of blacks just did not believe that that was important, or that it was important enough to join in a boycott in downtown Memphis to force the city fathers to open these public facilities.

From that point on I began to dream about being with an organization that would put something together and make something happen, that would not be dependent upon white leadership but would not be opposed to white participation. I didn't want a situation where everyone would say, "Well, he's there, but the white folks are runnin' the thing." I wanted black folks to be able to say, "Well, you just gotta admit, shit, we runnin' that one."

I had grown more convinced that while there were many white folks who were certainly agreeable to the ideal that blacks should be treated as equals, there were not many who agreed that there was any reason to help black folks catch up, that is, that blacks had started out with a major handicap having come out of slavery and the Jim Crow years. I felt that what blacks had to do was to be in a position to stand up on their own.

We Worked Hard to Get the Clinic Started

Trenton Trice: The Neighborhood Action Councils [NACs] were chiefly responsible for getting the health care programs and clinic started in Lee County. The NACs began as an organization around 1969. It was an organization meant to allow people—blacks and whites, males and females, and rich or poor—to come together and discuss the needs of their communities. The NACs were the offspring of East Central Arkansas Economic Opportunity Council, the OEO [Office of Economic Opportunity] agency for this

Trenton Trice

area, which covered five counties—Lee, Cross, Crittenden, Woodruff, and St. Francis. It was through East Central that the VISTA volunteers came to work with us.

Theressa Ramey: Dan Blumenthal was the doctor, and he had to practice several months out of his car. We had problems finding housing for the center. This was pitiful. Besides this, we were required to have medical personnel on the clinic board, but the only medical people that we had in Marianna and Lee County were the ones who were fighting the center.

Olly Neal, Jr.: I remember in one instance that Dan Blumenthal and others had arranged to rent out the old train depot, but it was bought out from under them. We had other trouble like this in trying to rent out spaces, numerous times. We finally ended up renting out an old house owned by Lacy Kennedy, which we remodeled with the help of volunteer labor. Nobody really wanted to rent out an old house, but there was literally no other space available in Marianna, particularly commercial space. At that time, you couldn't buy or lease a lot of property downtown; that was for white people only.

Pitson Brady: Most of the doctors would not wait on you. You had to tell them how you were going to pay first before they would wait on you. I was never in that shape because I made enough money, so I could pay for my children. I was also able to help others. But there were so many that you couldn't help. Some women lost their lives having their children on account of not being able to get doctors. There were midwives, but sometimes there would be trouble and the midwives would call the doctor, but the doctor wouldn't come unless the people lived on some man's property who would pay.

Dan Blumenthal: I had applied for membership in the four-member Lee County Medical Society, because membership carried with it staff privileges at Lee Memorial Hospital. But by now the local doctors no longer considered me a member of the clan. By majority vote I was refused medical society membership and the use of the hospital, including its laboratory and X-ray facilities.

By mid-November 1969 the story of the rejection hit the papers. "Medical Society Locks Out Physician to Poor" read a headline in the Memphis *Commercial-Appeal*: "Dr. Mac McLendon, a Marianna physician, said the medical society refused Dr. Blumenthal admittance partly because he had 'agitated' local Negroes to demand more rights." In a subsequent newspaper story Dr. Gray explained, "We object to a group financed by the Federal government coming into the community and, in effect, practicing medicine as a group."

National media coverage of the Lee County situation soon led to rapid polarization of the community.[4] The pharmacists, the minister of the First Baptist Church, some of the large farmers, and other white establishment figures lined up publicly against the VISTA project and the proposed clinic. The black community, on the other hand, solidified its support. The fund-raising drive produced nearly $2,000, mostly in one- and two-dollar donations contributed at church functions. Attendance at NAC meetings grew. The poor, who had for so long been recipients of paternalism and the beneficiaries of occasional charity, began to realize that the Lee County Cooperative Clinic would not come into existence of its own accord, the way other government programs had. A struggle would be required.

Sara Sauls: I got involved with the clinic by being chosen as a member of the board for the clinic by the Neighborhood Action Council. They chose me because I had already been working in the community for twenty-five years as a midwife. I used to work day and night as a midwife. I can't remember how many babies I delivered in all during that time. I would go out at night in all weather—rain and mud. I never did get stopped; my truck just went through mud and water. I never would drive anything but a Ford. Still do. I really enjoyed being a midwife. Not a lot of people could get doctors around here. So I could really help people. And people really needed me.

We worked hard to get it started. I solicited the first dollar for it, and Ms. Ramey got the second dollar. I just went into the community and around to the churches to help raise money. Our goal was to raise $500, but we made much more than that. We got over at least $2,000 from people in Lee County.

Dan Blumenthal: OEO granted initial funding for the Lee County Cooperative Clinic (a relatively miniscule $39,875) in December 1969. We were pleasantly surprised and speculated that perhaps OEO thought things could be kept quiet in the Delta by infusing a bit of health money. If that was the reasoning, the agency could not have been more mistaken. In February 1970 the board of directors selected as clinic administrator Olly Neal, Jr.

Other Things to Do with Health

Olly Neal, Jr.: I thought that I was given more credit than I deserved for the conceptual design of the clinic and the health care program. I think I deserve credit for helping to make it happen, but not for the design. The credit for the design should go to the white kids who came here and helped. Dan Blumenthal, his wife Janet, Jan Wrede, Coreen Cass—Coreen was here with us for ten years—and also Steve Warner. What they were not able to do, and where I was fortunate enough to be able to help out, was in taking these ideas to the community and convincing people in the community that this was the best way to get things done.

We worked extremely well together because the commitments and aims were the same, namely, that there be meaningful participation—some of us called it control—by the patients themselves and the direction that their own health program would take. What we tried to do was to take the work of the experts and adopt it to our own needs. We recognized that the medical model of health care provided by super experts would in no way solve our health problems, but that the kinds of preventive measures and activities that people could do themselves would have more of an impact on the community.

We learned from the outside expertise that came in to work with the clinic most of the technical aspects that were necessary. Putting together a health center is a lot more than people simply standing around. You have to have the technical know-how to implement the ideas for improvement. We felt very strongly, for example, that a substantial number of the health problems of children were related to their contact with human waste. But how do you most economically and effectively design a sewage treatment system in a rural setting? An answer to such a question as this required more than street knowledge. In this instance we arrived at plans for the construction of outhouses. This is just one example of plans that required formal knowledge and training. In this respect Jack Geiger was such a tremendous guy because he had no qualms about sharing whatever information he had.

There was a common thread that ran through the leadership of the health care programs in the late 1960s and the early 1970s. It was not by coincidence that I visited Lowndes County, Alabama, and saw what was happening there, or attended health fairs in Haywood County, Tennessee. Steve Wilson in Lowndes County, Alabama, Tom Barnwell in Beaufort-Jasper, and I were involved in the management of health centers, and yet all of us had very little technical background in health management. I had a national reputation for the little background I had in health, but Steve was probably the only person in the country that had less than I did. We needed the contribution of these outside experts. The only major philosophical difference was over how a health care program should be implemented: to what degree experts and officials from outside should help to bring along the potential leadership of the community; and what size the program should be to allow effective community leadership to grow with it.

My position was that the people in the community who are capable of really running the clinic could take care of the health care needs in the community, as well as become active in community politics. [Pitson] Brady is an example of this kind of effectiveness. This to me was the essence of what the program was all about; not that health was limited to the absence of medical maladies, but rather that people were involved in the life of their community. That has so much to do with your head, you know. When you do something that you know makes good sense, then you get the pride of knowing that you participated in something and made it happen. Anything less than this kind of mental and physical involvement and control over the community in which one resides is not good health. The clinic represented a real milestone and opportunity for me to try some things that I might never have done otherwise.

Dan Blumenthal, M.D.: Neal's commitment to the community part of the clinic was total, and his organizational efforts on its behalf, tireless. He talked to people about the clinic—what it was, and what it could be—in his office, at NAC meetings, at board meetings, and in the little country bars that dotted the county. And sometimes there was a political message in what he said: if the county officials did not support this clinic, then perhaps replacing them would have something to do with health.

Pitson Brady

Pitson Brady: There was a lot happening in 1970, running for office and voter registration, among other things, and I helped in most of these. I was not active in the community before I started on the Neighborhood Action Council. I had been busy helping to raise a family; we have ten children. We started the Neighborhood Action Councils in 1970, and I was on the one in Marianna.

Before 1970 I was farming. I bought land with my family around 1948. There used to be more black people who owned land than there are now. It's gotten to be now where a little farmer like me can hardly make a living. I used to be able to do well with a couple hundred acres of land, but you can't do that now; you can't buy the equipment, it's so expensive. When I first started out farming, about 50 percent of the blacks in the area I was from owned land; now there are about 20 percent. Most still own their homes, but they had to sell their land when the price of the land went up to about $1,000 or $1,500 an acre. Often when the old people in the family died, the children would sell. We have some partition sales of the land. I have been with the Neighborhood Action Council ever since it started. I knew we needed these things in the community, and that's the reason I got involved. A lot of people wanted to help to make this community a better place for themselves and their children.

I also ran for justice of the peace in 1970. I got elected, and I've been justice of the peace ever since then except for one year when they said that a white man and I tied for votes and the next time around he had about 20 more votes than I did; but I won it back the next election. There were about four of us elected that year, and we were the first black people since Reconstruction days to be elected to public office in Lee County. I ran because we decided we needed representation, 'cause we didn't have none then. We decided that we should have a part of what was going on; we didn't want all of it, just a part of it. People hadn't run for public office before this, except for something like the school board.

Concerned Citizens was the organization that supported us in running. They were already around before I became a member in 1970. Concerned Citizens was not responsible for getting the clinic started; that was the Neighborhood Action Council. But a lot of the people in Concerned Citizens were the same as the ones in the Neighborhood Action Council. Thomas Ishmael was another person who ran for county judge at that time.

Thomas Ishmael: I was one of the first blacks to run for public office in Lee County when I ran. I was awful fearful, but on into the campaign I realized that I had more white friends than I thought. I had to move my phone to my bedside, I'd get so many phone calls at night. And they would ask me, "Thomas, we heard you're running for judge. If you're elected what will be your stand?" And I told them, "Now look, I have only one promise, and I can keep this promise and I guarantee it, and that's that I'll be fair to all citizens, that's my promise." Then they would ask my stand on particular issues, and I'd tell them. And they would ask, "Do you really mean that?" And I'd say, "Yes." Then they told me that they couldn't vote for me in the primaries because they were Democrats and I was running as a Republican. But they said that if I made it through the primaries that I could count on their votes.

I had a lot of support, but they took my votes away from me and the other man won. Some of my votes were in boxes that fell into the Mississippi River on the way to being counted. I protested and wanted a revote. But at this time my lawyer didn't have much time because he was defending a man on death row, and he asked me to drop my claim, because I could have another chance to run again in two years but this was the last chance for the man he was defending. So I dropped my case.

Olly Neal, Jr.: It may seem strange to you, but blacks control the Republican party in this county. One of the more important features of the Arkansas political system is that each county controls its own elections. These elections are controlled by a commission, made up of one person who is the chairman of the Democratic party or his designee, one person who is chairman of the Republican party or his designee, and one person from the majority party, which in Arkansas is the Democratic party. Blacks can't win control of the Democratic party, but our numbers make control of the Lee County Republican party easy. This means we have one member of the election commission. With one black among those three, that should guarantee us at least one judge and one clerk in every polling place. But we know that in the past they have stolen the elections from us in ways that are subtle and hard to take to court. For example, older black people simply did not want to challenge white judges, and they did what they were told to do. What we did was to put the meanest black folks in those precincts where whites controlled the polling process until that policy changed.

Dan Blumenthal, M.D.: The appearance of a black slate of candidates kindled racial fears in the whites of this majority-black county; at the same time it gave the black community a feeling of some potential political muscle. Then, in April 1971 the white power structure suffered another jolt when the Lee Memorial Hospital Board agreed to an out-of-court settlement of the clinic's suit demanding hospital staff privileges for clinic doctors. The hospital consented to the agreement when it realized it would lose its suit if it went to trial.

Three months later Quincy Tillman, a young black social worker employed by the county welfare department, got into an argument with a white counterman over what flavor of pizza she had ordered. The dispute grew heated and Tillman was arrested. In days gone by the incident might have been overlooked, but now the black community, particularly the Concerned Citizens, was in no mood to ignore further injustices. The Concerned Citizens proclaimed a boycott of all white-owned downtown Marianna businesses and declared that the boycott would continue until a list of forty-one demands, mostly for more jobs in both the private and public sectors, was met.

By January 1972 a dozen stores, a third of the downtown business district, had closed. Racial tension ran high and spilled into the school system when black students in the newly integrated high school demanded of the white superintendent of schools that the birthday of Dr. Martin Luther King, Jr., be declared a school holiday; that one white teacher be fired, and that a black teacher, suspended for excessive force in spanking a white child, be reinstated. Refused, the black students—80 percent of the enrolled students—walked out of school en masse and began a protest demonstration. The police and fire department arrived, turned a fire hose on the students in subfreezing weather, and arrested one hundred of them. With injury added to insult, the black students declared a school boycott that lasted the rest of the term.[5]

For the first time since the organized black political activity had begun in Lee County, violence reared its ugly head. County Judge Adams, driving a pickup truck, narrowly missed running over two black boycott picketers on the sidewalk in downtown Marianna. (Later, he testified that his brakes had failed.) When the two picketers went to the county courthouse to file charges, Adams threatened them with a pistol. Cooler heads restrained the county judge and he was eventually arrested, convicted of assault and carrying a prohibited weapon, and fined $100.

Subsequent incidents were more serious. The house of one of the boycott leaders was fire bombed; shots were fired at another boycott leader. In January the headquarters of the Concerned Citizens was burned; the fire spread, destroying ten businesses, seven black owned, three white owned. Another white-owned store burned a few weeks later. A white deputy sheriff was shot at and his house fire bombed. A shot was fired at the president of the school board. Miraculously, despite the numerous incidents, there were no deaths, no serious injuries.

The white establishment complained to Washington about the clinic's assumed role in the boycott and in the county's politics, and Washington responded by investigating and auditing the clinic and its funds, the VISTAs, and Neal. No wrongdoing was found.

That Was Some Times, Then

Alice Morganfield: The establishment of Lee County really got interested in the clinic in 1972 when that $1.2 million grant was available. OEO had agreed to build permanent facilities for the health clinic. All of a sudden everyone wanted to be on the board. We were starting to open the doors for people to be real citizens. Governor [Dale] Bumpers was under pressure from the establishment not to approve the grant if we were going to be in control of the money. People from Washington came down and told the establishment that there would be no other way that Lee County could get the money.

Thomas Ishmael: Some people around here didn't want that much money going through our hands. The co-op gin of the past had been a big business, but it had not made all that much of a difference in bringing about change in

Lucille and Thomas Ishmael

the county. But the clinic was a big money operation that we controlled even though we had struggles. My wife and I had both done volunteer work in the community prior to the start of the clinic. One thing I did was canvassing for people in office. Because I had done all that canvassing for white officials, I was surprised when these same people I had campaigned for later refused to serve on the governing board for the clinic. The law required us to have some of them on the governing board. I had worked in the campaigns of these white elected officials, not for money, because I didn't want that kind of payment, but for recognition as a citizen with equal rights. But when it came time to support and help us, they didn't.

They were against our clinic, and they tried to set up their own. And when I went to Forrest City, where they were organizing their own, so as to tell them what the law required, they said to go on, that they didn't want any part of it. What they did instead was to try to block the one and a quarter million dollars in federal aid that was to be given to us. This power bloc had been trying to set up their own clinic. But when they had gotten to the point where they were required to have two colored people on their governing board, they said, "We don't want any part of this. Let us out."

But by the time we had the chance to get the clinic here I had made it up in my mind that live or die, sink or swim, I was going to stand up for my folks. I could have gone to a private doctor because I had insurance, but I had so many friends who weren't blessed like that.

In the end we were told by the federal officials that we had done all we could to get the local officials to help us and to go on and form our own governing board. They finally told the people who refused to serve on the board, "All right, gentlemen, you've had your chance. That money is coming on here." After that they were told that the only way they could serve on the board in the future was to be chosen by the Neighborhood Action Councils that we had formed.

Olly Neal, Jr.: This grant would have made the clinic the largest organization in the community, and there were some folks in the community who were up in arms about this. One opposition group was the local branch of the Citizens Council, a group which in my opinion is akin to the Ku Klux Klan. Among other things, they filed a lawsuit that tried to kill the clinic. The Citizens Council had met with Governor Dale Bumpers three times, and it was the governor who was responsible for releasing the OEO money to us.

I remember how we used to have so many conference calls and how me first, and then members of the board, would get on the phone and talk to people in Washington or how our lawyers in Little Rock would get on the phone with Dale Bumpers and his lawyer. I remember one time when Sonny Walker and I and some other folks were meeting with Leon Cooper in Atlanta at night. We were sitting there trying to figure out how to get past something and drinking this whiskey and all of us getting kind of high. The higher I got, the more relaxed I became, and I ended up calling Dale Bumpers at 2:00 in the morning. Arkansas time! We had a conference call going at two in the morning! I remember those calls to Leon and him saying, "Now damn it, Olly, we're not going to do that!" And I'd say to him, "Well, Dr. Cooper, I understand but my problem is that I gotta get my board. . . ." "Oh, hell, I don't want to hear about that damn board!" Whenever I could tell that Leon was getting really upset, I started calling him Dr. Cooper. Shit, that was some times, then, I'm telling you!

John Wilson: What was at stake on the other side of the tracks was that whites were not used to blacks running things. They had controlled the county all down through the years, and now we were moving in their territory. There might have been two or three blacks on the school board, but they were told what to say and what to do. We were doing what the people in the community, the poor folks, wanted to be done. We had some rich folks on our side, and if it wasn't for them we couldn't have managed; they let us know when traps were set. If we had said that we were going to take Mr. Charley and Mr. Frank and put them on the board and let them run things, then there wouldn't have been any problems. But when they found out that members of the board were to be chosen from the Neighborhood Action Council, they couldn't stoop that low.

Alice Morganfield: When school desegregation occurred here, the white communities would select the black families in their communities whose children they considered to be "good enough" to go to school with their children, and these were the ones that went to the white schools. Here at Marianna it was the Kennedys who were chosen. In Aubrey my family was chosen. And this was how it was done throughout the county.

Olly Neal, Jr.: We finally lined up a meeting with the governor one Sunday afternoon. At this time the governor assumed that we were a rabble-rousing group lead by Olly Neal. What he didn't understand was that there was already a large number of people committed to the clinic, although they might not be able to articulate this commitment.

The governor was agreeable to releasing the money on the condition that we reorganize the clinic board and bring onto the board some of the same people who had been fighting the clinic so that they could manage this money. After sitting a while in this meeting at the governor's mansion and drinking from these little cups, you know the kind you can't get a finger through and you have to hold the saucer with one hand and squeeze the handle with the fingers of your other hand, I remember Ms. Sauls telling the governor, "Mr. Governor, we just sure appreciate you inviting us over to your house on Sunday, after church. And we sure want you to be happy with us, but Mr. Governor, we just can't put them folks on our board. We can't just let them come in there and destroy us from the inside. And if that's what we're going to have to do, you'll just have to keep your money."

After this, then we had a changed relationship with Dale Bumpers, and I've had an excellent relationship with him since that time. He realized that the way the clinic was developing truly reflected what was wanted by a significant proportion of the people in the community here. We had whites on the board, but they were not the whites who the so-called leading citizens of the community wanted on the board.

Sara Sauls: The governor's expression looked like he thought I was crazy. But he eventually released the money.

Sara Sauls

I've seen blacks afraid, afraid to speak up for themselves. I've never been afraid to say anything, to say what's right. My husband wasn't afraid either. My father passed when I was young, so I don't remember him too well, but my mother was this way, and she taught me. She was never afraid to say anything to anybody no matter where they came from or no matter what color they were.

We worked real hard after that meeting to get the money. On the last night we had stayed up all night long; if we hadn't gotten the money then, we wouldn't have gotten it at all. But we got it, we sure did.

I dreamed about something like the clinic one time. This was before the clinic started, when I was still a midwife. I had seen people so poor, poorer than I was. Some people weren't able to pay me for delivering their babies. I dreamed that something would come along to help people. I never forgot that dream. I remembered that dream when the clinic got started and I told my husband, "That's what my dream was about."

Theressa Ramey: I remember the meeting. I was not nervous. I'm not nervous about meeting anybody. I think this is because of the way my parents brought me up. They brought their children up to feel that they were as important as anybody else. To me, people are just people.

We've Tried to Address the Preventive
Aspect of Health Care

Alice Morganfield: When the clinic got started, we had all sorts of ideas on how we could improve our community. One of the things that was lacking in the county was enough adequate housing. So the housing project got started as something related to the aims of the clinic in that we were trying to improve the health of the entire community. The housing project has thirty or forty units. Again, the concern was with preventive medicine. We used to have a rural water project, but this program fell by the wayside when government funding for it was discontinued. However, the countywide water system that was installed under the program is still in operation.

We've reached people miles out in the country who used to be cut off and isolated. We've tried to address the preventive aspect of health care. For example, the environmental services has in the past sprayed for mosquitoes and checked for contaminated water so as to prevent illnesses and diseases. The incidence of major problems like heart disease, hypertension, and infant mortality has been greatly reduced.

The organizational structure of the clinic is composed of the Neighborhood Action Councils, who are responsible for selecting the board members, who are in turn responsible for choosing the administrator, and under the administrator are the supervisors of the various clinic services. The supervisors keep up with the day-to-day operations and then report to the administrator, who reports to the board, who reports to the community. The various services over which there are supervisors are medical services, finance, allied services, dental services, transportation, aging program, housing program, marketing, and environmental services.

John Wilson: Although I'm in transportation services now, I used to be in environmental services. There is still a need for a number of the environmental projects, but there's been a cut in funds starting in 1981. We used to be able to go to people's homes and build outhouses, install screens to keep out insects from the house, as well as repair windows and spray homes for insects and pests.

Gloria New: When I first started out in environmental services, the conditions I found people living in surprised me. I didn't think people in the United States or in Lee County were living any longer without things I took to be basic. Some were still living without running water. They would have to walk and get their water from a pump. There are degrees of being poor, I found out. And some degrees were severer than I knew.

John Wilson: We found out that we were about half-way poor, not all-the-way poor.

Alice Morganfield: Under allied services fall the services of nursing, lab, pharmacy, X-ray, nutrition, medical records, child care and development. To make such services available to people in Lee County, we have the transportation service. Lee County is 618 square miles, and the majority of the people living here do not own their own transportation. We take the calls from patients requiring transportation, and we will pick them up individually, though we do try to travel by routes so as to cut down on transportation costs. We also make scheduled runs to Little Rock for people needing special medical care, and this is at no charge to them. Occasionally, we might take people to Memphis or somewhere else, depending upon the case.

Our aging program is designed to cut down on loneliness and encourage independence by providing alternatives to institutionalization. Each day we provide one meal to help satisfy nutritional requirements. There will be tours and recreational activities such as a senior citizens' olympics. The senior citizens have a choir that has traveled to Little Rock to sing in the governor's inauguration. A lot of these activities for the aging program are funded separately from the regular HHS [Department of Health and Human Services] medical budget.

In the case of the aging program, the clinic took over community services for the elderly that were originally carried out by the hospital here. Women on the hospital board had been responsible for delivering meals to the homes of the elderly on a daily basis, as well as providing transportation so that they could go shopping; this was within the city limits. When these services started to expand, the hospital wasn't equipped to administer them. But the clinic did have the capacity to handle the expanded operations, so Olly Neal and some other people sat down and wrote the proposal for the grant, and the program got started.

John Wilson: When the hospital was in charge of services for the elderly, they were serving seven home delivery meals a day. Right now we're serving seventy-nine home delivery meals per day, and about seventy to eighty people come each day for meals.

Cleola Bursey: As long as Lee County stays short on health care, there will remain people who can't be reached through health services. Nevertheless, the clinic has been able to reach a wide range of people. Every year in Lee County, I think we see at least 7,500 different patients. I can remember at one time in Lee County there were people who lived so far off the beaten path they hardly knew what a doctor was; that's almost nonexistent now. Still, there is a shortage of manpower.

Gloria New: Our patients include all ages and all types of ethnic groups.

Alice Morganfield: The black-white ratio among the patients is about 70 to 30. About 66 percent of our patients fall within the poverty index. For them we charge two dollars per visit, and for anyone else we have a sliding fee scale.

Gloria New: A new patient can become a member of the clinic by paying the annual membership fee of six dollars. This membership is why the clinic is a cooperative clinic. We also, of course, see nonmembers as well, although in 1984 we made a rule that all members had to be from Lee County. We just couldn't see all the people who wanted to come, after the budget cuts.

Eliza Dobbins: That's right, we had and still have a variety of services that the regular doctors just don't offer, like nutrition counseling, dental care, environmental services, and other things like the pharmacy, home health care, transportation services, X-ray, and the lab, which people didn't have before.

Frances Fields: I don't know of anything in Lee County to compare the clinic to in respect to integration and the employment of blacks and whites. But here at the clinic we have a fully integrated staff.

Lillie Mouton: One other thing worth mentioning is that we had Head Start programs, and all of these grew out of the Neighborhood Action Councils. As far as the clinic goes and how I feel about being part of it, you may as well not ask me how I feel, you may as well cut my finger off and ask whether or not I bleed.

Olly Neal, Jr.: The health program here is known both nationally and internationally. When I was working with the clinic, I was also the president of what was known as the National Administration Water Project, which was involved in improving the drinking water and human waste disposal in low-income rural communities throughout the country. We were in about twenty-eight separate states,[6] and this is one way by which people learned about the Lee County Cooperative Clinic.

Internationally, we had the good fortune to get involved with Meharry in

Olly Neal, Jr.

Nashville in the training of people from several African countries, and many of these people spent part of their time in training at the health center here in Marianna. They even made a movie comparing our program with a program in Tanzania. It was shown on national television, on *Nova*, about 1977.[7]

To Build the Clinic from Community People

Alice Morganfield: The idea has been to build the clinic up from community people so that these people would stay with the clinic. To this end, we've gotten educational loan grants to train people in different areas. Once these people received their training, they could in turn train others. The idea to train people who would stay with the clinic has not always worked out in practice. Many have since left the clinic and gone elsewhere.

Olly Neal, Jr.: We also took the position—and I think this applies to other health centers around the nation—that we needed blacks in top positions with the clinic. This was not hatred of whites. But we could not have a situation where the only people in those roles were whites of good will. We had to have blacks in these roles so that children and younger people in the community could see that this was something to which they could aspire.

My former wife Ethelane was the first black physician to come to the health center, and at that time she was the only pediatrician in Marianna. She probably had more academic training than any other physician, black or white, in this seven- or eight-county area. Now, I remember well how this young girl who lived across the street from us at the time and who was one of six children raised by her father would come and visit us. She may never be of any outstanding consequence, but she was the only one of her brothers and sisters to graduate from high school, and then later she went on and got her LPN. This girl saw that she could do something like Ethelane had done.

What a lot of black kids don't see is that some black individuals who have done well have come from way down. If this girl would ever had seen where I used to live, she might not have believed it. So one of our main goals was also to improve the image children had of themselves, and I think this was common in all the health centers around the country. I know Steve Wilson told me that he had to have at least one black doctor in Lowndes County that the kids there could see.

Eliza Dobbins: Most of the staff are natives of Lee County. We didn't have any active involvement in community affairs before our work with the clinic. Before the clinic got started, I was a housewife with a family.

Lillie Mouton: I was also aware of the health needs in the county from having served as a midwife for thirty years. So I feel real good about the Mother Infant Care program that the clinic has now.

I came to the clinic in 1972. I was hired at that time as one of about eight health aids chosen by the NACs. I was selected by the Marianna NAC. I began working as a nurse's aid and then was transferred to nutrition, and that's where I've been ever since. The nutrition program includes different services to the community. Among these are diet counseling, supplying milk to newborn infants, managing a community garden, which is not as big now as it once was. In the past we have been responsible for organizing the elderly for the senior citizens' program at the clinic. We used to make home visits and provide transportation for people to and from the stores so that they could do their shopping. We have conducted classes for diabetes, hypertension, and mother and infant care. A lot of our programs, like other services at the clinic, have had to be cut back because of lack of government funding.

Lucille Ishmael: I was a VISTA worker at the time the clinic was in its early stages. We would visit people in their homes and tell them about the clinic and what it stood for. A lot of people in Lee County at this time did not even know that the clinic was there. We would also find people in need. We found poor families and provided clothing for them, especially their children. One of the VISTAs got in touch with an organization where she could get clothing. We also used to take the elderly ladies shopping for groceries. My work with VISTA lasted two years, around 1971 to 1973.

We would go to the homes of whites and blacks. I visited a white woman one day. This is the story. She had been to a private doctor, and after he had finished examining her, he had told her to go out and sit on the front porch— he wouldn't let her wait in the office. He would not even give her a chair to sit down. While she was waiting for her daughter to come back and pick her up, a young colored woman drove up in her car and saw her and said, "You come and sit in the car with me and wait." So this woman told me that she would not go back to that doctor after the way he treated her. I could understand; the lady was a human being just like he was, and she wanted to be treated like one. So like with other people, I encouraged her to come to the clinic. I asked her later what she thought of the clinic, and she said, "A fine institution."

Frances Fields: I had been away from Lee County for sixteen years. When I returned, I was at home with my husband who was ill. It was after that that I started at the clinic.

After I was here for two years, the clinic sent me to school to become a licensed nurse. The clinic supported me and paid for my schooling. Otherwise, I don't think I would have gotten this training. I vowed that for every year I went to school I would give two years back to the clinic. Of course, as you can see I'm still here more than ten years later.

I love the clinic and my work here. In the early years we were trained to do just about anything that needed to be done. There wasn't any one of us who couldn't go from pushing a broom to assisting in other ways. There's been a real sense of togetherness working here, and it's still here. We enjoy what we do.

I'm an LPN, and I work in the Home Health Services Division of the clinic. In Home Health Services we do a lot of teaching, trying to instruct people how to take better care of themselves. We do rehabilitative exercises with patients, such as those who have suffered from a stroke. We are responsible for mother and infant care. There are many who aren't sick enough to be in hospitals but who still need care, and we try to meet their needs.

Alice Morganfield: I got back to Lee County on March 5, 1970, the same day we got the Kennedy house for the clinic. I remember that day because that was the day I came back home. I can't remember why, but for some reason my daddy gave me something to give to Olly Neal, and the Kennedy house is where I found him. I had no idea at that time that I would eventually be working with the clinic. I later became involved when I was working as a manager of a political campaign office downtown. Olly asked me if I would like to keep the books for the clinic. I told him that I didn't know anything about that kind of work, but he told me that I was smart and could learn, so I did.

Annie Green: I worked in a TV [assembly] plant in Forrest City before the clinic got started. I commuted there and back each day.

I'm the assistant lab technician now. My education for this position and others here at the clinic has come through on-the-job training. I came here fifteen years ago when the clinic first started. At that time I would fill in wherever I was needed, from doing general maintenance to working as a home health aide.

Gloria New: The clinic had been in operation quite some time before I came. I've been here at the clinic seven years now. Marianna is my home. I was born just outside of town, and I graduated from high school here. I have long been interested in what the clinic has done for the people of Lee County. My main job at the clinic is to direct the medical records department and to be sure that the records for the ancillary services, such as transportation, are coordinated. The first contact which a patient at the clinic has when he or she comes through the door is with my department.

Cleola Bursey: I've been in Lee County most all of my life. I taught school for thirteen years before I came here to be assistant administrator.

I would think that the clinic has made some difference in terms of people's education and their aspirations, if no more than that more kids are interested today in the field of medicine because of the clinic. We help sponsor Career Days with the school system. The kids can come out here and see people at the clinic in different lines of work and see how they get on-the-job training. They can see how people can start out with nothing and get somewhere.

My younger sister and I are the children in my immediate family. I was the first in my immediate family to complete college. I was followed by my younger sister. My mother was raised on a farm, and she finished seventh grade. My father died when I was about four, and my mother raised both of us. Apart from a small amount of my father's Social Security, my mother did this without any government assistance. We had grown up with the expectation that we would go to college, and when I graduated from high school, my mother moved from Marianna to Chicago to get work there and to pay for college tuition.

There's been tremendous change and progress over the past years for myself and the county. There is a much better working relationship among social organizations and services today. I'm sure there are things that used to be done in the school system that just aren't done anymore. For instance, books that used to be bought for the black schools were given to the white schools, and books that had been in the white schools were passed on to the black schools. I know that this happened because I worked in the libraries. That just doesn't happen anymore. In the past the city officials did not want to work with certain organizations, and the clinic was one of them. Now we have a beautiful working relationship. As a matter of fact, we're working with the city for a grant for an aging program. And if the money runs out for this program, the city is willing to pick up the tab. Even with the hospital we have a good working relationship. We may have our differences, but it's nothing major that we can't work out. We now get support from the medical society and local physicians where we didn't before. This also applies to the banks, too.

I think there's been changes for women. There used to be a time, and it lasted for a long time, when most people used to think that the woman's place was in the home. For example, when I came to the clinic, I took over a position that had previously been held by a man, and for a little while at the beginning this took time for some people to get used to. I was paid the same salary as the man before me.

People Today Should Be Fighting for More

Alice Morganfield: When the clinic started off, there was a real family feeling. When we were working on the grant proposal for our present facilities, there were times when we would be up all night long; there wouldn't be any going to bed, you wouldn't think of going to bed. I remember when we were working that late how we would call one woman here in town who owned a hamburger stand, and we would ask her to open her stand at three o'clock in the morning to feed us. That woman has never held a job at the clinic, but that was the kind of community participation it took to get the clinic to where it is now. I don't know of any other effort like this in Lee County. I've never seen before the kind of closeness we have here at the clinic. You know, if something happens to you, it happens to me.

Mildred Broadway: When the clinic started, we didn't have anything to lose and everything to gain.

Alice Morganfield: What was at stake then was our right to a better way of life; our right to vote, our right to a good education, our right to health.

Frances Fields: I can remember in the early years when the grant money ran out and we worked for nothing, and we got paid later. This was sometime around 1971.

Olly Neal, Jr.: It's my opinion that all too frequently our newly educated blacks are not as committed to doing things that take some sacrifice and don't bring immediate benefits to them. There is a style that's recently been learned by blacks—I don't know where it comes from—that I find very frustrating. I've seen it over at the health clinic, in the working habits of some of the younger black folks. When I went back as director of the clinic in 1976, one of the first things that I did was fire about four people who had master's degrees. They had the notion that because they had degrees, they ought not to have to produce anything.

But we had a health center where people needed to work to make it superior to other health centers around the country because we knew that we were controversial and that we would be eaten up if we weren't the best we could be. We've kept our head above water because we've tried to do what they've required us to do better than they required. And they've acknowledged this. Just last year I got an award from the HHS for the contributions I've made to the health center movement in this country.

During the years when the clinic got started, I think there was a more prevalent attitude running throughout the nation that the government and people could make a better world. I think you can compare this to a more widespread attitude now of "Let me get mine and you can get yours." I don't mean this in a pejorative sense. But I do think that the climate of the nation has moved some from the late 1960s and the response of people to Martin Luther King's and other's exposure of the way blacks were being treated with "We can do better." Now even among young blacks there seems to be more of an attitude of "I better save myself and get my own business in order."

After LCCC, We Were Part of White Folks' Business

Olly Neal, Jr.: The greatest pride I have about the clinic is that I think that there are very few people in this community who would ever question that black folks run Lee County Cooperative Clinic and have managed budgets in excess of a million dollars for several years and have never had a major complication with our funding source. Even though we have been as controversial as any clinic in the nation, nobody has ever come down on us because of mismanagement.

My greatest pride is that no one can say that black folks, in fact, didn't run that organization. The board was about 90 percent black; I was the administrator, and those who came into the clinic came in through the board and me, and it was clear that the funding source could not dictate who we hired or who we fired. We completely managed our own money and selected our own auditors—this was the first time that white folks in Arkansas knew there was such a thing as a black CPA—so there was no government decision as to who we should use.

I regret that we did not do some things that we should have done, and my greatest disappointment is that we never did create a permanent economic venture.

Andrew Williams: We started the Lee County Vegetable Growers Association about 1970. It was when Dan Blumenthal was with the clinic; he helped

Dan Blumenthal, M.D., as VISTA volunteer.—*Photo courtesy of Dan Blumenthal*

us start it. I was one of the first three board members. We had been selling our vegetables to a local buyer who was getting all the profit.

We borrowed money from the Farmers Home Administration to build a shed by the clinic for the produce. We put the organization together so that we could have a guaranteed farm product to sell. At that time we worked with the Birds Eye company. The association is still in existence today, but it is not as strong as it used to be. One of the reasons for this is that we have marketing problems. The companies can buy cheaper from Mexico now. When soybeans became a big commodity, everyone went into this, and as a result the vegetable crops got smaller, too small for companies buying large scale. Now, instead of selling to frozen food companies, we have what we call fresh market, so that we can market our small vegetable crops. We sell to a cooperative that in turn sells to a retail or wholesale store.

Olly Neal, Jr.: It's unfortunate the clinic was not more successful in economics. The clinic is the only organization in the community that can bring in the top experts and skilled professionals in its field. It's the only organization that can make an aggressive, serious, and direct effort to bring in blacks at this level. The school district does this to some degree, particularly since 1979 when blacks came to represent a majority of the school board; I served as president of the school board for a couple of years, and I was the first black man in Marianna's history to hold this position.

The problems we have here are not unique to Marianna, and they are not entirely unique to blacks. The problem is how to create permanent kinds of work that are sufficiently tied to the community so that they don't leave the community any time that there is an upheaval in the economy. I'm not talking about having an industry in Marianna that will survive only so long as the defense budget stays high.

A problem for all small communities is how to create and develop industrial prospects with such ties to the community that they do not depend on the good will of someone keeping them there. Marianna has been a farming community and used to have a substantial number of folks who owned small parcels of land; can we develop here some sort of activity that revolves around processing, manufacturing, and relating to the raw materials that are grown here? What is it that is unique to Marianna that will allow for this kind of economic development? I think that if any answer comes to this question, it will come from someone who is not a full-time job developer but from someone who is an expert in his or her field yet whose vision and professional outlook extends beyond that field.

I have books on rural development, but they are based on a narrow perspective. I don't mean this negatively; it's only that the thinking in these books is not as free and uninhibited as it could be if it wasn't so concerned with scholarly opinion. That's why the health center is important; it brings in people like this, whose reading and travel and thinking is not narrowly limited to what the book tells you is the proper direction for rural development.

My thinking is that every time you put money down there, I want to use it for a definite purpose and to show at the end that it accomplished something because I don't want anyone to ever be able to point their finger and say, "They let them niggers have that money, and look how they screwed up those federal dollars." Don't let niggers be in charge—that's what our folks have been taught. And we've accepted the idea that we can't do some things.

Thomas Ishmael: The clinic has improved relations between whites and blacks in the county. We have whites coming in to the clinic as patients who are good comfortable living people and who could pay private doctors, but they give the clinic their support. We didn't have white support with the gin. Excepting my church activities, I feel that my involvement with the clinic is about the best thing I've ever done to help people less fortunate than myself. Today, in Lee County, black elected officials serve on the school board, and there are black justices of the peace. I think my running for county judge helped to make this possible because it broke down fear. The clinic has done this as well in its determination to stand up for people and their needs.

John Wilson: Lee County Cooperative Clinic opened up the eyes of people. It's been an inspiration for a lot of things we never dreamed of: water, sewers, paved streets. We never thought of things like that except in Marianna. But even in the black section of Marianna we had streets that turned to mud with rain. You couldn't get through with a John Deere tractor. We had a man die because we couldn't get him out and to a hospital.

But we saw those things as white folks' business. But after LCCC we were part of it. It was like having an old house you wouldn't let a cat live in. We take it down and start building it over. We had 408 people in Haynes and 200 people in Aubrey. I would never have considered being mayor of Haynes, or even incorporating. I've been mayor for four years now. We've helped white people, too. A lot of them, the poor and the middle class, they didn't know they were free people, too. The powerful people fought change. They fought new jobs because jobs might take Mr. Charlie's best tractor driver. They still fight change. You'll see, I'll have a plant in Haynes before Marianna.

Theressa
Ramey

Measures of Progress

Theressa Ramey: The Lee County Clinic is not a black clinic; it is a clinic for all people. Changes that have occurred as a result of the clinic include housing projects, an environmental program for the control of pests and insects, and a supply of clean water, training and family health care, a meals-on-wheels program for senior citizens that assures them of one balanced meal per day, and transportation services for people. I don't think these things would exist in the community were it not for the clinic.

Pitson Brady: Since 1970 we've been able to get some things, but not enough. The clinic is about all we really have because we still don't have that much say-so in policies even though we might be talked to nicer now. In 1970 we had four justices of the peace; now we only have three. We've been able to get some roads and some housing in the black community, but this hasn't been enough. So we've had to get things like housing and a sanitation project through the clinic that we haven't been able to get through the county court.

My work with the clinic is a lot different than my justice of the peace work. We don't always get what we want, but we know we have that federal money. So we have more say-so over what we want and need. It's different working with the federal government than with the local government, even though we have lost some things with the Reagan administration.

I would encourage blacks to run for office as a way of helping the community. It's a way of getting things we need. We could win if enough people who don't vote would vote. We're ready for this now. A lot of blacks used to be scared to do things like vote, but now they're living more on their own, and they are not as scared. When we first got to be justice of the peace, there wasn't too much that we could do. There are more duties now, but there is still not much we can do, especially as far as blacks are concerned, because we don't form a majority. There are nine justices of the peace, and there's never been more than four blacks as justices of the peace. We've tried to do things for the community, like getting roads in black areas. We've tried to get blacks hired at the county courthouse, but apart from one who used to be in the sheriff's office and one who is now in the county clerk's office, we haven't had much luck.

Olly Neal, Jr.: I left the clinic finally in 1976, because I never did want to be there permanently. I had always felt that in order to effectively manage a major health program, you had to have a good and strong background in certain specialized areas of health care. I think that I have a good background in community health and organization, but I don't have that kind of medical expertise. I had an opportunity to get a master's in public health, but I just didn't want to do it; I felt like it was too limiting. I also knew that I was controversial and that there might come a time, although it has not come yet, that people would come onto the clinic board who would be anti-Olly Neal. So I didn't want to be solely dependent on the health center as my only way to stay in Marianna, and I sure wasn't going to work at the hospital. I went into law school because it provided a way for me to pay my bills and remain in Marianna.

HEW [the Department of Health, Education, and Welfare] laid all sorts of evaluative tools and mechanisms on us to measure the impact and change that resulted from the program, but how the hell do you measure some of these things? You couldn't measure what it meant when the vice president of the clinic board was elected seven times straight to the county legislature after having served on the clinic board. Or that the chairman of the board has assumed one of the primary leadership roles in the economic development of small black farmers in the county, again occurring after several years of service with the clinic. Are these measures of an improved quality of health in Lee County? Well, some people, like the people John Eason sends those reports to, couldn't say that it is. I can.

What about Olly Neal? Am I any measure of the progress of health in the community? I would like to think that I am. But these are the kinds of things that can't be put into those statistical reports that John Eason, clinic administrator, tells me they do out there now. I don't have any objections to these reports insofar as the clinic has to be run like a business and you have objective criteria to measure change and progress. But I don't know if the experts will ever be able to take an intangible like improved self-worth and put a value on that.

CHAPTER 3

The Time for Waiting Had Been Used Up

Lowndes County, Alabama

The Place

Lowndes County is low lying and divided among large farms, small towns, and swamps. Hayneville, the county seat, has a population of about 500. In 1970, just after the clinic began, the county had 12,897 inhabitants, 75 percent of whom were African American. About 62 percent of the county's population had poverty-level incomes or less. The median African American family income was $2,810, or about 30 percent of the national median income figure for all families and 75 percent of the county's median. Sixty-one percent of the housing was substandard. There were three doctors in the county, all of whom were white.[1] These doctors provided the staff of the first federally funded health program. The county's population continues to decline. There are now 12,700 residents. The county's overall per capita income in 1980 was $2,164, or 23 percent of the national overall per capita income.

The People

William S. (Sam) Bradley graduated from Tuskegee in the 1930s and worked in federal programs, including the Farm Security Administration and Head Start. His skills as a hunting-dog trainer won acclaim from whites and blacks and provided him a living for several years. His position as a Seventh Day Adventist preacher enhanced his reputation in the African American community. He served on the board of the original Lowndes County OEO health program, led the reorganization of the health services after its suspension by the OEO, and stimulated other programs from the newly organized Lowndes County Health Services Association.

Uralee A. Haynes has taught and administered schools in Lowndes County since World War II. She participated in the programs of both the Farm Security Administration and the OEO. She first registered to vote in 1965 and ran for the office of superintendent of schools in 1972. She lost by 112 votes. In 1975 the woman who had been superintendent and Mrs. Haynes's employer for thirty years resigned, and Mrs. Haynes was appointed to succeed her. She won elections in 1976 and 1980. She did not run in 1984 and retired. She considers this "an interesting time to live."

Annie Hrabowski was in her sixties when the movement came to Lowndes County, and she welcomed it with youthful enthusiasm. She assisted civil rights workers in the conduct of meetings and fed and sheltered them. She still heard from them occasionally, including a visit from two of them the day before we interviewed her at her home. She died in 1988.

John Hulett is the first African American man to win election to public office in Lowndes County. He was prominent in the early organizing efforts in Lowndes County at the time of the Selma March. His arrest in 1965 on a traffic violation resulted in the statewide reform of the practices of justices of the peace. At the time justices of the peace earned their support from fines levied on people they found guilty in trials they conducted.

Parthenia Kelly is medical records supervisor of the Lowndes County Health Services. Now in her forties, she has worked with the clinic from its inception, supervising home health aides initially.

Robert Mants first came to Lowndes County in 1965 as a young SNCC field worker. He had worked for SNCC before in Georgia, and after his work with SNCC he worked for Save the Children in Alabama and Arkansas. He has remained in Lowndes County working on economic development projects. In 1984 he was elected county commissioner. He did not seek reelection because he felt more effective outside of elected office.

Kenneth McConnochie, M.D., now practices pediatric medicine at Rochester (New York) General Hospital. His first medical practice was as a National Health Service Corps physician in the OEO-funded program and later in the reorganized Lowndes County Health Services Association. His continued service under trying circumstances and in makeshift quarters made the transition in services possible. The esteem he acquired is expressed in the Dr. Kenneth McConnochie Award, given each year to the outstanding employee of the Lowndes County Health Services Association by the board and staff, "In fond recognition for exceptional performance, dedication and loyalty." His comments are taken from a paper he wrote.[2]

Mattie Lee Holcombe Moorer housed civil rights workers and was very active in community development efforts and programs, including a credit union, since 1965. She was a VISTA worker in the early days of the clinic and served as a community outreach worker. She has lived in Lowndes County for all her seventy years.

Charles Smith heads the county commission in Lowndes County. He grew up in the Calhoun area of the county. During World War II he worked in shipyards of Mississippi and Mobile. In 1965 he was the first African American man to register to vote in Lowndes County and led efforts for voter registration and political change. He worked in other parts of the rural South on community organizing projects. He was elected to the county commission in 1972 and was reelected every time since then until 1990.

Mary Smith presently serves as juvenile probation officer for Lowndes County. After college, she served as the Women, Infants, and Children program (WIC) supervisor in the Lowndes County Health Services Association. She was on the staff during the difficult transition when the clinic was conducted from an abandoned building in Moss. Her father is Charles Smith.

Steve Wilson became manager of the *Green County Democrat* newspaper in January 1985. This was a return to journalism for this Philadelphia native, who worked with *Newsday* before coming south as a young man in the late 1960s to work in various media campaigns. In 1973 he went to work for the Southeast Alabama Self-Help Association (SEASHA) at Tuskegee. He worked in Lowndes County and administered the reorganized Lowndes County Health Services Association from 1973 to 1978.

The Time Had Come in Lowndes County

Robert Mants: I was one of the first civil rights workers here in 1965. I was a field secretary for SNCC. Lowndes County held the reputation of being the most violent county in the state and perhaps in the black belt. There were people who went east or west between Montgomery and Selma but who would refuse to drive through this county by Highway 80. They would go some thirty to forty miles out of the way so as not to come through this county. Stokely Carmichael, Jimmy Richardson, and myself decided we wanted to try to organize Lowndes County. We saw an opportunity to capitalize on the Selma-to-Montgomery march and organize this county.

What we found when we got here in 1965 was that blacks lived in abject fear of whites. There was open violence, racial violence. There were no black people registered to vote here. In 1860 this county was 70 percent slave. So this county always had a black majority, but black people were not involved in the political process. The basic source of income was from tenant farming, sharecropping, during those years.

The biggest problem was that the power structure in this county was not amenable to change, not just political change but any kind of change. Part of the reason is, that is the way they maintain control. If, for example, the number of people have the opportunity to make higher wages, hey, they wouldn't be able to control them. They would have opportunities to travel and see new kinds of circumstances and have opportunities for education and that kind of thing. This would mean that they most likely would not be content with being sharecroppers. These power structures understand that.

Mattie Lee Holcombe Moorer: I birthed in a place called Gordonville in Lowndes County, and I birthed June 20, 1915. I was one child. I attended school three months out of the year until I was in the sixth grade, then they allowed us four months. There was plenty of slavery-time people living then, and that is where you would find me. I would always go and hear their stories about how they come and how they were sold. I just loved to hear it. My great grandmother lived to see me. She died at 105. She put part of her name, Melinda, into mine, but I have never used it. She was sold from five boys, her sons, in Charleston, South Carolina, and when slaves were free, she went back trying to locate her boys. Some went to war and there were two to Arkansas; she never saw them no more. The rest of the children she birthed, she birthed here in slavery. She was sold three times. They say they never could make a slave out of her, never could.

Stokely, Bob Mants, Courtland Cox, William Hix, all them, they stayed with me. We prepared food special for them. They mostly stayed in a little place down in White Hall, but they would come in and we would prepare food for them and we would travel with them. Mr. Jackson was the first person to let the SNCC people stay with them; he lived in White Hall. His son is the mayor in White Hall now.

There was fear among people at that time. Yes, Lord! But we were at a point that there was so much that we were tired of, and we were willing to risk our lives to get to vote and whatever else went with voting. There is a time for everything according to Ecclesiastes 3, and the time had come in Lowndes County.

How was I able to deal with my fear? I was born in Lowndes County. I was raised in Lowndes County; not figuring on going nowhere else to live but Lowndes County. I was not feeling fear like a lot of people was. If I thought I was right, believed I was right, I stood on that principle. So that is how I dealt with fear.

Mattie Lee Holcombe Moorer

I remember when a white man come on me, he said, "Mattie Lee, quit going to these mass meetings." He did me a favor once, and I did him one. He lent me some money, and I paid him exactly what I owed him and 25 cents on the dollar. And I did not borrow the money but for a month. I ain't talking about no year. So I looked at him, and I said, "Let me tell you something." I said, "I may be dead when I leave Lowndes County, but I am going to be the last one alive." He found out to get me from Lowndes County he was going to have to get me killed. Cause you see, this is my home. I never lived nowhere but here.

Robert Mants: The leadership for the most part in this county and most places came from the grassroots people. In few instances were the leaders —those up front and outwardly involved—professionals and teachers. Most of the people in the local leadership were independent farmers, people who owned their own land.

A lot came out of the rural communities, like Lowndes, in the civil rights movement in the South. Particularly in those areas in which blacks owned the land you had the most activity, and the movement was present to a considerable extent. These were communities created by the Farm Security Administration like White Hall, Alabama, and Lakeview, Arkansas. There were whole communities that were established by it. Generally, there was a house, a barn, an outhouse, a smokehouse, a chickenhouse, all of them pretty much the same. Some of those structures are still around. When children grew up, those with higher education came from those communities in which the blacks owned land. And education is important in their struggle.

Charles Smith: The reason that landownership made a difference was because people that were living on the plantation, they were ordered by the landlord not to go down there to get involved in what they called "that mess." Well, the landlords had that economic kind of swing you couldn't do without. That backed off some people, who by their own convictions would have liked to have gotten involved. Landownership really put leadership in the hands of the people who were determined to get registered and to teach their sisters and brothers the importance of it. That did make a difference.

Some of the leadership came from the Calhoun area. Calhoun School was founded by people from the New England region of the United States. They came down after Reconstruction in the 1890s. It's my understanding Booker Washington played a role in directing these people—Miss Charlotte Thorne and Miss Dillingham—to Calhoun at that time. They then proceeded to buy several hundred acres of the rural land and establish what we call two-horse or small farms, family kinds of farms. I think the intent there was to make sure the school would have a growing human reproduction so that they could continue the things that they were famous for. The mere fact that the Calhoun people owned their place made them a little bit more secure in their well-being, in their person.

It wasn't easy for a black person to buy land. One, you had to find someone willing to sell a black person some land. Number two, financing was hard to come by. The average two-horse farmer just had enough money to get by, maybe, from one year to another.

My father acquired forty acres from the Calhoun Land Trust, but that was way late, in the late 1930s. I bought some land also from that land trust, in 1943. They were going out, but they left a part of their business in the hands of the people coming in. My dad bought his land in 1938.

The other thing about it, the Calhoun folks had some teaching. They were just a little bit further along in terms of their education. Now, of course, Lowndes County at that time was owned by the large landowners. As far as public schools were concerned, they were very sad. The students who finished at Calhoun had a higher I.Q. than the children in the surrounding areas.

It was a scary thing registering black people at that time back in Lowndes County. I can't put in words the countless ways one was supposed to fear. We knew as citizens we had these rights, but then how were we going about articulating that and registering people to vote? For one reason or another, they turned us down. This was a delaying tactic. This was to wear our patience. This was immediately after the Selma March. We had talked about it, but this was the first time we tried to register. Somehow that march relieved us of some of the fear and oppression we originally had. Whatever it cost, we were going to do it. The organizing work of SNCC was responsible for us going down to vote.

Uralee A. Haynes: It was mostly grassroots people who did it rather than any of the professionals. Most of the local black professionals were, well, they were kind of intimidated. They thought they would lose their jobs and what have you. So they didn't do as much participating outwardly. They did some participating under the table I call it. They would make contributions and give advice to people on the QT without going to the meeting because there was a concerted effort among even some of the blacks to report everybody who was at a meeting and things of that sort. You didn't feel free. As if you really could do it, even though you really wanted to.

I did not go to the meetings at first. I certainly did not! My husband and I did do things like giving advice and making contributions as much as we possibly could. Of course, when they came here in the 1960s, we weren't making that much money. But we did share what we had because we felt that we were a little better off than some of the other people who were doing the work. At any time, whenever transportation was needed, we would let somebody drive our car or something of that sort.

We really just could not openly work with them. My husband had gone to the service, and when he came back from service in 1945, he worked and tried to register to vote at that point. Of course, we had always wanted to register and to vote. I came up with a family that had been registered voters all of my life. I don't remember when my people were not registered voters. We lived in Arkansas, too, and so it wasn't up North. We went to the school superintendent to ask her about registering. Of course, the school superintendent told him that if he registered, he would not have a job. He was a teacher like me, and that was the thing that made us know that we would be intimidated.

But we really had always wanted to be registered voters here, but we knew we couldn't break the ice. My husband had already been told that if he did register, he would not have a job. I understand it was pressure on the superintendent—it was not necessarily her individual feeling about it.

When the ice was broken and people began to register, we realized that if we didn't go then, that we would be cursed by these people here as people not interested in any improvement at all. So we thought, it would be best that we would go over and register, and the two of us went at the same time. Before any other professional went to register. My husband and I went up and registered, and I think that was the thing that made them know that we were really with them. We went to the old jail and took the test and registered.

That test had such terrible questions about the constitution of the United States. There were all kinds of—I don't remember the questions now, but there were catchy questions. Whites and blacks had to take that test. I know blacks did. Of course they had different sets of questions, and if you and I went in together, we would not have the same set of questions. Yours would be different from what I had. We would have to pass that test before we were eligible to vote.

After registering, the people leading the organizing came to me and asked me to be on the board of the OEO program. I just immediately told them that I would work with them but in the meantime I knew that there would be repercussions if I did not let the superintendent know. I agreed to work, and then I went directly to her office the next day to tell her that I was working with them. My husband and I had decided that if she said that I could not work with the OEO, I would just have to stop teaching. It had just gotten down to that point.

Annie Hrabowski: When Carmichael and Mants came into the community, well, people were not so hot about it. I had two girls stay with me here, and they would come and we would have meetings here. We would have night meetings and get the people together, and these two girls lived with me. There were no danger to me in taking those students in. The whites never said anything to me. I would have just told them, "Time has changed now." I could see so much that was coming in that was coming fast in Lowndes County. Having these meetings, I could see then that a change was coming about. There was a lot of fear in the county because some people had been treated bad. There is so many under the whites that they could not venture out.

My daddy, he wasn't afraid of anything. I remember the time my daddy carried me to Hayneville. I was a little kid. He would always take me by the hand and go to different places. He carried me to Hayneville one day to the courthouse, and I saw we were passing the front door. There was four deputies sitting in front of the door, and I said to my dad, "Poppa, why are you passing the door? Here is the door." And he shook me. We kept going around the side of the building, and when we got around there, he said, "Listen. You can't go into the front door. You got to go into the back." I said I didn't know. He said, "When I get you into there, don't you have nothing to say." He said, "You are talking too much, you can't do that." I was about ten or eleven, something like that.

The Lord has opened the door for us. If you do things right, you can do things that you couldn't do back then. The right way is the best way. If you do right, you go with the light. There have been a lot of change since the civil rights days.

Robert Mants: The movement here and elsewhere represented prophetic truth to a lot of people who were motivated by religious beliefs. Contrary to a lot of them being so-called communist, what inspired them was belief in God. People saw themselves pretty much like the children of Israel in the biblical days.

The Selma March Meant Things
Were Going to Be Better

Annie Hrabowski: I remember the Selma March; I remember that day very well. I kept seeing the airplanes, helicopters flying over the people that was marching. People was afraid to go out and march. I didn't go because my brother would not come get me. I asked him, would he come get me. He said, "I am going to be watching at there from the road."

Later, he said it was a good thing that I did not go down there. I could not have joined in. I said, if I would of gone down there, I would have joined right in there with King, with Martin Luther King; right there in front. He said, "How you going to get there?" I said, "I'll walk up there." I said, "The time has come from change." It was a long time, people could see that, a long time.

Mary Smith: The Selma March meant a lot for me like it did for any person living in Lowndes County or for the United States. It meant a change. Things were going to be better, for us, and if things were going to be better, I surely wanted to be a part of making it better.

Parthenia Kelly: The right to vote came with the march. I registered the same year that the march came.

I was happy, but really it was dangerous. We were threatened. They were going to throw us in jail and beat us up. I was afraid because I had three little

Annie Hrabowski

ones, and I didn't want to go to jail and be away from my children. During that time I even regretted I voted because of what we had to go up against, but now that it's over, I'm glad I did.

I was really thinking about my children. I wanted things to be better for them. I went and talked to my sisters and brothers, and they all felt the same way about it.

Annie Hrabowski: The first time I went to the polls, there was a man who lived there at White Hall. He asked me that day, "Annie, what you doing down here?" I just looked at him and said, "I am down here just like you are to do the same job that you are doing today." That is the way I left it. He just looked at me and smiled, and he did not say no more to me. Since then, I've been working around the polls, taking people in, showing which lever to pull, and stuff like that. I've been doing that ever since we got this voting rights thing.

John Hulett: Let me say that during the same time our jury system in our county was completely male. Black men could serve on the jury, but very few in fact did. So there were all-male, predominately white juries. We filed a suit in Birmingham, I believe, in order that women might have an opportunity to serve on the jury as well. The result is that today we have both white and black women on juries.

Mary Smith: In general, the movement helped at first. It helped the blacks to register to vote. It gave us some of the key positions by votes here in Lowndes County. You can see that. There are black faces in high places.

Sam Bradley: I was not part of the Selma March, but I remember it, sure. For years, a number of years, I've had dealings with our white people in one way or another, and it's not been too turbulent, except in extreme cases. Back then, before the march, I had been told a number of times by them, "You're a good citizen, you're a good citizen." I was working with the local board of registration—I knew most of the members on the board—to bring it to pass that they would voluntarily register black people. And I got many promises that it was going to happen, but it never really happened. It was always something that came up and it didn't happen.

Then the fight began to develop in the South about registering to vote and that sort of stuff. So at the time, I looked up every county in the state of Alabama, and only three were not beginning to register black voters: Lowndes, Wilcox, and Russell.

By that time, a little before the march, I got thoroughly disgusted. I said, "I'm going to settle it. I'm a good citizen, and I've been told by a number of whites I am a good citizen, and I think I am a law-abiding citizen. I don't know of any serious violations of any laws I have ever committed. And all I lack being a full-fledged citizen of this county is the privilege to vote, and I'm going to ask for it." When I made up my mind to do that, then my wife attempted to discourage me, but she couldn't. And I said, "No, I'm going. I have children, and if that's the last good deed in this life I can do to make it better for them, I'm going to do it." I decided to go, and she said, "Well, can I go with you?"

I got a group from our area of the county, and we planned to meet the board, and I had a promise that the board would register us that first Monday. Others asked about whether or not we ought to invite Dr. King to come in and demonstrate. I said, "No, this is not for demonstration. We have what I think seems to be a bona fide promise. Let's see how it works. If we do that, I think it will be much smoother. If it doesn't happen, I promise you, I'll be the first to holler the loudest for the demonstration. But until that happens, let's just see and give it a chance."

Somehow the news got to Dr. King. On the appointed day the group of people came in, and Dr. King and eight or ten other persons came by also just to observe, not to demonstrate. But the minute they were known to be on the scene, the board of registrars got frustrated. All the persons there were to write their names down in a composition book, notebook, and come back the next board day and register. They closed up shop.

Shortly after that, I did get registered. We started registration down in the old jail house, which sat right where the clinic is today. That's where I signed my registration papers. In a few weeks after we got started, we got federal registrars in here, and I was told by I guess two or three dozen local whites that they wished they had allowed us to be registered like they promised us, but it was too late. And all of this was taking place right after the Selma March.

Charles Smith: I was among the first five blacks to get registered. At that time we had to pass the literacy test. That test was pretty tough. I passed it somehow. I not sure just exactly how. You not only had to read it, but you had to interpret some section of the Constitution. They'd grab some random questions and throw them at you. The questions that sort of boggled me were: how often is the census taken? and how often is the state supposed to reapportion itself? Now, the state was supposed to reapportion itself every ten years. But, of course, it was a very long time since it had done that. A whole lot of the reapportioning was just got done most recently.

I got registered the same day as Sam Bradley. Mr. Bradley and I and few people from the Gordonville community.

John Hulett: The Lowndes County Christian Movement was organized, I believe, in April of 1965, right after the Selma March. There was a connection in some sense. First, we got a group together to try to register. After we got organized, we made a choice of which leadership we would work with, and we chose Stokely Carmichael and SNCC over Martin Luther King and SCLC [Southern Christian Leadership Conference].

In doing this we began to work toward the needs of the people in our area. We set up workshops and educated people about registration and voting. We talked about land and how people should maintain and hold their land; how they could lose their land by not making wills and deeds. We were also very much concerned with people getting decent jobs. Most people were just sharecroppers, and a few were small independent farmers.

During that time I would go off on speaking engagements with different groups, and whatever donation they would give we would put toward buying land. During the harvest time of the year, families were being evicted from the plantations because they registered to vote, this was 1965 and early

John Hulett

1966. Stokely Carmichael and SNCC secured some tents from people all over the country, and we went to Montgomery and bought some second-hand lumber to build a platform where these tents could be placed. The land was bought through Stokely Carmichael doing speaking engagements. That was Tent City located near U.S. 80 and set up for people who were evicted from their land. Families lived there until most of them were able to buy land. Some of them stayed over a year until they were able to secure land in other places and have houses built on them.

The land was bought for a second purpose. We were going to have a business on it, but we never were really successful. We got the business started. We had a service station first. Then we started to build a supermarket, but we never finished the building.

Parthenia Kelly: My daughter was the first black enrolled in the school here. A lot of children made application to attend the white school, but there were only five accepted during that time. That was 1972, and she was entering the ninth grade. During that year it was very hard for me to even get her to school. They would not even provide transportation in the beginning. They said that the white school bus did not rotate and couldn't come here. At first I had to take her down to Highway 80 to catch the bus and then go back in the afternoon to pick her up to bring her home. Later on, they decided they would provide transportation. They decided that the bus that was coming through picking up kids that went to Lowndes County Training School, which was all black, could pick her up and take her down to Highway 80 to catch the white bus. Transportation from one bus to another, from the black bus to the white bus.

It was real rough on my daughter at first. Going to a place where you know you don't have any friends, it was really hard. And during that year, out of the five students, she was the only one that made the grades to stay. Really, during that time there really wasn't any fun. Anything could happen; it was frightening. It really wasn't too safe. It was a fearful feeling. I had to do it, though, because the school was much better there. The white school there was giving more quality education over there than at the rest of the schools.

John Hulett: The OEO was really important in bringing about changes in Lowndes County! We started with a housing program. Housing was one of our major concerns. During that time there were programs under the OEO, the Farmers Home Administration, called self-help housing. We finally got a grant and started working on one. Wilcox County had a program in that area, and so I was hired to work with them to develop a housing program here in this county. I had some problems at first with the Farmers Home Administration, and after we got things straightened out, it was pretty successful here in the county.

Another thing we tried to develop then was some type of economic enterprise. We organized and tried to get a handbag factory in this county. It started off pretty good and then fell through. We tried also to maintain a pallet factory, and it was real successful until its last two years, when economic conditions were so bad that people just didn't buy a lot, and it had to fold up.

Community Leadership Doesn't Parachute Out of the Sky

John Hulett: Community leadership: it doesn't just appear as if somebody parachutes out of the sky and you have a community leader. There are a lot of factors that go to establish community leadership. For myself, I didn't just wake up one day and say, I'm gonna move on for freedom today. It didn't happen like that.

When I was rather young, I lived in Birmingham where I worked for the NAACP. I believe it was in 1949 when the governor of Alabama outlawed the NAACP, and that's when I first got involved in working with people. We organized a statewide organization, the Alabama Christian Movement, to try to take the place of the NAACP and do some of the same things they were doing. The later bus boycott organized under Reverend Shuttlesworth in Birmingham, I worked with. I worked with him also with the registration of black voters. This gave me some general ideas about leadership and what we ought to be doing. This was in the 1950s. Later, I came back to Lowndes County, in 1959, I believe.

I came back here, and I began to talk to people about pulling ourselves together, registering to vote, and starting some other things. It was hard to convince people. They were just really afraid at that time. Around 1964 we tried to register to vote, and at that time they wouldn't let us. I came over to pay the poll tax so I could register, and they wouldn't take the poll tax. We just kept pushing till finally we started getting large numbers of people—hundreds—coming over on the first and third Tuesdays to try to get registered to vote.

It was the type of thing that just didn't happen overnight. I had been around other groups and knew that all we needed was some help in pulling this together and doing it. Stokely Carmichael and others gave us the kind of encouragement that we needed.

Uralee A. Haynes: The Christian Movement that brought the OEO program in thought that they needed some people who had a little training to be on the board of directors, and they asked me to be on the board.

I came here as a teacher in 1940. And I have been teaching here ever since. Three of those years I worked with the Farm Security Administration. The Farm Security program helped individual farmers get on their feet. It was during the 1940s, the early 1940s. I worked with them in helping the wives learn to can fruits and vegetables and do some of the same things at the extension services. They bought homes some of them, and some of them are still in those homes. It was really very, very helpful. After that program stopped, I went back to teaching.

Mattie Lee Holcombe Moorer: I remember. I was in Roosevelt's program that brought in ladies to teach us how to prepare commodities and raise chickens. Mrs. Haynes came out, that is how I got to know her. She was one of the ladies. Now, some white ladies were ahead of her, but I recall her because she was a black lady who came out.

I remember Hoover. We were so patchy. Back then, if I could get a penny to put into church, I thought I had something. It was the country store that would take my mother's eggs. We could not eat eggs; we had to sell them. She would give me a nickel back. She would let me divide the nickel between a treat and church. I still go to church. I still believe in the church. After Roosevelt, we began to put nickels and dollars in church, and today, we put what we want in church.

Uralee A. Haynes: From that time until the OEO programs came in, I don't believe there was anything, really, that tried to help people get themselves back on their feet. About 10 percent of the people here have 90 percent of the wealth and the land, too. The 90 percent of the people who are poor people just go in two phases, you know. You couldn't say prosperity because they never really had prosperity, but you would call it being better off. So they go from depression to being a little better off. Since I've been here, about the only two things that have come in to try to help people support themselves have been the Farm Security program and the OEO.

I am sure the OEO program would not have been as effective without the voter registration drive and some of the Farm Security Administration work. See, what had happened with those farmers who worked with Farm Security, they were deeply in debt; the government came along, paid whoever it was that they owed, gave them a start with a mule or a plow and whatever equipment they needed, and a decent house to live in. Those same people who succeeded in paying the government back were the same people who would work with the OEO program later, who really wanted something but had not had the opportunity. The Farm Security helped them get out from under the debts they had, and the OEO helped with problems that they had acquired over the years. Some of them were doing leadership roles and some were trying to work with the OEO to try to improve whatever it was that could be improved. One set of federal programs twenty years previously helped generate the leadership of the next.

Most of the same people participated in the OEO, Farm Security, and voter registration. In almost every program these were usually the same families. You know, there are some things that are in your blood. Some people are just happy and content no matter what happens—they are just satisfied. Then, there are others who always want to see things improve and be better if they possibly can, and they'll participate in most programs that are trying to be uplifting or making the change for people. Most of the same families, the people who did well with the Farm Security program, are the

Charles Smith

ones who really came along and worked with the OEO programs and other programs.

Sam Bradley: There were several hundred families like that in Lowndes County. We did find that the families we worked with in the Farm Security Administration program were prominent in later voter registration drives and other activities.

Charles Smith: I spent three terms at Calhoun School, 1933–34, 1934–35, 1935–36, in the middle of my schooling. They were great years. It was very different from the other schools. Some of the kinds of things that were taught in the sixth, seventh, and eighth grade at Calhoun were almost unheard of in the regular public school system. I didn't finish at Calhoun; dropped out, married, and started a family. That was the end of my school as it was.

When I left Calhoun, I started a small farm. When the war broke out in Europe, I left my family at Calhoun and went to Mobile. I moved from common laborer to first-class hull erector. I bought my land from the Calhoun Land Trust while I was working in Mobile. By 1944 I had gone to the top level in the hull erector department.

I came back to the county in 1945 and tried farming for a little while. I went back to Mobile and worked in the yard. I came back home and started a little business of my own, logging.

When I came back, I understood things a little differently. One, I didn't understand why the financial institutions and banks place a different value on a person who is in his own business. I was able to work up some credit when I got back. If I wanted a truck or needed some machinery, I could go down and get a loan, buy the machinery, and make payments.

Prior to the war, there was a whole lot of resistance to lending money. You could only get very small loans before the war. You couldn't get up enough money to do very much of anything. It was hard to pay back. It was limited how much the bank would lend you.

As time moved on, in getting involved in the civil rights movement, I was recommended for one or two different grants and scholarships. One of them took me as far away as the University of Wisconsin in Madison, Wisconsin. From there I went another fifteen weeks for further development at Frogmore, South Carolina. The movement was my school.

I first went to Penn Center to study how to organize cooperatives. But the director said that he didn't think that would be all that helpful. So, they transferred me to the education committee, to learn how to organize a local school system and how it gets recognized—its accreditation.

We also had what I call group orientation of the kinds of things we would like to see developed: voter registration; civic kinds of things that the ordinary citizen ought to be about; study what his rights were under the law. We were divided into groups to go out into the community to actually do the kinds of things that had been discussed in these group sessions. While we were at Penn Center, we organized, or helped organize, a rural health center, similar to the one that we have here, that served multiple counties, the Beaufort-Jasper center. This was 1968 and 1969.

While I was at Penn Center, they had a temporary position open on the staff. They gave me that. They sent me out to Louisiana to recruit some potential community leaders. When that program ended, I had already applied for the Ford grant, a scholarship or a fellowship for six months, which I got.

I spent a few months at Tuskegee. I did a lot of research on a lot of things, and I became interested in how the governing body of a county could render greater services that's not been provided its citizens, such as road improvement, home improvement, health care, and so forth. All those things that could be addressed through their governing body. It was a very limited kind of thing that the governing body was doing up to that point in time. While everyone was only talking about those kinds of services then, Lowndes County now has a countywide rural water authority. We now have water all over the county.

Sam Bradley: I've had a few positions in the county. I worked for the Veterans Farm Training program. Before that, the first work I did in the county was with the old Alabama Rural Rehabilitation Corporation; that was back in 1934 and '35.

Now, the Alabama Rural Rehabilitation program ended, and on the heels of it the Resettlement program came, and from the Resettlement program to Farm Security, from Farm Security to Farmers Home Administration. We still have Farmers Home Administration. I've worked in all those programs. I was the assistant supervisor in the Alabama Rural Rehabilitation program.

With the resettlement program I was assistant supervisor; the same with Farm Security and the Farmers Home Administration. I was with all those programs right through, until one went out and the other took over.

I think back to the Farm Security Administration days and all the changes that have happened since then. I was brought on the job for Macon County, this was right after the Alabama Rural Rehabilitation program. The day I left that program, I joined the Farm Security program in Macon County.

After three or four days I met with the state director to be oriented to the job. He took me on a tour, and we went to see the seed dealers, the equipment dealers, all the people that I would be dealing with, you know. They were all white. He put forward all types of foul language and oaths: nigger this, nigger that. I did not show my resentment outwardly. I thought it wouldn't help to show it outwardly. But there was something in my stomach. It kept twisting and hurting with every oath and every time he used the word "nigger."

When it was over, he said, "Bradley, I told you in the beginning that your success or lack of it would get similar positions for other blacks. If you make it go, black people can come on board. If you fail, you'll slow the process up. You'll make it. I know you will. I want you to forget any oath and every time I said 'nigger.' I wanted to make sure you were equal to the task. I know now. I know that you'll make it."

Charles Smith: These were the most recognized organizing efforts in the county: that short-lived political period during the Reconstruction era; this attempted organizing effort of the sharecropper's union in the 1930s; and immediately after the Selma-Montgomery March. These were the major revolutionary turning points in terms of black action in the county. It seems to be a reoccurring thing. It may not be exactly the same kind of activity, but some radical movement of some kind becomes somehow necessary.

I was very young at the time of the sharecropper's union; I was still at Calhoun School, but I do remember that there was an attempt to do some organizing. The landowners got into it and squelched it before it got real muscles. Black people were driven off the farms and in some cases murdered. It was a period of fear. I was enrolled at the Calhoun School at that time. It was the last year I was in school. When the local power structure attempted to come onto Calhoun lands, it is my understanding that the Calhoun Trust made it clear that they would not tolerate the harassment of their people. It wasn't the school but the land trust that was important in the organizing. But the school started the land trust long ago. I remember that the resistance was being attacked by the powers. I attended a few meetings just prior to the attempted strike at the plantation, which just about shattered the movement.

The truth of the matter is that the leaders who were organizing were arrested and driven off, so forth. It pretty well died out.

Sam Bradley: The sharecroppers had passwords, "Put a nickel in your pocket and meet me tonight." I remember that. I stopped in Calhoun to get gas the day it started and heard them talking. I didn't think they'd succeed. They didn't have anything to fall back on.

Charles Smith: But, I can't help but believe that this organizing in 1965 was kind of a holdover for many of these people that were originally into that sharecropper's movement. It wasn't the same recognizable people, but it was the same concept that was formed in people's minds. The people were glad to see this togetherness in 1965, which means that some came out of, I'd say, hiding and really got involved again. But I was glad to see the day when enough folks wanted to do the same thing, to exercise their civic muscles and so forth. I thought the time to wait had pretty well been used up.

I don't know what happened. It happened so fast. When the opportunity came, why it just moved us. The time to wait had been used up. Stokely said it. Lowndes was the fastest moving place he'd ever organized. Stokely was hated by the power structure and loved by the black community—still is.

We Chose the Panther as Our Symbol

John Hulett: After we organized the Lowndes County Christian Movement, we decided to run people for office in 1966. We found out that the Democratic party in this county had raised the candidates' fees; so, if someone had to pay a hundred dollars to run for sheriff before, it was now five hundred

A VOTE FOR THE LOWNDES COUNTY

FREEDOM ORGANIZATION

Mr. Sidney Logan, Jr.
Sheriff

Mrs. Alice Moore
Tax Assesor

Mr. Emory Ross
Coroner

Mr. Frank Myles, Jr.
Tax Collector

Mr. John Henson
Bd. of Education

Mr. Robert Logan
Bd. of Education

Mrs. Willie Mae Strickland
Board of Education

IS A VOTE FOR US

Cover of voter education pamphlet of the Lowndes County Freedom Organization, 1966.

dollars. So to avoid the candidates' fee, we organized our political group called the Lowndes County Freedom Organization. We chose the panther for our symbol. The symbol later spread to California and other places, but started here. Everybody called it the Black Panther party, but Lowndes County Freedom Organization was the name of the party at first. The original purpose was a party by which we could run our candidates. Later we coordinated our efforts with the National Democratic party.

Robert Mants: Several of the people around the state had indicated to me their frustration in trying to get people to register to vote. Plus, when they got people registered and they started voting, they found the same white people were in charge. We tried to get into the Democratic party, but once we tried to get in, they raised the candidate fees by 1000 percent. And what people decided was that what we needed was a party of our own.

I wrote a one-page position paper with SNCC that talked about this high frustration and that in those counties where black people were the majority of the county, they needed to be in control of the decision making. Our research department in Atlanta did some research on independent political parties in Alabama.

The Code of Alabama has a specific provision for the creation of independent parties. One of the requirements is that the party have an emblem. One night over at McGill's house, a girl named Ruth Howard drew this panther at that kitchen table. One of the reasons that she drew it is that one of the other fellows working here was Courtland Cox. He, Ruth, Carmichael, and some other people had gone to college at Howard in Washington, D.C. Courtland was a big, dark, intelligent-looking fellow. At Howard he used to wear a big cape. They said he looked like a black panther. That's the way the name black panther came about. That panther became the emblem of the Lowndes County Freedom Organization.

After the first election it became an official party, and it was called Lowndes County Freedom party. Everybody started calling it the Black Panther party. Huey Newton and Bobby Seals asked Stokely about the use of the emblem of our party for the party they were putting together. As I recall, Carmichael did speak with some of the black leadership about it, and that's how the Black Panther party took our emblem. They were one thing, and we were another.

Charles Smith: There was never a Black Panther party. There was the Freedom party, using the black panther as its emblem. In 1968 I ran as part of the Freedom party. I ran in 1968 and lost; came back in 1972 and won. I've been reelected three times.

I ran for public office because I wanted to help address some of the unmet needs that I had lived with. I wasn't frightened. People tried to frighten me; the fright was just about gone. It was used up, like the time for waiting.

We tried to join the Democratic party, but they wouldn't have us. The way we got on the ballot was that on the date of the Democratic primary you had to hold a convention, or however you want to call it, and come up with at least 20 percent of the total vote. Well, on May 3 we captured 42 percent of the total vote. And, until the November election, we could put a candidate on the ballot because the party had established itself. We had become a legal party. We elected John Hulett with the Freedom party in 1970. In 1972 I got elected. The Freedom party then had merged with the National Democratic party of Alabama. We became part of that party so that we could run people for state office. Hulett was elected by the regular Democratic party in 1974. When I ran in 1976, I was elected by the regular Democratic party. We have run all our candidates since on the regular Democratic party.

John Hulett: So the political organization went through three steps, Lowndes County Freedom Organization, the National Democratic organization, and the regular Democratic party.

I was drafted into running for sheriff. I never was interested in running for political office. During that time I was working as a housing specialist with a group out of Washington doing construction work, called Rural Housing Alliance. One night I was at a meeting of people who were trying to come up with somebody to run for sheriff. We had run people since 1966, and we just wasn't successful in getting people elected. They asked me if I would run. I accepted the idea, and I ran for sheriff on the Freedom Organization.

Black People's Needs and White People's Funds

John Hulett: Health became an issue during that time. We started off by having doctors come to examine and screen people. They were doing screening to find out nutrition needs and the number of people with high blood pressure, for instance. That was the beginning of the whole idea of health care program here in our area.

We put a plan together to try to get the OEO health program in our area. We got money to do a survey of the needs of people in the county. Ethel Seals was one of the women who did the survey. We found out that about 800 people tested needed some type of health care. We pulled together a board of doctors and leaders in the community, mostly whites and few blacks, and public meetings were held. That's how our ideas first started coming together.

Kenneth McConnochie, M.D.: The organization of this and other Alabama health services was strongly influenced by a state law that establishes the county medical society as the local board of health. The medical society is legally bound to review and evaluate all health care activities affecting county residents. The Lowndes County Medical Society included the two GPs, Dr. Griffin, approximately forty-five, and Dr. Staggers, approximately eighty-two. In 1967 Howard Meadows, M.D., joined the society. Approximately sixty and noticeably symptomatic from coronary artery disease, he had just retired to Lowndes, his family home since the early 1800s, following a career as an administrator in the Navy.

John Hulett: We had a case of black people's needs attracting lots of federal money for white officials to administer. This was exactly the case with our program.

Sam Bradley: There were several meetings held before we ever got the OEO project. The last meeting where the community people were involved was held in Hayneville in a little brick building where the Davis Drug Store presently is housed. One of the local doctors asked this question, "If we, the Board of Health, do not take this program, could it inevitably come into the county anyway?" The Washington representative said, "It could." The response was, "We'll take it, then." You see, there again was the gulf between whites and blacks. This program was not to be controlled by blacks; it was to be controlled by whites. The board of health was all white.

At the time I was working with Lowndes County Board of Education, and the superintendent of education appointed me to represent the Board of Education on the health council.

I was glad to serve. I had a neighbor woman get sick one night, and I took her to the doctor. She was in a great deal of pain and was crying and hollering. He yelled at her, cursed her, and told her to stop carrying on like that. That's when I determined there would be change. He treated her no better than an animal.

Kenneth McConnochie, M.D.: The opening of the new center in Hayneville in 1970, built with OEO funds, was a major event. The architectural inspiration for the building was unmistakable. Columnar structures running the full height of the two-story facade, though not physically separate from the brick building, were a dominant feature. The building contained the only elevator in the county and offered 16,000 square feet of floor space. When fully staffed, there were one hundred employees including approximately fifteen community health aides and five drivers, one for each of the station wagons used in patient transportation. The LCCHP [Lowndes County Comprehensive Health Program] was the largest employer in the county and achieved an annual budget as high as $1,377,212.

Sam Bradley: From the inception of the program, we had, in my opinion, if not a unique, then a very undesirable kind of organization. The county board of health became the grantee for the program. The county board of health became the administrators of the program. The county board of health became the providers of the services. To me, you know, that's a very definite conflict of interest. So that is really the reason why the program never got off the ground to the kinds of things that the OEO had hoped it would do. Because the board of health didn't want that kind of program, or that kind of delivery health care in the county.

We made very little progress. The persons who were charged with doing that were not really ready for it. They were not ready for the change. After a number of years prompting on the part of the OEO, others, and local people, we came down to the nuts and bolts of the thing—either you do this or there will be no program.

Kenneth McConnochie, M.D.: On both quantitative evaluations performed, those of 1970 and 1971, the OEO found the Lowndes CCHP as a whole to be providing worse care than any other health center that it had evaluated. Though the score achieved by the Hayneville center in 1971 approached the OEO average in the area of adult medicine, most scores from the two physician's offices were as low, or lower, than any scores earned elsewhere in the nation. One of the many consumers interviewed stated: "I was in so much pain until I just couldn't keep quiet and he [the doctor] hit me. . . . he slapped me again."

In 1972 evaluators noted separate and unequal bathroom facilities for blacks in one physician's office. Also, there was "still an invisible dividing line between blacks and whites [in the waiting room], the blacks being relegated to a relatively unlit corner of the room."

Starting Over

Sam Bradley: The OEO had committed itself not to refund the board of health as grantee. I never will forget the last time I was in Dr. Cooper's office in Washington trying to save the program. The administrator, two

William S. (Sam) Bradley

doctors, and one or two other persons and myself went in to see him about some funds. He was at his desk, sitting in a swivel chair, and he just turned that chair and looked from one person to another. He looked at this one for a while and he looked at that one and right on down the line. Nobody said a word. We were just sitting there like dummies. I sort of got embarrassed.

Finally, after five minutes had elapsed, I attempted to tell Dr. Cooper what we were there for. The administrator took over soon as I broke the ice and went on for nearly an hour. Dr. Cooper never said a word. Finally, when he had heard all he wanted to hear, he stood up and said, "Let me tell you folks something. Now, you people go back down to Lowndes County and put together a program that I can buy, and I will buy it." He said, "I'm not talking dollars right now. I'm talking about the kind of program that I can buy. If you put that kind of program together, I'll buy it." And with that he dismissed us.

So we went on out, and as soon as we got out of the door, the administrator asked me, "Sam, what does he mean?" I said, "I think he meant what he said." He said, "What is that?" I said, "Well, he wants programs to do the kinds of things that they had hoped the program would do in the beginning. That's all he's talking about. We now have an opportunity to really do something down in that county, but we are not fenced in with dollars. He gave us a green light to do the program, and he'll buy it at whatever the cost." I guarantee you, I told them that fifty times between Washington and Lowndes County.

Nothing ever happened when we got back to Lowndes County. Nothing ever happened toward developing that kind of program. So the 1972 funds were spent. I think we probably had about $125,000 to $130,000 when the program year was over, and of course the administrator and his secretary stayed around long enough to use that up in the process of closing out the program.

On June 8, 1972, we, the council, decided, voted unanimously, that we would go ahead, at my recommendation, to develop a new broad-based board because it was getting late in the game to be ready by a funding cycle that began in October. I proposed at this particular time a series of community meetings with grassroots people.

The administrators said there was no point in doing that, because those people didn't know what they wanted. That bothered me a little bit. I said, "Well, look here, I tell you what, those people know what they want. They know lots more about what they want than you or maybe I. The only difference is they don't know how to put it on paper and make it look pretty, and that's why you are in the picture. That's your job to write it up into a proposal or whatever, the whole works. If you will listen to them, they can tell you what they want, what they need, and they'll tell you what they will support. It's just that simple."

It was a tremendous battle finding anybody to support us in efforts with the health program. Here I was again spearheading a health program that was entirely against the will of the county board of health—the administrators, and the whole outfit. To begin with, there was nobody. The administrator of the project dared any of the employees to even talk to me, or to even be seen talking to me. They were really wanting to get me off the council, too. But the superintendent was at odds with them. See, she was one of the biggest politicians in the county, and she used the school system really for a lot of support in that whole thing. She had appointed me, and she was afraid of repercussions if she dropped me after having appointed me. They put all kinds of pressure on her to get me off that council, but she never did. I just stayed there. I was steady. I lasted.

I became the bad guy. That's how the administrator of the project made it look; I was gonna tear up the program. He knew as well as I did that the OEO was not going to re-fund the program. He was telling the black employees, "Don't pay any attention to that Bradley, and we will have a program here, and you'll have a job, and blah, blah, blah." I became a bad guy even to the blacks. I was an "Uncle Tom." Whites saw to it that I was "Uncle Tom" to all the rest of the blacks, so blacks wouldn't pay any attention to me. I got a copy of the letter that the OEO had written—"we will not refund the board of health as grantee." I showed it to the staff, and that was the only way I got the reorganization started.

Kenneth McConnochie, M.D.: The OEO gave Bradley and the new board members an unparalleled political issue and a forum. The OEO created opportunity for them; it produced the "carrot." Effects of the loss of the old program were felt by all Lowndes' blacks and were attributed to the medical society. The OEO rendered the verdict that the medical society had failed. By enhancing Bradley's financial security, another federal program, Head Start, removed a threat that would have precluded response to such allurement in the past. Also, credit Bradley with extraordinary wisdom, restraint, and perseverance in gaining influence and using it well.

It Was Exciting, Doing Good

Sam Bradley: We were not eligible for re-funding as the old program, but we did stay in business as a new program. We got an agreement with Dr. Ken McConnochie. He had been working with the OEO project for about six months, and he agreed to stay with our regional board to provide health care for the people.

There are more stories behind that. He had to move out of the county into Montgomery because his landlord, a doctor, refused to rent to him. He commuted. His first patients were seen on the tailgate of his station wagon. He didn't even have a place. We were looking for a place while he was doing that. We found an old community building six or eight miles out of Hayneville that we rented and renovated and made a clinic. Our first health care was provided out of that building.

Mary Smith: First we had this old building, over in the Moss Community Center, which was a center for the OEO project. We didn't have anything to work with at first. We had to go through a transition trying to get a building. We cleaned it up, and then got that place fixed up for a doctor's office for when we would move there. We got donations of sheets and bandages and gauze and stuff like that that we might need to operate a doctor's office. Local community people and agencies gave us equipment. I think most of the materials came from the National Health Services Corps [NHSC], and

SEASHA provided us with an acting director, Steve Wilson, and we set up in the local centers in the communities and operated out of these, with the NHSC paying us a stipend for our services and paying for the expense of a doctor. A lot of the pharmaceutical agencies provided us with medicine and supplies, and we operated there until the board and some other people got us the building.

I continued to work as a nurse's aide. It was just an aide, myself, a nurse, and the assistance of a doctor. We had no set job responsibilities. We did anything we had to do. I would be the receptionist for a while and then go back and assist with the patients.

It was exciting! I loved it just being out there doing good, really doing something to help people. At that time people were so much in need. I guess you would just have to be there to see it: the old building, goats always around it, and the people coming in with no transportation of their own, not having money to get the kind of care that they needed.

Sam Bradley: In the meantime we were trying to negotiate with the county commission to get the building where the old OEO health program had operated. They were bitterly against that, and they were most determined that we would not get it, and we were definitely determined to get it. Of course we knew, first of all, it was built with tax dollars, and it was built for the people in Lowndes County. We felt like if it was built for us and we wanted to have a health program and we needed one, then it should come out of that building. Charles Smith became the first black county commissioner in 1972. Without having him where he was, our move to reorganize the health services would not have been successful.

The county commission was trying to maintain status quo. We actually had a battle. Mr. Smith was the only black member on the county commission. We got people together and forced the county commission to meet with people. They recognized the organization we were proposing as an agency to provide health care for the people in Lowndes County. We got it in writing. Sent their letter to Washington and several others to the governor.

Then they wrote another letter and sent it to the same persons rescinding that letter. They said that the county commission had met and unanimously agreed that we had no need for this program in the county. I got a copy from Washington. I asked Charles Smith about it, and he didn't know anything about the letter.

I said, "Man. You are discriminated against. They said it was unanimous. It couldn't have been." I also questioned the fact that he knew that this meeting was even being held. I asked him if he would stand up and say that he was being discriminated against, and he said, "Yes." I said, "Would you sign a letter to that effect?" He said, "Yes." I said, "Could you come to Hayneville?" He said, "Yes." I told him I would write a rough draft. Then he could read it and we would formalize it, and we did just that. That was in 1972. We began to provide health care in 1973.

Charles Smith: They wrote that letter without my knowledge. They said that this was the unanimous decision of the county commission. I said to myself, those boys got trouble without knowing it. They voted for me without my consent and represented me without my permission or my knowledge.

So that was a turning point. I didn't tell them, but I had made my mind up that there was bias in the county commission. I made my argument strong enough to the point that it turned things around. The peoples got the clinic now. It was a long, hot summer to get that building in hand, but the peoples got it now.

Mary Smith: There was a supplemental feeding program for women and children called WIC. I supervised WIC in 1973 and 1974. I believe we had 1,368 participants at that time. That was the case load during that time. And we provided them with cereal, juice, eggs, and milk. I believe Steve Wilson wrote a grant, and it was approved. We were the grantee for the WIC program at the Lowndes County Community Health project, and I became supervisor of that program.

Steve Wilson: McConnochie had read somewhere that the government had approved this feeding program, but he didn't know how it worked. He went to Bradley and said, "Here, this is something that would really be good for us." I mean, he wasn't thinking administratively or anything, you know; he asked Bradley if we could get this program, and Bradley came to SEASHA and said, "We need someone who can write this application for us."

I was working for SEASHA, which was out of Tuskegee. Their primary purpose was rural development through self-help techniques, small farms, housing, water systems, land retention, so it was a conglomerate of community development programs thrust at a twelve-county rural black-belt area. It was a community-based program. It was originally a Tuskegee Institute Community Education Program [TICEP], part of the literacy and cultural enrichment program and remedial in its approach. The TICEP became sort of an extension of the Freedom Schools of Mississippi in the early 1960s. The TICEP naturally got political and had to start dealing with economic questions. This was beyond the scope of Tuskegee Institute as an educational institution, so Dean Philips and John Brown, Jr., who was previously

Steve Wilson

a school principal who had come to work for the TICEP, conceived of the idea of the spinoff and the creating of this new organization. They were successful in getting other kinds of federal monies, and they got large support for a number of years as one of Ford Foundation's Community Development Corporations [CDC]. It was one of the few rural CDCs that they got funded.

I was dispatched by SEASHA. I hadn't worked there for more than just three or four days when they said, "Go to Lowndes County and go help these people. They want to get a nutrition proposal together." They said, "Go down there and see what it's all about." That's basically how it all got started. And within three or four months Lowndes was taking all of my time because you had the dynamics of the building being padlocked and the equipment being reassigned, and the conditions that the clinic was operating in were not tolerable. The next thing you needed was to get access to the building. You know, one thing just sort of followed another.

I had to work with McConnochie from the medical side of the WIC proposal and with limited information that was in the regs to figure out how to meet the requirements for Lowndes County. It was the sort of thing that you sort of made up because there weren't particular instructions or anything. We hit on the mark so well that when the program was funded, the USDA went to people in Montgomery and told them that they should set up the state program based on our model. This did not make our critics happy at all. It was one of those opportunities that you have to set something up right.

The need we found, well, it was powerful. I had seen a lot. I'd lived in a lot of places. But the poverty situation in Lowndes County was so concentrated, so pervasive, that it was shocking even to me. I got passionate about it. You could see the poverty. But that wasn't the motivation for me. What moved me was the level to which these people had been abused by the system of care that by its own philosophy is supposed to be humane. That was new to me. These people were walking around sick and dying, and they were being ripped off for prescriptions and office visits and things like that. I can understand racism and lynchings from a political standpoint, but I couldn't see it from treating other humans inhumanely and the exploitation that took place. So the clinic and these people deserved whatever I could do. They needed a lot more than what I could do, but we just did what we could. Some of it worked, and, well, some of it didn't.

Another battle was for dental services. What I was faced with was that the Alabama Dental Association [ADA] had, across the board, denounced the National Health Service Corps as a communist organization. So there were big scuffles all over Alabama because the Certificate of Need dental regulation reads that the professional dental society in the area has to certify the need for an additional health professional. I went to the ADA two or three times to meet with them and provided them with data: if we had three dentists working full-time for a year, we couldn't fill all the cavities in Lowndes County. It was just exhausting. I got nowhere.

I woke up one night and said, "Damn, I know what to do." So I set up a meeting with Sullivan Jackson. Martin Luther King stayed in his home during the Selma March, and Dr. Jackson is a dentist, and at that time he was president of the Alabama Chapter of the National Dental Association. It was the black dental association. I met with them at a chapter meeting in Selma. I said, "Now, you are the area professional society. It doesn't say whether it's a white one or a black one and you have just as much authorization to certify as the Alabama Dental Association." So they were glad to do it. It hurt them more than anybody else because it meant that a lot of people that used to go to Selma and Montgomery for dental care and pay for it would now get dental care here subsidized by the government and wouldn't come to a black dentist. But these guys were glad to do it.

I went to Washington with this certification and saw the director of the dental services within the National Health Service Corps, and he said, "You've got us now, don't you? Nobody has pulled that on us." So I said, "This is a Certificate of Need signed by the appropriate professional people." And he just said, "What kind of equipment do you need?"

The dentist we finally got was so vitriolic and hostile and problematic and pretentious that the board fired her. That was sort of the ultimate audacity, you know; Wilson fired her. He fires dentists! After I kicked their asses to get the dentist, then I was going to fire her. They felt I was playing fast and loose with the rules and not giving them any respect.

That's not the only problem I had. We also had a black nurse practitioner who came in and freaked out because people stank. I took her for a ride, "to show her the county," and I gave her lemonade and iced tea at two or three stops until she just had to use the bathroom. But every place I went just didn't have a bathroom until she had to use an outhouse and get some idea of how her patients lived.

Some of these things you could stop and some you just couldn't take care of. I could never stop one woman from spraying disinfectant every time she went into the examining rooms to see a patient.

The problems with the docs was that the community board exercised its authority to decide the manner in which people would be treated at the clinic and not to merely accept the manner in which the staff treated people at the clinic. That rubbed against the grain of the medical professional people at the PHS [Public Health Services], who didn't have any of these experiences. They hadn't treated a patient in ten or fifteen years, and the doctor was supposed to be always right. So that began to put cracks in our armor also. The corps began to relate to the new physicians independent of me, and my reaction to that was not positive.

If this had happened three or four years earlier, I would have figured out a deal, a way to get around it, but there was a fatigue factor and a burn-out attitude that in retrospect I would have done things less confrontationally. But I was also working as the president of the Southern Association of Community Health Centers, and I was carrying too heavy a load. Because I had tried a year or more before to get out of the health center, I told Bradley I could not continue to bite the hand that feeds us. I got to get out of the way. I knew that I had passed the tolerance point.

I knew I should get out of the way and let some new personalities take over. Then I got sick in January 1978, and when I came back in March, I quit. They got along for six weeks without me, and I came back and said, "Well, I'm not coming back." That reduced the pressure.

Because of Working Together, We Have Done Something for the People

Sam Bradley: Every service in the county which we now have wasn't there before the movement, not even Head Start. We have a senior citizens program, rural transportation—we've never had one before—it's a brand-new program. We have the housing program. All of these things are really post-movement services.

My philosophy is, know where you want to go and work toward getting there. Nothing takes my eye off that goal. I may have to change course and go this way or that, but my eye is on the goal. I don't know that I've done any great things, but I've been able to work with people at most levels. I've resisted what was illegal. I've maintained the respect of people I resisted.

John Hulett: Well, let me say this. Number one, these programs and other changes came through them because of organization. People used to gather and work for it and do it. It has brought about a service to the people. They now have a clinic they can go to at reduced rates or no charge in some instances. It's brought about a sense of honor to our young people who, because of organization, because of working together, we have done something for the people in this county.

It's interesting that the clinic is located right on site where the first registration went on. That's where the jail was. They moved the jail and built this clinic.

Charles Smith: When I was thirty or forty, I couldn't even dream of nothing like my being county commissioner in Lowndes County. I couldn't even dream of nothing like that in Lowndes County.

I would like to see the black folks and the white folks in Lowndes County lay aside their racial differences, and let's together do the kind of thing that would move Lowndes County forward and get her in the mainstream of productive kinds of activities. Whoever happens to be the kind of person who has the best ideas, that idea ought to then be adopted by all people, most particularly the business folks. Let's upgrade the educational system.

We might have some of these kids walking around here who can't hardly get enough to eat from day to day. What happens to these kids who go around from day to day who barely have enough to eat from day to day? If we got them well enough prepared, they might make a real contribution. Let me make an observation, had Dr. George Washington Carver not come along, we're not sure that we would have had all those uses of peanuts. All those uses of peanuts would have laid dormant until he came along. Well, looking at just that one thing, if we were to develop all of the people and utilize that human resource, together we could do some of the kinds of things that need to be done. If we could really develop people, it is possible that we could really develop Lowndes County to the point to where it wasn't last in prepared people. We just might have some of the best people.

Robert Mants: We find ourselves in the same economic shape. The tax base is not able to provide the kinds of public services—health, sanitation, not being able to afford decent housing, and not being able to afford a decent kind of quality educational system. About 85 percent of the people in this county are on some kind of public assistance of one form or another. The reason being that the opportunity for jobs is simply not here. There is a $1.5 billion General Electric plant going in here. The problem is that people here will get very few, if any, of the jobs because it's a high-tech plant, and our county, given its poor educational system and lack of capable skills, cannot provide the labor market for that kind of industry. The labor that is being proposed by GE is going to come from outside this county, within a one hour's, one-way commute.

The problem of the rural community is that there's been no parallel to that cotton dollar. There are black faces in high places, but the fact of the matter is that the county is still economically bound to the same power structure. The people who controlled the economics and the politics twenty years ago still control the economics today. And in a lot of instances, they speak through a lot of these black faces in high places. There has been no meaningful alternative to the cotton dollar. We've had social programs in everything, but there's no meaningful alternative to a rural economy whose basic source of wealth is cotton. Many of these wealthier persons in these rural communities made money primarily through low black wages, three dollars a day. That cotton dollar still speaks in these rural communities.

When we talk about an industry, we're not talking about big or small, we're talking about appropriate. And an appropriate industry is an industry where our people can provide the labor force. This county was bypassed by the Industrial Revolution. And if we, both black and white, don't move to meet the challenge at this time, we will find ourselves again being left out of this technological age.

CHAPTER 4

The People Are Trying to Do Something

Sea Islands, South Carolina

The Place

Johns, Edisto, and Wadmalaw islands form part of a chain of large islands, the Sea Islands, that extend from Charleston to Florida. These three islands begin near Charleston and extend southward about two-thirds of the distance to Beaufort. Johns Island is the largest island, about 240 square miles and second in size only to Long Island among islands of the continental United States. The islands are entirely rural, with few population centers. About 7,000 African Americans live on these islands. Wadmalaw and Edisto are about 80 percent African American and Johns Island, about 45 percent. The islands have acquired attention time and again for the poverty of its residents, about 40 percent of whom are at or below poverty level. In 1980 the per capita income of African Americans on Edisto Island was $3,588, or 38 percent of the per capita income of all other Americans. On Johns Island it was higher because of the number of more affluent African Americans who live there. The per capita income was $5,484, or 58 percent of the national per capita income.[1] Much of the area had undergone resort development. Kiawah Island with its beach-front condominiums, manicured lawns, jet-port, and equestrian center offers a stark contrast to adjoining Johns Island. Before the Sea Island Comprehensive Health Care Corporation and related efforts began, there were no medical services on these islands.

The People

Septima Clark lived in Charleston, where she was born. Few people had as important a role in the voter registration of African Americans in the South during the civil rights movement. She has been described as "one of SCLC's wisest senior staff persons"[2] and accompanied Martin Luther King, Jr., to

Stockholm when he received the Nobel Prize for peace. Her father had been a slave on the Poinsettia plantation and "fought on the side of his masters" in the Civil War. Her mother was orphaned as a young girl, and an English church group took her to be raised in Haiti. Clark acquired meticulous dress and speech from her mother. Clark died in the Sea Island Comprehensive Health Care Corporation's nursing home in 1986.

Ophie Franklin, the second president of the Sea Island Comprehensive Health Care Corporation, held that position from 1979 to 1984. A middle-aged college graduate from outside the area, he was an agent of change both for the corporation and within it. He tended to calculate explicitly the economic and political ramifications of events and to express them more than other narrators. His speech is slow, soft, and precise.

The Reverend Willis Goodwin first came to Johns Island as a sophomore in college to work in a program for migrant farm workers. He later served as a chaplain to migrant workers from Florida to Massachusetts, including Johns Island from 1956 to 1966. After that time he began his duties as pastor of five Methodist churches on the islands. After twenty-six years of ministry on the islands he was appointed pastor of the Emmanuel United Methodist Church in Sumter, South Carolina, in 1984.

Marybelle Howe's name suggests the southern gentlelady she was. Her laugh and manner, however, evoke an image of the salt of the earth rather than Scarlett O'Hara. She worked with the Reverend Mr. Goodwin and migrant laborers on Johns Island through the Church Women United and became an important and powerful ally of many of the African American community leaders on the islands. Like the bridges between Charleston and Johns Island, she was a link between the two. She lived her last years in an antebellum mansion in Charleston's Battery section. She died in 1988.

Abraham (Bill) Jenkins is the son of Esau Jenkins and vice president of the Sea Island Comprehensive Health Care Corporation. He began working with the project upon his return to Johns Island in 1971 after twenty years in the Air Force. He is one of thirteen children, seven of whom are still living. His father, Esau Jenkins, is prominent in the narratives. An entrepreneur, Esau Jenkins operated transportation services on Johns Island. With the assistance of Septima Clark, Bernice Robinson, and Highlander Folk School, Jenkins began Citizenship Schools and a local voter-registration effort. He ran for elected office in 1956, a bold and dangerous act at the time. His portrait now hangs in the Charleston County courthouse.

Linda Lingle came to Edisto Island as a VISTA volunteer fresh from college to work for the South Carolina Commission for Farm Workers. She was an original member of the board of the Sea Island Comprehensive Health Care Corporation. She works as director of development at Trident Technical College and serves on the Human Affairs Commission of South Carolina.

William (Bill) Runyon is an attorney from Charleston who has devoted a large portion of his law practice to low-income clients. Initially, he founded and served as an attorney with Legal Services. He has been attorney for the Sea Island Comprehensive Health Care Corporation since its beginning. He is in his forties.

William (Bill) Saunders was born on Johns Island, where he still lives. He is president and general manager of WPAL in Charleston. He has been active for political change since returning from the Korean War. He led a strike of hospital workers in Charleston. His activities include founding and directing a number of programs, including the Committee on Better Racial Assurances (COBRA), which serves three counties and of which he is executive director. He is also chairman of the Charleston Democratic party.

The Reverend McKinley Washington is the pastor for the Presbyterian churches on Edisto Island. He has been a member of the state legislature since 1974. He first came to the islands as a student intern in 1964 and remained. He served as the chairman of the Sea Island Comprehensive Health Care Corporation at the time of his interview.

We Had So Many Children Die

Septima Clark: I taught on Johns Island from 1916 to 1918 one time, and then I went back from 1926 to 1929. There were ten black schools on the island, and I taught at a place called Promised Land. Esau [Jenkins] was at another school. He was a little boy about six years of age when I was teaching there. I left because the pay was terrible. It was $25 a month, and that's why I went up to McClellanville, where they were paying $60 a month. When I went back in 1926, I was getting $175 a month. The conditions in 1926 were much better than when I went in 1916. In 1916 I had a room in an attic; I had a lantern for light. Starting in 1954 we had electric lights. There was very little water, and I had to use the same water to bathe in and wash my clothes. They had those surface wells, and there were no indoor toilets, so the toilets ran into those surface wells. But in 1926 the law had come and said they had to dig down into the dirt for their toilets.

In 1948 we had so many children die on the island that we made our first effort to improve health care. We had the first immunization program. Do you know some of the white nurses did not want to roll up the sleeves of the black school children? Myles Horton from Highlander helped us out by sending some girls from Antioch College, who helped with the immunization program. They would roll the sleeves up and then the nurses would give them the shot. Those girls pushed up those sleeves very nicely. Esau Jenkins had a bus then, and he would take the bus all around the island to get these people for the immunization program.

The school board decided in 1956 that if I was a member of the NAACP, I couldn't be a teacher. I taught for forty-one years, from 1916 to 1956, before they dismissed me. The state passed a law that said that no employee of the city or state could be a member of the NAACP. A lot of people decided that they were not members, but I said, "Yes, I am a member." I joined in 1909. I said if they are going to tell me what organization to be a member of, then they'll tell me what religion I ought to be. But that's the reason that the pilgrims came over. The state of South Carolina took away my pay and dismissed me. That's when I went to Highlander and stayed and started working there.

After we saved those babies from dying in 1948, we started with the

Septima Clark, center, at Citizenship School on Johns Island, 1959. Bernice Robinson is standing behind the group.—*Courtesy Ida Berman*

men because they had pellegra since they didn't eat vegetables. That was around 1956 or 1957, and the women from the Presbyterian Church came to the school house where we were working and they would start showing the people how to cook. They used a charcoal pot to show them how to fix the vegetables that they grew. They fixed them so that they could eat them themselves. You see, the boats would be at the northern end of the island, and they would take their vegetables straight to New York and Philadelphia to the markets.

Marybelle Howe: The World Council of Churches and Protestant organizations had been interested in the plight of migrant workers for years, and it had been a particular concern of Church Women United. This work with the migrants began around 1959. I was then president of the local chapter of Church Women United. We would drive along the roads to get to the sites where we would work, and once we were there, not enough work could be done. The need was so great.

The local group of Church Women United was not integrated at the time. The school board said that we could use Haut Gap School as a permanent facility where we could take the children during the day, provided that the black women looked after the black children and that we, the white women volunteers, supervised. Of course, it turned out to be everyone working together; you couldn't tell a supervisor from a worker.

One of the reasons, I suspect, that some of the women were interested in migrants was exactly because they migrated. They would come, but then they would be gone. That way you could contain what you were doing, if you know what I mean. Whereas, if you went around the corner, there would be needs and people there all the time. It's interesting—kids from elsewhere would come here to Charleston and work with the migrants. But the kids here in Charleston would go to Costa Rica and work. It's like there's something in our psyche that says it's all right if you do this thing—but not at home. There were, however, a few young people from Charleston who worked with us. It's just that we never had trouble recruiting people from other areas.

Esau Jenkins had been opening up Johns Island to new ideas and possibilities. He was our bus driver for the migrant children's program at the time. Each day he would pick the children up at the various camps and bring them to the school. He did this with considerable sacrifice to himself. He did get some money for his work, but not enough to compensate for the use of his bus or his time. One of the things that I admire about him was that he treated everyone the same. He was even sweet and thoughtful with children of the migrants; can you imagine carrying a busload of children of all ages and stages?

He was a very nice and courteous man, but he was also a very stubborn man—otherwise, he would not have gotten where he did! He was difficult to convince of anything, but he was not hard to work with. When you are working for the same things, you just don't have that many difficulties.

We Got Us an Engineer

Bill Jenkins: My daddy Esau had been active on the island before most other work got started. He was really interested in education. His whole emphasis, everything he did, was with education in the background of his mind. One of the reasons was because he didn't get a chance to go through no more than the fourth grade initially. There were no schools out here until 1953 for blacks to go beyond elementary school. So, any blacks who wanted to go beyond elementary school had to get to Charleston and go through one of the public schools in Charleston.

When we were small, Daddy used to read anything from a dictionary to black history books; I don't care how old the books might have been. He used to teach us so much about Frederick Douglass and all of the black people that he knew of. He read just like he used to teach us Greek—whatever he knew he tried to pass it on. He used to stay up still reading until it was almost time to go to work. My mother and he had thirteen children; seven of us are still alive.

He had an organization set up as far as the family was concerned for Sunday morning. Come hell or high water, there was a service, and if it was your time to lead the service, you had better have your stuff ready. You had better start about Wednesday if Sunday was your time to lead service, because he would have so many questions to ask you, you had to be prepared. It was quite a chore to go through, but looking back now, I'm glad it happened.

He was so religious when it came to those kinds of things. His name was Esau, his brother's name was Jacob, his father's name was Peter—all biblical names. And of course my given name is Abraham. My brother that died was named Peter; my other brother is named James. He did not follow the biblical names with the girls, but with the boys he did.

His mother died when he was only eight. His father married a woman with two kids already from a previous marriage. In my father's estimation, he was getting more of the hard chores and he figured that he was being unjustly taken advantage of in that family mix. He started living with one of

Esau Jenkins—*Courtesy*
Ida Berman

his relatives and quit school at fourth grade. He began working as a deck hand on a Greek ferry boat in the city of Charleston. He couldn't have been more than twelve or fourteen years old.

I would hear him tell the story how one of the best things that ever happened to him as a boy was when he met the Greek engineer. When he finished cleaning up on the deck, he would go downstairs, and this Greek engineer would teach him the ropes about engines and what they did. He just observed, and after a couple of years he got to the place that he knew almost as much about that engine, and what to do with it, as the fellow that was teaching him.

This engineer took sick one time, and so the skipper was saying that they could not go out because they did not have the engineer. My daddy told him that he knew how to run the boat. They started laughing—he was just a young fellow. He went down and started up the engine. The skipper told him to trim it, and he trimmed it. Then he told him to put it in reverse, he put it in reverse. He told him to rev it up a little; he revved it up. The skipper told the crew, "Come on, let's go. We got us an engineer." When the Greek fellow came back, he refused to take his job back. He told them to let Esau run the boat and to let him get on another boat. So that's how he got to be like an engineer, as a boat mechanic.

One of those Greek fellows told him, "You know, it was a good thing that you got to be an engineer on that boat, but where do you think you are going from there? You need to start looking for bigger things." They were in the market that day, and there was a lady there with a bushel of plums. She was from the island. She had a doctor's appointment. So she had to leave, and she just wanted someone to pay her seventy-five cents for that bushel of plums so she could leave. Daddy gave the lady seventy-five cents for the bushel of plums. And while he was there talking with the Greek sailors, he filled up the three baskets she had also given him along with the plums. People came and looked at them, and bought them. I know he said he made more money off that bushel of plums than what he would make sometimes in two days working on that boat. And he never went back on that boat.

He started hustling out of the market in Charleston. He had learned some Greek from the fellow on the boat, so when he would see the fellows coming through the market, he would call out to them in Greek, "Kalimera. Ela edho. Echo frouta na poulesa." And they would come to him. Imagine this black man speaking Greek with all this accent! With the profits he bought a Model A Ford truck. And then he would come out to the islands and buy out of the fields, which was even cheaper. He bought the truck when he was sixteen. He started doing a little bit of farming, too, and then supplemented his produce with that of other farmers, and what he couldn't get out on the islands, he would go to the market for. From that, he started making smaller stops around Charleston making deliveries, and this led him into other things.

My dad got some of his land from his father, and some of it they bought together. He was never a big landowner. He had probably six acres. That was about all he ever owned. He would plant that and then buy from other people, their vegetables. He was a truck farmer. He never had a whole lot of money.

His daddy was a carpenter. People would get him to build houses every once in a while. He would scrape some money together. He had a Model T Ford, I remember. There were other black folks on the island that had a lot more than he did. There were people who owned seventy-nine or eighty acres and who ran ferries. They were the leaders of the black folks, economically.

During World War II plants were looking for people to make fertilizer, and a lot of people out here who had been doing almost unskilled work were looking for other jobs because farming didn't pay that well. They started getting jobs in Charleston, and Daddy started using his truck to carry people to the fertilizer plant. By that time we, his children, had started going to school in Charleston. We used to go in with these people to work in the morning. Then other kids started riding the truck. After a while we had many, many kids from the island going to school in Charleston. He took one of his trucks and traded it in on a small bus. With that bus he used to carry people to work and kids to school.

I don't have any sympathy at all when they start talking about busing. We didn't even have the opportunity to get on any bus but my daddy's. We had these one-room schools in different communities that taught everything from first grade right through to the seventh grade, one teacher for sometimes fifty kids. The teacher had to have it set up so she could have the small kids up on the front row and try to get to the seventh graders on the back. All during the winter time we sat behind one potbelly stove, and she used to have the older kids make sure the fire was started prior to 8:30 or 9:00 in the morning. When it was your week, you would be there a little earlier than the rest to start the fire. The windows were those board windows, no panes—you just opened it up like a door. Looking back, we had some good teachers. I learned more there than any other place that I have been, I think, because the teacher just had a pride that she was from the island and had gone to Avery Institute. Her father was one of the people who had a big ferry boat, so she got a chance to go to private school in Charleston at Avery Institute. When she finished, she came back over here and started teaching. At the time it was fun. But looking back now, I get angry.

My father started being a fighter. People gave him all kinds of problems because he just started saying to the county school board, "If y'all don't have a school out here, then y'all gonna pay me to carry my children and other people's children to Charleston's schools." He just started fighting everybody. They started calling him a communist and other things. This was 1943.

He got really involved in the community when a black man got shot by a white in the late 1940s. The black man had a male dog, and this white person who lived on the other side of the road had a female dog. This dog, I guess, was in heat, crossed the road, and the two dogs started having intercourse. The white man's wife came over and told the black fellow to get his dog off her dog, and he just flat told her, "Lady, I didn't put them together and Lord knows I'm not going to try to take them apart." And he went on to work. The woman went and told her husband that this guy cursed her. He got in his car, stopped the black man in his truck, called this young man off the truck, and shot him in the stomach. At that time my daddy was at the market, and when the word got to Charleston, that this young man got shot because of a dog, he and some others got an investigation with a lawyer started. There was to be a trial, but it was always being postponed until the intensity of that incident really died out. We never saw the white man punished. That's when my dad really got involved and started telling people the reason we were treated like that was because we didn't register to vote. We did nothing. We just accepted it.

Since he had the bus, he started transporting people who did domestic work into Charleston. Those people didn't have to be at work until about an hour or an hour and a half after he'd take the people to the fertilizer plant. They just sat on the bus since there was no place to go. So he started teaching them on the bus that portion of the Constitution you had to read in order to be a registered voter. One lady said she could not read it but could memorize it. And she used to help everyone else when they would start reading it and start stumbling; she had it so memorized that she could just tell them what the word was. That was a big thing around here for a long time—she couldn't even read but she could help tutor these other people who could read. Five or six people registered, and then the number doubled, and doubled again.

We Had Developed a Model Here

Bill Jenkins: Then my daddy started getting involved with Highlander Center in Tennessee. He went out there and met with Septima Clark. Septima Clark, Bernice Robinson, my sister, my dad, and some more people came out here and started adult education.

Septima Clark: He went to Highlander, and he saw whites and blacks together like he hadn't seen before attending these classes. He got ideas there, and with a little help from Myles Horton he got money to set up a school to teach people to read and write. The Marshall Field Foundation supplied a little money, and we set the first schools up. The first schools were for two months and later for three months, and we got people out of the fields. We developed the first Citizenship Schools in about 1954 and 1955, and from there we went through all the southern states; I have an article here that says 50,000 people in eleven states. The first one was right here on Johns Island.[3]

Bill Jenkins: He used to be up trying to get people organized. He used to do a lot of traveling, going all over Charleston, especially with adult education and voter registration. When he got with the Citizen's Committee of Charleston County, that used to take him from McClellanville all the way to Edisto Island. Many times, attempts were made to take his life. Besides trying to run him off the road, people would try to stop him, but he just wouldn't stop. I know Momma and the rest of us would be fearful until we heard the truck come into the yard.

Daddy caught purely hell when he was alive from black and white. He got more recognition after he died than when he was alive. Blacks didn't want to be identified with him because they were fearful that they would lose their jobs, and whites didn't want him because he would not bow down to them. Some thought he was crazy. People even hired black folks to come out here to try to kill him. One guy just came and told him, "One of the prominent white fellows on the Island had offered to pay one guy $500 if he gets rid of Esau Jenkins." One of the guys they tried to hire came back and said, "I may be a fool, but I'm not that much of a fool." He just came back and told him, "Watch out because some people are trying to get rid of you."

When Martin Luther King finished in Montgomery and went to Albany, Georgia, to get the people organized there, he was lacking the grass roots. He came down here, and my daddy taught not only him but taught that whole group how to organize. Ms. Clark, Bernice Robinson, and my daddy used to go all the way to Louisiana and teach adult education. They used to go along ahead of Martin Luther King and get the people organized, and when King got there, the people were ready, because King was more on an upper level than with the grass roots.

You can hear Andrew Young tell it. Andrew Young will tell you that he did not become involved because of Martin Luther King. He became involved because of Septima Clark and Esau Jenkins. Then he got tied up with Martin Luther King. But they all started out working together, even with the Selma March and all those other marches.

Septima Clark: Andy was a highly, middle-class black boy. He had been to Europe and all around the world. We had to teach him how to work with our low-income and indigent people.

I Wanted to Be Free

Bill Saunders: I've certainly thought back on why I got involved in all the ways that I have. It was because I wanted to be free. When I finished elementary school, I was bused like everyone else at the time to the inner-city school for blacks in Charleston, Burke High School. Burke was the only school for blacks, although you had St. Johns right here on the island, but St. Johns was for whites.

I wasn't free, and I wanted to see what price I had to pay to get that freedom, and whether or not I could make the down payment and the last payment on it. This came to me when I was in the military. I served in the Army in Korea until 1954. I was about fifteen or sixteen years old when I went to the war. Afterward I felt like a fool when I realized that I had gone and said I was fighting for the freedom of the Koreans and I wasn't free myself. I experienced more racism in the military than anywhere else I've been in my life. But what was worse was to fight in Korea, to get wounded there, and then to return to the States to find that I couldn't ride in the same train coach with those I fought with there. Or to come back to Columbia, South Carolina, and to go into the bus station to get my ticket, not knowing I was not supposed to do this, and to have a cop with a gun come up to me and say, "Boy, you don't know what you're doing." To find that blacks were supposed to get their tickets in the hole cut in the back of the station; to stand outside in the weather with no shelter while waiting for the bus; and finally to find that blacks got any seats that were left over once all the whites had loaded on the bus—all this made it crazy to say that I was fighting for the freedom of Koreans.

When I returned home, I joined the Progressive Club. A group of us at the Progressive Club bought an old school house and turned it into an adult school. The school we bought was the one I had gone to as a kid. It had no lights or restrooms. After the 1954 Supreme Court decision, they decided that they better build us some better schools, so they built a new elementary school and sold the old one.

We worked strictly on voter registration. We worked with the Highlander School, which at this time was in Monteagle, Tennessee, in running workshops on the island, and this was the first time that blacks and whites really came together.

The Progressive Club kept growing. We borrowed money and built a gym as part of the Progressive Club where our kids could play basketball and skate. None of the schools on Johns Island had gyms. This was another stupid thing that white leaders did; they would deprive their own children

Myles Horton, director of Highlander Folk School, and Esau Jenkins in store adjoining Progressive Club, 1959.—*Courtesy Ida Berman*

of places to play basketball, etcetera, just to be sure that blacks didn't have these same things. They would make their own kids suffer just to make sure that blacks didn't get anything. We also built some rooms in the Progressive Club as places where we could hold more workshops. Being part of the effort had its dangerous side; my wife and I got shot at at the Progressive Club on the same day that Kennedy was shot. We never found out who did it, but the bullet hole is still in the window to mark the spot.

Besides doing a lot of community organizing after I got back from Korea, I spent eighteen years working in a mattress factory, from 1956 to 1975. We started a press, *The Low Country*. We had a big press hidden out in the woods. Because of my work and commitments, people brought their problems to me. In 1968 I was also organizing the hospital workers, and in 1969 we had a strike that lasted one hundred days. The city of Charleston was closed down for one hundred days. We started the strike at a good time. It started about April and went into July. It was the tourist season, and the whole city was empty. You can just imagine the economic problem with that. We shut down the whole city because the medical university is pretty large. But the second thing is the strike was so well organized. The students who were in school came out and demonstrated, marched, and went to jail. The SCLC and 1199 [health care workers' union] came. There were just so many people. We had thousands and thousands of people marching. The jails were full. Abernathy did a real good job. He went to jail. It really caused a lot of emotion. They had the state troopers, the local police, and the national guard, in addition. There was very little violence. We had a heck of a chief of police. A retired marine major had just become chief. He handled the thing pretty much. He locked me up, but he was a pretty good guy. We got to be pretty good friends. He was responsible for doing a lot of good things.

It got national attention. The Nixon administration finally got involved, Harry Dent. They told people in South Carolina to settle the strike. "You can say we made you do it. You can say you're doing it because you love your state and your people. But do it."

We were dealing with issues of justice. We were dealing with what was going on when black nurses had to get the key from the white nurses to go to the restroom. They had to eat their lunches in the boiler room. And the state said that they didn't come under the minimum-wage law. The city of Charleston and the state of South Carolina were not paying people minimum wage. At that time minimum wage was about $1.60 an hour, and they were paying people 80 or 90 cents an hour. My idea was and still is that the best way to help people is to help them make more money. We went after the medical university here because we saw if we won with the medical university, the entire state would have to follow its lead because it was a state institution. We did eventually win, and the state signed an agreement that they would always pay at least 10 cents above minimum wage, that they would have job descriptions, that everyone working for the state would have a grievance mechanism all the way up to the governor.

Whites were making that same money. That gave me a rude awakening during the strike. Whites were dumb enough to think that because they got access to the restroom and a special place to sit for lunch, they were above the black workers. In fact, they were all making the same money. We had some of them come to join the union. We had one guy, white, who came in and said he'd been working there fifteen years and was making $1.25 an hour. The blacks that were in the union thought that the whites were making a hell of a lot of money.

That's when my attitude changed. We do live in a class system. It really is rich or poor. It begins to be a racial situation when we get to the bottom. Even if you don't have as much as you need, as long as you have more than somebody else, you think you're well off. Especially when there's an orchestrated effort to make you think that.

Even today, my biggest enemy is poor white people. They're the ones who see blacks somehow standing in their way or somehow stopping them from getting what they want. They never look at the system. They're my enemy in the sense of people who would give me the most opposition. They're not my enemy in terms of my target. In the 1960s the poor whites were in the Klan, and I used to say they weren't my enemy because they didn't have power. My target has always been the people with power, in the statehouse and city hall. The poor whites in the Klan were powerless. They had nothing. They had no power.

A lot of things changed at this particular point. The Human Affairs Commission came into being as a result of the hospital strike. Right after the hospital strike we had a sanitation strike that helped workers here in the Sanitation Department. Up until that point blacks were not allowed to drive the trucks, and they worked six days a week and those sorts of things. As a result of the strike they began working five days a week, received at least minimum wage, and got uniforms.

In 1968, when the militant movement was on, a group of people on the island known as Concerned Citizens, for which I was the chair, laid down an ultimatum. We demanded that three people that we would select be appointed to the seven-member school board by a certain date, and that if this wasn't done, we would hold our own elections, and there would end up being a black school board and a white school board. In 1956 Esau Jenkins ran for the school board in District 9 on Johns Island. Esau almost won, and this shocked the hell out of a lot of people. There was not another school board election held on Johns Island until 1972. This was complete disregard for the law. The response to our demand was the appointment of Esau Jenkins and one other person we recommended to the school board.

Now, at this time Esau Jenkins and I were really having a conflict. Esau

Jenkins was cofounder along with Martin Luther King of the SCLC. I was very close to Stokely Carmichael, SNCC, and Malcolm. I used to keep people from SNCC who used to come to John's Island for a rest. Stokely came from Cuba around Christmas time 1968. Esau preached nonviolence, but I didn't believe in nonviolence and I still don't. Esau was fighting from one position, and I was fighting from another.

The power structure had appointed Esau because they hoped that the conflict between him and myself would continue and hurt the movement. I went to Esau and spoke with him, and I said, "People are asking you whether you are against me or not because of this so-called militant stand. I'm not violent or nonviolent. I'm just not going to let anyone tell me to be either one of those things. But I have never been as militant as you. The kinds of things that you have done on the Island are strictly militant. I've done things backed up by an armed bodyguard, but you've done things alone and without any of that." He realized what I meant, and after this we worked together, and he made some real important policy changes on the school board.

Most of us who took part in that effort were called communists. When I ran for the state senate here in 1980, that was the label which my opponent used against me. That was something I never fought against too much because all the sufferings of blacks in this country had nothing to do with communism. It was all under democracy. What has been so stupid is that the gains blacks have made have been given to the credit of communism, whereas democracy was flexible enough to make those necessary changes.

Waiting on Bridges to Open and Close

Bill Jenkins: From my recollection I think the highway road was built in the 1930s or the late 1920s, and that aided us in getting to Charleston. There was no medical care here, so everybody had to go to the emergency room in Charleston. The people were treated so badly by some of the nurses, and sometimes by the physicians, but especially the nurses. It was segregated there.

Sometimes they would be riding to or from Charleston, and the bridges would open and it would take so long to close at that time. They were manually opened. A man would have to walk around and crank it open. That went on until the 1960s before they put in a motor that would swing it open. Many people died trying to get to medical care waiting on the bridges to open and close.

The Reverend Mr. Goodwin: People in Charleston had given up on health care for the islands. They could not envision the possibility of a health center here. They didn't know how to go about getting one, even though some doctors saw the necessity of some kind of health service. So we would carry people in need of care to Charleston and would often wait on the bridges to let the tourist boats pass through. I helped to carry people to medical services and hospitals in Charleston. I remember carrying migrant workers who had no money to the emergency rooms. Sometimes I had to promise that they would pay. Pregnant mothers in labor would sometimes be turned away. Several people died in my car when we had to wait on the bridge for the beautiful ships to pass through. The absence of health facilities on the island was sorely felt. When we made it to the hospitals, there were segregated waiting rooms for whites and blacks. The white patients were served first and the blacks last. I am glad those days are gone, and I hope they never come back.

We attempted to talk to people so as to get things changed, but to little avail. Some of the groups who opposed us included the big farmers, some of the white churches, and the medical society of Charleston. I served as a member of the county council, but they were insensitive to the plight of the people on the islands. I remember telling them about people dying in my car while we waited on the bridges, and they replied that the sea lanes had the right of way. The islands were a forgotten land.

This was the time when the civil rights movement was getting started in the area. Stokely Carmichael and Martin Luther King were coming here. Some of these people let me know that the church was not taking an active enough role in the movement, and they were right.

Bill Saunders: I was very hard on ministers because I thought they were hard on black people, making arrangements for them to go to heaven, but not giving too much of a damn whether they ate or not.

Marybelle Howe: Esau Jenkins pushed the Farm Commission to upgrade the lives of the people on the Island. He wanted to do more than the Farm Commission. That's how Rural Mission came about. It was adult education, housing, and some health care. There wasn't any room for a big health clinic. There weren't any doctors. A doctor came on Saturdays, but there was no major health clinic.

The doctors like Dr. Heisel that we got through the Methodist church would come here under the auspices of the Charleston County Health Department. We didn't go through the local medical establishment, the Charleston Medical Society. They were against the clinic then, and many of them

Join

Rural Mission, Inc

in an exciting ministry of
Christain concern: the
comprehensive development of
the Sea Islands of Charleston
County...

..."Inasmuch as ye have done
it unto the least of these,
my brethren, ye have done it
unto me."

The Rev. Willis
Goodwin, on front
portion of pamphlet of
Rural Mission, Inc.

still are against it. Why are they against it? Don't ask me to explain the mind of a doctor.

Everything at first came through voluntary effort until we got the federal OEO grant, and the Sea Island Comprehensive Health Care Corporation was established. I am not sure if we could have gotten the Sea Island Comprehensive Health Care Corporation if one wing of the Bethlehem Church on Bohicket Road had not already been operating as a clinic on Saturdays when Dr. Heisel would fly in from Indiana. That wing was built with volunteer labor drawn from many churches. The first doctors we got through the Methodist church. After we had gotten the OEO grant, I developed back problems and had to resign from my position on the local commission.

The Reverend Mr. Goodwin: The people really needed the health center. Dr. Heisel was the only doctor on the island at this time. He knew of a hospital in Washington, D.C., that was going out of business, so we drove up there and got a lot of their medical equipment. This was around 1968 or 1969, I believe. There were no doctors on the island, and there would still be no doctors were it not for the center. There had been widespread illness on the island before the center got started. For instance, smallpox was an acute problem and was one of the reasons why it was so difficult to get ministers to come in and reside here. Before Reverend Brown became the first resident minister in 1933, there had been a history of preachers dying when they came here. Besides smallpox, there were a lot of parasite diseases, like worms, hypertension, and maladies related to dietary and sanitation habits, on and on. There was no such thing as preventive medicine.

The move toward the health center really got underway around 1970 or 1971. Dr. Heisel had not been able to continue coming in on weekends, and Dr. Elliott, who had been a missionary in Africa with the Methodist church, took his place. Dr. Elliott lived with me for a while, and later he moved into a trailer. Dr. Elliott compared the conditions he found here on the Island with those he had experienced in Africa. I myself became aware of these parallels when I went to Africa some years ago, and I have made a commitment to return to Africa every year since then. The year before last I was in Central America. I was the only black man in the group that visited countries there, and I was asked by reporters what I thought of what I saw. I told them that I was not surprised by what I saw since there were similar conditions in America. So there have been and are still parallels between places in the United States like Johns Island and Third World countries.

Linda Lingle: I came here in 1970 as a VISTA volunteer with the Farm Commission and lived out on Edisto Island. There were six of us in VISTA,

Linda Lingle

three women and three men, in the group in Charleston. One was a woman from Oregon and a little older than me. The other woman was seventy years old then. She was the most conservative member. She grew up in a wealthy black family. She would always say we were being racist. She was a snob. She could be very kind, and I loved her in a lot of ways. It was a real experience. We were more like the people in the community than she was. She would go up to a kid and say, "Why don't you have braces on your teeth?" She would ask why people didn't have flowers on the table. Flowers! They didn't even have food!

I was acting as a nurse with Dr. Elliott even though I knew very little about medicine. It was really an incredible experience. Dr. Elliott would come in to the clinic once a week, and there would be waiting to see him a long line of people with all sorts of illnesses and complaints. It was the first time that a resident doctor had come to the island. There had been a doctor over on the beach, but he would not see a black person unless he or she were 90 percent dead. So people began to think that something could get started.

We got help from all sorts of people and places. There was one white man whose family owned one of the larger grocery stores here on the island. He was a member of the National Guard Medical Corps. When he would return from weekend duty, he would bring back with him medical supplies which he would donate to the clinic. For instance, he would salvage supplies that might have otherwise been thrown away, such as the syringes which they were required to dispose after one use. So the federal government was supporting the clinic in ways which they did not know! Since he was in the medical corps with some medical knowledge, this man also helped directly with the work at the clinic. What was interesting was that he got flack from the white community for doing this.

As it turned out, there were connections between my VISTA work here on the islands and events of the same period in Lee County, especially with respect to my mother's concern for these developments. I still get emotional about this. My mother knew some people from the medical establishment in Lee County. She went and spoke to board members of the hospital there to solicit their support for the clinic in Lee County that was similar to the clinic that was starting here. This didn't represent a major action, but she did it.

Bill Jenkins: Senator Hollings got a copy of an article about hunger in Beaufort and Jasper counties.[4] Since it was talking about his state and his area, he and part of his staff came on a fact-finding mission to see what was really going on in Beaufort and Jasper counties. They also got Lieutenant Governor West at that time and part of his staff to go along. When my daddy and some of the people here heard they were going to Jasper and Beaufort counties, they formed a committee and they went to Beaufort and Jasper counties. The fact-finding team found out that the conditions were worse in Beaufort and Jasper than stated in the paper.

My daddy and others said to them, "Senator Hollings, Lieutenant Governor West, before you go back, we want you to stop on Johns Island, and whatever you saw here in Beaufort and Jasper counties we can duplicate on Johns Island. The people there are trying to do something about it, but we don't have the means." Senator Hollings and Lieutenant Governor West came to Johns Island and took a tour. We took them around to Peter's Field on Johns Island and some other places. Lieutenant Governor West just couldn't believe it, and he said, "How can we have a country as abundant as ours sending money all over the world and people living like this in this county and in this state?"

Senator Hollings told Esau and the rest to find someone who could put a proposal together and send a personal copy to him.

Progress Was Like Patching Pieces of a Quilt

Bill Saunders: When they got the package for the grant together, they found out that they had to come through me since I was on the OEO commission that had to approve it. I was on the countywide commission for the OEO program. I represented the poor from Johns Island, James Island, and one other island.

Even though commissioners were elected by the people, they had to be certified by the governor to serve on the commission. The governor refused to certify me. I continued to serve anyway. They tried to call for another election, but I refused because I had been legitimately elected by the people on the islands. Finally, in 1968 an OEO representative came here from Atlanta, and during her review I told her that I was not certified. She told the group, "Ya'll don't get a nickle until this man is certified." She then packed up her stuff and walked out of the room and went back to Atlanta. Charleston County, at this time, had been receiving about $3 million in federal funds through an OEO program. So this really put the state in a bind, and they came up with a rule from that day on that the governor would never be responsible for certifying anyone again. The county became responsible for appointments. We got back on track and got the money.

Nineteen seventy-one was when we applied for the grant that established the Sea Island Corporation. I was not part of the process as it related to Rural Mission because a lot of people on the islands, especially ministers, did not like me at the time. I was considered the black militant leader in the state, and as a consequence a lot of people, including blacks, avoided having much to do with me.

But I was the commissioner for this area, and if I had opposed it, they would not have gotten the grant. What Reverend Goodwin and other leaders did, therefore, was to make me chair of the Rural Mission Health Committee! This is how I got directly involved when we got the funding.

Bill Jenkins: In my case I retired from the service in 1971 and moved back home. I figured I'd come back to give my daddy help. I was in a position now to help him do some things. I grew up around this work, and I guess I would have come back eventually. I spoke to my daddy. He never said I should come back, but just the way he spoke, I knew I should. Then after talking to some other people, I knew the work needed to be done.

Marybelle Howe: The progress was like patching together pieces of a quilt. Esau Jenkins, of course, was the overriding big power, but he sparked others like Bill Saunders and Reverend Goodwin into doing other things as well. So a lot of these other little things added up to pretty good things. The fact that people on Johns Island now have health care where before they had none at all represents a tremendous step forward. There were a lot of other little steps taken.

Linda Lingle: Interestingly enough, most of the community leadership that served on the clinic board were there as representatives of other local organizations. The influence of Esau Jenkins, who had died before the clinic got started, was felt by almost everyone because he had been such a powerful community leader. It seems that community representatives who served on the clinic board were already on the path of community leadership, and that their involvement on the board enhanced their abilities. Even though mistakes were made, the board training process was valuable because we had people there from varied backgrounds who had never actually served on a board.

The majority, or at least close to 50 percent of the people who trained for the board, were black women. The black women involved were Mrs. Clark and Mrs. Robinson. Bernice Robinson was a supervisor. We were fortunate to have her because of her strong background. Mary Frances Brown is still with the program. She's sort of behind the scenes. Also Rosa Nesbitt was on the board. She was very active. She was a strong force on Yonges Island. Mrs. Alan Wood was the second chairman of the board on the island. She was very involved with the people. She helped start a school and was the director of the Head Start program. She is still very active and must be about ninety. She was perhaps the foremost community activist. Most board members were representatives of local organizations.

Bill Jenkins: What we did was to try to get a local health council on each of these islands. Either we created or we got to be a part of an existing organization on each island. In most cases we became a part of an existing organization. We started getting input from all of the islands, and we started trying to meet their needs.

The first thing we did was get a film on Mound Bayou. It showed them that this was a possibility. When it looked like it was going to be feasible, we began using that to organize local health councils. We tried to get people we could rely on.

Some of the organizations included the Citizens Committee of Charleston County, which was an organization that my daddy formed a long time ago to get people to vote and be politically united for what they needed to do. Out of the Citizens Committee came the credit union, which taught people to be thrifty and how to do some banking because trying to borrow money in this area was hard. You had to go to the loan sharks if you did not have the kind of track record anyone would loan you large money for. So they had to come up with something through the Citizens Committee—the credit union—and it's still in existence. The Rural Mission Health Corporation was another

Abraham (Bill) Jenkins

organization. It was first organized as the Rural Mission Health Planning Program.

We went through a six-month board training process. We took a couple of thousand of dollars and bought two vans. Then we were still working out of the wing of the United Methodist church on Johns Island. We just started running up and down the roads on all these islands to pick up people so they could see the doctor. Then we also would go to all the church services to tell people about the program. I think we went to so many churches in one week getting on the agenda for five minutes, and then on to the next and their agenda, till we covered sixty-six churches one time.

A lot of places we couldn't penetrate. People had such bitter feelings for government projects. One guy asked, "Is this one of those projects that offers you everything but doesn't deliver? We had too many of those already." We said, "No, man! We are going to have a clinic out here." He said, "We have heard that so many times. As a matter of fact, let me tell you where I'm coming from to see if you are going to really deal with the issues. We walk using hip boots to get through the mud from my house to the road trying to thumb a ride into Charleston just to make a living, and come back home and we ain't even got a place to take a bath. The tub we've got is filled up with diapers. If you are going to start dealing with these kinds of things, you don't have to worry, I will be your number one advocate in this area. I know I got some people who will listen to me. But you are going to have to demonstrate that you're for real. We've had too many promises."

As Long as We Were in Those Trailers, There Were No Problems

Ophie Franklin: Eventually, the activities of the Sea Island Health Center program included two health centers, in brand-new buildings: a nursing home, housing for the elderly, a laboratory, a pharmacy, a nutrition program for the aging, and a sewage treatment plant on Johns Island. Alongside the Sea Island Comprehensive Health Care Corporation was a related corporation called the Community Development Fund, which was originally set up to handle the construction and other developmental activities that were not permitted through the health center.

When we were operating the clinic, it cost us about $3 million annually. We got $1.8 million of that from the federal government, and we generated about $800,000. We had a sliding fee scale. Most of the people we saw were indigent. Among the major illnesses were hypertension, diabetes, obesity, and sickle-cell anemia. About 50 percent of our registered patients fell beneath the guidelines for the sliding fee scale, so they were receiving free services. Sea Islands has an approximate total population of 60,000, but a large portion of those people belong to the densely populated bedroom community of James Island. So we are probably talking about more in the range of 26,000 to 30,000 people, 22,000 of whom were registered with the clinic at the height of its operation.

We had many people here who observed our efforts. Right now we have a group of students here from Africa and Saudia Arabia, and we have worked with different groups every year from 1978 to 1981. For the past five years we have worked closely with the University of North Carolina at Chapel Hill. They came down here once conducting an extensive study on health care and health administration. Dr. John Hatch from Chapel Hill wrote a letter to the Department of Health and Human Services saying what a fine operation we have here and how it should be a model for the whole country. We were ranked fifth of all health centers in the country one year prior to the defunding. We even got money, an extra bonus, for a well-run organization until the local medical society got involved and started trying to discredit us. We still work with the University of North Carolina at Chapel Hill. The Albert Einstein Medical School Evaluation Team evaluated us also. We have received all kinds of compliments.[5] That's why we know we were doing the job.

The history of the corporation and its ability to serve as a focus for the social and political development of this community has shifted, depending on the source of federal funding. For example, with the OEO, which funded the planning and initial operation of the clinic and bricks and mortar, the focus was to redress the inequities of the past. When the funding shifted to the HEW [the Department of Health, Education, and Welfare], there was an additional emphasis on the provision of jobs as a legitimate concern for community health. There was likewise an emphasis on community control. With the Reagan administration, there was a dramatic shift to emphasis on state control and a correlative deemphasis on jobs as a factor of a healthy community. As a consequence of this we have suffered severely, both economically with respect to cutbacks and politically with respect to control of the operations of the health program. To the extent that the whims of the funding sources change, so our own activities change.

Bill Jenkins: I would have to put our dealings with the federal government in three categories. First, when we got started, the OEO was more people-oriented. You could apply for aid, especially poor people in rural areas where they were denied health care. Health was just a privilege there. When we got started, we had many people who came down who tried to assist us in doing the planning and those kinds of things; this was under the OEO.

We got the Esau Jenkins Clinic on Yonges Island through the OEO, and we were supposed to get a clinic built on Johns Island the following year through the OEO. But when Nixon became president and said he was going to disband the OEO and transfer all these health centers over to the HEW, the HEW was a different ball game. "We don't deal in construction. You'll have to go and seek it in order to get construction. We will give you equipment and those kinds of things, but not any construction." We ended up with a clinic on Yonges Island but then couldn't get a clinic over here, so we ended up in trailers because we could buy trailers as "equipment." So we ended up in a lot of trailers. And we stayed in those trailers until we started branching out in nursing homes and housing and all this kind of stuff and went to Farmers Home Administration and started borrowing money to put up structures. One of the structures was the permanent health facility over on Johns Island, through Farmers Home but not through the HEW or HHS. That was under Carter.

The third phase is now. As long as we were in those trailers, there were no problems. As soon as we started coming up with the construction, there started all kinds of investigations and audits. We bought fifty-five acres of land to put the nursing home and clinic on, and they wanted to find out how could you buy fifty-five acres of land if you didn't have any money. "They" were the federal government, the politicians and the medical society. Everybody we've been fighting ever since.

To Disrupt and Destroy

Bill Runyon: The corporation's most severe problems began with a dedication ceremony of the new facilities, the nursing home and other buildings. Reagan had just been elected, and along with him a Republican, Tommy Hartnett, had been elected to the U.S. Congress from this district. The Reverend McKinley Washington, our state legislator, was giving a speech at the ceremony before Hartnett was due to give his. In his speech Washington was being critical of the Reagan administration. Hartnett rose from his seat, walked past the podium in front of everyone assembled there, gesturing with his hands to show his disapproval, and then he left.

The Reverend Mr. Washington: I spoke at the ceremony, and in my speech I criticized Reaganomics and the cutbacks on local health care programs. Representative Hartnett, who was also scheduled to speak, said, "To hell with this" and got up and left the program. I later told him that if he was not able to take criticisms of Reagan's programs, then he should not be going to Washington where he would hear this every day whether from Republicans or Democrats. I don't think that this incident made all that much of a difference, although it might have speeded up things already underway. Tom Hartnett was already after the local health care centers. He had already gone after Fetter Health Center in Charleston by this time.

Bill Runyon: After this occurred, I knew that we were going to have trouble. Suddenly, all our financial operations were being questioned, despite excellent reviews in the past with the HEW and HHS. It should be noted that this began after the urban health center, Franklin C. Fetter, had been determined to be, if not corrupt, then mismanaged. The entire board there had been removed and replaced by a board that was dominated indirectly and directly by the local medical establishment. We knew after this coup of Fetter that we were next, although we did not know exactly what to expect.

William (Bill) Runyon

Bill Jenkins: The medical society was trying to compare a medical encounter here with an office visit to a doctor. That's apples and oranges. When a person walks through the door here with a medical encounter, that may be five or six different things. When they walk in for an office visit, if they come for an ear ache, that's what they get. That's what you get, an ear ache exam. That's all you get. When they come here, they get everything that we can do. Everything that we can find wrong, we deal with even if we have to make a referral. That comes under that one encounter. You can't compare the price for an office visit with an encounter. But they didn't want to hear that.

The GAO [General Accounting Office] looked at us and found out that they couldn't find anything wrong, but by that time the local newspaper had crucified us. They even talked about the president driving a $40,000 Buick— Buick didn't even make a car for $40,000 back in 1982—and how we misused government money. It was all over the paper. All this was just to discredit us. They took a little bit of fact, put a lot of fiction with it, and just blew it out of proportion. Though they couldn't find anything wrong, you would never see any apology. If it came, it came in such a part of the paper that no one reads. The main objective was to disrupt and destroy.

Bill Runyon: The only thing that the investigators could turn up as even remotely questionable were the business arrangements between the corporation and its lawyer, myself. The HEW, for about three years, had been granting $25,000 in the annual budget to the corporation for legal services. Because the corporation needed money for land development projects, I volunteered to use only a portion of this $25,000 for expenses, leaving whatever was the difference for the corporation to use in its land development projects. It was a voluntary donation; everyone knew about it, and the agreement was in writing.

I remember when during this period of investigation, two HHS representatives came by my office and asked me why I was not taking the $25,000 payment in full. I tried to give them a sense of what was happening. I told them, "You're talking to the town liberal. My son has gotten beat up on the school bus because his daddy's a 'nigger lover.' Why do I do what I do? I was there at the clinic's start, and if you plant the seed you want to help it to grow."

GAO rendered extremely technical interpretations of the regulations for the corporation's activities, activities that had been approved by the Program Review Divisions of the HHS and HEW. But the GAO investigators said that they differed with the judgments of the HHS and HEW and that these things should never have been done. But it was not corruption. No trace of corruption was ever turned up.[6]

The Sea Island Corporation gave the government its money's worth and achieved maximum results on the dollar. On paper it might have averaged out that services were provided at the cost of $50 per visit. This could fail to show that these included services not normally provided by private medical care: home nursing, health care centers, housing for the elderly and handicapped, a lab and a pharmacy, a sewage treatment system, an alcohol program, speech pathology treatment, and dental services. These were things that did not receive the attention that they deserved.

The press stories made it look like here were a bunch of blacks stealing from people. It was a witch hunt.

All of a Sudden Everything Was Wrong

Bill Runyon: What caused all of this? The general feeling was, "You black folks can't run things." So this "blue ribbon," white majority board was to be put in charge of things. I think the bottom line was racial prejudice. I think there were some people who could not tolerate the idea that a black community-based organization was operating a federally sponsored multimillion-dollar health project, even though the need for health care on

Johns Island and the other islands had been enormous before the program had started.

It had happened to the Beaufort-Jasper Health Center as well as to others, and we knew that sooner or later it would be approaching our turn. When the smoke cleared, Fetter, the center in Charleston, with a board dominated by the local medical profession, had its hands in our operations.

I also think that the Republicans, both nationally with the Reagan administration and locally with figures like Tommy Hartnett, were playing a game of "catch the minority by the toe." They were out to discredit Democrats and Democratic programs so as to prepare the way for the eventual dissolution of these programs. I remember calling Tommy Hartnett to voice my displeasure to him, and he just responded that these people, these blacks, had never done anything for him and never would do anything for him.

Ophie Franklin: Even at the height of the controversy, Dr. Ed Martin in Washington admitted that this was one of the best-run health clinics in the country. The GAO auditors indicated unofficially that, despite the allegations of mismanagement of funds, the federal government was getting three times worth the dollar value it was putting in to the operation. Since this was a politically inappropriate statement, it never got into print.

Prior to the HHS and GAO investigations, we had received glowing reports, both written and oral, from the federal government. The HHS had always given us high marks. This is why the investigations were so weird and Kafkaesque. All of a sudden everything was wrong, yet the strength of the program was the reason why HUD in conjunction with the HHS had funded the program. Five million dollars in federal grants must indicate some level of confidence. From 1981 to the takeover by Fetter in the spring of 1982, there was a flurry of audits—seventeen audits in seventeen months—by the GAO, HHS, and state representatives. No one was ever indicted, nor was the corporation sued by the government. Of course, just the audits' starts, not the results, got into the press.

Bill Runyon: I don't think Ophie Franklin's being appointed director of the Sea Island Corporation made all that much of a difference, although it probably sent some shivers down people's spines. Looking back now with the advantage of hindsight, I would say that we could have avoided a lot of our troubles had we appointed someone from the local medical establishment. That Mr. Franklin was not part of the local establishment was what made a difference, even though he was quite qualified. Having a black director did help to increase the fears of this black organization, as if this was a Malcolm

X-like, black power group. Those fears were completely unfounded. Both the board of the corporation, the staff, and the patient population were all integrated. We never tried to present ourselves as a black movement, but as a community-based effort. The publicity played on the typical white stereotypes of blacks; blacks were either incompetent or militant.

Ophie Franklin: Changes since the 1960s in black-white relations in Charleston seem superficial and minimal in light of the lack of interest or desire to let blacks share power. For the most part, only those representatives of the black community who have been sufficiently acculturated into the white community will step up or be allowed to enter into positions of influence. Where they are able to exercise such power or authority, their conditioning is such that they act in the interest of the establishment. Leaders who come into the community from elsewhere face a life of resistance and suspicion. They are never really accepted.

The black professional and middle classes were supportive but not as active or overt as they could have been because a social system has been set up in which individual self-interest takes priority over the needs of the community. Though people's lives may no longer be threatened as in the 1960s when they registered to vote, they still may suffer the loss of their jobs if they do not act in accordance with the demands of the establishment. When an outsider comes in who does not adhere to this code of behavior, it can place an institution in jeopardy, and I think this has a lot to do with what has happened with the corporation since 1980.

The final objective of the bureaucracy and the county administration was to gain total control of the Sea Island Comprehensive Health Care Corporation, but someone didn't do their homework, and they ended up with just the funding for the operations while we were able to retain ownership and possession of the facilities. This was largely thanks to the design of the corporation, which my predecessor, Jim Martin, and myself had implemented.

So we managed to survive on a shoestring until September of 1982, when we negotiated a settlement with the Department of Health and Human Services on the basis of the investigations conducted by both the HHS and GAO, which had failed to turn up any evidence supporting the allegations that had been made against us. There was never, however, any admission that the accusations made were false, and there was neither a reply to our own rebuttal of the charges. As a result of the settlement we were paid $261,000. No one seems to want to admit, though, the irony and the revealing truth that the government, which claimed we supposedly owed them a quarter of a million dollars, turned around and paid us that same amount. Nonetheless, there are still unresolved matters from that period, particularly as to who has legitimate ownership of the clinic on Johns Island.

The white blue-ribbon committee that took Fetter over is operating the clinic, and though we do not get any income from that site, we maintain that we own the clinic. The HHS maintains that they own the clinic, and others argue that they have a share in the operations.

Bill Jenkins: We still have the nursing home, eighty-eight units, forty-four skilled and forty-four semi-skilled. We have housing, eighty-eight units. We have the laboratory, the pharmacy, and the home health agency. We have the nutrition program. Our budget still runs somewhere around $3 million a year.

As far as our relationship with Fetter goes, we're still holding on. Fetter runs the clinic here, but they're supposed to use our pharmacy and laboratory. But more and more we see less of the lab work from the Esau Jenkins clinic on Yonges Island. We still own the building, and we're paying Farmers Home Administration for the building. Fetter pays us rent, because we own the building here and the Esau Jenkins clinic on Yonges Island. That clinic was built with OEO money, so there are no payments on it now. They give us something like a dollar a year for the lease. They also pay a share of the sewer plant, which is the lifeline of the clinic, the nursing home, and the housing project. There's no other sewer system out here yet, although the city is taking all of this in here now.

Ophie Franklin: Land development undoubtedly has a crucial role to play in this whole question of permanent black ownership of organizations and institutions on the island. Charleston is expanding, and as it does so, more and more people want to move onto the island, which is after all a nice place to live. It is going to be very difficult for blacks to hold on to their land when their land acquires so much worth. I think the only thing that slowed this process down so far is the presence of heirs' property and the title to the land tied up in this.

Bill Jenkins: Our land is a threat to further development.

Access to the System, Blacks and Whites Working Together

Bill Saunders: But it got to the point that certain members on the board was pushing the idea that a black should be executive director of the corporation.

Esau Jenkins and I and others were satisfied, however, in having Jim Martin, a white man, as executive director and Bill Jenkins, a black man, as vice president under him. This allowed us double access. Bill Jenkins had access to the black community in ways that Jim Martin could not have. But Jim Martin could deal with hospitals, clinics, the medical association, and other social levels which a black man did not normally have access to. In 1980 this conflict culminated in the appointment of a black man to the position of executive director of the corporation, and I resigned as vice chairman of the board. I resigned because the chairman of the board, David Richardson, someone with whom I am still friends, and others on the board had forced an issue that I was against.

I now regret having resigned. About three Sundays ago at the church where I teach Sunday school we were asked what decisions we had made in our lives that we really regret, and I think that the biggest mistake that I ever made was resigning from the board of Sea Islands. You cannot fight anything from the outside; you've got to be a part of it to fight it. Although there was a lot of fighting on the board, as long as I was on the board, I could at least educate new members as to past history. I sincerely believe that if people get all of the information, they will make the right decision, but people don't always get enough of the facts.

My position of black militancy is not and has never been "Black is always right." This was not the meaning of black militancy, but because of the press it became equated with violence and the like. We did not have the opportunity to educate the press. I've never burned anyone's buildings or taken part in a riot. At the first news conference I ever had someone asked me to describe black militancy. I said, "It's very easy to describe; if I were white, I would be called a patriot."

The Sea Island Corporation worked well for a long period of time in terms of having access to the system and in terms of blacks and whites working together.

We have black leaders in the country, in the state, and in Charleston County and on the islands who have an academic and professional orientation. They are lawyers or doctors or highly accomplished in some way. They believe that a black person of their caliber should be in charge, or else they want to be the top people in some organization. This can cause problems.

The black middle class, they were resistant to all our efforts except voter registration. The black middle class has never accepted me. I can remember the first radio program I ever did—they said that what I was saying made sense but that my English was so bad that I should write down what

I wanted to say and let someone else restate it. Of course, if I couldn't say it, I sure wasn't going to be able to write it! It was tough for the kids from Johns Island, like myself when we went to school, because we spoke a special language, Gullah, and the teachers who knew nothing about our language worked from the assumption that we couldn't speak English because we were just stupid. I was the commencement speaker in May of this last year at graduation ceremonies for master's degree students at the Citadel, and members of the black middle class were angry that I had been selected, especially since I had no degree myself.

You Need Some People Who Don't Have the History

Bill Saunders: I've witnessed a hell of a lot of changes over the years. In 1974 my wife ran for the school board and won. She has been chair of the school board for the last six years. This is a school board that blacks at one time could not be on. At St. Johns High School, a school that I could not attend, three of my kids have been presidents of the student body.

William (Bill) Saunders

After all the changes that have taken place, I don't think that I have become like the people in the system whom I used to warn others against. That's something to always be careful about, but I don't think people ever change that much. My position, my fight, has always been for the right to be a part of the system. Some people might say that I don't raise hell anymore. But hell, I have access to the conference table. I can pick up the phone and call the mayor or the governor or someone else. I couldn't do that twelve or fourteen years ago. I can do more for people now than I ever dreamed I would be able to do, simply by having access to and impact on the system.

Linda Lingle: I know things have changed to see Bill Saunders as head of the county Democratic party; that would not have been possible fifteen years ago. If the redistricting goes through, McKinley Washington may be state senator from this area. Things have changed. On the other hand, sometimes I wonder if I think things have changed because I am now part of the way things get done.

There are some who say things haven't changed. The way Jackson delegates booed Andy Young, that's what that's about. Some of those people wouldn't have been at the Democratic convention in 1984 except for Andy Young, and yet they booed him. I guess they see him as part of the establishment.

The Reverend Mr. Washington: The incident at the Democratic convention this year [1984] when delegates of Jesse Jackson booed Andrew Young indicates some division between younger blacks and blacks who grew up in the civil rights movement, though I am not sure how significant this division is. But a number of young people did not go through the struggle, and as a result they do not understand the need for their continued participation and support.

There has always been black control of the Sea Island Corporation, and some sensitivity has grown among the people of the black community to the importance of this black control, that this is their organization and that it belongs to them. Yet blacks have not financially supported the organization as much as they could have. Many still do not understand the importance of this organization because they did not go through the struggle to establish the health program, and that goes back to the Democratic convention and what happened there.

Although it wasn't a majority of the Jackson delegates who booed Andy Young, there were a good number of blacks at the convention who didn't know who he was. I remember after he had been booed, Young spoke to the South Carolina delegation the next morning. He went through with them some of the things that had happened in the 1960s with the civil rights movement. He told them how he used to be scared to drive through the state of Georgia, and how today he is the mayor of Atlanta. He recounted to them how at one time he had worked with Septima Clark and Esau Jenkins in Beaufort County to teach people how to read and write so they could register to vote. He explained to them how what others and he had done then made it possible now for blacks to take part in the convention and for Jesse Jackson to address the delegates. The people in the South Carolina delegation were then saddened because they had discovered that they had done something wrong.

However, there were those who did not take the time to listen and who did not realize that this man Andrew Young was more "black" than Jesse Jackson and had done more than Jesse Jackson had ever done. I remember that same morning at the black caucus meeting when Coretta Scott King asked the audience to apologize to Andrew Young, and people booed her. Clarence Mitchell, who was standing next to me, said, "Y'all don't even know where you came from. If it hadn't been for this woman and her husband, or Andy Young, or my daddy ("old man Mitchell," who was director of the NAACP and helped write the Civil Rights bill) and others like them, y'all wouldn't be standing here and neither would Jesse Jackson."

I had no problem attending the convention as a Mondale delegate. Even with all the emotionalism the other people from my precinct followed me as Mondale delegates in a committee meeting. They were people from this community who trusted me because they knew who I was, where I had come from, and what I had done. They thought that whatever I was doing was in the interest of the black community. When I returned from San Francisco, I discussed some of the issues of the convention on a radio talk show at WPAL called "Open Rap." People called in and said they were glad that I was explaining things that some people might not be educated enough on. Jesse Jackson's minority plank made it possible for blacks on the Mondale platform committee to get a middle-of-the-road plank in which their voices were heard. People have to understand that Jesse Jackson didn't lose. He knew that he wasn't going to get what he was pushing for anyway. So he helped us.

In the same way that Jesse Jackson's campaign has brought vision and hope to people, the Sea Islands health program brought visions and new aspirations to the people of the island. This is why the dismantling of the program was so tragic, and a lot of people have failed to realize just what this means for the delivery of health care services and preventive medicine on the islands. The program was such a life-line because it improved the total community. This is also the bottom line why white politicians went after the program. The Sea Island program was involved in voter registration, education, and all sorts of training projects that this community would never have experienced had it not been for the Sea Island program. The program has been more than a health care center. It has been a way for people to come together and talk about political, social, and economic issues affecting their lives.

A lesson that has been learned about working with the federal government as a result of the experiences of the Sea Island program is that you can't depend on the government. The federal government may be supporting you today, but tomorrow with a new administration it may not, and you have to prepare for this. This is a lesson learned in our community and others throughout the nation, and some learned it the hard way. We fared better than others because we were prepared when the government came down on us with the intent to wipe us out completely. They weren't able to do this because of the way we had structured the organization of Sea Island as a development corporation. They could take the money out of the programs, but they could not remove the services from the buildings, which we owned.

Things started rolling in 1965 when we got OEO support for programs on the island like day care centers, Talent Search, and summer projects, and these later branched out into other activities. This was when the mayor was saying that we didn't need any OEO money in Charleston County and Strom Thurmond was calling it dirty money.

Today there are still housing and education needs on the island.

Bill Jenkins: Daddy died before he could see it in its present form, but he had come many times to the clinic when we were in trailers. He thought it was one of those things that was needed, but not the only thing. He was still looking for much more in education, especially with kids not going any further in school because of economic conditions. He wanted them to have some kind of trade so that they could get out of school and be viable in the community. One thing that he really was against was kids with aspirations and talents being drained out of this community and going and helping other communities because either they couldn't go to school here or couldn't get a job here. That was one of his concerns—to keep some of these people here. Otherwise, we are going to have a dying community. We are still trying to deal with this. Now that we have engineers, lawyers, doctors, and everything else, we have to try to make sure that we can make room for those people back here.

Bill Runyon: White folks fear black folks, and there were people around here who were afraid of what Sea Island Corporation was doing. At one point Sea Island was the largest employer on the islands, employing as many as 200 people, if not more. These weren't just black employees; there were whites and Mexican Americans; Sea Island was an equal-opportunity employer. A lot of people were concerned about blacks operating a multimillion-dollar enterprise. They were doing a pretty good job at it, too. With the Reagan administration there had begun racist attacks on organizations nationwide, and by racist I mean attacks on organizations controlled by minority groups. Various threats such as those of indictment have been used.

The Reverend Willis Goodwin: This change from a period when we were receiving aid from the federal government to a time when financial inquests were being made began when the Reagan administration took office. When we went to Washington at this time, we spoke with Ed Martin, who told me that he had a mandate to close down health centers. With this administration everything that poor people—not just black people—have gained for themselves has either been abolished or cut back. The only good thing about having elected Reagan is that he's cut federal funding, which has forced the church to be the church again and start taking care of the sick and the poor.

Linda Lingle: My feelings about the federal government have changed from the days when the clinic was first established and supported by the OEO. For example, back in the 1960s when governors stood in the doorways of the schools, the federal government took the side of those who were fighting for voter registration and desegregation against the local and state authorities. Now they're taking the side of the local and state authorities when they lay down restrictions on voter registration, for instance. Back then the federal government seemed like our friend. We had run-ins with the local police, but we felt that there was someone we could call.

Bill Jenkins: I wonder about the progress because I think everything is just moving. I don't think we're closing the gap.

Every time you think you're making progress, the next thing you know is that somebody's changing things. Reagan tried to change everything around. Most of the people he's had the chance to put on the Supreme Court, they may change later, but right now they're showing that conservative philosophy. I wrote a letter to Senator Hollings about Bork's nomination. Hollings,

Thurmond. I wrote from the point of view of the Citizen's Committee. Hollings responded, saying that he was close to the situation and that he would look at both sides. He didn't say he was for him or against him. We wanted to let him know that we had reservations about Bork.

This is the same Citizen's Committee that my daddy started and was president. We are not as active now as when he was in it. Right now, we try to do some of the same things, but we don't do them on the scale that we used to. Self-esteem—that's what we're working on now. Kids are losing self-esteem. The reason they're losing their self-esteem is that most of us don't know our own history. We think our history begins with the slavery. We don't even want to look past then. We have people looking at how we can better address black history, because I know we're going to have to do that. We're doing this work mainly through the churches and in each other's house.

Bill Saunders: Black people know we can go backward. We've seen it. I think the difference in 1990 and 1890 is that we—when I'm talking about *we* I'm speaking of minorities, I'm talking about women who were not a part of the 1890 situation—we're better equipped to deal with the situation. We have enough power, if we can maintain it, within the system itself to make it work. That has always been my dream, anyway.

My dream has always been not to have any special laws for black people. But let the laws of the country work. To make those laws work, blacks are going to have enough power, because the only way things work in our country is by power. We're talking about all kinds of power. We're talking about the vote, education, economics. We're talking about politics.

I believe that we have enough political power right now to impact state and local government. When I speak of political power, I'm not referring to blacks alone. There is such a beautiful political alliance that blacks could make with women. There are other groups, like poor whites, who share the same problems that blacks suffer from. I feel that blacks are going to have to quit locking ourselves into fighting for things we call black when they really benefit everybody. Food stamps were fought for by blacks, but they benefited everybody; the whole country needed the program. The South has not done a good job in elementary and secondary education. The whole system needs to be upgraded, from textbooks to teachers. Education is not a black issue alone.

I've been very careful to say what progress blacks have made in America. But when I look at the progress of blacks in America, first I have to kick out the progress that America has made. A lot of times when I take out the progress that America has made, the progress that blacks have made is very little.

I think affirmative action is a necessary thing. It deals with the past misdeeds of people. Although a lot of my white friends, who I meet on the corporate level, they say that they had nothing to do with this, so they shouldn't be held responsible for it. But they had something to do with it because the company that they have and the rights that they own came out of those segregated arrangements of their fathers and grandfathers. So I see that they are responsible now to undo what's going on now because of what went on before. I see affirmative action as a necessary tool to at least try to bring people up to give us a chance to compete. That is one of the things that we have not really had, a chance to compete. When I say a chance, I mean with all of the tools that I need to compete.

That includes health care. The medical profession in this state and America has not been a good partner with poor people in providing health care. We probably have the best medical establishment in the world in this country, but we have the poorest health care system. Preventive medicine has always been neglected by doctors in this country. It's all right for me to have hypertension or a stroke, then I'll be treated. But no one cares how I got to that point. That is why Sea Island program provided us with an opportunity to change things for the better for ourselves.

PART II

The Elusion of Emancipation

As John Hulett explained, leadership does not parachute from the sky. The life experience of the narrators prepared them for their later efforts. Those experiences were fashioned by conditions of subordination and repression as well as their own and others' efforts at change. The chapters of this section outline some of those conditions and efforts as foundations for the later change efforts that the narrators recount. Each chapter begins with Reconstruction and works forward to at least 1940, when the oldest narrators were young adults. The community health centers expressed a portion of the promise of the civil rights movement. But the civil rights movement itself demanded some of the promise of emancipation that had eluded African Americans in the rural South for a hundred years, as the chapters of this section show.

CHAPTER 5

Economics: Land Reform and

Landless Farmers

For Tom Rice, the other narrators, and most African Americans in the rural South, the economic promise of Emancipation was in landownership. Other rights and freedoms were linked to that economic promise. Landownership meant that Tom Rice could send his son, Earl, and his other children to school. It permitted him and others to register to vote with less fear of reprisal from disapproving landlords. Because landownership was central to other changes, it was withheld. Twice the federal government distributed land to African Americans in the South, in the 1860s and the 1930s. Between these federal efforts, other land-reform efforts occurred in places like Lowndes County. The largest number of African Americans in the South, however, were landless farmers. In places like eastern Arkansas, they rebelled frequently from the repression and subordination that marked their landless condition. Their efforts exposed the violence beneath their economic condition.

The various land-reform efforts were successful in various ways, even though they served a very small portion of people who needed them. Part of their success was to supply an economic base for later organized efforts at change. Bob Mants, who worked in two different areas of the South during the civil rights movement, remembered finding a set of landowners behind every organized change effort in the rural South. Bill Saunders attributed the success of Esau Jenkins's efforts in literacy, voter registration, and political campaigns to the large number of small landowners on Johns Island. The political change efforts were, as the narrators indicated, preludes to the development of the health services, except for Lee County where the health center came first. Even in that instance, landownership was a crucial element of the leadership of both efforts.

This chapter covers land-reforms efforts from the time of Reconstruction on the Sea Islands to the New Deal in Haywood, Lee, and Lowndes counties. It also surveys the labor conditions of African Americans in the agricultural economy of the rural South. These conditions were the base from which the older narrators began as young adults. The land reforms, of which some of them were part, began with a broad and dramatic vision of change but were compromised with more powerful competing economic and political interests. This is a common characteristic of the health centers and the reforms that we will examine.

Forty Acres and Sometimes a Mule

General William T. Sherman's arrival in Savannah at Christmas time, 1864, began a large-scale program of land redistribution. Sherman had in his company some 40,000 freedpeople who had joined him at one place or another during his march of destruction. These freedpeople presented a problem for Sherman, who was anxious to continue without his unwanted entourage. This was merely the latest dilemma the former slaves of the South presented the Union forces. Lincoln had moved slowly to resolve the status of the slaves. As Union troops entered the South, tens of thousands of slaves were behind their lines. Others made their way to the Union positions. Without direction from the president about the status of slaves, military commanders adopted a host of conflicting policies. Some turned fleeing slaves away from their camps. Some established refugee camps for them. One commander, ingeniously, termed the fleeing slaves "contraband." This term preserved the property status of slaves but entitled the federal forces to keep them behind their lines because they would otherwise be used by the enemy in its war effort.[1] On September 22, 1862, in the midst of military setbacks, increasing casualties, and the need for new troops, Lincoln proclaimed all slaves in states still in rebellion by January 1, 1863, to be free. This declaration had the immediate effect of opening the ranks of the Union forces to the freedmen. By mid-October 1862 the First South Carolina Volunteers, from Beaufort, was on parade. By November the company was in combat. By the time of Sherman's arrival in Savannah, some matters had been resolved; the slaves were emancipated, freedpeople. But what that meant in practice and specifically for his unwanted 40,000 freedpeople was not clear.

Secretary of War Stanton visited Sherman in January 1865. They talked with twenty African American religious and civic leaders of Savannah, who assured the general and the secretary that the best way for the freedmen to care for themselves and to aid the government was "to have land, and turn it and till it by our own labor." The group also expressed a preference for separate communities because of "the prejudice against us in the South that will take years to get over."[2] Sherman issued Field Order No. 15 on January 16, 1865, four days after the meeting. The order declared all of the Sea Islands, from Savannah to Charleston, 485,000 acres, abandoned land. It provided for the islands to be divided into forty-acre plots and distributed to the freedpeople on the islands, who would receive a possessory title issued by the army. This dramatic new policy and the equally dramatic new process of participation of freedpeople in policy making, Stanton suggested, would "electrify the nation."[3]

Ironically, the man responsible for implementing Sherman's order, Brigadier General Rufus Saxton, was not excited at the prospect initially. This new order renewed Saxton's previous attempts to establish landownership for freed families and opened up new possibilities of the same crushing disappointment that followed his previous efforts. Saxton had supervised an extensive experiment in freedom for the "contraband" since April 1862.

When the Union forces captured Beaufort and the nearby Sea Islands in November 1861, they unexpectedly assumed responsibility for 10,000 slaves left behind by their fleeing masters. Northern abolitionists found in this circumstance an opportunity to demonstrate that the slaves of the South, if provided assistance, could labor for wages, acquire education, and thus merit the status of freedom. Edward L. Pierce conducted an initial study for Treasury Secretary Salmon P. Chase about these ideas. Pierce explained to the "contraband" of the Sea Islands that many northerners assumed that they were lazy and would not work unless whipped. "Mr. Lincoln has sent us down here to see if it was so." Moreover, Pierce promised the "contraband" that if they worked hard, "By and by they would be as well off as white people."[4] This was probably not the first time, and it would certainly not be the last time, that public policy would offer the opportunity for African Americans to disprove the prejudice of white Americans. It would also not be the last time that hard work, frugality, and morality were offered as the measure of differences between white and black Americans. On February 3, 1862, Pierce recommended to Chase an experiment in a "guided transition to freedom" on the Sea Island as a national model.[5] In late April, Saxton assumed responsibility for it.

Saxton was the firm ally of the "contraband" and a primary advocate of policies within federal agencies that assumed and promoted equality and new services.[6] During 1863, impelled by the free status of former slaves conferred by the Declaration of Emancipation, Saxton proposed to divide 60,000 acres of government land into small plots of twenty to forty acres and to sell them to the heads of freedfamilies for not less than $1.25 an acre. Others opposed Saxton's plan and preferred an auction sale of the 60,000 acres to raise money for the war. Without capital, freedpeople could not buy land at the auction. The auction was scheduled for early 1864, and Saxton attempted to sabotage it. He encouraged freedpeople to stake out plots and erect homes on the land in the hope that a cabin on land would "be considered as having a preemption right in equity to the soil." He introduced a model of a rude small house approximately sixteen by twenty feet that could be erected quickly on the plots that he anticipated selling. Such preemption was applicable only to 16,000 acres of the government's 60,000 acres set aside for charitable purposes, but Saxton's plans spilled over to all 60,000 acres. In late December 1863 Saxton's gamble paid off. President Lincoln and Secretary Chase ordered the 60,000 acres be sold to the freedpeople.

This order inspired a vision of change that Saxton shared at a celebration on January 1, 1864, the first anniversary of Emancipation. He contrasted the destitution and ignorance of two years previous with the great progress that freedpeople had made during the experiment on the Sea Islands. Looking forward in time, two more years, he told the freedpeople, "You may see these islands covered with neat cottages each the centre of a happy home, little farms well tilled, school houses built and teachers hired to instruct your children."[7]

His enthusiasm was short lived. In early February 1864 Secretary of Treasury Chase reversed himself and ordered the public lands to go up for sale at auction. Only land set aside for charitable purposes, the 16,000 acres, would be for sale on terms of preemption and reserved for heads of freedfamilies at the price of $1.25 per acre.[8] The terms of the auction were very costly in terms of trust. Some freedpeople confronted the superintendents returning from the sale. They protested the sale of their land from them and promised that they would not work for the new owners. As a sign of their belief and the legality of their claims, they refused to take back the money that they had paid as part of establishing a preemption right. Saxton had proceeded in his belief that he could successfully win support for his preemption plan. He did, temporarily. In selecting his strategy, he ignored the example set in an earlier sale when some freedfamilies pooled their capital and bought land collectively. Saxton's plan deprived the freedpeople of leadership on this issue. The disappointing results of the preemption plan left them frustrated and bitter with federal policies and white people.[9]

Saxton was frustrated, too, and disappointed not only with the failed land reform but other broken promises as well. Saxton wrote Stanton a letter on December 30, 1864, outlining his frustrations and complaints. Where Saxton assured freedpeople that there would be no conscription, there was wholesale conscription and coercion. Where Saxton assured the freedmen who were conscripted that they would receive full wages for their military service, the military paid them one-half of white soldiers' wages. Where Saxton promised the freedpeople land, the government auctioned it away. This string of promises and contradictory policies, Saxton wrote to Stanton, created "uncertainty in the minds of the freed men . . . as to our ultimate purposes toward them."[10] It also bothered Saxton that he had raised the expectations of the freedpeople many times, only to dash them. Saxton tendered his resignation to Stanton.

Saxton worried about the commitment behind Sherman's field order and the new promise of land reform. He traveled with Stanton from Savannah to Beaufort after Stanton's meeting with Sherman. Stanton gave Saxton an assurance that the freedmen would maintain possession of the land according to Sherman's order. Consequently, Saxton withdrew his resignation and accepted responsibility for the program outlined in Sherman's field order.[11]

By mid-1865, because of the quick and effective administration of the program, Saxton had settled 40,000 freedpeople on forty-acre plots on the Sea Islands. Sherman also gave Saxton horses and mules that were in excess of his army's needs or no longer capable of service. Saxton gave these animals to freedmen as they settled their new land.[12] Thus, Saxton, for one-half of a year, carried out a formal federal policy of forty acres that sometimes also included a mule. Sherman's order and Saxton's administration were the most extensive land-redistribution effort on behalf of African Americans ever undertaken, and the most direct economic benefit of emancipation that federal policy provided.

While Saxton carried out Sherman's order on the Sea Islands, Stanton, Chase, and radical Republicans within Congress were moving to extend the lessons from the Sea Islands into national legislation and to provide the guarantee of law to Sherman's field order on the Sea Islands. On March 3, 1865, President Lincoln approved legislation to establish the Bureau of Refugees, Freedmen and Abandoned Lands, the Freedmen's Bureau, and selected General Oliver Otis Howard as commissioner. A clause in the legislation promised every male citizen, whether refugee or freedman, forty acres of land at rental for three years with an option to buy.[13]

Reversing Reform

Subsequent events unraveled land-reform measures. Lincoln's assassination brought Andrew Johnson to the White House. Johnson's liberal terms of amnesty for former Confederates included restoration of their lands, which created much confusion about Sherman's order. Howard issued a circular to his Freedmen's Bureau staff on July 28, 1865, to make clear that "the pardon of the President will not be understood to extend to surrender of abandoned or confiscated property which by law has been 'set apart for refugees and freed men'."[14] By late summer, however, Johnson's plans for pardon clearly specified the return of all property, except for slaves, including confiscated lands like those sold on the islands.[15] This put the former planters and slaves of the Sea Islands squarely in the middle of conflicting orders. Complicating matters more, Saxton had moved with incredible speed to implement Sherman's order to accomplish a land redistribution that, he felt, officials would not dare undo. Saxton was repeating his tactics and again underestimating the forces of reaction.

Johnson ordered Howard on September 12, 1865, to carry out his amnesty policies that restored all lands to those who had been pardoned and to reverse Saxton's actions on the Sea Islands. Accordingly, Howard sent out circulars instructing freedmen that they could acquire land only by purchase and instructed his staff to correct any impression of government provision of forty acres. This action reversed his circular of clarification of July 28, six weeks previous.[16] On October 17 Howard held a mass meeting at the Episcopal church on Edisto Island with 2,000 freedpeople, most of them new landowners. Howard explained to the people who had assembled that they would have to give up their lands that they had cultivated as their own. He attempted to soften the blow for the freedpeople. Families would be allowed to stay on the land to tend and harvest existing crops. Freedpeople who had settled on land would be allowed also to stay there as long as they were willing to work the land through a contract or lease from the restored white owner. Finally, the schools that had been started had to continue.[17] Howard set up a board representing planters, freedmen, and the bureau to oversee this policy.

The new landowners, soon to be dispossessed, were not happy with Howard's decision. Howard assured them that working for wages or shares would enable them to achieve the same ends as possession of the soil. This sounded to the freedpeople like an unlikely rationalization for an unpopular policy, which it was. As one freedman responded at the time, "He had lived all his life with a basket over his head, and now that it had been taken off and air and some light had come to him, he could not consent to have the basket on him again."[18]

A few days after Howard's appearance, a committee of three freedmen wrote the president of the United States.

Dear President Johnson of the United States

We the freedmen of South Carlina wish to address you with a few lines Conserning the sad feelings that is now resting upon our minds wee pray that god may guive you helth & good spirets that when you receive theas few notasis that you may receive them as the father did the prodical son wee have for the last four yars ben studing with justis and the best of our ability what step wee should take to be a peple: wee have lernt to respect all Just Causes that ever came from the union.

Mag genrl howard has paid the freedmen of South Carlinah a visit & caled a meating on Edisto Island South Carliner in the Centrel part of the island at the piskple Church thair hee beutifly addressed the freedmen of this island after his adress a grate many of the peple understanding what was said they got aroused and awoke to perfict sense to stody for them Selves what part of this law would rest against us, wee said in rafarence to what he said that nothing did apier at that time to bee very opressing upon us but the one thing that is wee freedmen should work for wages for our former oners or eny other man president Johnson of u st I do say . . . man that have stud upon the feal of battle & have shot there master & sons now Going to ask ether one for bread or for shelter or Comfortable for his wife & children sunch a thing the u st should not aught to Expect a man (to do) . . . .

Here is Plenty Whidow and Fatherles that have serve you as slave now losen a home . . . .

[As] the wise presidon that sets on his seat . . . [please give us] a Chance to Recover out of this trubble . . . . these 3 Committee has Pleg the Trouth to you dis day. Oct. 25 1865.[19]

Their letter came from organized discussion among the freedpeople and spoke of the aspirations of the most ordinary among them, and not an elite. The committee of three explained in another letter that its sentiments were deeply rooted in the community. Some petitions that they sent had up to sixty names, and others, such as the petition they sent the president in 1865 to remove a bureau official, had no names. "It was thought by the majority unnecessary [to have names], as it was the sentiments of not a few, but the People of the [Edisto] island."[20]

This committee of three, and others, worked with freedpeople on the other islands as well, where similar sentiments led to other letters to President Johnson. In simple terms, these newly schooled freedpeople articulated clearly the profound dilemma that Howard's order caused them. The order asked them to work for men who at one time owned them and whom some of them had fought in battle. This dependence for work and wages on former owners and battlefield adversaries jeopardized their opportunity to support their wives and children and removed the hope of buying land at reasonable prices. Their petition also clearly stated the aspiration of the freedpeople on the Islands and on the Sherman lands at this time. They wanted land because without it they were not truly free. Second, they were willing to pay for it. Third, they made claim to the land because their toil had made it productive. Fourth, they had fought for the Union Army but now were asked to return land, given them by the government they fought to defend, to those who fought against the Union Army.

> This is our home. We have made these lands what they are. We were the only true and Loyal people that were found in possession of these Lands. We have been always ready to strike for liberty and humanity yea to fight if needs be to preserve this glorious Union. Shall not we who are freedman and have always been true to this Union have the same rights as are enjoyed by others? Have we broken any Law of these United States? Have we forfeited our rights of property in land?— If not, then, are not our rights as a free people and good citizens of these United States to be considered before the rights of those who were found in rebellion against this good and just Government (and now being conquered) come (as they seem) with penitent hearts and beg forgiveness for past offenses and also ask if their lands cannot be restored to them[?] . . . If the Government does not make some provision by which we as Freedmen can obtain a homestead, we have not bettered our condition.
>
> We have been encouraged by the Government to take up these lands in small tracts, receiving Certificates for the same. We have thus far taken sixteen thousand (16000) acres of land here on this Island. We are ready to pay for this land when the Government calls for it. And now after what has been done will the good and just government take from us as this right and make us subject to the will of those who cheated and oppressed us for many years God Forbid! Land monopoly is injurious to the advancement of the course of freedom.
>
> We the freedmen of this Island and of the State of South Carolina—Do therefore petition to you as the President of these United States, that some provisions be made by which every colored man can purchase and hold it as his own. We wish to have home if it be but a few acres . . . . We therefore look to you . . . for protection and Equal Rights, with the privilege of purchasing homestead right here in the heart of South Carolina.[21]

Howard used these letters as grounds for continuing his efforts to acquire legal status for Sherman's order and to reverse the president. In December of 1865, as the new Congress convened, Saxton also suggested "a practical solution" to the conflicting policies of land restoration and land distribution. He suggested that "Congress purchase the entire tract set aside by Sherman's order, and offer to pay to the former owner that sum or, give him possession of the land, as he may elect. In case he should prefer the land to the money, then pay the money over to the freedman who occupies it." The proposal, a limited version of Thaddeus Stevens's redistributive proposals, now exceeded the financial commitment to equality that the radical Republican Senator Charles Sumner assessed Congress was willing to make. Sumner did not act on Saxton's suggestion. He did introduce language in the Freedmen's Bureau bill to validate the Sherman land grants, but legislators conceded this part of the bill in compromises among themselves and with the president in early 1866.[22]

The hope of the freedpeople for land of their own had spread far beyond the Sea Islands and was now expiring in Washington. Reports came from military commanders of the Freedmen's Bureau in Georgia, North Carolina, and Alabama in the last half of 1865 of the expectation that land would be distributed to the freedpeople of those states. The military in other states took measures to end the hopes of landownership. The Alabama commissioner, for example, issued a circular assuring the freedpeople that the plantations would not be broken up and distributed to them. He told them further that they "must go to work and behave themselves."[23] Ending the landownership among the freedpeople on the Sea Islands was part of ending the hope of freedpeople everywhere for forty acres and a mule.

If people in Washington were ready for compromise, the freedpeople on the Sea Island were not. In January and February 1866 residents repeatedly defended their claims to landownership. Two former planters accompanied by a bureau official were surrounded when they landed on Wadmalaw Island in early January 1866. The freedmen demanded to know the authority of the bureau official, at which point he drew his revolver and declared it to be his authority. The freedmen overpowered the small party of white men. They convinced the visitors to talk without a show of force and to leave when unsuccessful in convincing the freedmen of the merits of their position. A northern teacher recounted the words of one freedman involved in the foray who had been wounded nine times in the war. "Oh . . . it was shaking the pistol in the mans face that has made us come here, such things kill us, if they had treated us as men we would not have harmed them."[24] Four men from Philadelphia landed on Johns Island on January 28 and were arrested by a patrol of freedmen, who marched them twelve miles to be interrogated by their commander.[25] Governor James L. Orr of South Carolina wrote to President Johnson describing the series of events on the Sea Islands as "Serious disturbances."[26] The new landowners used the training that they had acquired in the Union Army to organize themselves along military lines to hold onto their lands. But they now fought the government that they had previously defended over something the government had given them but was now taking away.[27] Freedmen and women also barricaded roads to plantations and resisted, with arms, attempts to repossess plantations and the lands that they had been given by Saxton under the authority of Sherman's order. The army responded to the numerous confrontations of freedpeople with former landowners and speculators who would be new landowners. Travel to the islands was restricted for white people, and soldiers escorted those groups permitted to travel.[28]

Events in Washington proceeded to remove ambiguity about federal policies toward landownership in general and on the Sea Islands in particular. Johnson acquired from General Sherman a statement that he had not intended his field order to be permanent. The president also removed Saxton from his command. Finally, Johnson vetoed the Freedmen's Bureau bill on February 19, 1866, and began a public battle with those proposing radical land-redistribution measures and other liberal policies of reconstruction. Congress passed the Freedmen's Bureau bill over Johnson's veto in July of 1866, but the land provisions were watered down. "Sherman's Negroes" were given permission to lease property on government land with a six-year option to buy. But such land was very scarce, given the policy of restoration, and could not come close to accommodating the dispossessed. Congress made clear it would not propose land reform in general or in the South, particularly on the Sea Islands.[29]

With clearer direction from President Johnson to take the lands on the Sea Islands from the freedpeople, with fewer officials to obfuscate policy or delay its implementation, and with the active intervention of federal troops, the battle over land possession became a matter of mopping up pockets of armed resistance and imposing the new set of policies. The army invoked the strictest criteria for valid claims. Squads from the 35th United States Colored Infantry visited each new landowner and examined the landowner's documents that established claim to land. Only eleven of the four thousand claims on Johns and Wadmalaw islands passed this scrutiny.[30]

Eventually, the bureau determined by more liberal criteria that some 450 land claims of the freedpeople were valid. These valid claims on Edisto, Wadmalaw, Johns, and James islands were exchanged for leases on government-owned tax lands near Beaufort. Settlers without a valid claim could enter into a labor contract with the restored owners or were forcibly removed and marched to an employment office that the Freedmen's Bureau had established. There, contracts for labor on the lands of pardoned Confederates, whose lands were restored, were drawn up for the former landowners.[31]

While losing their land, the freedpeople attempted to hold on to other rights. In October 1866 the "people of Edisto Island," still expressing themselves as a group, petitioned General Howard to dismiss Robert K. Scott, Saxton's successor as assistant commissioner of the bureau in the area. Scott had ordered an end to mass meetings or conventions. The leaders on Edisto Island pointed out that only by such meetings did people receive information on events and about the new political rights and freedoms of the freedpeople. Among these rights and freedoms were the "Articles of the Constitution, & Civil Rights Bill," which Scott's order contradicted, in their view.[32]

As late as 1867 there was still resistance to the restoration policy, and military force was needed. In January 1867 a corporal and five soldiers sent to dispossess freedpeople found themselves surrounded by 200 freedmen armed and determined to die "rather than contract with Captain Barnwell or depart for St. Helena Island." The troops withdrew. A detail of fifty soldiers returned, only to find themselves confronting the entire plantation's population, including women and children, organized in military fashion and even more determined to serve only Jesus, who would "never come here to collect taxes or drive us off."[33] The resistance grew more sporadic as the restoration became complete.

President Johnson discredited the policies of Saxton that he reversed. He sent two investigators to South Carolina in late spring of 1866 to inspect the work of the bureau. In effect, they would kick dirt on the embers of reform there to assure that they would not smolder or ignite again. The presidential emissaries, generals Joseph S. Fullerton and James B. Steedman, reported that Saxton's administration had been characterized by "mistakes and blunders" with "extremely pernicious" results.

> Our personal observations, the evidence we have taken and the inquiries we have been obliged to make to supply the place of the records, have convinced us that the condition of the freedmen of these settlements, while in charge of General Saxton, was such as to give but little hope that under the policy pursued by that

officer they would ever have become self-supporting, even with fertile lands on which they were located placed at their disposal free of rent or taxes. The failure of General Saxton's administration resulted from a variety of causes, among which may be enumerated:

The unnecessary continuance of Government support to the freedmen, which tended to increase their natural improvidence and to encourage habits of idleness.

Keeping them under such guardianship and tutelage that they were disinclined to make proper exertion for their own support or improvement.

Teaching them to distrust all white men but those who had immediate authority over them or who came among them with passes from the Bureau, thus preparing them to fall an easy prey to the sharpers who afterwards obtained access to them under the guise of friendship, took advantage of their credulity and fraudulently appropriated their crops.

Their inexperience in providing for their own support and in managing business for themselves.[34]

In the short space of eighteen months the federal government had started a program and a process that it retracted and then discredited. This would happen again, but seldom in such a short time.

To assure that these damaging reports had maximum circulation and impact, Fullerton and Steedman publicized their presence and purpose, and released their reports to the local press.[35] The editors of the *Charleston Daily Courier* praised the generals' "able report" for its "strict fidelity to truth" and as "a more reliable record" than "those false and irritating slanders which so often have been circulated by evil and vicious persons." The generals' report supported the newspaper's recommendation that the lands of the islands be restored to the former planters by the end of the year so that they may "be made available hereafter for agriculture and the freedmen obtain proper compensation for their toil." Most importantly, the editors hoped that the islands would be restored to precedent and delivered from experiment. "The frauds committed upon the freedmen by those who claimed to be their friends and especial advocates are exposed with an open and unsparing hand. The plea of philanthropy was but the cover for self-interest. And the small crops that were made by the improvident and careless freedmen were bought up at a nominal price and paid for in goods at the most exorbitant rates."[36]

The generals' report also cited an instance of success. On Edisto Island "freedmen exclusively, working under the direction of one of their own number, a superintendent chosen by themselves . . . are apparently doing well, and have a fair prospect of a good crop." This, however, was almost the only instance that they surveyed "where the freedmen cultivating exclusively for themselves, without the direction of whites, were doing even tolerably well."[37] The generals, like the editors of the *Charleston Daily Courier*, treated this success as an exception to the rule rather than a program to analyze and disseminate.

If some federal policies did not give the freedpeople what they needed, at least one program, the Freedmen's Bank, took away what was already theirs. Saxton, among his many reforms, began a bank in August 1864 in which freedmen soldiers and other freedpeople could deposit their wages and savings. A savings institution for the freedpeople captured the imagination of national leaders, who instituted a Freedmen's Saving and Trust Company on March 3, 1865. The bank grew quickly. It served some 100,000 depositors in its nine-year history and handled some $57 million in deposits, mostly in small accounts. The average account was $60, the price of six acres of land. Mismanagement and fraud brought the bank to insolvency and an unprecedented failure for a bank of its size. Some depositors recovered as much as 62 percent of their savings, but the majority, especially those far from Washington, illiterate, and unknowledgeable of banking practices, received far less or nothing at all.[38]

There were severe consequences to this banking debacle for freedpeople. They demonstrated their industry and thrift as they were asked, but those who challenged them proved to be devoid of the virtues they preached. Some bank officers even proved to be paragons of the vices against which they railed. Those freedpeople most faithful to the bank lost the most. Frederick Douglass, brought on to save the bank after it was too late, explained metaphorically that although the bank had been the black man's cow, it was the white man's milk.[39] The savings of freedpeople were largely gone on the eve of the severe economic depression that began in 1875.

Despite federal land policy and the loss of savings, some freedpeople still succeeded in acquiring land after Reconstruction. Land prices were low, and income sometimes permitted freedpeople to accumulate enough money to buy land, especially on the Sea Islands. Acre by acre, freedpeople, most often pooling their resources, acquired land on Johns, Wadmalaw, and Edisto islands. By 1880 a survey of the islands estimated a population of 10,800 African American men, women, and children and 8,800 acres of land under their ownership. In 1910 some 60 percent of the African American farmers in Beaufort and Charleston counties were landowners.[40] The legacy of Sea Island land-reform programs lingered on in other ways as well. In 1916, for example, Septima Clark went to teach on Johns Island, at the Promised

Land School, a name that was not biblical in reference but a reminder of the federal policies of a half-century before.

In other parts of the South landownership was far less prevalent but not uncommon. In those places, according to Du Bois, it became the mark of "individual efforts of exceptional and lucky Negroes."[41] Some African Americans acquired land because their white fathers left it to them or some white benefactor was willing to sell them some. But apart from the Sea Islands, landownership in the South was beyond the ordinary grasp of freedpeople. The conditions of their work kept landownership beyond the reach of their children and their children's children as well.

Debt, Fraud, and Coercion

The overwhelming majority of freedpeople entered the agricultural economy of the post–Civil War South as landless farmers, wage laborers. But the restored landlords had little capital to provide for wages. Landlords and laborers arranged a system of sharecropping that provided the freedpeople some appearance of independent, economic stature and required minimal cash wages of the landlords. The Freedmen's Bureau sanctified this surrogate of landownership for the freedpeople and of the plantation system for the landlords with contracts. Both northerners and southerners venerated contracts. They suggested a semblance of equality between landlord and laborer and an agreement of mutual benefit.[42] Behind this appearance, there were coercive forces premised on inequality and subordination. Laws passed in eight southern states between 1865 and 1867, the Black Codes, combined the new reality of emancipation with the old subordination of slavery.[43] Congress later abrogated these codes, but other forms of coercion remained. The Freedmen's Bureau and northern philanthropies reduced relief measures to prevent the freedpeople from becoming "indigent, fault finding and lazy."[44] The bureau arrested freedmen without signed contracts for labor, and state and local law officials also arrested and imprisoned freedmen in transit from one place to another. The prisons of the South changed drastically as a consequence. Between 1865 and 1880 the prison population in Tennessee, for example, increased from 200 to 1,241. The number of incarcerated freedmen went from 67 to 800, and from one-third to two-thirds of the prison population. Once in prison, the freedman found labor worse than slavery. In some instances half of the prisoners leased for labor were dead within a year.[45]

The best means for a freedman to escape the snares of the law was the protection of a white person of some status in the community. This protection proceeded from a landlord-tenant relationship and the satisfactory completion of tenant responsibilities.[46] A planter in Lowndes County, Alabama, explained the nature of the new free labor to a group of African American workers.

> Formerly, you were my slaves; you worked for me and I provided for you. You had no thought of the morrow, for I thought of that for you. If you were sick, I had the doctor come to you. When you needed clothes, clothes were forthcoming; and you never went hungry for lack of meal and pork. You had little more responsibility than my mules.
>
> But now all that is changed. Being free men, you assume the responsibility of free men. You sell me your labor, I pay you money and with that money you provide for yourselves. You must look out for your own clothes and foods, and the wants of your children. If I advance these things for you, I shall charge them to you, for I cannot give them like I once did, now I pay you wages. Once if you were ugly or lazy I had you whipped, and that was the end of it. Now if you are ugly or lazy, your wages will be paid to others, and you will be turned off to go about the country with bundles on your backs, like the miserable low down niggers you see that nobody will hire. But if you are well behaved and industrious, you will be prosperous and respected and happy.[47]

Whatever the promise of wage labor, debt was its ordinary outcome. African American agricultural workers worked in anticipation of a share of the crop, and in the meantime they borrowed heavily for food and the necessities for farming. These loans came with high rates of interest from the only source from which African American borrowers could get credit, their landowners who had a vested interest in their labor, their crop, and their debt. They purchased their necessities at inflated prices from those who were nearby, again, their landowners.[48] When it came time to settle debts and pay accounts, these workers were again at a disadvantage. The written records of the white landlord determined the settlement, and disputing these records with contrary evidence often was an invitation for reprisal, from murder to unemployment. Sharecroppers had little recourse for the equitable enforcement of the contract. They did not dare dispute the landlord's word given the lack of economic alternatives, other mechanisms of coercion, and the possibility of violence. Complaints from freedmen became legendary, in a literal sense, in a short period of time. As one bureau agent recounted before 1870, "The old story has been repeated thousands of times, no definite bargain made—no wages promised; but 'massa said, stay till the crop is made and he would do what was right'."[49] This story, already old by 1870, would be repeated endlessly until the system ended.

The common experience of fraud and coercion provided African American agricultural laborers bitter lessons about the double standard that enforced the inequities of their position. A freedman writing from Helena, Arkansas, in early 1866 observed that freedpeople had been "thoroughly acquainted with that system of morals, that teaches the negro to observe and fulfill the moral obligations of a contract, but has no meaning or significance when applied to the white man."[50] This lesson was expressed in a couplet that was recited for three-quarters of a century.

> Ought's an ought and figger's a figger;
> All fer de white man an' none fer de nigger.[51]

Shadows of Slavery

The economic depression in 1929 brought new attention to southern agriculture and the peonage and serfdom that continued to be part of the sharecropping system. Few of the 2,000 tenants interviewed in one study reported cash incomes of any amount in thirteen previous years.[52] Another study of tenant families in Missouri, Tennessee, Arkansas, and Mississippi reported an average debt for supplies and food of $70.70 in 1933. The average settlement payment of the families was $62.30.[53] Some better-off families, like Mattie Lee Moorer's in Lowndes County, supplemented their earnings from crops by selling milk and eggs, which amounted to an annual average of about $300.[54] The study of Norman Thomas and the Tyronza Socialist party concluded that the rural agricultural workers and their families they surveyed lived and worked on "an economic plane so low that . . . [their] buying power was completely exhausted in obtaining the most basic necessities of life, food and shelter." Thomas extrapolated that the conditions they uncovered described as much as 50 percent of rural agricultural workers in the southern states.[55] Similarly, a study of the Department of Labor of more than 1,000 Alabama farm households that were on relief in 1933 estimated that the families had spent 89 percent of all their years in sharecropping either at a break-even point or in debt.[56]

There were four categories of workers, a hierarchy of misery in the agricultural economy. Each category differed in the degree of dependence on the landlord to supply what was necessary to make a crop. Correspondingly, each category differed in the degree of debt. Although whites and blacks were caught in this hierarchy, the proportion of African Americans increased in each lower rank of the economic pecking order. In bad economic times agricultural workers might move down a rung or two, and white workers invariably displaced black workers in this downward move.

The first category of tenant farmer, cash tenant, paid a fixed amount of rent to the landlord in cash or an equivalent amount in crop values. These workers provided their labor and that of family members, food for the work animals, tools, seed, and fertilizer. The landlord provided land for farming, a house, and fuel. The number of these relatively independent and well-off tenant farmers was small compared with the tenant farmers with other arrangements.

The second category, share tenant, included many more farm laborers. They pledged to the landlord their labor and that of their families and one-fourth to one-third of their crop. In exchange, the landlord provided some portion of tools, seed, fertilizer, and food for stock, whatever the tenant could not provide. In addition, the landlord provided the land, a house, and fuel.

The third tenancy arrangement is appropriately termed sharecropping. In this arrangement the landlord furnished almost all the requirements for the crop in addition to a house and fuel for the farmer and his family. In exchange, the sharecropper provided labor, perhaps a portion of the fertilizer, and pledged one-half or more of the crop to the landlord.

A fourth category of rural agricultural worker, often neglected in the analysis of cotton tenancy, was the wage laborer. Wage laborers worked seasonally and occupied the bottom rung of the labor ladder, lacking even the semblance of the security of sharecropping and tenant-farming arrangements. These workers were largely unskilled and in competition with each other. They were at greatest risk for incomes below the subsistence level during hard economic times.[57]

The studies of southern agricultural labor of the 1930s disclosed once again the continuing mechanisms of control over labor through the credit system, debt, jail, and the established social customs of the plantation order that had been in place since Reconstruction. Myrdal termed the system "a public scandal" and found that the greatest prospect for security for African American tenant farmers in the 1930s was in a contracted relation with a landlord, just as it had been in Reconstruction.[58] White landlords still maintained the records of furnishings and debt for their largely illiterate African American workers and limited their workers' capacity to sell their portion of the crop to anyone but them. This inevitably meant a balance of accounts at settlement time, around the end of the year, which left the tenant farmer or sharecropper in debt. Complaints about settlement and the unfair treatment of workers continued, but it was still dangerous to challenge the settlement terms of a white landlord. Esau Jenkins recounted a calculated challenge he made, his fear, and that of his father.

> My father was a man who believed in whatever the white folks said. He didn't want to hurt them a bit. . . . One day we went to carry some cotton to sell. The white man who figured what the cotton come to, he gave us a certain price. I started to figure mine.
>
> Daddy told me, "Don't do that. The white folks never like that, son."
>
> I say, "Well, I'm not figuring for the white folks at this point, I'm figuring for my own benefit."
>
> . . . I waited until everybody got the money, including my daddy, and I went to him. "According to what you paid me, my money didn't come to what it should come to for the amount of cotton I had."
>
> So he said, "Well, let me see." Sure enough, he found out that he made a mistake.
>
> . . . I told my daddy, say "Now Daddy, you see I don't know how long this man doing it, but this figuring was wrong, and I don't know how many other person was wrong, but I didn't say it because I was afraid that everybody would say the same thing, and then he would blame me for it. But can't you see it's good to do your own figuring?"
>
> Of course, I convinced him at that time, but he never would do it.[59]

Henry Roberts, a laborer in Lowndes County, recounted conditions there in 1935. These included settlements in which "the landlords just tell us so much was spent but we never see it on paper"; schooling which "run about 2 months and 3 months at the highest"; children who had a total of three months of schooling at the age of ten; and chronic conditions of indebtedness.

> Those who have large families always owe at the end of the year. If you owe, the landlord takes all your corn, cotton and peas and carry it someplace else and lock it up. If we move when we are in debt the landlord gets the Sheriff to carry us back. Sometimes a landlord will take over our debt to another landlord and get us to move to his plantation. If we owe too much we cannot get anyone to buy off our debt and take us on their place and we have to keep on at the same place.[60]

Labor Movements of Resistance

The conditions of the African American agricultural workers in the South remained unchanged, but so did their resistance to the system that kept them
poor, ill, and uneducated. The Alabama Sharecroppers Union conducted a
strike at the J. R. Bell Plantation in Lowndes County in September 1935
to protest and change the conditions that Henry Roberts described.[61] The
strike ended unsuccessfully, and workers returned to the fields with unchanged wages. The union was dead after the strike and its reprisal. Twenty-
five union leaders fled the county for fear of their lives and their livelihood.
The strike surfaced the violence constantly at hand to enforce the system
of scarcity and to suppress attempts to organize to improve conditions. Six
people were killed by police and "deputies."[62]

The organizing effort among tenant farmers that won the greatest national
attention at the time of the Depression occurred in Phillips County, which adjoins Lee County in eastern Arkansas. The Southern Tenant Farmers Union
(STFU) sprang from a set of grievances similar to those that inspired the
Alabama Sharecroppers Union at the same time in Lowndes County. These
grievances had inspired the Progressive Farmers and Household Union in
1919 as well as the Cotton Pickers League in 1891 in eastern Arkansas.

The three organizations marked a succession of efforts to bring about
change. The Cotton Pickers League was a splinter group of the Colored
Alliance, the first major African American organization with a mass following since the 1860s, apart from the church. The Colored Alliance began
in 1886 and claimed 1.2 million members in the South by 1890, four years
after its start.[63] The Colored Alliance demanded policies that African American agricultural workers had advocated since Reconstruction. They included
a program to provide loans for mortgages and land purchases for African
American farm workers and longer school terms for their children.

R. M. Humphrey, the white superintendent of the Colored Alliance, proposed a nationwide strike of cotton pickers in 1891. He explained that the
collusion of planters in Charleston and Memphis to reduce the price for picking had "induced" the strike. He proposed to withhold the labor of landless
cotton pickers until planters agreed to pay $1.00 per 100 pounds of picked
cotton. Some members of the Colored Alliance endorsed the call for a strike
and sided with the pickers, but the landowning majority in the alliance did
not. Humphrey persisted. He set a date of September 12, 1891, for the strike
and began the Cotton Pickers League as a more appropriate vehicle than the
Colored Alliance for the organization and conduct of the strike. The Cotton

Pickers League initiated passwords, ritual handshakes, and other gestures to identify themselves to fellow members and to conceal their identity from the uninitiated.[64]

One of the few places that a strike occurred was Lee County, Arkansas. Ben Patterson, probably brought to Lee County by police from Memphis as convict labor, began the strike in Lee County with the support of twenty-five men on September 20. They struck the plantation of Colonel H. P. Rodgers, who dismissed the pickers' demand for $.75 per 100 pounds. The strikers appealed to other pickers to leave the fields but with very limited success and began to use force to keep them out of the fields. A band of strikers eventually encountered a deputy, an overseer on another plantation, on his way to join the posse hunting them, and they killed him in a gun fight.

After several days' search the posse found and fought thirteen strikers. In the gun fight that ensued, two strikers were killed, two escaped, and nine were captured and immediately lynched. Patterson, the leader, had escaped but was later captured by police. He was being brought to Helena by riverboat for trial, but a lynch mob hailed the boat ashore. Fifteen men boarded the boat, carried Patterson, who was wounded and could not walk, off the boat, laid him on the river bank, stood over him, and shot him to death.[65]

The Lee County strike achieved little for local workers but had far-reaching adverse consequences. The strike strained the relations of the landless and landowning African Americans in the Colored Alliance and between the Colored Alliance and the all-white National Alliance that had spawned it. Humphrey was discredited and the ranks of the Colored Alliance depleted.

After World War I, African American farmers in the area of Lee County again acted to improve their terms of work and life conditions. They organized the Progressive Farmers and Household Union of America, or the Progressive Union, in 1918. Because such an organization still invited reprisal, its members, like those in the Cotton Pickers League, adopted passwords, grips, signs, and other secret measures to communicate with each other and to provide for their security. These were changed every three months to reduce the chance of infiltration by nonmembers. Locals of the Progressive Union sprang up in small communities in Phillips County, which adjoins Lee County. The Progressive Union had as its purpose "to advance the interest of the Negro, morally and intellectually and to make him a better citizen and a better farmer." Both men and women belonged to the union, and efforts were made on behalf of both sexes. The union was exclusively African American and for the benefit of African Americans.[66]

With the encouragement of his organization, Ed Ware, who was secretary of the Progressive Union Lodge at Hoop Spur, Arkansas, refused to sell his cotton at $.22 to $.33 a pound to his landlord at settlement time. Other farmers were selling for $.43 a pound. Ware also took the highly unusual step of seeking legal assistance to reach a fairer settlement with his landlord. U. S. Bratton, an attorney in Helena, had worked against peonage during the administration of Theodore Roosevelt. Bratton agreed to take the case and to conduct a trial for debt peonage but required the members of the union to raise a $50 retainer fee. On September 30, 1919, the local of the Progressive Union at Hoop Spur met to show that they were "tired of being expected and forced to act like children"; to organize the withholding of cotton at settlement time to achieve better settlements; and to raise money for a retainer fee in Ware's case. Sometime between 11:00 P.M. and 12:30 A.M., gunfire broke out between the men at the meeting and special agent W. A. Atkins of the Missouri Pacific Railroad and sheriff's deputy Charles Pratt. Atkins was killed and Pratt wounded. Later, Pratt testified that they were in the vicinity to arrest a bootlegger. According to his story, while they were trying to fix a flat tire on their car, they were fired upon by members of the meeting in the church.[67]

However it started, the conflict continued in a bloody manner. The next morning a posse of white men began a general campaign of terror in the Elaine area. White men from Tennessee, Mississippi, and Arkansas streamed into Phillips County to fight the insurrection. One report lists five whites killed and twenty-five blacks. Other estimates of African American deaths range from forty to more than a hundred. The posse and mobs ransacked homes and arrested African American men, women, and children without discrimination. White women and children were evacuated. The governor dispatched 500 national guard troops armed with twelve machine guns to occupy Elaine and Helena. All African Americans in Elaine were rounded up and placed in a stockade. Troops combed a fifty-mile radius for other African Americans, who were arrested. Their release depended upon the word of a white citizen or their satisfying their interrogators. The authorities gave a pass to each person released that they needed for identification or risk rearrest.[68]

With military order imposed on Phillips County, the governor appointed secretly a group of seven local leaders, including two plantation owners, to examine the cause of the violence. The committee reported that the September 30 meeting in the Hoop Spur church was part of the planning process, close to completion, of a campaign of insurrection and violence by the Progressive Farmers and Household Union members against the white population of Phillips County. The committee reported that the uprising was to take place on October 6 and that twenty-one white men had been marked for death.[69] In early November, less than a month after the violence, trials were held for seventy-nine African American men to determine their guilt or innocence for the initial violence at the Hoop Spur church in which Atkins was killed and Pratt was wounded.

The trials became a benchmark of legal travesty. The defendants' court-appointed attorneys requested no change of venue despite the rabid emotions stirred by the special committee's report released at the time of the trial. African American witnesses testified to the insurrectionist plot both to the committee and at the trial. In addition to the ordinary forms of intimidation to acquire such testimony, reports indicated that some witnesses had been beaten until they consented to testify.[70] The courtroom was a legal backdrop for mob action, and there was little doubt that lynchings would occur if anything but guilty verdicts were delivered. The defense counsel called no witnesses and put few of the defendants on the stand. The trials lasted no more than four hours. The all-white, all-male juries then deliberated no more than eight minutes. Eventually, all seventy-nine defendants were found guilty. The judge sentenced twelve to death by electrocution on December 27, 1919. The jury recommended jail sentences ranging from one to twenty-one years for the sixty-seven other defendants. Eventually, the case went to the U.S. Supreme Court. On February 19, 1923, in *Moore v. Dempsey,* the Supreme Court ordered a new trial for all the defendants of the Elaine trial. Justice Holmes writing for the majority explained that a trial dominated by a mob is not justice. The state did not retry the seventy-nine defendants, and by mid-January 1924 all the defendants had been released.[71]

As important as that outcome was, the larger matters were unchanged. The union was destroyed, and the sharecroppers had no more legal protection in the settlements with their landlords than they had prior to their efforts to organize. It was Bratton's opinion that the Elaine massacre was a preconceived plan of whites "to put a stop to the Negro ever asking for a settlement." Bratton expressed his opinion from afar. He left Arkansas in response to the retaliation against him, his law practice, and his family that his defense of the union members incurred.[72]

The efforts of the Progressive Union at Elaine served as a precedent to later organizing in counties just north of Lee County in the 1930s. They provided lessons to white and black tenant farmers and sharecroppers who organized the Southern Tenant Farmers Union. Twenty-seven black and white men met in the Sunnyside school house near Tyronza in Poinsett County, Arkansas, in early July 1934 and founded the STFU. An initial question at the meeting was whether or not to form two unions, one for blacks and one for whites. After some initial discussion in which members of the meeting drew parallels to separate institutions for the races including schools and churches, an old man stood and began to explain reasons for having one union. He explained that for the previous seventy years African Americans had built unions and other forms of organized resistance only to have them broken up by planters and the law. He recounted his membership in the Progressive Farmers and Household Union and how that union had been wiped out and many of its members massacred in Elaine in 1919.

> We colored people can't organize without you . . . and you white folks can't organize without us. . . . Aren't we all brothers and ain't God the Father of us all? We live under the same sun, eat the same food, wear the same kind of clothing, work on the same land, raise the same crop for the same landlord who oppresses and cheats us both. For a long time now the white folks and the colored folks have been fighting each other and both of us have been getting whipped all the time. We don't have nothing against one another but we got plenty against the landlord. The same chain that holds my people holds your people too. If we are chained together on the outside we ought to stay chained together in the union. It won't do no good for us to divide because there's where the trouble has been all the time. The landlord is always betwixt us, beatin' us and starvin' us and makin' us fight each other. There ain't but one way for us to get him where he can't help himself and that's for us to get together and stay together.[73]

The union asked for improvements in the contract for tenants and sharecroppers. These improvements included better financial terms on furnishings; the right to trade for food, tools, and other goods where tenants pleased; and reimbursement for improvements made on the property of a landowner. In addition, the STFU demanded a certain portion of land, rent free, for the purpose of growing food for the family and livestock and access to nearby woodlands to secure fuel. Finally, the workers demanded the right to sell cotton at market prices to whom they pleased. This last issue, of course, was the issue around which the Progressive Farmers Union organized and which brought the reprisal of the Elaine massacre in 1919.[74]

Reprisals came again. Rumors that planters were arming themselves with automatic weapons were matched with rumors that union members were doing the same. Police arrested strike leaders and reinstated the subordination of convict labor. Three of four union leaders who had been sent to jail were leased as farm laborers for 75 cents a day. In the most blatant form of peonage, Paul Preacher, town sheriff in Earle, stopped a march of union members, arrested thirteen strikers, and put them to work on his own farm. Eventually, the Justice Department arrested, convicted, and punished him.[75]

These events occurred against the backdrop of another STFU strike in May 1936 to increase wages for planting tasks from 70 cents a day, 5 cents less than the cost of convict labor, to $1.00 a day. Initially, the strike was 80 percent successful, and few workers went to the fields. The state governor sent in troops, and the planters began transporting strike breakers from Memphis. New violence occurred. The Reverend William Bennett, of Wynn, a union officer, was beaten to death, two strikers were injured and one was reportedly killed when a picket line was broken in Earle. The reprisal to this strike was so strong that the union found it impossible and unwise to hold a meeting until the strike was called off in July.

The national publicity surrounding these events achieved far more than the strike. The union's advocates in Washington, who had been dismissed from the legal staff at the Agricultural Adjustment Administration a year earlier for defending the STFU's positions, now found more receptivity for changes of federal programs in the administration. The policies they advocated and lost their jobs over were now adopted. The government began mailing checks to tenants and sharecroppers directly and increased their share of benefits.[76] It was this policy that gave Jesse Cannon claim to his check and why it was addressed to him. Still, the policy did not eliminate conflict with his landlord.

From Tenant Farmers to Landowners

Slowly and modestly, federal policies began to redress the grievances that had sparked organized efforts of labor in the South. The STFU advocated a national land authority to take over idle farmlands and lease them to displaced tenants.[77] The Alabama Sharecroppers Union had made similar demands. Numerous studies, individuals, and agencies also recommended the idea of a modest form of land redistribution by the federal government. President Roosevelt's committee on farm tenancy eventually recommended directed-community programs, an echo of the call for a "guided transition to freedom" heard on the Sea Islands. This new plan involved cooperative farm colonies and the development of schools, health care, and recreation facilities, incubators, breeding stock, and marketing facilities. Charles Johnson, a member of the committee and coauthor of a study on tenant farming, suggested a re-homesteading project. He reported wide consensus among those familiar with the problem for the program. It would buy up huge tracts of land and provide supervision, guidance, and aid to new homesteaders.[78]

The Resettlement Administration of the New Deal resembled the land authority that the STFU envisioned and was comprehensive, as the presidential committee had suggested it needed to be. Seventy years after Saxton's hurried attempts to implement a policy of forty acres and a mule on the Sea Islands, the Resettlement Administration and its successor organization, the Farm Security Administration (FSA), began thirteen programs to establish farm communities for African American tenant farmers. Altogether, 1,151 families were involved and 91,992 acres of land in nine southern states. An almost equal number, 1,117, of white and black families were served similarly in programs in which the participants were scattered rather than concentrated in a community. These projects entailed 70,000 acres of land. Fifteen percent of the program's participants were located in eastern Arkansas, in recognition, perhaps, of the problem there which the STFU had made known nationally. The Lakeview Project, in Lee and Phillips counties, was the third largest project of the FSA, 135 African American families and 8,095 acres. The FSA conducted other large projects in Wilcox County, Alabama, which borders Lowndes. Ninety-nine African American families participated in that 10,188-acre program at Gee's Bend. Another large program that would become noteworthy in the civil rights movement involved 110 African American families and 9,350 acres in Holmes County, Mississippi, near Mileston.[79] The Tennessee Farm Tenant Security Program included an all-African American project in Haywood County, the Haywood County Farms Project, which got underway later than the others, 1938. It included 39 African American families and 3,358 acres of land and, of course, is central to ensuing political changes in Haywood County.

By October 1942 there were obvious results and very positive changes to report from Haywood County. The annual income of the members of the project quadrupled in four years; their total net assets tripled from $13,086 to $44,438. Their production of meat, fruit, and vegetables for their own use increased fourfold. Each family grew at least a half-acre of strawberries, which proved a lucrative cash crop. The families were growing more cotton on fewer acres, had more "live-at-home" crops, and were meeting their loan repayments satisfactorily. This history of the project substantiated the FSA's belief and fulfilled its purpose, "To show how small farmers can improve their living conditions through better tenure, adequate credit for equipment needed to carry out a balanced farming plan, and technical advice and guidance in sound farm and home management practices." Given that the nation, in October 1942, was at war, the project was also important because it meant "increased capacity to produce food and fibre for the Nation's war effort."[80]

The FSA worked in Lowndes County on a more modest scale. Fifteen African American families, in an area near White Hall in Lowndes County, participated in the Alabama Farm Tenant Security Project. White Hall had the largest concentration of families in the project. The project statewide included 113 black and white families in twenty counties and 10,926 acres. The program called for a home economist and a farm management specialist. The widely scattered nature of the program precluded the provision of community facilities or cooperative arrangements of buying and selling. The project was termed "a broad infiltration one," but it had the same purpose of other FSA programs. "The project was initiated for the purpose of demonstrating the practicability of selecting highclass white and colored tenant families and through the advantages of credit at a low interest rate, coupled with efficient farm supervision elevating them from tenancy to ownership."[81]

Discrediting Reform

Just as the land-reform efforts of Saxton were discredited, so was the work of the FSA. The determined opposition of the American Farm Bureau Federation led to several investigations of the FSA and its various programs. These investigations began in 1940 and culminated in a year-long set of hearings by a select committee of the House of Representatives Committee on Agriculture that finished in 1944.

The committee concluded that the FSA was used as "an experiment station of un-American ideas." "Honest, hard-working, low-income farmers" became "colonized and regimented" "guinea pigs" in the "communal or communistic" experiments of the FSA that were patterned after the collectivization in Russian agriculture. The FSA "tortured" tenant farmers with stories of "intolerant and mercenary" landlords and "intrigued" them with stories of "electric lights and bathtubs," only to remind them of "their low standard of living and of the hardships which they were constantly encountering." To make matters worse, the FSA used contracts "more harsh and far more exacting than the ordinary contracts between landlords and tenants." The work of the FSA was rehabilitation, such as its work in Lowndes County. But it "flagrantly abused" its authority and set out to raise "the living standards of its clients to somewhere near the highest prevailing in a community." The FSA offered "the promised land" but provided "desolation and disappointment" beyond what their clients had known before.[82]

The committee concluded that the FSA construed its enabling legislation "with great liberality and legal and administrative ingenuity" to permit it to do "just about everything under the sun they wanted to do." The report listed some specific transgressions of the FSA.

> They established, maintained, and operated communities and villages in rural and suburban areas, built and maintained streets, roads, and highways, shops, stores, and warehouses, hotels and inns, recreational halls and community houses and playgrounds, and other places of amusement. They built power plants and water systems. They built hospitals and rest homes, sewage-disposal plants and irrigation systems, creameries and canneries, packing plants, and factories for the manufacturing of numerous articles, including pants for men and full-fashioned hosiery for women. They built and financed dairies and grain elevators, cotton gins, potato houses, and other storage facilities. They provided modernly equipped homes, with all conveniences and facilities. They made loans and grants of Federal funds for the payment of lodge dues and poll taxes, for work stock, tractors and plows, and for farm implements of every kind and description. They furnished money with which to buy cows and sows, and bulls and boars, and with which to pay for family subsistence and for feed, seed, and fertilizer, and for the purchase of stock in corporations and for the payment of dues in cooperatives.[83]

The committee relied on the investigations of the American Farm Bureau that had sent investigators throughout the country, as President Johnson had done. The committee, with assistance from the Farm Bureau, traced the excess of the FSA to the presidential committee on farm tenancy. The Farm Bureau had a member on that committee just as the Southern Tenant Farmers Union had. Both dissented from the report. The Farm Bureau dissented because the report went too far and the STFU because it did not go far enough. Seven years after the report the Farm Bureau, unlike the STFU, had the power to discredit the report. The committee traced the ills of the FSA to the determination of the agency's administrators to circumvent the efforts of Congress to limit the scope of its programs, their size, and to concentrate on loans to farm buyers.[84] The committee proposed removing the "rotten apples" from the good programs in the barrel of the FSA and began the legislative process that would convert the FSA into a lending program for home and farm purchases, the Farmers Home Administration.[85]

The Farmers Home Administration, successor to the weakened FSA, underwent change in time. African American farmers charged it with racial discrimination in its lending policies and bias toward large farmers.[86] During the Carter administration the FHA entered into a special arrangement with the Department of Health and Human Services. By this agreement, loans were made for the construction of rural community health centers. Two such centers were the Douglas Community Center in Haywood County and the center on Johns Island. In addition, the FHA provided loans for the sewerage plant, clinic building, and nursing home on Johns Island.

Leaving the Land and Later Changes

By World War II the changes in the southern agricultural economy brought about massive changes far greater than either federal programs or the organized efforts of resistance among tenant farmers could. Machines replaced humans in the agricultural economy of the South. Mechanization, steel mules, not only reduced the demand for labor in the cotton economy, it created incentives for removing tenants from the land. Tractors and mechanized cotton pickers would do the work that poor, uneducated laborers did before and on the land their cabins had occupied.[87] Indicative of that change, from 1940 to 1970 rural farm agricultural workers in the four counties of our study declined by 544 percent, from 24,503 to 4,503.

These changes promoted a mass migration of millions of African Americans from the rural South, first to the cities of the South and then to the urban areas of the North. In the all-rural Haywood, Lee, and Lowndes counties the decline in African American population was from 66,575 to 31,508, or 41 percent, between 1940 and 1970. The total population, white and black, of these three counties decreased by 33 percent during this same time.

The vast majority of these migrants arrived in northern and southern cities with few resources. Like their family members before them who left slavery for the Union lines, Cleola Bursey's mother and other migrants left their place in the agricultural economy of the South with very little. Like their forebears, they left in hopes of finding something better than the economic position they had left behind. These migrants, like the tenant farmer and sharecropper who was now vanishing, served as the ultimate shock absorbers of economic swings and capital flow. In this particular case, the shocks were the mechanization of one sector of the American economy, the drastic decrease in demand for labor of millions of low-skilled workers, and an expanding wartime economy. The strategy of individual improvement, which migration represented, dwarfed federal interventions such as the FSA as a mechanism to improve the conditions of African Americans in the rural South in a drastically changed economy. The new economic and political status of migrants in the North would eventually stimulate national policies to address many of the social and political factors that contributed to their exodus.

Simultaneously, the modest land-reform efforts would support change efforts locally. African Americans owned more than half of the farms on Johns Island and the other Sea Islands from 1880 to the 1960s. This land was a critical foundation for the early voter registration efforts in the rural South, as we shall see. In Lee County the portion of African American farms ranged from 10 to 20 percent of all farms from 1900 to 1960, although African Americans were about 65 to 75 percent of the population. In Haywood County that range was from about 5 to 12 percent of all farms during that same time and about 70 percent of the population. In Lowndes County the portion of African American farms rose slightly above 10 percent only in 1950, when the African American population was 82 percent of the county. In 1940 only 908 African American farmers owned their land in these three counties. On this narrow base leaders like Tom Rice, Jesse Cannon, Charles Smith, Annie Hrabowski, Pitson Brady, and many others stood and established their own economic security and then built organizations and movements for civil rights and increased social services.

CHAPTER 6

Education: Instruction and

Incrementalism

The older narrators of this book have pleasant and angry memories of their education and their schools. Several claim they received their best instruction in the elementary grades of segregated one-room schools. But they also remember the inadequate provision for their schooling. Dilapidated buildings, discarded textbooks, and a short school year of three or four months established a curriculum in low expectations. Whatever lessons this curriculum imposed on them, their parents taught lessons in higher expectations. Tom Rice was willing to work "by the moonshine" for the money for his son's college education. Esau Jenkins transported his and other children to Charleston to attend the only school available for them. Parthenia Kelley supported her daughter's attendance at previously all-white schools in Lowndes County. Dr. C. P. Boyd and Olly Neal recalled their mothers' emphasis on education and efforts to acquire education for themselves and their children.

Many narrators taught school: Uralee Haynes, Mary Smith, and Sam Bradley in Lowndes County; Cleola Bursey in Lee County; Septima Clark on the Sea Islands; and Dr. C. P. Boyd, like his mother, in Haywood County. They recounted some of the injustices of their work in segregated systems, especially inequalities in responsibilities and pay. As with other aspects of racial inequality, these disadvantages were always recognized, occasionally protested, but never accepted. The schools in which they taught were more completely segregated by law in the 1940s than they had been in the 1860s. The hard work and aspirations for education expressed in the narratives mirror the extraordinary efforts of almost a century to make education for African American children available in the rural South. With little or no ordinary access to landownership, the best hope for improvement for African Americans in the rural South was vested in the schools they attended. Many efforts to conduct their schools proceeded from the premise that African American children have normal abilities and aspirations. This pitted them against notions of the inferiority of African Americans and their subordinate place in the economy. The heroic efforts to conduct schools were repeated time and again and from place to place. Among other things, the schools provided a haven of hope for changes that would come later.

New Schooling for New Freedom

During Sherman's bivouac at the Sea Islands in late 1864, General Howard, who was serving under Sherman and would become the commissioner of the Freedmen's Bureau in a few months, visited five schools for the freedpeople around Beaufort. He found "children sparkling with intelligence" and "not the stuff of which to make slaves."[1] The schools Howard visited were part of the "guided transition to freedom" on the Sea Islands. After Pierce made his report to Washington officials, he returned to Boston and assisted his abolitionist colleagues to begin the Education Commission.[2] Simultaneously, the Reverend Mr. Mansfield French, who had met Pierce on the Sea Islands during his visit, worked in New York to recruit volunteers to staff the experiment in freedom on the Sea Islands, as well. French was replicating work that his organization, the American Missionary Association, had already begun further up the Atlantic coast at Fortress Monroe near Hampton, Virginia.[3] On March 3, 1862, fifty-six men and women recruited by Pierce and French embarked from Boston and New York for the Sea Islands. One month later, additional abolitionist volunteers from Philadelphia sailed for the Sea Islands. Among the latter were Laura M. Towne, who began Penn School at Frogmore on St. Helena Island. It was one of thirty schools on the islands that enrolled 3,000 students by 1865. In the beginning of that year Howard visited this and other schools and drew inspiration from the children who were their pupils. In his new role within the Freedmen's Bureau, Howard disseminated information about these schools, describing them as models, and he gave education more attention than any other of his duties. He parlayed authority to rent and repair school houses and $500,000 in appropriations into a construction program for school houses. The bureau then turned the much-needed buildings over to other groups to conduct the actual education program.

The schools, like land-reform measures, were caught in a crossfire of the Freedman's Bureau, Congress, and President Johnson. They fared better than land reform, however. The president vetoed the Freedmen's Bureau bill in February 1866 with very sweeping language. He cited a lack of precedent for the federal government to conduct the work of the Freedmen's

Bureau and singled out education as especially inappropriate. The president preferred to leave education, like other matters of relief and provisions for welfare, to the "competent and efficient control" of state and local authorities, and to private philanthropy.[4] However, Johnson's opponents in Congress and within his own cabinet understood that entrusting education to the local authorities in the South meant the restoration of an antebellum system of no free public education system and only extraordinary access to education for African American children and children of the white laboring class. Congress overrode the veto and supported explicitly the Freedmen's Bureau's development of schools.

Howard's assistants also showed enthusiasm for the bureau's work in education. The monthly reports of the Freedmen Bureau's officers always carried news of the schools of the district, and the semi-annual report included the numbers of schools and their enrollments.[5] The assistant commissioner for Alabama, Major General Wager Swayne, did his best to dissuade the freedpeople of their hopes for land but worked hard and well to support the initiation and conduct of schools.[6] Often the army protected the buildings and staffs of the schools against violent opposition, which the bureau officials hoped would soften with time. However, by 1870 it was still evident to a bureau official in Tennessee that if the bureau withdrew its school effort, "the cause will droop and its defenders will become discouraged."[7]

Between 1866 and 1872 the Freedmen's Bureau spent $3,771,132 on school construction and repair and rent of thousands of schools.[8] Johns, Wadmalaw, and Edisto islands had a concentration of them. Only one bureau school began in Haywood County, in Brownsville, and Helena was as close as a bureau school ever reached Lee County. A school did reach Lowndes County. From there, one teacher in Hayneville wrote Howard in April 1868, relating an average class day and her ambition.

> We teach four hours per day without room recess, varying the exercises with concert repetition and singing, and then dismiss for the day. Besides Reading and Spelling, they are paying great attention to Penmanship, and I give them Bible lessons, teach them Geography of their own State, the tables of Arithmetic in concert, something of the proceedings of a court of justice, many particulars of good manners; and I design giving them oral lessons upon United States History and Physiology.[9]

This class was typical of the effort going on throughout the South, but it was not typical of the experience of freedchildren. By 1870, 4,000 schools with 9,000 teachers enrolled and taught 200,000 students. Impressive as this accomplishment was, it meant that only 12 percent of the estimated 1.7 million freedchildren in the South were enrolled in schools. At no time during the Freedmen's Bureau's program did enrollment exceed this proportion.[10] The bureau's superintendent of education in Alabama estimated that the number of school-age freedpeople of the state was 173,000 and that 100,000 of them had never entered a school house and probably had no knowledge of the alphabet.[11] The effort of the bureau was dwarfed by the problem it addressed. There were hundreds of thousands of children and adults to educate for the first time, few resources, little local cooperation from the white political leaders, and in some cases outright opposition. The bureau educational superintendent for Alabama suggested that the bureau had done well but that little was accomplished.[12] Nonetheless, the bureau's modest achicvemenl was monumental compared with what had preceded it.

The critically short supply of teachers hampered the bureau in its efforts to begin schools for the freedpeople. A bureau official in Tennessee lamented that only one in forty-five potential students was in the schools and exasperatedly explained, "We have not the teachers." He had places for one hundred competent African American teachers immediately who could go to rural and isolated places where "places of safety, and comparative comfort to board" were not available to attract white ladies from the North.[13] In Alabama as well, the demand for schools was great. "Everywhere, to open a school has been to have it filled."[14] The bureau aided in the recruitment of teachers and other workers among the freedpeople by paying their transportation costs to the South. It assisted about 4,000 of them in this way at a cost of $385,307.[15]

The bureau's educational program gave abolitionist societies a new agenda after the war that reanimated the enthusiasm of the freedmen's aid societies and provided a target for northern philanthropy.[16] In 1865 fifty groups in the North, both secular and religious, were supporting education work in the South. Between 1863 and 1875 these societies contributed $7.5 million to this work.[17] The American Missionary Association (AMA) provided the most support for thc cduɔation of the treedpeople in the South. Between 1861 and 1890 the AMA contributed about one-third of the $20 million of all of benevolent associations' aid.[18] In the first decade of its work the AMA supported 3,470 ministers, missionaries, and teachers—one in seven of them African American—and provided instruction to 322,000 men, women, and children in 350 day, night, and Sabbath schools.[19] The AMA worked with the African Civilization Society, a freedmen's aid association led by African Americans who espoused racial pride and training African Americans to teach and lead the freedpeople.[20] The African Civilization Society was especially active in promoting the education of the freedpeople in the District of Columbia and assisted in establishing Howard University.[21]

The Freedmen's Bureau and the AMA had close ties that bound them not only to each other but each to the earlier abolitionist movement. John W. Alvord, the bureau's general superintendent of schools, attended Lane Seminary with the AMA's corresponding secretary, George Whipple. They were among the students who left Lane along with supporting faculty to go to Oberlin, where they had more freedom to express and develop their abolitionist views.[22] The bureau and AMA had an "old boy" network that developed into close working relations after the war. AMA principals and agents were sometimes paid and employed for their work by the bureau, and bureau officials, including Howard's brother, took positions within the AMA. Howard would serve as the first president of the Washington university named in his honor, Howard University. Certainly, without the financial support of the bureau, including the rent the bureau paid the AMA for some school properties, the AMA would have had too few resources for its work. In fact, the year the bureau's support ended, 1872, the number of AMA teachers dropped from 461 to 309.[23]

The AMA approached its work as political salvation and with a spirit of redeeming action. Caste was the particular sin that the AMA purged.[24] Caste, like slavery, locked individuals into a level of privilege or deprivation, precluded social mobility and individual improvement based on merit, and degraded people. Opposed to caste and enlightened far beyond their contemporaries about race, the workers of the AMA challenged the dominant racial prejudices of others. For example, inquiries about the superior intelligence of mulattoes compared with African Americans received convincing negative replies from classrooms all over the South.[25] Also, from the first, African American men and women staffed AMA schools and took leading roles in changing the educational level of the freedpeople. Mary Peake, an African American woman, taught slaves secretly in Hampton before the Union occupation and directed the first AMA school after occupation. She was assisted by two other African Americans from the North. African American men and women were directors of schools such as Avery Institute and heads of departments at Straight. Thomas Cardoza hired six African American teachers for Avery, and his brother, Francis L. Carodza, who succeeded him, kept the racial balance of teachers equal for the time he served.[26]

This challenge to dominant prejudices was successful enough to earn criticism and rebuttal from those firm in their knowledge about the low intelligence of the freedpeople. The *Charleston Daily News* reported in May 1866 that the Avery Institute "must not be considered a fair average of colored education in the city." Many of the children, one-fourth, had been born free and "scarcely a pure black" could be found in some classes. "The best material has been retained as far as practicable and the remainder sent to other schools." [27]

Other groups joined the AMA in educational work among the freedpeople, including the freedpeople themselves. Of the 165 teachers in Tennessee's bureau's schools in 1869, for example, the AMA supplied 26, the Presbyterian Committee of Home Missions 36, and five other church-related associations 27. The American Freedmen's Union Commission supplied 4 teachers. Freedpeople were supporting 22 teachers with their own resources in schools known to the bureau. [28]

This support indicates the drive for education that came from the freedpeople at their first opportunity. The same freedfamilies that bought property at the Direct Tax Commission sales in 1863 on the Sea Islands also opened schools for their children at their own expense. [29] Likewise, some teachers from the North arrived at their assigned sites on the Sea Islands to find that the freedpeople had begun schools already. A former slavewoman, Hettie, who had "stolen a knowledge of letters from time to time," began a day school on Edisto Island. In general, freedpeople taught in school before white teachers arrived, during their absence, and in places they did not reach. [30] Altogether, 500 African Americans participated in the ranks of AMA teachers, more than half of them from the South. By and large, these teachers like those in other associations were relegated to the least important positions and were often sent to the most dangerous and isolated locations. [31] In general, they performed their duties differently. They spent more time in the location, on average, and did not take summers off to return to the North. They also encouraged more ancillary development efforts, including other forms of instruction, crafts, and alternative economic activities. Given the dangers they faced, they were also less inclined to express hostility to local white leaders and in general expressed fewer explicitly political views. [32]

Integrated staffs presented problems for the schools. Controversy over policies and practices often turned to charges of racism when whites and blacks were on different sides. African Americans from the North, in particular, complained about their treatment as second-class members of school faculties for the sake of local mores. By the early 1870s local freedpeople were also asking for more control over the schools and for more African American teachers. Their requests conflicted with the authority of the white AMA school directors, who claimed that other freedpeople preferred northern white teachers to either northern or southern black teachers. They also maintained that northern white teachers were essential to uphold the reputation of the schools.[33] Although dead-set against caste, AMA officials continued to distinguish among their staffs by race and among African Americans by skin color and class manners.[34]

Between 1866 and 1870 freedpeople contributed $785,700 to support their own schools in the South. This, plus the contribution of the several freedmen's aid societies, equalled approximately one-half of the total cost of the schools. The Freedmen's Bureau contributed the other half of the cost of conducting the education programs.[35] Some associations made matching funds from freedmen a condition of their contribution. Bureau reports from Tennessee indicate that the freedpeople there made an average contribution of $400 per school and provided board for teachers and incidental expenses for the school's operation. Average monthly support for all schools from the freedmen was $1,862 a month in 1867 when they owned forty-four school buildings. Expectations were that they would double that number in the coming year.[36]

In addition to these reported efforts, other efforts never received public notice. In remote areas throughout the South freedpeople began their own schools that bureau officials knew nothing about until they accidently discovered them, as they did constantly. In November 1869 a bureau assistant commissioner for Alabama found twelve schools previously unreported in one county.[37] Alvord, bureau superintendent for schools, estimated that there were at least five hundred schools for freed children that white people never visited or supported in the South.

> A cellar, a shed, a private room, perhaps an old school-house, is the place and, in the midst of a group of thirty or forty children, an old negro in spectacles, or two or three young men surrounded by a hundred or more, themselves only in the rudiments of a spelling-book, and yet with a passion to teach what they do know; or a colored woman, who as a family servant had some privileges, and with a woman's compassion for her race—these are the institutions and the agencies. . . . In truth, these spontaneous efforts of the colored people would start up everywhere if books could be sent them.[38]

But books were not sent to them in proportion to the need or their own efforts. Resources did not match the enthusiasm of freedpeople for education or their willingness to sacrifice to establish schools. In some places freedpeople were sometimes cheated by men who exploited their hopes for a school by promising classes, collecting money, and leaving. In other places the freedpeople supported schools with inadequate teachers. In one instance in Tennessee the freedpeople were put in the unfortunate position of having to defend, by force, a teacher, whom the bureau judged a tolerable teacher but "really an immoral, bad man." Those who would have taken him away would have also left the freedpeople with no one to teach and conduct the school.[39]

Resources and Reprisals

If support for the education of freedpeople was inadequate, hostility toward it was abundant. Alvord traced the support of education to the accurate calculation of freedpeople that people with influence and power had education and that education was necessary to their improvement, influence, and increased power.[40] Opposition to the schools came from the same calculation by a different group. This opposition deterred the development of some schools and led to the destruction of others. In Haywood County in April 1867 the Freedmen's Bureau officer reported some support among whites for schools for freedchildren, "but the opposition is strong enough to deter any person from engaging in it, they do not feel safe." If whites felt unsafe, black leaders had more reason to fear. Earlier that month a "squad of guerillas or outlaws," the nascent Ku Klux Klan, burned a school that was started and conducted by a freedman. Despite the fear and the reprisals, the bureau officer reported two schools in Haywood County that the freedpeople organized, even though they had no teacher and no prospect of securing one without the aid of the bureau.[41] Another bureau official in west Tennessee deployed troops to sustain the local school and estimated that without white hostility there would be at least four other schools in the county.[42] In the first six months of 1869 three schools in Tennessee were destroyed by fire, and there was little doubt in the mind of the reporting bureau officer that in each case the fire was deliberately set.[43]

Howard noted similar incidents in Alabama in 1868, and anguished: "People from a distance could not comprehend the feeling; schoolhouses were burned, and those left standing were in danger; teachers were hated and maltreated, two being driven from their work. 'The truth is,' they cried, 'we are in the midst of a reign of terror.'"[44]

Churches that housed schools were destroyed to remove spaces and institutions of the freedpeople. In addition to this violent interdiction, communities of freedpeople were sometimes dispossessed of school buildings through financial means, and local officials interfered with teachers, including charging them with crimes.[45] There were many different types of teachers in the early schools of the freedpeople: white and black, northern and southern, male and female, as well as qualified and unqualified. The white teachers from the North were the explicit target of deepest suspicion and distrust from white southerners. Just as their work started, one bureau official in Alabama reported the local suspicions that the northern teachers promulgated ideas of "negro suffrage, of social equality, of miscegenation, of agrarianism, and every mischievous outgrowth of the fanaticism of that clime."[46]

As a group, the white northern female teachers taught far less equality than their critics feared but far more than their critics wanted. They did not encourage social equality but did encourage expanded opportunities for learning and landownership among the freedpeople. A yeomen's democracy of Jefferson and mythical New England was their "fanaticism," as it had been Saxton's. It was radical only in contrast to the subordination of slavery. Most of these teachers accepted the limited preparation of the freedpeople for their new freedom but understood the limits as temporary and imposed by politics, the economy, and culture. They advised patience, work, and learning as the surest means of improvement for the freedpeople and trusted little in the possibility or efficacy of sweeping and lasting reform. Some of them had doubts about the wisdom of enfranchising freedmen and their qualifications for public office. At least one of them complained about the injustice of extending the vote to unqualified freedmen while denying it to qualified women. As in any group, they were divided on the issues of equality, charity, and the role of freedpeople in American society. The clearest political message to their work was support for increased and new forms of government intervention such as the bureau's schools for the social welfare of the freedpeople of the South. This set of teachers was much more likely to express antipathy to local whites and to challenge their racial attitudes directly.[47]

It was this challenge more than their characteristics that engendered hostility to teachers of the freedpeople's schools. Whatever their skin color, education, origin, or gender, teachers were disturbers of the peace and agents of "mischief" because they encouraged a degree of social equality beyond that allowed by the local mores and attitudes. Teachers by their mere presence, if not by their explicit lessons, offered the freedpeople a vision of a more equal role in society for them and of the opportunities that were available to them. Accordingly, some teachers encountered violent opposition. A white male teacher from the North and his African American assistant teachers were lynched in Alabama in 1870.[48] A white teacher, a native Tennessean, was driven away from his school because his father had served in the Union Army. Two African American men, graduates of Fisk University, were taken from their school in west Tennessee, beaten, threatened with death, and ordered to leave the area immediately, two months after they had started teaching in the summer of 1869.[49]

Skirmishes over individual schools were part of a larger political battle. Violence toward teachers and the meeting places of the freedpeople increased before elections and were part of an effort to disorganize and discourage freedmen from voting. When elections restored the former Confederates to power, as they did in west Tennessee in the summer of 1869, violence against schools and teachers increased because the likelihood of legal punishment had declined.[50] Events in Tennessee after the elections of 1869 and the restoration of control to former political and economic leaders portended what was to come in other parts of the South. Overt forms of violence subsided and new forms of subversion succeeded them. Teachers were chosen whom the local authorities could depend upon to accept the inequalities of the separate school systems and to practice the caste norms of inequality that segregation inferred. Finances were meager for public schools in general and distributed disproportionately.

Public schooling was consistent with the place of the freedpeople in the agricultural economy of the South and a caste system that assumed racial inferiority. Even the Union men and the "better class of disloyal" who favored or at least did not oppose the schools in fact were "bitterly opposed to any action looking to what they are pleased to call *equality*."[51] Although emancipation had ended slavery, the practice of deciding essential and personal matters for the freedpeople, including education, was still a prerogative of white people, at least according to some white people.[52]

The state constitutions established in the 1860s and some African American political leaders impeded gross inequalities in education from developing too rapidly. Taxation for schools, unknown before the constitutions of the Reconstruction era, became part of the constitutions of Alabama, Arkansas, and South Carolina. Very quickly, publicly supported schools became legally mandated for whites and blacks.[53] Important African American leaders supported public education and the entitlement of African American children to that education. James T. Rapier, who represented Lowndes County, Alabama, in the United States Congress in 1874, was one such political leader.[54] So was Samuel A. McElwee, who represented Haywood County in the Tennessee General Assembly for three terms in the 1880s. Like other African

American legislators, McElwee made the distribution of public educational funds a major item on Tennessee's legislative agendas.[55] These legislators met with little success but impeded regressive measures until the 1890s, when African American political participation was suppressed and unequal provision for the services to African Americans became the practice.

In the 1890s the finances of the public schools in the South grew more unequal. White political leaders from the black-belt counties of Alabama, including Lowndes County, for example, brought about substantial changes in the funding of the public education. They fought increases in funding for public education in 1888 and 1891, arguing that the intelligence of African American people was not as advanced as the intelligence of white people, and consequently they did not need as much education or expenditures on education.[56] In addition, they complained that whites paid property taxes almost exclusively that supported county schools that had predominantly African American enrollments. This "onerous" burden was, of course, the consequence of the imposed paucity of landownership among African Americans in the county.

Laws passed in 1891 permitted local authorities in Alabama, rather than state officials, to disperse state funds for education, which made matters worse. Lowndes County's officials began a disbursement policy that reached extreme proportions. In 1930 Lowndes County received $53,525 in state funds for its 11,014 children of school age, $4.86 each. Officials divided the state support $22,049 for the 10,039 African American children or $2.20 per African American child, and $31,476 for 975 white children or $32.28 each. Local authorities distributed other local, state, and federal revenues for education, over which they had discretion, so that $4.76 was spent on each African American pupil in Lowndes County in 1930 and $95.93 for each white pupil.[57]

When Myrdal visited the rural African American schools during his study, after some six decades of local control, he found them and the entire southern educational structure for African American children in "a pathological state." Like Howard and other bureau officials, he visited schools in rural areas. But in the 1930s he did not find inspiration; instead, he "hardly believed his eyes and ears when he ascertained the primitive school building, the lack of practically all equipment, the extreme lack of contact with modern American civilization on the part of the untrained, poorly paid, Negro woman serving as teacher and the bottomless ignorance of the pupils."[58] Although such schools were not typical, they were too frequently encountered to be isolated instances or even exceptions. The existence of such schools, Myrdal concluded, was a "remarkable, and a significant characteristic of the whole system."[59] Educational conditions for African American children in Haywood County were deplorable in 1938 according to the FSA supervisor there.

> The situation regarding the school facilities for colored families on Site I is entirely inadequate. There is one-teacher school on the Northern edge of the project which has, at times, had as high as 80 pupils enrolled. There is a two-teacher school approximately 1½ miles from the east side of the project. The school also has a heavy enrollment. Both are elementary schools. There is no high school closer than Brownsville, Tennessee, 17 miles from the project and no transportation to the high school is furnished by the county.[60]

The FSA supervisor, Stanley H. Rice, suggested a new six-room school with auditorium. The building would accommodate 200 elementary students and 100 high school students. Rice assured his regional and national superiors, "there is very little prospect of securing an adequate school building" except from the federal government. With the new building, Rice felt confident that he could acquire adequate assistance from the county and the state for teachers without additional cost to the project. Rice anticipated, correctly as it turns out, that the school and its auditorium would serve as a community building for the families of the project. One of the teachers, Theodore Giles, also worked with the farming families around the school and introduced new farming methods and crops. Giles's son would later serve as chairman of the Douglas Community Health Services, one of the many connections from the Douglas School to the development of the health center.

But the Douglas school had explicit backward linkages as well. In particular, the FSA officials knew of and emulated Penn School on St. Helena Island. T. J. Woofter, Jr., conducted a study of the island and described Penn School as a catalyst of services as well as a bond for local communities. Woofter found in Penn School an example of what might be done to improve the condition of rural African Americans in the South and a model of development for other nations as well.[61] Woofter worked for the Commission on Interracial Cooperation that Will W. Alexander directed. Alexander also helped start the Social Science Research Council that funded Woofter's study of St. Helena Island. Alexander became Rexford Tugwell's assistant at the Resettlement Administration and later succeeded him as director of that agency. But Penn was only one example of a school as an instrument of development. Each community of this study, in fact, had a school that played a prominent role in developing local leadership as the Douglas School was to do.

Penn School

Laura M. Towne began Penn School in March of 1862 and with her assistant, Ellen Murray, continued work at the school until 1905. Rossa B. Cooley and Grace B. House succeeded them as directors of Penn. Both Cooley and House came to Penn from Hampton Institute, bringing an industrial education curriculum that included carpentry, blacksmithing, wheelwrighting, harness making, shoe cobbling, mechanics, and agriculture. Penn changed its name to Penn Normal, Industrial and Agricultural School. This change ended an epoch of educational policies of Reconstruction. Hampton and Penn represented different approaches to the education of African Americans. President Andrew Johnson replaced Charles B. Wilder, who had conducted the Bureau of Negro Affairs at Hampton, Virginia, from 1863 to 1865, with General Samuel Chapman Armstrong. Wilder, like Saxton, had complied reluctantly with presidential orders to transfer lands from new landowners to the former white planters. Armstrong had far fewer problems with these policies. He devoted himself energetically to new forms of labor for the landless freedpeople in the area and to related educational programs. In 1868, with the assistance of the Freedmen's Bureau and the American Missionary Association, Armstrong founded the Hampton Normal Institute.

Booker T. Washington attended Hampton Normal Institute and become its most famous alumni. He would also become the prime African American exponent of the premises of the revised policies of the Freedmen's Bureau. These premises suggested that the condition of freedpeople in the South did not warrant wholesale reform of economic, political, and social arrangements. Rather, they required increased opportunities for education for freedpeople to acquire skills. These skills, coupled with hard work, thrift, and virtue, would win for freedpeople the admiration of whites and security for the political and economic rights of African Americans. Armstrong recognized that taking land from freed people put them "at the bottom of the ladder." But, he suggested, "It is not a bad thing for anyone to touch bottom early, if there is a good solid foundation under him and then climb from that."[62] Education was extolled as part of that solid foundation.

Towne and Murray and the early Penn School belonged to another tradition that attempted to transplant the northern pine of liberal arts education and yeomanry to southern soil and the freedpeople. Towne traveled to Washington in January 1866 to argue for the Freedmen's Bureau, Saxton, and the land-redistribution policies on the island.[63] This tradition also aspired to prepare freedpeople for the professions of law, medicine, teaching, and not the industrial arts exclusively. The school instructed York W. Bailey, for example, who proceeded, upon graduation, to Benedict College and Howard School of Medicine. He returned to St. Helena Island as the first full-time resident physician and practiced medicine until 1971 and the beginning of a community health center. Fisk, Meharry, and Howard expressed Towne's and Murray's educational aspirations better than Hampton or Washington's Tuskegee. When Cooley and House changed the curriculum at Penn School, they extended the hegemony of Washington's views of accommodation to subordinate political and economic roles for African Americans that went back to the retreat from Reconstruction reforms.[64]

Neither curriculum worked miracles on St. Helena Island. But Penn School did perform better than most other schools and contributed a great deal to the nearby African American community. The large numbers of landowners in the area, the remnant of land reforms of 1862 to 1866, created the unusual circumstance of African American families with the independence to send children to school. There is little doubt that the Penn School made the most of these circumstances. Instruction was more competent, teachers more qualified, and facilities better kept, even though they were underfunded and inadquate. Literacy was higher, although only one-eighth of the African American residents of St. Helena Island had gone beyond the sixth grade.

Cooley and House retired from their positions at Penn after forty years, in 1944, when the school began a new series of changes. Howard and Alice Kester became directors. Howard Kester had worked with the Southern Tenant Farmers Union in eastern Arkansas in the turbulent, violent days of the 1930s. The Kesters left Penn in 1948 when the county and state began providing public education for the African American children on the island. In 1951 the school became Penn Community Services, Inc., a community development program. Its activities included workshops, some of which trained civil rights workers like Charles Smith of Lowndes County, and conferences, one of which planned the March on Washington in 1963. Both Septima Clark and Bill Saunders worked in programs at Penn Center extensively in the 1960s. In 1969, 107 years after Penn School started, John W. Gadson, Sr., took charge of the program at Penn, the first African American to do so. Emery Campbell, a Penn School graduate, currently directs Penn Center and conducts a program of demonstration farms, advocacy to preserve African American landownership, and training, including the preparation of Peace Corps volunteers.

Calhoun Colored School

Lowndes County also had a notable school for African Americans, although less famous than Penn School. The Calhoun Colored School began in 1893 as an offspring of Hampton. Booker T. Washington visited Hampton Institute in 1891 and made a speech on the need for education on rural plantations in the black belt of Alabama. He quoted a letter from an African American preacher in Lowndes County that dramatized this need. The preacher recounted his congregation's members' reaction to a racial riot that took the lives of forty African Americans in Lowndes County. The members of the church in the aftermath of the riots began a prayer vigil to ask for deliverance in the specific form of a school from the North. The vigil was in its second week when the preacher wrote to Washington.[65]

Two white teachers at Hampton, Charlotte R. Thorn and Mabel W. Dillingham, expressed interest in returning with Washington to establish a school and to answer those prayers. Nothing came from that first discussion, but Thorn and Dillingham began work on a school, and in 1893 they came to Lowndes County at Calhoun. N. J. Bell, a white man, gave ten acres of land for the school and sold the two women another ten acres for $250. The women intended to establish a school based on the program at Hampton that would emphasize elementary school work, beginning with grade five, along with industrial and agricultural training, community work, and projects.[66]

At the time the school started the condition of public elementary education in Lowndes County was appalling by any standard. Thirteen dollars was spent for the education of a white child for every one dollar spent for the education of an African American child. The length of the school year was short for all children, but shorter for African American students. School did not start until the crops were harvested generally sometime in November. In February school was interrupted as the children joined their families in work to prepare the fields for spring planting. Tenant farmers depended on all family members for labor and withheld children from school frequently for harvesting, planting, and tending the crop.[67]

Like previous teachers from the North, Thorn was dependent on contributions from friends, family, and connections in the North for the funds to operate the school. She was a master of individual contributions, as evidenced by her success in keeping the school operating. She pursued contributions doggedly, even from those who had lapsed in their contributions. Before the computer and software programs for individualized appeal letters, she had perfected the personalized form letter. Her appeal for funds were especially moving because they were specific. Her letter to a lapsed donor in Jamaica Plains, Massachusetts, of December 1918 explained, for example, that an influenza epidemic had suspended school one month in October.

> Fifty-nine boarding students were ill at one time; ten with serious pneumonia complications. With a doctor coming only five times during the four weeks, all of the sick were cared for by teachers and officers of the school who gladly worked in day and night shifts so that everything possible could be done. We also accepted from the nearest doctor the charge of all families within a radius of three miles. What this means can be realized by the need of over seven hundred typewritten sets of directions.
>
> No lives were lost. WERE THESE LIVES WORTH SAVING? IS ALL OUR WORK WORTH DOING? After twenty-six years here at Calhoun I know we are working for and with a wonderful people who bravely if slowly have met and overcome difficulties and are uniting in helping others.

She then related Calhoun School's work and financial needs directly to this former contributor.

> You have very kindly assisted us in past years. Your last gift was received Dec. 1912. Will you aid us again. We know the tremendous demands during the past two years upon all generous and philanthropic people and realize why many had to suspend gifts to Calhoun. The omission of these gifts amounted to $4240.00 sorely needed by us. If possible will you help lift a burden? [68]

In addition to the conduct of the school, Thorn and her associates began conferences for the local farmers, calling them "a school for old people." At the first conference in 1896 farmers expressed their desire to grow white potatoes and then discussed their inability to do so. Since they owned no land, they had no say over land use and consequently were not free to plant white potatoes for their own food instead of the cash crop of cotton. Their inability to decide what crops to grow was indicative of the power that landlords had over them. Some farmers recounted threats they had received, including violence, designed to prevent them from even attending the conference.

Members of the conference decided that the key to acquiring more power over crop selection was landownership. The teachers who organized the conference had concluded that landownership was also key to an expanded school year and improved school attendance for the school children in Calhoun. Consequently, the farmer's conference, with the school's full support, decided to establish a land trust to acquire land. The conference began with capital contributed from individual farmers, $256.67. The officers of the trust bought a plot of forty acres and rented it to two shareholders in the trust. In December of 1896 the trust made a purchase of 1,040 acres and in November 1897 purchased another 2,110 acres. The money for these purchases came from northern individuals and philanthropies. By 1920 this land had been divided among sixty farmers.

Each participant signed a covenant, reminiscent of the AMA evangelistic ties with this work. They "recorded" that the objective before them "is not money or simply getting land but getting homes—living for our children, building up our neighborhood, becoming good citizens and Christians and with God's help we promise to do our best." As part of the covenant, they were requested to come to farmers' conferences; the women were requested to come to mothers' meetings and all other meetings on school grounds, when possible. In addition, the signers agreed to attend church and to send their children to Sunday school. The children of the newly created landowners were the largest contingent of pupils at the school.

It proved difficult even for these trust shareholders to become landowners quickly. The original plans called for each renter to become a landowner within three years. In fact, only one person did this in three years: Isaac Smith, one of the original two renters of trust land, whose plot was only ten acres. Some participants criticized early arrangements of the trust that permitted renters to buy land in theory although, because capital accumulation remained difficult, few people were able to buy land in practice and hardly anyone without a cash advance. Most farmers started and remained in a cash-poor position. Mr. Chestnut, a white man from Lowndes County, sold the land to the trust, supervised the project, and also lent supplies at 10 percent.[69]

The school provided a range of other services and activities for the benefit of the Calhoun community. Profits from the saw mill, along with profits of other activities and contributions received, supported the continuing education of some of its pupils once they had finished at Calhoun. The school also provided supervision in new agricultural techniques that were introduced slowly and with only limited success. The school had far more success with the introduction of housing, beginning in 1910. Farmers who had acquired land constructed new homes and could boast of the first homes of African Americans to have glass and paint in the Calhoun vicinity.[70] The school also had an integrated staff of black and white teachers,[71] which was an important, if intangible, form of service.

The integrated staff made Calhoun a space where races could relate on terms different from prevailing local, social norms. Likewise, such space provided the opportunity to better assess the relations of the races. In 1906 Du Bois used Calhoun Colored School as a base from which to study the division of land among the races, the distribution of labor, the relationship of landlord and tenant, political organizations, and family life of the African Americans in Lowndes County. His study was funded by the U.S. Department of Labor. The department did not publish the study and destroyed it because it "touched on political matters."[72] Whatever accommodations Miss Thorn and others at the school made to the racism of their contemporaries in their work, they showed more courage in providing space for the work of Du Bois than the U.S. Department of Labor, which had far less to fear in terms of physical violence and reprisals.

Du Bois was obviously deeply impressed by Thorn and the Calhoun School. His book, *Quest of the Silver Fleece,* was a fictionalized account that praised the efforts of a school like Calhoun, the heroism of women like Thorn, and the abilities of the students whom the school trained. It also depicted the hostile and racist environment in which the school worked and worked to change. Calhoun School, in Du Bois's account, challenged the foundation of the Lowndes County and national economy: cheap labor for cheap cotton. Despite the school's ties to Washington, Du Bois described it as reluctantly accommodationist. Du Bois even portrays Thorn's fictional counterpart as refusing an endowment for the school from a northern bene-factor who required a local landlord to become a member of the school's board. "I cannot accept your offer," Thorn's model replied, "his relation to the forces of evil in this community has been such that he can direct no school of mine."[73] Du Bois portrayed Calhoun as a school that encouraged and prepared students for larger roles and even provided the means for those new roles, education and landownership. He related the land-buying effort of the school, then in progress, directly to the effort of Thorn to provide an alternative to the fraud of sharecropping for at least a small number of African American farmers.

The land trust began to dissipate after 1920 as African American land-ownership was declining throughout the South. Another 2,200 acres was purchased but at much higher rates than the previous land. By 1930 only three lots from this new purchase had been sold. The other sixteen lots were being rented or leased, and only three farmers were managing to keep up with their debts. The combination of low prices for crops, increased price for land, interest rates on loans, and increased taxes combined to make land purchasing much more difficult after 1920 and brought the period of slow but important success of the Calhoun Land Trust to an end. At this point, in 1930, the first African American to be in charge of the Calhoun Land Trust, A. W. Roper, assumed the position of supervisor.

By the mid-1930s the idea that the Calhoun Land Trust embodied and that it had carried on from the original promise of forty acres and a mule from Reconstruction was taken up and implemented by another federal program of the New Deal, the Resettlement Administration. Will W. Alexander, the director of the Resettlement Administration, explained, "The program which has been carried on for a number of years [at Calhoun] is the most successful demonstration that has been made of a thing of which the Resettlement Administration is now attempting to do on a nationwide basis." [74] Both Sam Bradley and Charles Smith became landowners in Lowndes County because of the Calhoun Land Trust.

Fargo Agricultural School

Yet another offshoot of Booker T. Washington's pedagogy took root near Lee County, Arkansas. The Fargo Agricultural School began in 1920, later than most schools. It initially enrolled fifteen students. It operated until 1949, at which time 165 boarding students and 15 day students were enrolled. Its founder, Floyd Brown, attended Tuskegee and knew Washington personally. At the age of twenty-one in 1912 he went to Tuskegee completely unprepared. He had little previous education; he had not formally applied; and he had no money for tuition. Initially, he was set to work on the farm at Tuskegee and was eventually tested to determine the appropriate level to begin his education. Washington established a special C Prep class for Brown and several others in his situation. At the age of twenty-one Brown began fifth-grade work. He advanced rapidly. He also studied at Phelps Hall Bible School and Tennessee Agricultural & Industrial State Normal School For Negroes and finished his studies in 1919.

Brown first visited Fargo in 1915 during summer vacation. Washington had died shortly before, and Brown was in eastern Arkansas that summer selling a book on the life and times of Washington. He returned to Fargo in 1919 with $2.85 to begin an industrial school because of the great need he found in the community for such a school. He borrowed $50.00 from his land-owning stepmother in Mound Bayou and used $40.00 of it to buy four acres of land from the Reverend E. M. Garrison, in Fargo. With other donations from local merchants, saw mill operators, and farmers, Brown and others completed the facilities in time to welcome the first group of fifteen students in January 1920. In subsequent years Brown added 546 acres of land and eleven more buildings. The school enrolled 180 students who were charged $2.00 a month tuition and room and board but could attend even if unable to afford this fee. The school was a center of development and boasted of electricity, telephone service, and an improved water system before other areas of eastern Arkansas had them and certainly before they were common among African American residents of the area.

Brown was a protégé of Washington as well as a student at Tuskegee. He internalized the virtues that Washington extolled for him and that Armstrong had offered Washington at Hampton. For example, Brown would later explain to his students at Fargo that life was a ladder and one proceeds step by step, "round by round, safe and sure, from the bottom."

> Do not live above your means, and do not attempt to become successful over night. Make good on the small jobs and you will have a chance to make good on the large ones. If things do not go your way and you do not succeed the first time you attempt, keep trying.
> We build the ladder by which we rise out of our own material. Learn to manage a little money and it will enable you some day to manage big money. We climb the ladder of life round by round and not by flights.[75]

Brown repeated "Work will Win" and offered examples of people like Henry Ford who worked hard "day by day with courage and strong determination" to his students. Sixty years after Armstrong had extolled the virtues of starting at the bottom of the ladder, Brown recommended the same starting point to another generation of African Americans in the rural South as "common sense." If not common sense, starting at the bottom of the ladder was the undeniable reality of his students.

Despite the starting point, Brown encouraged his students to be great. He strongly opposed the ideas of those who equated education and dignity with freedom from the necessity of work. "Greatness comes through service, service comes through work, and work comes through efforts. . . . An opportunity to work is an opportunity to live." Examples to imitate were important. He, of course, provided one, and he urged parents, "Hold up to your children the names of great men and women of your race."

Fargo Agricultural School provided community service as well. It was a meeting place for the Southern Tenant Farmers Union in the mid-1930s. It conducted conferences for African American farmers, as had Hampton, Tuskegee, and Calhoun. These conferences were opportunities for the school leaders to inject into the parents of their students and other farmers of the area the ideas and aspirations that were the day-to-day curriculum of the school. The school leaders asked the 1945 conference participants a set of questions that seem like an examination of conscience intended to promote moral behavior, self-improvement, and self-reliance.

> Do you own your own home? Do you attend church? Do you attend the Negro Farmers' Conference? Do all your children attend school? Does your boy belong to a corn club? Do you have a year round garden? Do you have milk and butter all year? Have you any hogs? Do you buy corn, hay or meat? Do you cooperate with your neighbors? How many rooms in your house? Is your house screened? Do you have a pump? How far does your wife have to carry water? Do you get wood in the summer? Do you use your money for the things you borrowed it for? Do you get the Agricultural Farm Bulletin? Do you have a sanitary toilet? Do you encourage your children to be thrifty and honest? Do you take your son into your planning and farming account? Do you cooperate with the farm and home agents? Is your attitude what it should be? [76]

The influence of Fargo continued after its doors closed. E. C. Burnett, agricultural instructor at Fargo, left there in 1946 and taught at Moton High School in Marianna. Burnett had attended Fargo and was supported by Brown for his tuition, room, and board, as Brown had been supported before him by Washington. Burnett taught at Fargo for ten years before beginning to teach industrial arts at Moton. In his position Burnett taught every boy in Marianna who attended school. He passed on the values he had acquired at Fargo as adages he repeated in class: "Work will Win," "More Work and Less Talk." Among Burnett's students were Olly Neal, Jr., and the present administrator of the Lee County Cooperative Clinic, John Eason.

Calvin R. King is another of Burnett's students who carries on one specific part of the work of Fargo Agricultural School. King is executive director of the Arkansas Land and Farm Development Corporation (ALFDC). Beginning in 1980 the ALFDC has conducted a program to address the need for credit, and the legal and economic causes of the loss of African American-owned land in Arkansas and the declining number of African American farmers. The ALFDC conducts workshops for farmers and provides technical assistance on farm management, developing markets, converting to new nontraditional crops, and developing new ownership forms such as land trusts and cooperatives to reduce the barrier of capital accumulation for African American farmers. It conducts advocacy work to improve the access to capital for African American farmers and provides emergency financial support in small amounts. Since 1983 the headquarters of the ALFDC have been at the former campus of Fargo Agricultural School. There, the ALFDC intends to expand its work to create a community center, not unlike Penn Center, and to conduct demonstration projects for farmers of eastern Arkansas as well as Third World nations. The MacArthur Foundation recognized Calvin King for his work with ALFDC in 1990 and awarded him five years of support to further his work.

Havens of Hope

However bright these schools may have shined, they were distinct especially because they appeared against a bleak background of abysmal education for African American children in the rural South. A tide of reaction reversed the reforms of the nineteenth century and produced poor public educational programs in places like those of this study. Some characteristics of the school system had not changed. Dr. C. P. Boyd, for example, recalled his mother's teaching one hundred students one summer in a single class. That same class size was reported to Laura Towne at the Penn School in 1864.[77] Similarly, the poor condition of school facilities in the black belt of Alabama prompted African American families who could to move from the rural areas of the black belt to towns where schools were better, just as Olly Neal's family did in Arkansas.[78] Penn School, Calhoun, Fargo, and Douglas continued the Reconstruction efforts to teach African American children for expanded opportunity and were part of what Du Bois termed "one of the marvelous occurrences of the modern world, almost without parallel in the history of civilization."[79]

African American colleges and universities are another element of those Reconstruction reforms that remained to renew both modest and major reform efforts later. Howard University was the alma mater of Stokely Carmichael and other SNCC workers in Lowndes County. The name "Black Panther" was a nickname for one of them, going back to their college days at Howard. The law school at Howard, under Charles Houston from 1929 to 1935, trained a cadre of lawyers who would defend or challenge the law to protect the civil rights of African Americans. Thurgood Marshall, who succeeded Houston as special counsel of the NAACP, was one.[80] Pauli Murray, whose distinguished career included defending John Hulett against the fine-levying practices, was another. Bob Mants went to Morehouse in Atlanta. In Tennessee, Fisk University, named after the assistant commissioner of the Freedmen's Bureau for Tennessee, opened in 1866 and became a university a year later. Central Tennessee College began in 1865 and opened Meharry Medical College in 1876 as its medical department. In west Tennessee LeMoyne Normal and Commercial School began in 1871 as a school for freedpeople that had antecedents going back to 1862. Like other schools springing up in the South, LeMoyne educated teachers primarily. In November 1882 the Colored Methodist Episcopal High School began its first classes in Jackson, Tennessee, in Madison County, adjoining Haywood County. The school had been planned for four years by church officials. Its planning and staffing came from an African American institution and African American leadership. In 1883 the school's name was changed to Lane Institute in honor of the church's presiding bishop, Isaac Lane.[81] It was this college that Earl Rice attended, for which his father put in "many a hard day's work." Similar developments took place in black belt Alabama, South Carolina, and Arkansas; they provided the other educational institutions that the narratives of Part I mention such as Tuskegee, Avery Institute, and Philander Smith. By 1879 there were eighty-four normal and high schools and sixteen colleges enrolling some 12,000 African American students in the South. These colleges and universities appear in the narratives.

Unlike the movement to give the freedpeople an independent hold in the southern land-based economy, which had not taken root, the attempt to plant New England colleges in southern soil bloomed. Du Bois is emphatic about their significance as "the salvation of the South and the Negro" and a place where African American people "built an inner culture."

> Had it not been for the Negro school and college the Negro would, to all intents and purposes, have been driven back to slavery. . . . His Reconstruction leadership had come from Negroes educated in the North and white politicians, capitalist and philanthropic teachers. The counter-revolution of 1876 drove most of these, save the teachers, away. But already, through established public schools and private colleges and by organizing the Negro church, the Negro had acquired enough leadership and knowledge to thwart the worse designs of the new slave drivers.[82]

The schools established "a little group of trained leadership" that grew and provided leadership for the mass of African Americans by the end of the century, according to Du Bois.

Myrdal also found that education nourished and strengthened African American protest.[83] The New Deal proved to be far friendlier to college-educated African Americans than any previous political era since Reconstruction. It improved their employment opportunities more than any set of federal policies and programs since that time. African American social workers increased their numbers from 1930 to 1940 from 1,000 to 4,000. Most of them worked outside of the South but within the federal government. Howard University and Atlanta University, institutions started during Reconstruction, graduated the largest portion of these new African American professionals. The New Deal was setting precedent in the South as well. Myrdal pointed to the FSA as one of the fairest of the New Deal agencies in its employment of African Americans. True, the agency limited the services of its African American staff, like Sam Bradley and Uralee Haynes, to its African American clients. But even with this limited practice, these new positions placed them in official roles in larger numbers than at any time since Reconstruction.[84]

Education offered hope for new and better economic roles for young African American people of these communities and an escape from the dependence of landless farmers. For that reason, it was kept in limited supply. Even as late as the 1950s the school calendar was organized around the cotton crop. The change that education produced was painfully slow. But by 1940 the agricultural economy of the South was undergoing evident transformation, and changes in education would follow swiftly on its heels, as the Douglas School symbolized. There was political change as well. By 1949 new high schools for African American children began appearing on Johns Island and in Lee County, primarily in an effort to stave off integration. Local officials could not claim equal education for children if they could not point to separate schools for them. But "separate but equal" was no longer adequate. The political movement behind school desegregation pursued the promise of political participation expressed in the Reconstruction reforms that "separate but equal" had ended.

CHAPTER 7

Politics: Civil Wrongs and Civil Rights

The narrators speak of violence and threats to their crops, their homes, and their lives. They recall considering that some course of action might incur a violent response or risk their lives, and determining to proceed with it anyway. Jesse Cannon, Jr., describes, for example, his parents and other adults at Stanton standing guard over their community at the time of their registering to vote. Bill Jenkins recalls an offer of $500 for the murder of his father, attempts to drive his father off the road, and the relief his family felt daily when they heard his father's truck approach their home each evening. Gunshots punctuate descriptions of voter registration efforts on Johns Island. Murder was the companion of those efforts in Lowndes County. Evictions are part of the story of voter registration in Haywood County and Lowndes County. Arson and firebombings enter accounts of conducting new health services in Lee County.

And there is fear in the narratives. Fear that law officers would not protect them from violent reprisals. Fear that law officers would conduct violent reprisals. There was much to fear. Political restrictions enforced the subordinate economic position of African Americans in the rural South and extra-legal restrictions enforced their caste subordination. Challenging those restrictions invited economic reprisals and violence. Registering to vote after World War II was a job-threatening act in Lowndes County for Uralee Haynes and her husband. It pushed people into tent cities in Lowndes and Haywood counties in the 1960s. By 1965, however, intimidation could no longer forestall the voter-registration movement, there or elsewhere. Somehow, as Jesse Cannon so simply and poignantly explains, people "lost the idea of being afraid."

As profound as these changes were, they had precedent in these counties and the South during Reconstruction, a century before. The demands of the civil rights movement articulated the restoration of legally established rights, liberties, and aspirations of the freedpeople during Reconstruction.

Political terror revoked those rights and liberties, and subsequently legal restriction placed those aspirations beyond the reach of ordinary African Americans in the rural South. The narrative accounts of registering to vote, integrating schools, and developing health services describe modest but courageous acts. They were part of a democratic revolution to overthrow Jim Crow, who had reigned as the monarch of race relations for a half-century. Unlike the fabled emperor who had no clothes, Jim Crow was invisible but his repressive raiment was plain to see.

Reconstruction and Counterrevolutions

The freedpeople had more enthusiasm to participate in a "guided transition to freedom" than federal officials had to conduct it. Secretary of War Stanton thought that the conversation he and Sherman had with a group of freedmen in Savannah in 1865 to plan measures to resettle the 40,000 freedpeople in Sherman's camp would "electrify" the nation. In reality, it was one of several efforts to provide political participation and economic opportunity that fell far short of its promise. The land reform failed, as we have seen, and new forms of political participation of the freedpeople were revoked as well. Nine months after the conversation at Savannah, for example, Howard appointed a freedman to the committee of three to arbitrate grievances between freedpeople and landlords arising from his policies of land restoration. The freedman was removed upon objections from the white landlords.[1]

Saxton provided freedmen additional opportunities for political participation. He assisted a committee of three freedmen to organize opposition on Edisto Island to the restoration policies of President Johnson. This committee generated letters, such as those quoted in Chapter 5, from throughout the Sea Islands to the president complaining about the policies.[2] Saxton's efforts resulted in his censure for "teaching them [freedmen] to distrust all whites" from the investigators President Johnson sent south to discredit the Freedmen's Bureau.[3]

African American soldiers of the Union Army were the most visible and incendiary indication of the new political role of the freedpeople. Despite their roles in quelling the resistance of freedpeople to new labor practices and in dispossessing freedpeople from their claims on the Sea Island, white landlords complained about them. They alleged that the soldiers undermined their authority with the freedpeople who worked for them. The legislature of Alabama wrote President Johnson that "a vague and indefinite idea" about land redistribution persisted among the freedpeople in 1866 and deterred the establishment of new contracted labor relations. The legislature, the same that produced Alabama's version of the Black Codes, blamed this problem on the "frequent intercourse and association with colored troops" that the freedpeople had.[4] Bureau officials endorsed this and similar positions, and the military began withdrawing African American troops throughout the South from their previous duties. This withdrawal occurred after the lynching of an African American private in Knoxville—in front of the Freedmen's Bureau and then reenacted at the army's command station. A riot in Memphis in May 1866 between white police and black soldiers also demonstrated how badly African American troops chafed white southerners.[5]

These changes in political roles in the South were modest indications of the changes taking place in Washington. The radical Republicans in Congress envisioned economic reform and educational programs as a foundation for the new political role of the freedpeople. The president denied them the land needed for broad economic reforms and unsuccessfully contested the school program of the Freedmen's Bureau. In response, the radical Republicans changed their policies. They sought political rights for freedpeople as the primary means to acquire what had previously been understood as necessary antecedents to their citizenship. Congress treated the vote for freedmen as having the political significance of Emancipation and the primary means to achieve and maintain public services, like schools. This change came from the compromise between the radicals and other Republicans in Congress that forged a united front among them in their conflict with President Johnson.[6]

The Republican majority in Congress proposed legislation in early 1866 to assure the civil status of freedpeople. The Civil Rights Act defined citizenship to include freedpeople and extended to them the right to sue and to testify in court, to hold and convey property, to equal protection under the law; and it placed jurisdiction of these matters within the federal courts.[7] This legislation, encased in the Fourteenth Amendment to protect it from political reaction, did more than extend political rights to freedpeople. It took away rights from white, southern political leaders who had sworn an oath to support the Constitution of the United States and who subsequently engaged in rebellion or insurrection. In addition, the legislature reduced congressional representation from states that denied freedmen the right to vote.

The radical Republicans had unwitting allies in the southern states who made it easier for them to forge opposition to the president's generous

terms of reconstruction. The legislatures of the South, under Johnson's liberal policies, had passed the Black Codes that measured, for some northern
observers, the unchanged attitudes of southern whites and the dim prospects of economic and civil liberties for the freedpeople of the South without
congressional action. Their actions also had very practical implications for
all Republicans in Congress. Southern representatives and senators elected
under the president's plan were likely to be Democrats. Because the freedpeople would now count as one full person each, not three-fifths of one,
these southern Democrats would increase their numbers in the House of
Representatives. In Congress, southern men like those who had drafted the
Black Codes might refuse to honor the war debts of the federal government,
vote to pay off the debts of the seceding and rebellious states, and move to
reimburse former slaveholders for the loss of their property.[8]

The Republican majority collided with the president on these political
reforms. Encouraged by the election results of 1866 that increased their
numbers, the Republican majority replaced the president's policy with their
Reconstruction Acts in 1867. This legislation replaced the state governments of the South that had not ratified the Fourteenth Amendment, all of
them except for Tennessee, with a new government supervised by the army
that extended the vote to freedmen and ratified the Fourteenth Amendment.
Radical Republicans remained a minority for impeachment of the president.
They failed to pass a resolution of impeachment in November 1867, after
ten months of hearings that included testimony from Rufus Saxton.[9] But a
few months later, the House passed a second and different resolution of impeachment. The Senate impeachment trial provided the radicals' leaders,
like Charles Sumner, "the last great battle with slavery," which they lost.
Sumner anticipated the defeat and described for his colleagues "another hell
of torment" for "that race so long oppressed, but at last redeemed from
bondage." He maintained hope, however. "I cannot despair of the Republic.
It is a life-boat which wind and wave cannot sink. So just a cause cannot
be lost."[10]

Congressional Republicans entrusted the cause of emancipation, and their
own fortunes, to the vote of the freedmen in the South. They had calculated that freedmen would vote Republican, and they did by overwhelming
margins. Their votes proved important in the election of 1868. Ulysses S.
Grant won by 300,000 votes nationwide in an election that saw as many as
500,000 freedmen vote for the first time. He carried Alabama and Arkansas,
with newly enfranchised black male voters, by slim margins of 4,000 and
3,000 votes.[11]

The Republican majority in Congress had much improved relations with the new president. Grant approved the legislation of Congress that increased the power of the federal government to protect the rights of freedpeople. From 1870 to 1875 Congress passed legislation to enforce the provisions of constitutional amendments it had passed previously. The first of this legislation, called Force Acts or Civil Rights Acts, responded to the Ku Klux Klan's terror. Just as no state could deny or abridge the right of freedmen to vote, this bill outlawed "force, fraud, intimidation or other unlawful means" of private individuals to prevent freedmen from voting.[12]

Senator John Poole introduced a sixth section to the legislation. His legislation was based on North Carolina laws to stop Klan terror. It made it a felony for "two or more persons [to] band or conspire together, or go in disguise upon the public highway or upon the premises of another" with the intention of depriving any citizen "of any right or privilege granted or secured to him by the Constitution of the United States." Poole also suggested a Section 7 that uniquely extended the police power of the federal government and provided that actions that violated Section 6, such as assault or murder, could be tried as violations of state law but in federal courts. Poole's proposed additions came late in the deliberation on the bill and were approved without debate.[13]

The provisions of Congress entailed an increase in the size as well as the powers of the federal government. It created the Justice Department to enforce the civil rights legislation it passed. The department depended on the secret service and private detectives for its investigatory powers and limited itself to enforcement, not investigation.[14] The last of the Force Acts of this period came in March 1875. The Congress, in tribute to Sumner who was dying, passed a law providing African Americans full and equal enjoyment of theaters, public transportation, hotels, and places of amusement. The bill contained no provisions for enforcement.

The Force Act of 1875 marked the death of a radical Republican, the passing of a Republican majority in Congress, and an end of the commitment of the federal government to establish and enforce the civil rights of freedpeople. The federal legislation of this period was a victory for the radicals, on the one hand, but an unsatisfactory compromise, on the other. They had wanted land redistribution but did not attain it. They had wanted civilian Reconstruction governments but legislated military ones. They had wanted an education program and time to prepare the freedpeople for citizenship but legislated political reforms as the best hope for educational reforms.[15] By 1876 the revolution for political participation had run its course in Washington. At the same time the counterrevolution in the South was reaching its climax, state by state, county by county, and district by district. This counterrevolution would eventually undermine the gains made during this time.

Union Leagues and Local Revolutions

Political counterrevolution first appeared in Tennessee because the revolution was advanced there. Tennessee, with its pro-Union government established during the war, was ahead of congressional Reconstruction. The Tennessee legislature ratified the Fourteenth Amendment in 1866, thus exempting Tennessee from military Reconstruction later. The ensuing Tennessee constitutional convention did not grant the vote to freedmen in 1865. The pro-Union Republicans of Tennessee were not necessarily abolitionists or advocates for enfranchising the freedmen. But the vote for freedmen would come sooner in Tennessee than in other states and for the same reason; Tennessee Republicans needed an expanded electorate to stave off the political comeback of former Confederates.

An organization of potential African American voters met at the time of the Tennessee constitutional convention and unsuccessfully requested the vote. Their terms were very similar to the request of freedpeople on the Sea Islands for land. They recounted the military service of freedmen and contrasted their loyalty with the rebellion of some white men whose rights exceeded their own.

> We know the burdens of citizenship and are ready to bear them. We know the duties of the good citizen and are ready to perform them cheerfully, and would ask to be put in a position in which we can discharge them more effectually. We do not ask for the privilege of citizenship, wishing to shun the obligations imposed by it.
>
> The government has asked the colored man to fight for its preservation and gladly has he done it. It can afford to trust him with a vote as safely as it trusted him with a bayonet.
>
> Will you declare in your revised constitution that a pardoned traitor may appear in court and his testimony be heard but that no colored loyalist shall be believed even upon oath? If this should be so, then will our last state be worse than our first, and we can look for no relief on this side of the grave.[16]

Their rhetoric did not sway the convention, but the dilemma of the Tennessee Republicans did. The preponderance of white voters in middle and west Tennessee, where secessionist sentiment had been strongest, was overwhelmingly Democratic, or Conservative, in the parlance of the day. The large number of Conservatives meant that Republicans could lose control of state government in the election of 1867. No other state had as rabidly Republican a leader as Tennessee's governor, William G. Brownlow, who took three steps to prevent electoral defeat. First, in 1866 the Brownlow administration disfranchised the majority of former Confederates in the state. Second, in February 1867, two months before similar national legislation, Tennessee granted the vote to freedmen. Third, Tennessee Republicans cultivated the political participation of freedmen and their Republican votes through Loyal Leagues or Union Leagues, local organizations of the new citizens and voters.[17]

The League was a political organization started in the North during the war and popular in the predominantly white, pro-Union sections of southern states. After the war the Leagues proliferated rapidly, especially where freedmen were concentrated. As early as May 21, 1865, Chief Justice Salmon P. Chase wrote, "Everywhere throughout the country colored citizens are organizing Union Leagues" and estimated that they represented "a power which no wise statesman will despise." There were Leagues in every election district and, when most active, they held weekly meetings. Two representatives from each county formed the state council. Northern abolitionist groups supplied the local chapters with pamphlets and other materials. As membership of the freedpeople increased, white membership declined.[18]

In some ways the Union Leagues represented the political tutelage for freedpersons that radical Republicans had sought but could not attain. With the enfranchisement of freedmen, the Leagues could inform and mobilize the new voters. Walking westward on the route that would be the Selma March about a century later, Stephen Powers was "constantly astonished at the quickness with which the freedmen pick up the catch words and slang of politics" and judged them "apter than any class of whites" in these matters. Other observers noted the extraordinary memories of some illiterate freedpeople. They could commit material to memory with one reading by others and then instruct upon it.[19]

If the new schools for freedpeople taught the three Rs, the Leagues taught the four Ls of Liberty, Lincoln, Loyal, and League. One pamphlet in wide use in 1865–67 explained that the Republicans were the party of Lincoln, Sumner, Stevens, "and all other men who favor giving colored men their rights." The party earned the term "Radical," this pamphlet explained, because the term described someone who "is in favor of going to the root of things; who is thoroughly in earnest; who desires that slavery should be *abolished,* that every disability connected therewith should be *obliterated,* not only from the national laws but from those of every State in the Union." The Democratic party, on the other hand, "has tried to keep them [freed-people] in slavery, and opposed giving them the benefit of the Freedmen's Bureau and Civil Rights Bill, and the right to vote." The Democratic party was the "enemy of freedom and the rights of man."[20]

For many white former Confederates and Conservatives, the Union Leagues were the smallest and most proximate unit of a conspiracy to deprive them of political participation and to mobilize Republican strength. In fact, the Leagues did organize the newly enfranchised freedmen. In Tennessee in 1867 more than 40,000 freedmen were eligible to vote for the first time, and the chapters worked to deliver that vote for candidates that would protect their interests in government. In other southern states the League chapters worked to prepare newly enfranchised freedmen for the selection of delegates to the 1867 constitutional conventions mandated by congressional Reconstruction.[21] The Union Leagues also worked to prevent splits among the new freedmen voters. League members sanctioned Democratic supporters among freedmen, for example. Before long however, the local Leagues became the arena where factions of moderate and radical Republicans, both white and black leaders, fought for party control and electoral support.[22]

The Union League, like the African American labor organizations that developed later, used secrecy to protect members from retribution. The 1,400 cases of assault on freedpeople by whites that the Freedmen's Bureau's courts dealt with from December 1865 to March 1866 suggests the extent of the reprisals that could be reasonably expected. League meeting places, including schools and churches, were burned to express local opposition to the new political organizations among the freedpeople. Secret handshakes and passwords, protected by solemn oaths not to divulge them, were precautions for League members against white reactions. The secrecy of the Leagues spurred rumors of plans for armed violence of blacks against whites and justified, in the minds of some local whites, the violence toward the League, its meeting places, and its members. Some Leagues combined military drills with their meetings, indicating that their members understood that they might have to fight to defend their new political freedoms. One chapter's name, "The Wide Awakers," suggests the vigilance the freedmen understood to be the price of their civil rights.[23]

But it was what the League was doing in public, not secret, that stimulated local white opposition and violent reaction. Political rallies of the League in Tennessee in 1867 and 1868 were often interrupted with Conservative gunfire. The Freedmen's Bureau officer in Memphis reported a Republican party convention in Brownsville on May 13, 1867, that was ended by a "party of lawless men." One Memphis newspaper blamed the "infamous teachings of Radical demagogues" for the riot. The immediate cause was banter and jeering between freedpeople supporters of Brownlow and his white opponents. One of the jeering white men fired several shots to disperse the Brownlow supporters, and then gunfire rang out for several minutes. The newspaper account expressed astonishment that the freedmen would shoot at the white men whose shots "it could be plainly seen . . . were not toward the crowd."[24]

In Franklin, Tennessee, in 1867, members of the local League conducted a political rally that Conservatives interrupted and turned into an hour-long gun battle in the center of town that left sixty-eight people wounded. This event fueled white fears of armed blacks in Tennessee and sobered a few about the growing white violence. The *Nashville Republic Banner* editorialized, "If the conduct of the colored League was censurable, what shall be said of those intelligent white men who deliberately planned and as deliberately executed what was intended to be a wholesale massacre?" The political banners of the Leagues, such as "Radicals build our schools, Conservatives burn them," were matched with Klan banners.

> No rations have we but the flesh of man,
> And love niggers best—The Ku Klux Klan;
> We catch 'em alive, and rost 'em whole
> Then hand them around with a sharpened pole;
> Whole leagues have we eaten, not leaving a man,
> And went away hungry, the Ku Klux Klan.
> Born of the night, and vanish by day,
> Leaguers and niggers get out of the way.[25]

The Ku Klux Klan and Political Terror

The Tennessee election of 1867 tested Republican strength in the new electorate recently constructed of disenfranchised white former Confederate men and enfranchised freedmen. Conservatives hoped that a combination of threatened economic reprisal and paternal kindness would win enough votes for a margin of victory. They were disappointed. Brownlow received about

75 percent of the votes. Republican candidates for Congress won their elections. And the Tennessee legislature remained in control of a Republican majority. An estimated 35,000 freedmen, 70 to 85 percent of those eligible to vote in the election, contributed to the solid Republic majorities.[26] The Union League was evidently effective.

The 1867 Tennessee election indicated the Republican victories that white southerners could expect from military Reconstruction just getting underway in other states. But it also demonstrated an important chink in the Republican armor. Several west Tennessee counties, with a majority of African American residents and voters, elected Democrats to the Tennessee legislature. The key to this outcome was violence. Whites intimidated freedmen either to stay away from the polls or to vote Democratic. Political terror could upset Republican strategies, and the Ku Klux Klan soon became the military arm of the political movement to end Republican rule in Tennessee.

As early as the spring of 1867 bands of night riders, based in Haywood County, had burned freedpeople's schools and churches, disrupted the meetings of the Union Leagues, and intimidated their organizers.[27] They represented an armed protest over the Brownlow administration that grew more organized and eventually claimed the political legitimacy that its members would not extend to the Republican administration of the state or the nation. The Klan took as its mission the restoration of the U.S. Constitution from the debilitating Fourteenth Amendment and the "unconstitutional" laws propelling Reconstruction in the South. Leaders of the various Klan dens met in Nashville, at the Maxwell House in May 1867, to organize the Klan and formulate its purposes and specific activities.[28]

As the presidential election of 1868 approached, the confrontation of the Klan and the Brownlow administration in Tennessee grew particularly severe. The violence of whites toward freedpeople became systematic, purposeful political terror. Counties like Haywood where the League was active had the greatest Klan activity. The burning of school houses and the intimidation of teachers and the leaders of the League became nightly events. Brownlow confronted the violence in middle and west Tennessee as warfare. In the spring the legislature, at Brownlow's request, passed a law giving local sheriffs, who were often Klan supporters if not members, authority to organize local citizens to suppress uprisings. This move was ineffective. Brownlow tried unsuccessfully to acquire federal troops to assist him. Finally, in July he called the legislature back into extraordinary session to provide legislation for a state militia.[29] Shortly after the legislature began this extraordinary session, Nathan Bedford Forrest, a very discreet man in public utterances, gave a newspaper interview that suggested that a new civil war was about to begin in Tennessee. Forrest, a former slave trader and Confederate officer, publicly denied his membership in the Klan and even its existence, but others recognized him as the leader of the Ku Klux Klan since the May 1867 meeting in Nashville.[30] Forrest did admit freely that he did not recognize the government of Brownlow and that he regarded it as oppressive and its laws as unconstitutional. He had gone to Nashville during the special 1868 session and talked with legislators requesting that they not organize a militia. He promised them he would make every effort to keep order and peace in west Tennessee. If, however, the militia was organized and deployed to carry out the orders of Governor Brownlow, he declared:

> There will be war, and a bloodier one than we have ever witnessed. I have told these radicals here what they might expect in such an event. I have no powder to kill negroes. I intend to kill the radicals. . . . But I want it distinctly understood that I am opposed to any war, and will fight in self-defense. If the militia attacks us, we will resist to the last; and if necessary, I think I could raise 40,000 men in five days, ready for the field.[31]

Forrest also offered his assessment of the role of the Klan as a "protective, political, military organization" and professed his own love for the federal government but the "old Government" of 1861 and its Constitution. Because of the military response of the Klan, Forrest suggested, "the leagues have quit killing and murdering our people." Klan members were under strict orders not to disturb or molest people, and three members were court-martialed and shot for their violation of that order in Haywood County, to Forrest's certain knowledge. Politically, the Klan was working through the process of law to end "oppressive" and "unconstitutional" laws. Forrest claimed a political organization, like the Union League, that reached down to the precinct level and gave its support to the Democratic party. He had just returned from New York and the national convention of the Democratic party at the time of his newspaper interview. This had been his first political activity since his pardon, which came with the general amnesty from President Johnson. He had urged the National Democratic party to take no position on suffrage for freedmen. He was opposed to it "under any and all circumstances," but once granted, he believed: "If the negroes vote to enfranchise us [former Confederates], I do not think I would favor their disfranchisement. We will stand by those who help us."[32]

The Freedmen's Bureau officer in Haywood County, Captain J. S. Porter, warned his superiors of the terror that might come with the presidential election in November 1868. Freedmen had taken a smaller part in politics, but the Ku Klux Klan wanted them to have no part at all. "Every law and order man in the county has serious fear as to what a few months will bring forth." Two months later the reports of the bureau indicated:

> Whipping freedmen now was as common in Haywood County as it was before the war; that outrages were committed on the freedmen nightly; and they were afraid to report the same to the civil officers or obtain warrants for the arrest of the parties. If they tried to do so, they would have to leave the county to save their lives.
>
> . . . Freedmen living in the vicinity of Brownsville cannot get justice, either in protection of person or property; at the bar; . . . it is the intention of the disfranchised to force the freedmen to vote as they wish them, or drive them from their homes and crops.

On the two nights immediately preceding the election the Klan, according to bureau reports, was out "in strong force"

> and roamed around the county visiting the Negro quarters and notifying the freedmen that if they went to the Polls and voted for *Grant* they would be visited again by them and punished for their timerity in so doing. This of course had the desired effect and as a general thing but few votes were polled at Precincts in the rural districts in those counties where they were not encouraged and protected by the presence of U.S. Troops.[33]

The Republicans carried Tennessee safely in 1868 for their candidate, Ulysses S. Grant, but they were clearly in political trouble. The total vote was some 14,000 less than 1867, and there was a decided shift in the proportions of those votes. The Republicans received 18,000 fewer votes and the Conservatives, or Democrtats, 4,000 more than 1867. The increased party support may have reflected the improved precinct political organization of the Klan. The decrease in Republican votes certainly reflected Klan tactics of terror, Forrest's protestations notwithstanding. The political trouble of the Republicans was a crisis in legitimacy, not merely election returns. Each action of the government to quell violence in west and middle Tennessee only incited more. By February 1869 Brownlow declared martial law in nine west Tennessee counties, including Haywood, and was about to deploy 1,600 militia. The war that Forrest envisioned seven months before now seemed imminent. Tensions eased when Brownlow resigned on February 25, 1869. His successor, DeWitt C. Senter, was more conciliatory to the Conservatives.

In May 1869 the Republican party of Tennessee split into two factions, each of which sponsored a candidate for governor. Democrats supported one of them, Senter, Brownlow's successor. Their support was a crucial new factor in the election because the Tennessee Supreme Court declared the state legislation of 1866 that had disfranchised white former Confederate men to be unconstitutional and void. As a consequence, many more former Confederates voted in 1869, and Senter won by a large margin, almost 70 percent of the greatly expanded electorate. The election, like most elections of the time, was marked by fraud. In addition, continued terror influenced the votes and decreased the participation of the freedmen.

The election results displayed the extent of the political counterrevolution that had occurred and suggested what was to follow. The Conservatives gained control of the State Senate, 20 to 5, and the General Assembly, 62 to 17. In four months the new legislature repealed the laws of the previous special session to keep the peace and suppress the Klan. It went further and repealed legislation protecting the rights of freedpeople at work, their access to public facilities and transportation, and the school law passed in 1867. In addition, the two chambers voted not to ratify the Fifteenth Amendment because "it is class legislation of the most odious character. It singles out the colored race as its special wards and favorites, and upon them it confers its immunity, bestows its bounty, confers its affection, and seals it love."[34] The newly elected legislature issued a call for a constitutional convention, and the new Democratic electoral majorities assured the dominance of Democrats at the convention and in the ratifying process. The new constitution prohibited schools from accepting white and black children together and prohibited interracial marriage. It provided for universal male suffrage but required a poll tax of not less than fifty cents or more than a dollar.

In a two-year period, August 1867 to August 1869, Tennessee had swung from solid Unionist-Republican control to a dominance by the former Confederate Democrats. The impetus of that swing came from the systemic, organized violence of the Klan, a deliberate plan of political terror that deterred the political participation of the freedpeople. It also came from increased participation of former Confederates. The momentum of that swing knocked down much of the legislation on behalf of the freedpeople of Tennessee. In the aftermath of these political changes, Forrest issued a call to disband the Klan because it "had, in large measure, accomplished the objects of its existence."[35] Before all of the southern states had completed the reconstruction of their constitutions and government, and before the revolution in Washington was complete, the counterrevolution in Tennessee was well underway. It would be imitated throughout the South.

Violence and systematic terror accompanied the Arkansas election of 1868, for example. Eastern Arkansas was particularly violent. Its proximity to West Tennessee and Forrest's work in eastern Arkansas, promoting the Memphis and Little Rock Railroad, facilitated the extension of the Klan and its tactics. Forrest developed a following there; the seat of St. Francis County was eventually named after him. In the three months before the election, 200 murders were reported in Arkansas. The victims were almost without exception Republicans, including a congressman from Little Rock. Both black and white Union supporters were killed. Some assassination efforts were unsuccessful, such as the attempt on the life of the Freedmen's Bureau agent in Crittenden County.[36]

Klan terror reached its highest level in South Carolina. In 1869 Governor Robert K. Scott, Saxton's successor as assistant commissioner for the Freedmen's Bureau in South Carolina, assembled a militia, mainly of African American troops, and dispatched them to York County to quell violence there. The presence of these troops was like extinguishing a fire with kerosene, and soon the central western tier of counties bordering Georgia was well into a civil war. In a year's time the violence, riots, and general lawlessness claimed 400 to 500 lives, including those of women and children. The violence alarmed planters. They feared it would drive their workers from the area. The fighting gave one county the name "Bloody Edgefield."[37]

Finally, in October 1871, President Grant used the powers recently conferred upon him by Congress and declared nine South Carolina counties in rebellion. He suspended habeas corpus and established a military government for the counties. Arrests followed this action and an unprecedented, and probably never repeated, rate of convictions in civil rights violation cases also occurred: 54 convictions in 122 cases in 1871 and 86 out of 96 cases in 1872. After that, the conviction rates dropped to 14 in more than a thousand cases. In 1875 trials ended altogether for two reasons. Federal circuit court decisions, beginning in 1873, cast doubts on the constitutionality of the federal Force Acts. Grant's pardon of local Klansmen who had been convicted undermined the importance of the cases. Grant's action, however, did end Klan activity, although violent intimidation continued to mark elections in South Carolina.[38]

By 1876 local counterrevolutions restored Democratic control state by state in the South.[39] They also influenced congressional representation and the federal government. In fact, the Democrats of South Carolina, elected in 1876 by a process marred by fraud, violence, and terror and embroiled in a controversy about the legitimate government within the state, certified Rutherford B. Hayes the winner in the presidential election and determined the national election.[40] This allocation of the Electoral College votes marked the end of Reconstruction. It culminated a political process and a series of elections that started in west Tennessee in 1867. In 1876 Republicans had lost their large congressional majorities of just two sessions earlier and their radical leaders like Sumner. Younger men with fewer memories of the abolitionist struggle and commitments to the freedpeople of the South became leaders of the Republican party and shaped a different agenda for it. The ambivalence of white Republicans to their party's African American candidates and officials and the cohesion of Democrats in their opposition to the political participation of freedpeople established a new and far different context for establishing the meaning of the new political status of the freedpeople.

Caste and Constitutions, 1877–1910

Public officials consolidated the new dominance of the white Democratic party in the South with extraordinary legal and illegal actions. A steady effort to reduce the number of African American voters eroded the base of support for the Republican party. By 1910 their number in the rural South was insignificant. In Lowndes County, for example, James T. Rapier, an African American, had polled about 4,000 votes in each of his three campaigns for Congress between 1872 and 1876. He was successful in 1872 but lost the two subsequent elections as former Confederates regained their right to vote and the white Democratic state legislature gerrymandered his district. By 1906 no African American candidate had a chance of victory or of polling 4,000 votes in the county. There were only fifty-seven registered African American voters in Lowndes County, and the number was declining.[41] This total disfranchisement process began with violence but then moved to legal and then constitutional restrictions on the registration of African American men as voters.

Despite the restoration of the Democrats to political power and the decline in their own ranks, African American voters occasionally could still determine an election when the Democrats were divided. Tennessee remained first in this political development. Events in the state also showed that when fissures among Democrats appeared, so did political terror to prevent African American voters from forming pluralities among or with factions of white voters. For example, tensions in west Tennessee intensified as Congress deliberated the Civil Rights bill. The congressional elections of August 1874 would influence passage or rejection of the bill. A riot took place in Fayette County at the time, and a massacre in Gibson County. The latter, the Trenton Massacre, wrote a bloody lesson that terror was part of continuing dominance of the Democratic party in the South and not merely part of its ascension to power. Violence would accompany elections in other parts of the South at other times, whenever Democratic party dominance was threatened by factional splits that could allow a bloc of African American voters to decide an election.[42]

That eventually happened in 1882 in Haywood County. Samuel A. McElwee slipped between divided Democrats to win a seat in the House of the Tennessee General Assembly. Twelve other African American men would serve in the House before 1888. Not one African American had served before. They fought the legislative retreat from the civil rights and public services for African Americans. McElwee was successful in acquiring appropriations of $3,300 for the training of African American teachers and $85,000 for an insane asylum in west Tennessee. But his and others' bills to reverse Jim Crow laws on public accommodations or to punish lynching were tabled or defeated in committee. McElwee won notice among African Americans and Republicans nationally. He nominated a candidate for vice president at the national convention in 1888 and influenced his party's presidential candidate, Benjamin Harrison, to pay increased attention to civil rights in the campaign. During his own campaign of that year McElwee encountered armed opposition from men who supported the all-white "citizens' ticket." McElwee lost his fourth campaign and fled Haywood County because of continuing threats to his life. At the age of thirty, McElwee's political career ended.[43] No African American would serve in the Tennessee General Assembly until the 1960s, and none have represented Haywood County since McElwee.

The Tennessee General Assembly elected in 1888 had no African American members to interfere with measures to reduce the political participation and power of blacks. Democrats controlled 97 of the 132 seats in the General Assembly after the 1888 election. Powerful Democrats in Haywood and neighboring Fayette County controlled key positions in the General Assembly and used their power to pass laws that reduced the need for extraordinary efforts such as the threat of violence to sway elections. The first law required voters to re-register at least twenty days before every election. This law would provide local officials frequent opportunities to exercise discretion in the registration policies. The second law provided for two separate ballot boxes, one for federal offices and one for state and local offices. The Lodge Elections bill, proposed federal legislation that was not successful, provided for inspectors in federal elections. By establishing separate ballot boxes, state legislators intended to remove state and local elections from the jurisdiction of the proposed new corps of federal inspectors. The third law provided for secret ballots in the thirty-seven counties that contained the state's African American population. It permitted local election officials to assist any person eligible to vote in or before 1857 with their secret ballot. This law, similar to one in Massachusetts, effectively barred illiterate African Americans from voting. The ballot was secret, and they could receive assistance with it only at the discretion of white election officials. The fourth law, passed in 1890, renewed the poll tax.

The consequence of this combination of laws was apparent immediately. The total number of voters dwindled, and a disproportionate number of Republican voters disappeared. African Americans soon became a miniscule component of the electorate. The *Memphis Appeal* found the laws' effects "from a Democratic standpoint most admirable. The vote has been cut down wofully [*sic*] and wonderfully to be sure, but the ratio of Democratic majorities has been raised at least four-fold. . . . The enemy is completely annihilated."[44]

Tennesseans may have been first in factional electoral disputes, but they borrowed lessons in disfranchisement from others. South Carolina, for example, pioneered in the law that permitted up to eight ballot boxes, a separate box for each contested office or set of offices. Local officials moved the boxes periodically during voting day to increase confusion. The legislature defeated efforts to assign numbers to each box and to ease their identification, but election officials were permitted to read the labels on the boxes to voters who requested their assistance. This permitted the officials another form of discretion and a great deal of control over the eventual resting place of the ballots of illiterate voters. Ballots deposited in the wrong box were disallowed. Beginning with South Carolina in 1882, each southern state became a laboratory for restricting suffrage. Each restriction narrowed the electorate to a group that would approve the next restriction. Eventually, the limited electorate incorporated voting restrictions in the states' constitutions that had been written during Reconstruction. These restrictions reduced the voting turnout among adult males of southern states to a minority within the first decade of the twentieth century. As the total number of voters went down, a limited Democratic oligarchy developed larger margins of dominance.[45]

Disfranchisement was important in Arkansas because Republicans and various agrarian protest parties had sufficient strength to challenge the

Democrats' plurality regularly in gubernatorial elections if they combined. Fraud was still a necessary element of Democratic victories in 1888 and 1890. A fusion of farmers and Republicans managed to elect two congressmen in the election. One of them was assassinated while investigating corruption in the election. Democrats took advantage of their solid control of the state legislature to introduce measures to reduce such threats to their control. Having the recent example of Tennessee, the Arkansas legislature, under the leadership of Senate Speaker James P. Clarke from Phillips County, passed a measure in 1891 to provide a secret ballot. Participation in the next election, in 1892, dropped, and so did the opposition to the Democrats. Republican ballots dwindled from 26,000 in 1890 to 9,000 in 1892, and the number of African American state legislators declined from nine to three.[46] Next, a referendum to institute a poll tax was conducted in 1892. With the changes in the electorate fashioned by the secret ballot, the poll tax was approved. This in turn reduced participation further, preserved the corps of Democratic voters, and continued to erode Democratic opposition.[47]

The disfranchisement of black voters in Arkansas followed the caste order of prohibitions and codified them into Jim Crow legislation. White legislative majorities passed legislation to segregate public accommodations to protect white people from interaction with offensive African Americans. Once separate facilities became a legislative reality, they implied defects in character among African Americans that required segregation. In turn, these character defects, the "negro nuisance," became rationale for disfranchisement.[48] "Mischief" had been the code word for practices of equality among teachers in the Freedmen's Bureau school. With those schools restored to local control, "mischief" was gone, but the "nuisance" that African Americans had access to public accommodations and to the ballot remained.

This "nuisance" was in Alabama as well, and made the Democrats there insecure in their power. Disgruntled members of the Democratic party, Republicans from the hill country, and the remaining African American voters posed a threat of fusion into a plurality. Fortunately for the Democrats, their opponents had important fissures among them. Alabama Republicans remained divided, as they had been when Rapier ran for Congress in Lowndes County, between the "lily-whites" and the "black and tans." But occasionally they came together with formidable strength. Reuben Kolb, for example, in 1892 and 1894 brought together Republicans, Jefferson Democrats, and Populists and received 48 percent of the total vote in 1892. Kolb may have actually won the election except for fraud. The aftermath of that 1892 election was electoral reform that reduced Kolb's strength and the number of African American voters in the 1894 election. The fraudulent manipulation of local elections had become a fact of political life in places like Lowndes County, but in the 1892 election, a white party, not only African American voters, had been "counted out" of electoral success. As a newspaper of the time suggested, "It is, to be exact, a necessity to find some legal and honest way of preventing Negro control in the black counties, the present 'system' having produced evils that threaten the existence of the [Democratic] party and the safety of the State."[49] The legislature found those "legal and honest" ways in 1893. The methods they selected had already been tested in other southern states and produced lower voter turnouts, larger numbers of disqualified ballots, and larger margins of Democratic victories. The Populist threat had peaked in Alabama in 1892, and the restriction of suffrage had been the means of averting its threat and providing larger electoral victory margins for regular Democrats in 1894 and subsequently.[50]

Predictably, with wider victory margins, Alabama's white political leaders imitated the action of others to disfranchise larger numbers of voters and nearly all blacks by constitutional amendments. In 1901 the constitutional convention of Alabama, under the leadership of Judge Thomas W. Coleman from Eutaw in Greene County of the black belt, incorporated a poll tax, a literacy test, and a cumulative property tax into the constitution as requirements to vote or to register to vote. The recurring exemptions for poor and illiterate whites were present in the form of a fighting grandfather clause that exempted veterans of the Civil War or their sons and grandsons and other men whom registrars find to be of "good character."[51] These changes resulted in the precipitious drop of registered black voters in Lowndes County by 1905. Out of 6,455 black men of voting age in Lowndes County, 57 were registered to vote, 0.9 percent. In contrast, 1,085 of 1,121 white men of voting age were registered voters, 97 percent.[52] These numbers measured both the changes that had occurred and those that had to come.

In four decades the country had moved from radical steps toward democratic equality for African Americans to their systematic exclusion from politics, education, and public accommodations. As the twentieth century began, the fight for democratic equality of African Americans contested measures to exclude them further from white-controlled institutions. Many individuals' lifetime spanned this change. One very telling and personal instance of this change was the life of Wager Swayne. Swayne had been chief of the Freedmen's Bureau in Alabama until removed by President Johnson in 1868. He had worked assiduously for the political freedoms and education of freedpeople, including support, in many indirect ways, of the Union Leagues in Alabama. In 1902, as an old man in frail health, he again acted to defend racial equality, albeit in the limited, restricted manner that was available in a system of total racial segregation and exclusion. The management committee of the Union League Club of New York City proposed to evict the club's African American servants and to replace them with an all-white staff. Swayne, vice president of the club, got up a petition for an open vote on the measure. At the meeting to discuss the measure he stood, supported by crutches, and spoke against it. The members overturned the management committee.[53] This was a small victory in a battle for racial equality that had long since lost momentum and changed direction.

Violence, Caste, and Subordination

The loss of the vote was important in itself, but its loss preceded new and restrictive legal measures for the total separation of the races and the subordination of black people. They extended to other caste prohibitions such as entering the Lowndes County courthouse by the wrong door. As an old woman, Annie Hrabowski could still remember her father's strong and angry reaction to her innocent insistence as a child that they enter the courthouse by the front, white only, entrance. The steadily deteriorating political status of African Americans had reached its lowest point, paradoxically, because of an American political reform movement. Populism divided the white voters in the South. Populists, like Kolb in Alabama, were defeated by the manipulation of black voters in counties like Lowndes. To prevent this manipulation of black voters in Lowndes County and other places, some Populists suggested disfranchising African Americans. African Americans fared just as poorly with Progressivism. The good government measures of the southern Progressives seemed possible only if the corruption associated with the manipulation of elections ended. The simplest means to do this, for whites, was the elimination of African American voters. African Americans paid for the sins of whites and prevented Democratic officials from stealing elections by yielding their right to vote. Fair elections were part of a social order of reduced racial violence and tension. The social stability that resulted, reformers reasoned, would assist African Americans to develop their own institutions parallel but apart, separate and supposedly equal, to white institutions.[54]

At the same time that rigid race restrictions solidified into the caste arrangements of Jim Crow in the South, African Americans there could look to Congress with less hope than before. The election laws of the 1880s eliminated most African American representatives from Congress and reduced the number of southern Republicans. As the southern Democrats grew in number, they constituted a bloc of votes that might decide the outcome of issues before Congress and that others courted. Republicans in the Northeast who sought higher tariffs and Republicans in the West who sought silver purchases, for example, gained southern Democratic support or at least no opposition to their measures. In exchange, these Republicans deserted their party's ranks in sufficient numbers in 1890 and did not oppose a Democratic filibuster that forced Republicans to withdraw legislation, such as the Lodge Fair Elections bill. With larger Democratic majorities in 1894, Congress repealed sections of the Force Acts providing for supervision of federal elections and other parts of the civil rights legislation that Congress had put together beginning in 1866. Most of what the courts had not declared unconstitutional about this legislation, Congress repealed at this time.[55]

The presidency also became a remote hope of African Americans. Theodore Roosevelt slowed the retreat of the White House on civil rights. His dinner with Booker T. Washington was a sensation in the white and black community precisely because even such modest interaction was extraordinary. The days had long passed since African American congressmen like Rapier met with presidents to discuss policy or when they could influence a party's candidate for president as McElwee did. Woodrow Wilson's administration introduced principles of southern caste into national life and relegated the few remaining African Americans in federal positions to segregated arrangements. Wilson shared and promulgated the by-then dominant view of Reconstruction as an epoch of northern adventurers and "ignorant Negroes," not an epoch of democratic equality.[56]

However legal the caste subordination achieved by the era of Jim Crow was, the violence that established it continued to enforce it. Lynching was the extreme and violent expression of caste subordination. Most often, the charge of rape justified lynchings. This coincided with the first tenet of caste: the prohibition of sex between black men and white women. But subordination, not punishment, was the systematic purpose of lynching. The disregard for the lawful punishment of an accused person and the effort to degrade the lynching victim by torture expressed a contempt for the legal rights of all African Americans and even their humanity.[57]

African Americans protested and resisted lynching as it emerged as a means and expression of political subordination. Samuel McElwee, for example, introduced antilynching legislation in the Tennessee General Assembly in 1887 after the lynching of Eliza Wood, an African American woman, in Madison County. A mob took her from her jail cell, where she awaited trial, stripped her clothes off, hung her from a nearby tree, riddled her body with bullets, and then left her naked corpse in full sight until late the following day. In introducing his proposal, McElwee decried the silence of the press in condemning lynching and the "sameness" of the lynchings. "It seems as if some man had the patent by which these reports are written." His measure was tabled by the General Assembly by a vote of forty-one to thirty-six. This vote was closer to a victory than most other legislative efforts, state or federal, would come.[58]

The following year, 1888, a lynching in Lowndes County elicited an unusual political controversy. Typically, accounts differed in white and black newspapers as to why Theo Calloway, an African American from the Calhoun section of Lowndes County, killed Mitchell Gresham, a young white man from the county. White newspapers described the shooting as an unprovoked, "brutal and cold blooded murder" related to an argument over a rubber coat. An African American newspaper in Selma described the shooting as self-defense in a fight started by Gresham and his brother. This article reported that Calloway shot only after being beaten and when Greshasm came at Calloway with a bowie knife.[59] All accounts agree that Calloway surrendered to his employer, who turned him over to the sheriff. More than a week later, on the night before his trial, Calloway was taken from the jail by a mob of 150 to 200 people and hung from a tree nearby. His corpse was riddled with bullets. When his family and friends came to Hayneville the next morning for Calloway's trial, they found that lynch justice had preceded a trial. His body still hung from the tree. Later, white residents explained to reporters that the mob took its action because of threats of African Americans to prevent a trial. The governor inquired of the Lowndes County sheriff what information the sheriff had about the prospect of a lynch mob and what steps he had taken to protect his prisoner. The sheriff replied "to beg to deny" the governor the authority to make this inquiry. He explained his view that the matter was under local jurisdiction and that a county grand jury could look into the exercise of his duties. Democrats around the state were meeting in convention in preparation for the state convention in mid-May, and the Democratic convention in Lowndes County supported the sheriff in his conflict with the governor.[60]

The rift ended with a joint effort of suppression in Lowndes County. Fearing reprisals to the lynching, white citizens, a month after the lynching, swore out warrants for the arrests of African Americans they felt were plan-ning an armed retaliation. The sheriff arrested twelve of twenty "suspects" for "conspiracy to raise a riot." He also shot and wounded one man who resisted arrest. Word of the shooting spurred fifty white men in the county to join the sheriff. This group encountered armed resistance in the vicinity of the Bell plantation, and two of the "deputies" were slightly wounded. The sheriff then requested state militia from the governor. He cited the danger of 100 or 200 armed negroes and the danger of mob violence. The sheriff attrib-uted the trouble to eight "bad negroes" in the area, including the father and two brothers of Theo Calloway. Fifty militia were dispatched. Many other armed white men proceeded to Lowndes County to assist the sheriff, his deputies, and the militia. Subsequent reports indicated the danger passed quickly and had probably been exaggerated. More African Americans were arrested, and several resistance leaders had been killed or surrendered after being wounded. By Sunday, after three days of posses and rumors of armed insurrection, a correspondent on the scene wrote, "As a rule, the negroes are here to-day pulling the bell cord over the flap-eared mule and the bob-tailed steer, and making corn and cotton just like they did twenty years ago."[61] Four days later, the state Democratic convention began with mem-bers united in the belief that an insurrection had been crushed by quick action and cooperation. A newspaper article, on the day before the convention, re-ported "confessions of several negroes" that suggested that had the sheriff's posse been two hours later in arriving, then "Sandy Ridge would have been burned to the ground and her [white] citizens slain without mercy."[62]

However legitimate the white officials thought their action to be, mem-bers of the African American community viewed lynchings, arrests, and the use of military force as the real violence to fear. Some of them gathered in fearful prayer for protection. The minister of this group wrote to Booker T. Washington about their fear and started a chain of events that led to the development of the Calhoun School. Land for the school came from the prop-erty where the posse had encountered resistance. Fifty years later, this area would be the center of the organizing efforts of the Alabama Sharecrop-pers Union.

Ida B. Wells-Barnett protested southern lynching over a lifetime and across the country and in Britain. She undertook an early, if not the first, systematic study of lynching. She cited 197 lynchings in the United States in 1894, a number that exceeded by 65 the number of legal executions that year. Surveying lynchings between 1892 and 1894, she explained and refuted the various justifications of violence against African Americans: the necessity to quell "race riots" during Reconstruction, the necessity to prevent "negro domination" after Reconstruction, and in her own time the necessity to punish rapists. To avoid any charge of bias, Wells-Barnett relied exclusively on white newspaper sources. Because of the lack of records for some lynchings and the white press's underreporting of lynchings, her figures are conservative estimates.[63]

She demonstrated how African Americans gradually became the predominant victims of lynching. It was 1886 before they outnumbered whites as victims of recorded lynchings. By 1892, however, 161 blacks were lynched, the largest annual number, in comparison with 69 whites. The accounts of lynching that she reported suggested to her a "programme" that eventually evolved into a gruesome ritual.[64] Hundreds and sometimes thousands of spectators might attend a lynching. Railroad lines even provided special excursion fares. Alleged victims of the crime might confront the victim of the lynching, who was generally paraded in a humiliating demeanor through the town. The lynching itself could take many different forms. A victim might be hung with a quick breaking of the neck or strangled slowly. After the hanging, the victim's body was often riddled with bullets. Lynchers might drag their victims for miles, cut them while alive, and then hang them. Some victims were shot. In any of these methods the mob hung its victim, naked and dead, in a public display. Several toes and fingers might be sent to people who supported or opposed the lynching, as proof of the act and as an indication of the contempt of the mobs' leaders for those who opposed them. Burning victims alive was a less frequent but common and spectacularly barbaric version of lynching.[65] Newspaper accounts sometimes stressed the bravery of the defenseless victims, stressing their merit as a worthy opponent and the honor they won for themselves by taking their murder in silence. Ben Patterson, the leader of the Cotton Pickers strike in Lee County, won the mob's admiration because of his silence, despite his pain, and his calm defiance of the mob gathered around and over him ready to shoot him to death.[66]

The final element of the ritual was the anonymity of the lynchers and a conspiracy of silence among whites about the mob members. Despite press coverage and even pictures, local law officers found that lynch victims died "from unknown causes at the hands of parties unknown." Lynchers were beyond legal punishment. Approximately one out of every 125 lynchings, 0.8 percent, between 1900 and 1930, were followed by criminal convictions of the lynchers.[67] Those who prosecuted them or in other ways took up the case of a lynching victim were likely to become entrapped in legal and personal entanglements that not only required time and expense to refute but cast aspersions on their personal and professional reputations.[68] Myrdal found frequent expressions of the "unfortunate" practice of lynching but few who would take any personal risk to hinder or punish lynchers.[69] The acquiescence of most white Americans to violence against African Americans added to the terror in caste subordination. Although the action of lynching was often attributed to lower-class whites, almost all people of all classes and both races found it advisable to let the incident pass without either defense of the victim or an attempt to bring the white lynchers before a court of justice.[70]

National events greatly influenced the number and nature of lynchings. As America subjugated and colonized foreign lands and peoples in the 1890s, the subordination of African Americans in the South incurred less opposition.[71] The Populist movement and the prospects of new political coalitions also contributed to lynchings of the 1890s. The military service of African American men in World War I invited lynchings to readjust them to their subordinate roles. In 1919 ten African American veterans were lynched, most of them in uniform.[72] Changes in the economy also contributed to lynching. African American men who migrated to urban, industrial areas came back less tolerant of the subordination of the rural South. In 1917 Will and Jesse Powell, for example, were returning to Birmingham from a visit with their father in Lowndes County and argued with a white man when his buggy and their father's wagon collided. They were taken from police custody and lynched by a mob of a hundred.[73] The Elaine riots in 1919 were at their core an effort to revoke the wartime prosperity and to reinstitute the deprivations of sharecropping.

Lynchings declined in the 1920s, in part because of organized pressure about them.[74] Wells-Barnett had started antilynching efforts in the 1890s, contributed to the origins of the NAACP, and led or participated in numerous instances to prevent lynchings, including the aftermath of the Elaine riots. By the 1930s and the time of Wells-Barnett's death other groups joined the efforts of the NAACP and made inquiries and protests about lynching. Two of these groups were the Commission on Interracial Cooperation, a group of white southern liberals headed by Will Alexander, and the Association of Southern Women for the Prevention of Lynchings, an affiliated group led by Jessie Daniels Ames. These efforts, as well as a change in some southern white newspapers, were indicative of the efforts of many southern whites to establish a new reputation for the South to attract investment and industry from the North. These efforts were not so new. McElwee invoked the

South's image in his protest of lynching. The reports of the white press of Alabama on Calloway's lynching in 1888 in Lowndes County included concern over lynching's impact on efforts to recruit capital and immigrants to the South. The protests of the 1930s coincided with a resurgence in lynchings and particularly brutal instances of them that came with the Depression and renewed economic pressure on low-income southern whites.

These new antilynching efforts reported again that lynchings had a pattern. Their frequency even showed monthly variations. February was the least likely month for a lynching, May through October more likely, and July was the most likely month. The work on the crops declined then and the idleness and heat offered more opportunity for a group of whites to be insulted by the behavior of a black male, about the only reason required for a lynching.[75] Such were the circumstances in the lynching of Neal Guinn, a young black man, near Hayneville in Lowndes County, Alabama, on August 5, 1931. Some unreported interaction with an eleven-year-old white girl became "an attempted attack" from which she escaped and ran home. For him, there was no escape. A mob captured the boy, tied him to a tree with ropes and chains, and shot him thirty-two times. As usual, no arrests were made.[76]

By the end of the decade lynching had not only declined but had changed. Ames had even declared a twelve-month period of 1939 and 1940 to be without a single lynching. When they did occur, like the lynching of Elbert Williams in Haywood County, they were less likely to be public. Williams was lynched as part of the repression of the fledgling NAACP in Brownsville. On March 12, 1939, about fifty black men and women, Williams among them, chartered a local chapter of the NAACP. Most of them were teachers, small business operators, and successful farmers, including Tom Sanderlin and his wife. The chapter functioned quietly for a year. In 1940 a few of the charter members began making inquiries about the procedure to register to vote. They had set the presidential election of that year as a target date for them to become registered voters.

The reaction to their inquiries surprised them. They began to get "friendly" advice to drop their efforts or they would be run out of town. At the chapter's meeting on June 14, a prominent African American business leader in the town was denied access to the NAACP meeting because he was not a member and because he was known as a confidant of white officials. His exclusion imparted an air of secrecy to their meeting that gave white officials grounds for reprisals. Over the course of a week mobs took NAACP leaders away from their homes at night, threatened them, and banished them from the county. A mob led by night marshall Tip Hunter took

Elbert Williams from his home on June 20 and interrogated him. On June 23, fishermen found Williams's body in the Hatchee River. His head was twice its normal size from the beating he had endured, and there were holes in each side of his chest from bullets or stab wounds. His hands and legs had been tied to a log. The coroner judged his death to be from unknown causes at the hands of parties unknown. A subsequent grand jury decided that there was not enough evidence for an indictment for his death.[77]

Williams's lynching was the only lynching in Tennessee between 1937 and 1944. The number of lynchings from Calloway in 1888 to Williams in 1940 had increased and then decreased, but the arbitrariness and lack of punishment for lynching maintained its subordinating purpose. If African Americans defended themselves in some minor matter, they could expect a major violent retaliation. This led them to avoid minor conflicts, the most common and dangerous one being a violation of place. Among the violations of place that could stimulate violence were visible signs of economic success or action for political change. Myrdal concluded that lynching remained "part of the inherited pattern of white society in the South not to respect the rights of Negroes on equal terms: the custom of tolerating the cheating of Negroes in economic deals and, generally, the insistence that he shall humbly pray for his due as a personal kindness, not profoundly demanded as a right."[78]

The Second Revolution: The National Front

The NAACP made Americans aware of lynchings and translated them into a civil rights measure. From 1922 until 1940 it championed federal legislation to prohibit lynching. It achieved success in the House of Representatives in 1922, 1937, and 1940 but was not successful in the Senate. Lynching, it was argued in the Senate, is murder and murder is a matter for the states to punish. Without new legislation, the NAACP fought lynching on the legal grounds provided by the anti-Klan legislation of 1870 and 1871. Eventually, legislation in the 1960s established jail terms and fines for anyone injuring or killing another person seeking to exercise a range of civil rights protected by the Fourteenth Amendment.[79]

Just as individuals and groups worked to end the overt violence toward blacks that lynching represented, so, too, did individuals and groups work to end the subordination of disfranchisement and Jim Crow. What had taken twenty-five years to construct would take a half-century to tear down. And as the wall of caste had gone up law by law, election by election, and court decision by court decision, so also it came down the same way. The first breach of black disfranchisement came in 1910 with the challenge to the grand-father clause of the Oklahoma Constitution. The U.S. Department of Justice prosecuted registrars in Oklahoma successfully for violation of the Enforce-ment Acts of 1870. The case was appealed all the way to the U.S. Supreme Court, where the fledgling NAACP filed a friend-of-the-court brief. Moor-field Storey, a white Bostonian constitutional lawyer, was the first president of the NAACP and the attorney in the case. As a Harvard undergraduate, he had left school for a time to serve as the secretary of Senator Sumner during Reconstruction. Now, he was in the process of restoring some of the legal protection for the civil rights of African Americans that Sumner had put in place. The Supreme Court upheld the convictions and the unconstitution-ality of the grandfather clause. Storey also participated in the Elaine appeals before the U.S. Supreme Court.[80]

On another matter, patiently, over eight cases before the Supreme Court, a string of NAACP lawyers beginning with Storey and ending with Thurgood Marshall established the unconstitutionality of the all-white primary. The legal ranks of the NAACP were reinforced with the lawyers graduating from Houston's revitalized Howard University Law School beginning with Mar-shall in 1933. By the 1940s, federal judges in the South at the appellate level joined in dismantling the all-white primary and other obstacles to African American enfranchisement.[81]

The poll tax was a very visible but now largely symbolic obstacle to vot-ing. The poverty of African Americans, and many whites, made the $1.00 or $1.50 tax to vote prohibitive. In addition, some states imposed a poll tax cumulatively from the time a person reached voting age, making the tax all the more prohibitive. The poll tax had more impact on black voters than white voters, but it was applied to voters of all races equally, technically. Consequently, the poll tax was fought by whites as well as blacks and for a decade, after 1938, liberal southern whites joined black leaders and organi-zations in a political campaign to end the poll tax. New organizations like the Southern Conference on Human Welfare and the National Coalition to Abol-ish the Poll Tax worked with the NAACP while still trying to keep their effort from being enveloped in larger concerns for civil rights. The U.S. House of Representatives debated and passed laws to end the poll tax, but the Senate did not. The stakes were clear. Arch-segregationist Senator Theodore Bilbo of Mississippi was candid about that. "If the poll tax bill passes, the next step will be an effort to remove the registration qualification, the education qualification of negroes. If that is done we will have no way of preventing negroes from voting."[82]

President Harry S. Truman included the end of the poll tax in the civil rights legislation he formulated in 1946. In that same year he appointed the Presidential Committee on Civil Rights. Congress renewed this committee in 1957, two years before it sent an investigator to examine C. P. Boyd's charges against officials in Haywood County. In February 1948 Truman became the first president since Grant to propose a comprehensive civil rights bill that included antilynching legislation. His actions led southern Democrats to bolt the national party that year and to run an alternative candidate for president, the governor of South Carolina and native of "Bloody Edgefield," Strom Thurmond.

The Twenty-Fourth Amendment of the Constitution abolished the poll tax. President John F. Kennedy supported the amendment in 1962, and it was ratified in 1964. It was largely an idea whose time had long passed. By 1964 no one needed to be told that the federal government had to deal with the race problem and civil rights. A long trail of events made that obvious. Slowly, African American voters had increased in numbers and influence, and with that increase it became more and more difficult to avoid civil rights issues. Caution changed to support of the inevitable by national leaders. Efforts by Thurgood Marshall to have the Justice Department prosecute Alabama officials for denying African Americans, like the Haynes and Sam Bradley, the right to vote in the Alabama Democratic primary had brought a response of caution in 1944. Jonathan Daniels, advisor to Roosevelt on race issues, talked with Lister Hill, by then a senator from Alabama, and reported to the president: "I strongly share his sentiments that any such action by the Federal government at this time might be the fact which would translate impotent rumblings against the New Deal into actual revolt at the polls. . . . Any such action . . . would be a very dangerous mistake."[83]

Accordingly, Roosevelt's attorney general Francis Biddle proceeded slowly on civil rights, trusting more to good will than new court rulings. Some new forms of political participation emerged. The New Deal, for example, required all farmers to vote on crop control measures of the Farm Security Administration.[84] This form of participation in a government program reinstated what the freedmen had temporarily on Edisto Island in 1865 under Saxton's and Howard's reforms, but not since then. The caution that Roosevelt's advisors expressed was similar to the explanations of political expediency that led to inaction when the Alabama Sharecroppers Union and the Southern Tenant Farmers Union sought his assistance.[85]

By 1948 the "rumblings" against the New Deal became a full-fledged revolt against the civil rights position of Truman and the Democratic party, just as Daniels had warned. But the result was surprising. Truman won his election bid of that year, and the decisive factor in his election was the African American vote. Not those in the South, but the 1.6 million who had left there. California, Illinois, and Ohio had received about 42 percent of these migrants who contributed to his slim plurality in the three states combined of 57,000 votes.[86] Even in 1944, had the nascent African American vote gone to Dewey, FDR would have been defeated. The outmigration from the South that the Depression, mechanization of agricultural production, and wartime industries fostered created African American electorates in states with fewer barriers to their registration. These new voters in states outside of the South created a new and significant factor in American electoral politics. With increased influence at the polls, African Americans were on the way to acquiring increased influence in American politics.[87]

The Second Revolution: The Local Front

Race still had a significant place in local politics, however, and it would be another decade and a half of struggle, violence, and terror before the most effective devices of disfranchisement were effectively dismantled locally. Despite the gains made up to the 1940s, African Americans in the rural South remained disfranchised and terrorized for any attempt to register to vote, as they had been traditionally. The literacy test and other measures that permitted registrars discretion and latitude in application kept new African American voters off the rolls. Only the Voting Rights Act of 1965, one hundred years after the Civil War, restricted by federal law the machinations that distinguished this southern tradition of political corruption. Before that, in places like Johns Island, Haywood County, and Lowndes County local residents sought to *regain* the right to vote that had been given almost a century previously and then taken away.

The Sea Islands that hosted the rehearsal for Reconstruction in the "guided transition to freedom" also hosted one of the formative elements of the civil rights movement in the rural South: Citizenship Schools. The Citizenship Schools began with the desire of residents of Johns Island to register to vote, the leadership of Esau Jenkins, and a program to instruct black adults sufficiently to pass the literacy test that was part of the voter-registration process.

Jenkins was approached first about literacy and voter registration by Mrs. Alice Wine in 1948. Wine, like many other old residents on Johns Island, remembered voting days for African Americans as a child when her father would load the family into the wagon and take everyone to the polling place while he voted. This was her first example of seeing a black man vote. As she grew older, the restrictions of the state's constitution impeded men like her father from continuing to vote and other people like her from starting. Jenkins began to give passengers on his bus literacy lessons. Eventually, Wine became an instructor. She could not read but memorized what she learned, as others had done before in the Union League, well enough to instruct others.[88] Accustomed to moving on an issue, Jenkins was impatient with progress on voter registration. By 1954 only 200 African Americans on Johns Island had managed to register to vote, and many of them did not bother to vote at election time. Jenkins took two significant steps to increase black political participation. He ran for school board trustee in 1955, and he began the Citizenship Schools.

He ran for public office primarily to show that an African American could do so without being killed, a hypothetical proposition at the time. He appealed to African Americans on Johns Island who paid taxes but were not getting the schools and educational programs for their children that they wanted. Of course, they were paying taxes because an extraordinary number of them, by rural southern standards, were property owners. He came in third among four candidates with 192 votes. His campaign had encouraged 100 African American residents to register to vote. With a bloc of black voters, Jenkins had finished ahead of a white man on the ballot. His showing was warning enough to white officials, who changed the office immediately from elected to appointed.[89] His campaign and subsequent organizing efforts ran set the stage for another man, LeRoy Brown, to run successfully for a seat on the Beaufort County Commission in 1960. His victory made him the first African American elected to public office in South Carolina in the twentieth century. The district he represented had much to do with his success. He was elected from a district near the Penn Community Center. Brown had attended Penn School and was a staff member of Penn Center. The legacy of black landownership and voting established firmly in this benchmark of Reconstruction provided the base for Brown's electoral success, almost a century later, and a modern precedent of an African American elected official in the South.

At the time of his campaign Jenkins began working with the Highlander Folk School to establish adult education schools, Citizenship Schools, on Johns Island. Jenkins first went to Highlander with Septima Clark. Clark had lost her teaching job in Charleston because her NAACP membership was prohibited by South Carolina law for teachers and she refused to yield it.

She began working for Highlander and brought Jenkins there for a workshop on the United Nations. But it was Jenkins who educated others at the workshop, including the Highlander staff, on the needs of the South. He soon interested Myles Horton, director of Highlander, and other staff members in the needs of the Sea Islands, especially literacy, education, and voting.

The first Citizenship School began on January 7, 1957, with a class of fourteen. Bernice Robinson, a former Charleston beautician and now a Highlander staff member, taught the first school under the direction of Jenkins. Enrollment grew to thirty-seven. The original fourteen students had a "final exam"—the literacy requirement to register to vote—and eight passed successfully. Classes incorporated reading material about matters familiar to the students and had a specific focus on voting requirements. The first school proved very successful, and the program was expanded in the winter of 1959. The schools enrolled 106 students on Johns, Wadmalaw, and Edisto islands and in North Charleston. Enrollments remained steady for the next several years, and the number of black voters increased. Johns Island gained 500 new black voters between 1956 and 1960. In 1961 Jenkins began a Second Step School in the same locations, which conducted monthly discussions on representation in the state legislature, the South Carolina congressional delegation, and federal money for housing, health care, and cooperatives. Altogether, the Citizenship Schools conducted thirty-seven projects around Charleston and the Sea Islands from 1957 to 1961 that included 1,300 students.[90]

Beginning in 1960 Highlander spread the model of Citizenship Schools throughout the South. First, schools were established in Huntsville, Alabama, and Savannah, Georgia, the latter under the direction of a local black chemist, Hosea Williams. By early 1961 Highlander turned the Citizenship School Project over to a special committee of the Southern Christian Leadership Conference (SCLC). Foundation funds could not come to the SCLC directly, and Highlander had a precarious existence because of state prosecution of its integrated functions, so a third organization was brought in to handle the foundation funds to support the Citizenship Schools. The organization was the American Missionary Association, which placed a young staff member, Andrew Young, in charge of the program.[91] One hundred years after beginning work at Hampton with the "contraband," the AMA now entered into a new educational program with the SCLC and Highlander. Young represented the black middle-class leadership that the AMA had hoped its educational and church work would produce, and he acquired his introduction to the civil rights movement and the SCLC through this work. An AMA school site, developed during Reconstruction at Dorchester, Georgia, became headquarters to the Citizenship Schools. For the next ten years black men and women throughout the South—2,350 of them—would come to Dorchester and Penn Center for training as teachers in the Citizenship Schools. These schools had earlier counterparts in the AMA adult and evening schools but especially in the Union Leagues.

Teachers in the Citizenship Schools differed from those of these earlier efforts. They were chosen from among African Americans who lived in the areas where the schools would be conducted by the people organizing the schools. Few had teaching experience, and most had only some high school education. It was important that they could read aloud well, write clearly on a chalkboard, and have some familiarity with voting and election laws as well as community services. In addition, the curriculum in the new schools was taken from the "lessons of oppression" and not the models of middle-class manners and aspirations.[92]

By 1967, 3,000 teachers had been trained and about 42,000 students; staff and enrollments equalled one-third and one-fifth of the respective totals of the Freedmen's Bureau's schools. The lessons of the Sea Islands, in the words of a foundation executive that supported and examined this program closely, "were being applied at least in part over a 600 mile radius where they had been worked out."[93] The registration of African Americans was well underway, in part, because the schools gave them a place to learn, to meet, and to organize for collective action. Steve Wilson credits the schools with providing Tuskegee a model of community development and the basis of the program for which he worked when he entered Lowndes County.

Leadership emerged in the conduct of the schools. Local leaders from communities throughout the South, like Charles Smith, came to Penn Center for instruction. Other leaders went to local Citizenship Schools. Students and teachers became leaders in the first African American organization for common action besides the church and the Colored Alliance since the Reconstruction era. The schools gave women, especially, a place of public leadership, and many, like Fannie Lou Hamer who would change the Democratic party of Mississippi in 1964, extended that role from the Citizenship Schools to the broader political arena. Some of the women who trained in the Johns Islands schools became staff at the OEO-funded child care programs in the mid-1960s.

A century after the political revolution for African Americans spread north on the Sea Islands from Port Royal, the second revolution spread south from Johns Island to Penn Center and from there throughout the South. In a movement unparalleled since the Union Leagues, African American people in the rural South were encouraged to participate in the political process and given the skills to do it.

Among the first places that the SCLC introduced Citizenship Schools were Haywood and Fayette counties in west Tennessee. In the very first SCLC class of 240 teachers in 1961, there were fifteen men and women from Fayette County and twelve students from Lane College. These students received training and staffed the Citizenship Schools in Haywood County because local officials had such a grip on the county that local residents could not come and go without fear of detection and reprisal. The two counties sponsored twelve Citizenship Schools with 141 adults, 95 of whom became enrolled voters in 1961. Second Step Schools, or workshops, were conducted in April 1964.[94]

As Haywood County had been among the last counties to be "redeemed" in the South in 1888, it would be among the first to announce the second coming of African American political participation. In early 1959 C. P. Boyd, Betty Douglas, Tom Rice, and others established the Haywood County Civic and Welfare League. This league was a direct descendant of the Union Leagues of almost one hundred years previous. It even resembled the Union League in structure with local chapters, each of which had representatives on the county organization. For a century African Americans in west Tennessee, Memphis, and then Nashville maintained political associations until the model of a league was offered by attorneys Estes and Z. Alexander Looby to organize in Fayette and Haywood counties, where they had flourished a century before.[95] Other events in other parts of the South and from a previous time also impacted events in Haywood County. The Citizenship Schools began with support from the Rural Advancement Fund, the remnant of the Sharecroppers' Fund derived from contributions to the Southern Tenant Farmers Union effort in Arkansas. Registration in Haywood County increased after the shooting death of a white sheriff, Jack Hunter, by a black man, Willie Jones, as Jesse Cannon, Sr., recounted. When Jones was not lynched on the spot for the shooting, people in Haywood County knew that something had changed.

But other things had not changed. Jack Hunter was succeeded as sheriff by his brother, Tip Hunter, the former night marshall implicated in the repression of the NAACP in 1940 and the abduction of Elbert Williams. The county conducted one of the nation's last all-white primaries in 1960, long after they had been declared unconstitutional. And there was recrimination for those who registered to vote. New registrants found themselves boycotted by store owners, doctors, and suppliers of bottled gas who supplied fuel for heating and cooking; they could not buy goods or services from them. White bankers denied black registered voters loans for their farming, and white gin operators refused to accept their cotton crop. Landlords began evicting sharecropper families on election night, 1960. Some gave the families up to January 1. More than 400 families were evicted in the two counties and took up residence with family members and friends. Their evictions once again brought the plight of the rural black agricultural worker to the attention of the nation and demonstrated their vulnerability because of their economic dependence. It also drove home to activists in SNCC, clearly and for the first time, the hardships of rural African Americans in the South and the need for organizing and assistance.[96]

Federal authorities had initiated legal action against the economic sanctions and boycott in Haywood County and increased their efforts after the evictions. On November 18, 1960, the Justice Department amended a suit it had brought in September to include thirty-six landowners evicting their tenants along with the original defendants, who included the mayor of Brownsville, the county sheriff, the superintendent of schools, and local merchants and bankers. With alacrity, the hearings, decisions, and appeals conducted between December 23 and December 30, resulted in a temporary restraining order enjoining landowners from carrying out the evictions scheduled for January 1, 1961. The Civil Rights Act of 1957 was being enforced, and people like Betty Douglas were testifying in federal court on their own behalf and that of their neighbors and friends. The Justice Department encouraged her, just as the Freedmen's Bureau had encouraged freedpeople one hundred years previously, to enter the courts as citizens.

In its report of 1961 the Commission on Civil Rights called these cases the most important to arise under the Civil Rights Act of 1957 to address the economic dependence of blacks. "How long and effectively the remedy in such cases can provide protection for a large group of Negroes so dependent economically on the whites is another question."[97] The civil rights legislation of the 1960s provided additional protection to African American voters in places like Haywood County. Eventually, some African Americans won elected offices in the county. There are now seven African American county commissioners, including Jean Carney and Dr. C. P. Boyd. There has not been an African American in the General Assembly representing Haywood County since McElwee, however. In 1988, a century after McElwee's loss, two African American candidates ran for the legislative seats that incorporate Haywood County: Jean Carney and Dr. C. P. Boyd. They were the first to do so since McElwee.

In other places like Lowndes County, African Americans would organize new and different remedies despite intense intimidation, repression, and violent reprisals, or more precisely because of them. Citizenship Schools, like the civil rights movement itself, came later to Lowndes County later than to Haywood County. The Selma March, the route of which ran the width of the county, brought the movement to the county and began a time warp there. Intransigent, unchanged racist attitudes of subordination clashed brutally against determined efforts, locally and nationally, for change. The tattered fragment of legal protections from Reconstruction provided some justice in the prosecution of the murderers of Viola Liuzzo. Liuzzo, a housewife from Detroit, came south to assist in the march from Selma. On the day of the march she shuttled back and forth, returning marchers from Montgomery to Selma. On a trip from Selma to Montgomery, a carload of men, four members of the United Klans of America, drove alongside Liuzzo's car and shot her dead. The murder took place on Highway 80 in Lowndes County, and so the trial of Collie LeRoy Wilkins, Jr., Liuzzo's accused murderer, took place in Hayneville. The first trial ended with a hung jury, and Wilkins's second trial ended with his acquittal. But on December 3, 1965, a jury in federal court found Wilkins and two accesories guilty of conspiring to go upon the highway to deny someone her civil rights. They received the maximum penalty under the law, ten years of prison. The law they were convicted of violating was a remnant of the Civil Rights Act of 1870, and the portion of that law that Senator John Poole introduced late in the deliberations, almost as an afterthought, to extend nationally what North Carolina had done, under Reconstruction, to curb the Klan.[98]

New laws of a second reconstruction went into effect that summer as well. In August, a few weeks after President Lyndon Johnson signed the Voting Rights Act, federal registrars, provided for by that legislation, came to Lowndes County to supervise registration efforts and offered the first federal presence to assure the voting rights of African Americans in Lowndes County since Reconstruction. Before their arrival, only fifty or sixty African American residents had successfully registered. The slow process began on the first Monday of March 1965, when thirty men and women, organized by Sam Bradley, John Hulett, and Charles Smith, defied more than a half-century of tradition and attempted to register to vote. Not one was successful. Many of them returned on the third Monday, and over the course of eight hours, sixteen were registered. Others failed because they could not answer questions like: "What part does the Vice President play in the Senate and House?" or "What legal and legislative steps would the States of Alabama and Mississippi have to take to combine into one state?"[99]

As more and more African American voters registered, it became evident that they would soon become a powerful voting bloc in the county. But it was not evident that their votes would bring about change. The Republicans had a shadow party, and the Democratic officials were part of an oppressive political structure that arrested, beat, tried, and sentenced African American people in Lowndes County with little justice. Trials were conducted in cases of the deaths of white civil rights workers, but all-white juries still found reason to acquit defendants in those trials, and not only in the Wilkins case. An all-white jury in Hayneville also acquitted Thomas L. Coleman, brother of the school superintendent, of the shooting death of Jonathan Daniels and the wounding of Father Richard Morrisroe.[100] The chairman of the county Democratic party was charged in federal court with evicting tenant farmers from his land because they registered to vote. Twenty-five families were evicted, spawning another tent city in Lowndes County. The days of the all-white primary were over, blacks could register to vote, but their political power seemed to amount to nothing more than the old tactic of waiting for factions to emerge among the white Democrats and then to control the balance.

Dissatisfaction with this condition stimulated the establishment of an independent political party for Lowndes County with which new voters could run candidates they selected. The new party was named the Lowndes County Freedom Organization (LCFO). John Hulett explained the symbol of the party, the black panther, in terms of pride and self-defense. "The black panther is an animal that when it is pressured it moves back until it is cornered then it comes out fighting for life or death. We felt we had been pushed back long enough and that it was time for Negroes to come out and take over."[101] Hulett credited the workers of SNCC for making this change.

> Nobody ever come to us and done for us what SNCC workers done. And people was afraid to let 'em come in their homes, so they walked the streets. This is the first time in our history Negroes can go to the courthouse and talk loud. And when we get scared and talked real weak, the SNCC boys with us took it up and talked real loud.[102]

The LCFO became the most organized and determined effort to achieve for African Americans political office and power at the local level in the black belt. On election eve 650 people met to listen and endorse candidates of the LCFO. This event was historic in a county where African Americans had never met as a group, except in secret, for any purpose other than to sing, dance, or pray. Speakers urged them to vote and let their voice be heard. Hulett spoke of gaining office and government power to rule "not in a spirit of vindictiveness" but "as a model for democracy."[103] The euphoria of the campaign ended with disappointment. All seven LCFO candidates lost. Their individual vote totals ranged from 1,602 to 1,669. Their margin of loss ranged from 200 to 600 votes and came from irregularities at the ballot boxes, the votes of African American tenant farmers brought to the polls by their plantation bosses, and other African Americans who were not ready to face possible detection and recrimination for not supporting the status quo. Despite the loss, it was clear that control in the county would change hands.[104]

It did in 1970. By then, the LCFO had merged with the National Democratic Party of Alabama (NDPA), the state's counterpart to the Mississippi Freedom Democratic party. As the NDPA's candidate, John Hulett won the election for county sheriff 2,082 to 1,864. Election observers calculated that some 200 whites, just about the margin of victory, had voted for Hulett. Alma Miller also won her race for clerk of the circuit court as the NDPA's candidate. Miller had formerly conducted a Citizenship School in Fort Deposit.[105] Charles Smith, the first African American to register to vote in 1965, gained a seat on the county commission later, in 1972, just in time to intervene on behalf of the group Sam Bradley organized to maintain the health center. In 1978 Hulett and Smith led a slate of eight black candidates for the regular Democratic party that won every office it sought. There were "black faces in high places."

The news of the early LCFO effort at organizing an independent political organization spread far and wide. Stokely Carmichael gained new prominence in SNCC after his work in Lowndes County. That work gave him, SNCC, and others a model of a freedom organization, just as work in Fayette and Haywood counties had shaped SNCC six years before. In the summer of 1966 Carmichael brought from the "blackest and most powerless place in America" the symbol and the strategy of an independent political party to Oakland, where the national party of black power and militancy, the Black Panther party, began. He spent Christmas on Johns Island in 1967, spreading the message further, and lent his support to the efforts of Bill Saunders and one hundred other people at Penn Center to change the existing educational system.[106]

From the time of the Citizenship Schools on the Sea Islands to the election of Hulett and Miller in Lowndes County, America undertook profound political change to restore the civil rights of African Americans in the South.

In the midst of that change, the federal government began programs to improve the welfare and health of all citizens, especially the poor. The development of community health centers was one such program. The civil rights movement and its demand for democratic equality and human dignity had a profound impact on the manner in which federal officials implemented and administered these programs. On the other hand, these programs gave new impetus and direction to the civil rights movement and brought it to some places, like Lee County, for the first time.

CHAPTER 8

Health: Contexts and Cures

For most of the narrators, health care was a minor concern before the work on the community health centers began. A few of them had addressed local health needs earlier. Sara Sauls and Lillie Mouton were midwives in Lee County. Uralee Haynes provided health education in Lowndes County as a home visitor in the Alabama Rural Rehabilitation Program. Septima Clark and others conducted immunization programs on Johns Island. But by and large, health was addressed after more pressing political and economic needs or as part of them. As Bill Saunders explained.

> Health care as an issue had no meaning at all to me before I went to the military, and it was not high priority until I had become more involved as I did. More than anything, when you're concerned about whether or not you're going to have enough to eat, health care is not that much of a priority.
>
> I, like a lot of the old people on the islands, was brought up to think that hospitals and doctors were for death, and that health care had nothing to do with bringing about a better quality of life. We still have problems like this with the older people on the islands. My grandmother made all of us in the family agree to let her stay home when she got sick and that's how she died. She felt like blacks got killed when they went to the hospitals.

Myrdal also dealt with health as part of the larger context of social, economic, and political matters. In 1,440 pages he had only two discussions of health care more than two pages long. Myrdal assumed that improvement of the economic and political status of African Americans would improve their health status and health care. This was true, in general. But with the community health centers, health care no longer trailed other changes; it strode alongside them and in some cases led them. The community health centers drew their inspiration from the civil rights movement. Poor health was a consequence of subordination, and the health centers were vehicles of desubordination. Moreover, they ended a century of almost uninterrupted neglect of the health of African Americans in the rural South.

That Their Condition Shall Not Be
Worse for Our Invasion

The first abolitionist volunteers on the Sea Islands anxiously attempted to provide the freedpeople with some tangible benefit of liberty. As the Education Commission pointed out, "The people of the North owe at least this much to the subject-people of the South—that their condition shall not be the worse for our invasion. . . . We hope . . . to do for these step-children of nature all their masters have failed to do."[1] This debt of the North extended to health care.

Masters had financial incentive to provide for the health and care of their slaves. By 1860 the average price of a human being in slavery reached $1,000 and a good field hand or house slave could bring twice as much. This form of human capital investment warranted attention. Some slaveowners contracted for health care. One slaveowner on a sea island close to Savannah, for example, paid a physician to care for one hundred slaves at $1.50 each annually. The slaveowner provided transportation for the physician for each visit but no additional expense for a visit. Other slaveowners paid by the visit. Slaveowners, members of their families, and other slaves also looked after, medicated, and nursed the sick among the slaves.[2]

The invasion by the federal army ended slavery on the Sea Islands and introduced new health care and new health problems. One early encounter of the freedmen with the new forms of health care came in the Army. It was not a good one. Many were conscripted despite poor health. The Union's need of troops was one reason for this, but recruitment officers enlisted fugitive slaves with marginal health status also to shelter them from recapture and renewed enslavement. Once in the military, freedmen had new risks to their health. Their cramped living conditions bred fatal contagious diseases. The Army diet posed a special threat to men leaving slavery. The rations were larger than the men were accustomed to, and the beef and wheat were new to them. The food caused several stomach and bowel disorders. In addition, the lack of fresh vegetables caused outbreaks of scurvy. Despite the evidence that the diet was contributing to the illness of southern African American soldiers and that appropriate substitutes would be cheaper, little change was made.

Army officers were another health risk to the freedmen. Commanders amplified the relative immunity of freedmen to malaria into an assessment that they were better disposed to hard work in an inhospitable environment. African American troops were more regularly assigned work digging ditches, constructing barriers, and similar hard labor for longer hours. Individual Army officers and special boards of inquiry pointed out the effects of changed diet, inadequate shelter, and excessive work details beginning in the fall of 1863 and continuing to the end of the war.[3] The official Army policy was a perverted egalitarianism. The African American troops would be treated equally and no special provision made for them except for occasional local efforts. Differences between northern and southern African American troops may have contributed to the Army's lack of action. Northerners preferred the regular rations of beef and wheat that they were accustomed to, and some southerners preferred them to the slave diet of pork and corn meal. Some Army officers assumed that the freedmen were feigning illness to shirk work, and like the masters and overseers of a time recently past, they imposed excessive discipline and demands, thereby deteriorating the health of the freedmen even further.[4]

The consequence of this policy was carnage. In a brutal war that killed more Americans than almost all other American wars combined, the African American troops bore a disproportionate brunt of the death. Fourteen percent of white soldiers who fought in the Union Army died. Most of them, 162,000, or 60 percent of the dead, succumbed to disease away from the battlefield. Twenty percent of all African American soldiers died. Most of them, 33,000, or 92 percent of the dead, succumbed to disease away from the battlefield. These figures varied from place to place and time to time. The medical director of the Army of the James in the closing months of the war calculated that disease struck four black soldiers for every white soldier and proved fatal seven times more frequently.[5]

The African American troops did not fare well when they got sick or wounded. Adjutant General Lorenzo Thomas wrote to the assistant surgeon general of his inspection of a Nashville hospital for African American troops on January 16, 1865.

> Words of mine cannot describe the utter filthiness of what I saw. . . . A soldier wounded Dec. 15, with leg amputated, was on a bed, the clothing of which had not been changed up to yesterday [January 15], and he was still in the dress in which he was carried from the battle-field, everything saturated with blood—and he complained that the lice were eating him up. . . . Other instances could be given but let this suffice.
>
> Had these men been white soldiers, think you this would have been their condition? No! And yet the Black fell side by side of the White with their faces to the

Foe, at the very apex of abbatis. One man was cared for in every respect:—the other suffered in filth for weeks.[6]

African American soldiers also wrote of the conditions of the sick and wounded and the inadequate care they received. One soldier described "the Ill treatment towards the Colored Soldiers in the line of medical attendance." He described how the sick men could be found in every other tent, too weak to wipe the sand from their face. Their friends could not help because they were on duty every day. The doctors visited three times a week, "and they do more harm than Good for they Poison the Soldiers." He asked only for a fact-finding effort "to investicate the matter you will find out matter Correctly nothing more." He requested confidentially "for there is So many ways to Seek revenge." And he apologized for his writing which was "none of the best for Slaves are poorly learned."[7]

Other writers directed their criticisms and requests to Secretary of War Stanton. One such letter came after the war, October 2, 1865, and indicated the disparity between the condition of the care of the sick and the ideals of freedom and equality.

> i Reealy thought that when i came out into the Servus that We Would be Honestly Dealte with but i find Since i have out that there has bin a Vase Differrances & a Conciderble Change in my officers We came out in 1(8)63 as Valent heated men for the Sacke of our Surffring Courntury. . . . We hve Never Refuces of Douiung any Duty that We war call on to Dou & when Ever We war orded to go we always Whent Like men but Mr. E. M. Stanton we Neven bin Treated as men. . . . & We are now in a Veary Hard & a Dreadful condishion. . . . We have come out Like men & we Expected to be Treeated as men but we have bin Treeated more Like Dogs then men. Sir alow me to Say that i hope that the Time Shall Soon come when Shall all be Eacklize as men hear our Hospital is full of sick men & our camp is a Laying one halfe of the men that in campe ar Cripples & Still they are Reporting 400 men for Duty. & they are Even Puting the fiffers and Drummars on guard.

The writer concluded with an assertion of his intelligence and his realization that liberty's promise was only as good as its exercise. "I Supose that because we are colored that they think that we Dont no any Better. . . . if we Ever Expect to be a Pepple & if we Dont Reply to some one of a thourety we Shall for Ever be Troden Down under foot of man."[8]

The dislocations of war, inadequate housing, and poor sanitation made illness and death commonplace among the freedpeople not in the military service as well. Laura Towne, the director of Penn School, wrote to a friend in January 1865 about the cold weather, her own illness, changes in personnel, the reoccupation of Edisto Island, and she mentioned, "The poor negroes die as fast as ever. The children are all emaciated to the last degree, and have such violent coughs and dysenteries that few survive. It is frightful to see such suffering among children."[9] Camps went up quickly on the Sea Islands and elsewhere, with minimal provision for sanitation and public health. These cramped, hastily provided living conditions of thousands of people incubated disease. In eastern Arkansas some slaves who reached the Union line in Helena returned to their former masters as a better alternative to the Union camps. Cholera and dysentery were common, and in one encampment these and other diseases took the lives of 117 of the camp's 700 inhabitants in May and June 1864. In some of these camps freedpeople who came looking for forty acres and a mule found only common graves for themselves, mules, and horses.[10] The mortality rate for freedpeople was so high in the first year after the war that some whites looked toward their extinction.[11] The death rate among the freedmen in the medical care of the Freedmen's Bureau in the spring of 1865 was 30 percent. The rate declined to 13 percent in the second half of the year, and by 1869 the mortality rate was 2.03 percent, approximately the rate that Myrdal found among African Americans in 1930.[12]

Howard initiated medical services through the Freedmen's Bureau, although legislation did not provide him specific authority to do so. The act creating the bureau gave the commissioner broad powers and discretion that Howard used in the face of horrendous suffering. Beginning in March 1865 with fourteen surgeons and three assistant surgeons, the bureau's medical program grew to forty-two hospitals with 4,500 beds, one hundred physicians, and 350 nurses by November 30, 1865. At its peak, 1867, the medical program had fifty-six hospitals with 5,292 beds in fourteen states and an annual budget of $500,000. The distribution of hospitals was very uneven and had a decidedly urban emphasis.[13]

In addition to its medical services, the bureau provided relief, clothing, and food for the freedmen. Howard dispersed this relief carefully and sparingly. He did not want to support the skeptics' view that the bureau would "feed niggers in idleness." He reduced the number of relief rations drastically by September 1865. The bureau was providing 75,000 relief rations a day, which was about one-half the number in March. Still, Howard remained ready to respond to need when others could or would not. In March 1867 he moved quickly, without congressional authorization, to relieve the famine and starvation that occurred in parts of Alabama, South Carolina, and

Tennessee. State legislatures, such as South Carolina's, took no action, but Howard sent a shipload of provisions and then requested congressional approval and appropriations for his action. He received them. One-half million dollars went to provide relief for 53,945 freedpeople and white refugees in the South, 30,000 of them children, in that year. Most of that money went to buy pork and corn, not beef and wheat as had been the problematic military diet.[14]

Howard recognized that the Freedmen's Bureau began in the wake of a social earthquake, "the actual, universal fact" of emancipation, and continued extraordinary government measures that Howard understood were "quite new . . . and hitherto always contended against by our leading spokesmen."[15] Before the Freedmen's Bureau, the federal government had social relief and service policies for only a few specific groups with whom the government has special relations: Native Americans, veterans, and their dependents. Howard expected his work on behalf of freedpeople and refugees to be temporary because it was extraordinary. He hastily concluded the bureau's broad program in October 1868. He focused on the education program of the Freedmen's Bureau after that and reduced his staff from 901 to 158 by October 1869.[16]

Howard's concern about possible criticism of his relief measures was justified. He had the benefit of Steedman and Fullerton's strident criticism of Saxton for his "excess" in having provided relief to the freedmen. Howard himself underwent two congressional investigations and one military court of inquiry about the finances of the bureau's relief provisions. The first investigation conducted by a committee of the House of Representatives, in 1870, lasted sixty days. The committee looked into fifteen charges. Nine of them dealth with alleged misdeeds surrounding the construction and administration of Howard University, four of them dealt with contributions and work of the bureau in and around Washington, and two of them dealt more generally with the bureau and its critics' central concerns.

> He [Howard] has discharged the duties of his office of commissioner of the bureau with extravagance, negligence, and in the interests of himself and family and intimate friends.
>
> That he is one of a ring known as the "freedmen's bureau ring," whose connections and influence with the freedmen's saving banks, the freedmen's schools of the south, the political machinery of a party in the southern states, and whose position has been to devote the official authority and power of the bureau to personal and political profit.[17]

The predominance of Republicans on the committee, eight Republicans out of ten members, assured Howard a sympathetic audience for his defense. The committee exonerated Howard of wrongdoing and waxed eloquent on his accomplishments.

> During the five years since the bureau has been established, General Howard has directed the expenditure of twelve million nine hundred and sixty-five thousand, three hundred and ninety-five dollars and forty cents; has exercised oversight and care for the freedmen and refugees in seventeen States and the District of Columbia, a territory of 350,000 square miles, and cooperated with benevolent societies, aiding in the education of hundreds of thousands of pupils, and in the relief of vast numbers of destitute and homeless persons of all ages and both sexes. . . .
>
> The world can point to nothing like it in all the history of emancipation. No thirteen millions of dollars were ever more wisely spent; yet, from the beginning this scheme has encountered the bitterest opposition and the most unrelenting hate. Scoffed at like a thing of shame, often struck and wounded, sometimes in the house of its friends, apologized for rather than defended; yet, with God on its side, the Freedmen's Bureau has triumphed; civilization has received a new impulse, and the friends of humanity may well rejoice. The Bureau work is being rapidly brought to a close, and its accomplishments will enter into history, while the unfounded accusations brought against will be forgotten.[18]

The bureau came under closer scrutiny later, however. In 1871 the Treasury Department began an investigation that involved nine clerks for more than a year. In 1872 the adjutant general's office seized all bureau records and spent two years poring over reports and expenditures. By 1873 Howard exasperatedly confessed his suspicion of a "concerted plan to treat my office with contempt and bring it into disgrace."[19] Preliminary findings dribbled from the adjutant general's office, feeding new suspicions that resulted in a second investigation in 1874, a court of inquiry that lasted forty days. This court also exonerated Howard. After three years and three months of investigation, the adjutant general's report found $131,431.39 of the Bureau's $18 million unaccounted for. In light of its size, its diverse tasks, its decentralization, and the often hostile environment in which it worked, this amount suggested that the administration of the bureau was evidently basically honest and efficient.[20]

Howard's assessment that the federal government would not conduct relief programs for long led him to pass on the responsibility for the health and medical care of the freedpeople to others quickly. The bureau attempted to coax local government into the provision of medical care and hospital services.[21] The bureau also made the provision of health care a clause in labor contracts, thus passing on responsibility for health care to employers. Saxton approved one version of the contract that required the planter to provide "all necessary Medical Attendance and Supplies in case of Sickness."[22] Another contract that Saxton approved provided that the freedmen would supply a nurse from among their number. In some cases former arrangements were restored. Thus, the workers on the Bascot plantation near Darlington, South Carolina, contracted to pay a physician four dollars per person annually for care and fifty cents for children. In some cases the freedpeople pooled resources to obtain and provide medical care, and their efforts nearly always exceeded those of aid societies.[23] The actual providers of care through these contracts remained the same antebellum physicians in many cases. Shortly, with the withdrawal of the Freedmen's Bureau, medical care was left to institutions, including labor contracts, that were dominated by whites. Health care became part of the subordination of freedpeople. Ordinary access to care depended on a relationship to a landlord who would pay.

The enduring contribution that the Freedmen's Bureau made to change in the medical care of African Americans in the rural South was through the schools it helped start and the education of African American physicians. By 1895 Meharry had trained 210 of the nation's 385 trained African American physicians, and Howard 54 of them. Both schools had ties to the Freedmen's Bureau, as we have seen. In 1905 five medical schools enrolled 816 African American medical students, and all other medical schools in the country combined had 66. The problem African American students had in gaining admission to medical schools was exemplified by the responses of deans of white medical schools to a survey that Du Bois conducted. Some deans of schools in the South simply stated that their schools did not enroll African American students, but some expressed the deep racism that excluded them.

If you are looking for "niggers" go to Boston or other "nigger" loving communities.

There are no niggers in this school and there never have been and there never will be as long as one of its stones remains upon another.
                                                    Medical Department University of Georgia

The Hospital College of Medicine never matriculated a "coon" in all its history and never will so long as I am Dean.   *Louisville, Kentucky*[24]

By 1940, 80 percent of all African American physicians in America were educated at Meharry Medical College or Howard University, not because they graduated so many but because other institutions graduated so few.[25]

Uninterrupted Neglect

After the bureau effort, the health status and care of African Americans in the rural South was primarily a consequence of their economic standing and a concomitant of the changes in education for them. Their work paid poorly. Poor housing, contaminated water supplies, inadequate sanitation, and poor nutrition were part of their wages. The schools set up for them were steadily and systematically robbed of financial and personnel resources, and so was their education on health matters. The Populist movement and the Progressive era came and went without benefit for the labor, education, or health of the rural southern African Americans. Presidential studies of both Roosevelts punctuated the seeming national indifference to the economic and educational plight of African Americans in the rural South that had such a devastating consequence for their health. But the federal government did little for them in general and on health care in particular.

Filling in the vacuum of federal efforts, there were philanthropic efforts that had mixed motives and results. The Rockefeller (Foundation) Sanitary Commission for the Eradication of Hookworm Disease proceeded in its successful public health program with motives not unlike those of antebellum planters. This disease affected a labor force and lowered its productivity. The maximum return on capital investment, now in manufacturing plants and not human beings, required an ample supply of healthy workers to run the industry.[26] Abraham Flexner, in work supported by the Carnegie Corporation, conducted a survey of American medical education. He concluded that a model of scientific medicine was needed as well as better educational preparation for medical students. He included in his report a list of medical schools most capable of meeting the challenge of the changes he recommended. Among the schools were Meharry and Howard universities. He did not include five other African American medical schools that existed at that time. His recommendations provided philanthropies and philanthropists targets for contributions and gave medical schools financial incentives to change their training because capital shortages and declining professional prestige would follow without such changes.

Flexner's recommendations had negative consequences for African

Americans. There was, of course, a class bias in his recommendation. The increased educational preparation of medical students adversely impacted all members of the lower classes who might aspire to a medical career, African Americans especially, who had less education and less educational opportunity. His recommendation was contrary to actions taken to change the little formal education available to African Americans. Educational reform for African Americans, including the General Education Board started in 1902 by Rockefeller,[27] had focused on the Hampton and Tuskegee model of education. Educational reform for African Americans emphasized preparation for a trade. Schools like Penn were changed to extend the hegemony of Washington's Tuskegee model for schools. At the same time however, Flexner recommended "liberal and disinterested educational experience" as preparation for medical school.[28] Reflecting the deep racism of his time, Flexner also recommended that African American doctors limit their practice to members of their race and presumed that segregated medical practice would contribute to the "mental and moral improvement" of their patients. In a short time the Flexner Report meant even fewer places for African American students in medical schools and more stringent criteria for admission to those remaining places. Fortunately, the General Education Board and the Rosenwald Fund provided generous support to Howard and Meharry, which permitted them to maintain their accreditation during this transition in medical training.

Still, the poor schooling for African American students and the generally inadequate resources of Howard and Meharry took their toll. Between 1902 and 1946 many more graduates of these schools than graduates of other medical schools failed to pass their medical boards. Fifty-four percent of Meharry graduates failed their medical boards the first time, and 26 percent of Howard's graduates, compared with 13 percent of students at all other southern medical schools.[29]

Flexner's report did have an important positive consequence for the health care of African Americans in the rural South. It credentialed medical providers and broadcast a belief that improvement in health status was possible by the improved practice of medicine. In time, the public accepted medical intervention in the event of illness as being better than no intervention. Improved medical treatment, improved public health programs, and general increases in the standard of living contributed to better health status for some and indicated the means by which the health status of others could be improved.

Carter G. Woodson's study of African Americans in the rural South of the 1920s, for example, starts with a chapter on health and an assertion that health is the "greatest problem of life." Woodson relates the problem of health to too few hospital beds and too few doctors. There was 1 hospital bed for every 2,000 African Americans, whereas whites had 1 bed for every 145 persons. The ratio of physicians to patients was 6 times greater for blacks than whites, 1: 3,000 and 1: 500, respectively. Even where there were doctors, there were problems. Rural practice did not attract the most qualified medical practitioners because of the distance from adequate facilities, the problem of deriving a physician's income from a practice among poor people, and the relative hardships of rural life. Woodson also examined public health measures in rural areas and found "almost nothing." Health education in the schools was hampered by problems of compensation and the preparation of the teachers of African American schools, which produced many teachers who were unqualified to teach health, among many other subjects.[30]

The paucity of health care reflected the general educationally and economically subordinate position of African Americans in the rural South but, occasionally, the provision of medical care was an explicit mechanism of control. For example, after a shootout between members of the Alabama Sharecroppers Union and police in Reeltown, Alabama, at least two wounded members of the union made it to the John A. Andrew Memorial Hospital at Tuskegee, one of the South's best facilities for African Americans, to acquire medical treatment for their wounds. One of them recalled judging it better to keep the cause of his three wounds to himself and told attending physicians it was just a riot between whites and blacks, without relating it to union action. After treating him, hospital officials refused him admission despite a serious loss of blood. "They had to treat me—but they wouldn't keep me there that night, a man of their own color. Scared the white folks would come after me and find me there and maybe tear the place up of accuse em of helpin me."[31]

Another union member, Cliff James, fared worse when he came to the hospital for treatment two days later. During the course of his treatment, staff members sent a student to summon the police. The attending physician thus reduced the risk to Tuskegee for aiding him. In addition, the physician testified against James to the police who arrested him. He told police that James had said, "He would have been fighting yet if his crowd hadn't run out on him" and that "He was sorry he didn't kill any of the officers." James denied making these statements.[32]

Amid this need, neglect, and control, Woodson mentioned one promising model to improve health care. The Julius Rosenwald Fund was considering establishing community health centers from which physicians and nurses could function like the teachers of the rural schools as providers of services and agents of broader forms of change. Woofter's study of St. Helena Island provided a model for such a community center. Woofter credited Penn School with the good health and longer life expectancy of African Americans on St. Helena Island. The effort of the nurse, her midwife-allies, and a public health program of the school refuted the assumption that rural African Americans were naturally sickly. The African Americans on St. Helena Island had a lower infant mortality rate than other groups. The eight-year average by 1929 was an incredibly low 48, compared with South Carolina's rate of 91 in 1925. In addition, typhoid was reduced despite the use of shallow wells, and the school provided demonstration projects on hookworm, pellegra, and filaria. Penn School conducted instruction and in-service training for midwives so that they could meet new state regulations in the 1920s. Weights and measures of the children were part of the work of the midwives, as well as health education for the mothers. Dysentery remained a large problem.[33]

There were other important although modest efforts at health improvement during this period of neglect. Septima Clark, for example, as she explained, conducted immunization programs on Johns Island. She recruited church groups, volunteers, and funding to provide primary health care, health education, and services to improve the diet and sanitation of residents of the island during the early 1930s. Modjeska Simkins, director of Negro affairs of the South Carolina Anti-Tuberculosis Association, mobilized African American teachers and preachers to prevent tuberculosis and raised funds for a mobile X-ray, conferences, and programs. Her work in the 1930s prepared the African American community to demand primary health care services from the public health department when they became available by the end of that decade. Simkins, like Clark, eventually lost her job because of her NAACP membership.[34]

Good Health for Better Credit Risks

Health care reform became an integral part of federal efforts of the New Deal, including the FSA. Will Alexander, its director, explained, "Quite aside from any humanitarian purposes, . . . the Farm Security Administration has found, as a lending agency, that a family in good health is a better credit risk than a family in bad health. It has developed plans for medical care because it has found that good health is a necessary part of a family's rehabilitation."[35]

The FSA created numerous prepayment medical plans. Local rural doctors and dentists entered into agreements to provide administration clients with care for a rate per person not unlike provisions made earlier by the Freedmen's Bureau, here and there. Eventually, the FSA's programs enrolled 117,000 farm families, or 600,000 people, in one-third of the counties of the United States. These plans provided a wealth of experience in the operation of prepayment plans of almost every conceivable pattern and were also notable for the cooperation of local rural doctors who participated. The program guaranteed them revenue from a group of very poor people in the Depression and thus had obvious financial incentive for them. Advocates of the program suggested that new doctors were attracted to rural areas because of the financial base the prepayment program represented.[36] Some physicians cried "socialized medicine." Alexander, as Howard had done seventy years earlier in the work of the Freedmen's Bureau, asked his regional directors for examples of the medical needs of clients. He used them to counter the charges of physicians "that the indigent now have adequate medical care." Regional directors obliged Alexander with the examples and anecdotal information he requested.[37]

The FSA bypassed local providers in some places and provided health services directly. It established health centers at about forty of its larger resettlement projects, for example. The FSA staffed these centers with a public health nurse, at a minimum, and in some cases a doctor or a dentist or both. The Taos County Coop Health Association was a showcase when it began in 1942. It had an elected board of local residents, a nonphysician executive director, professional staff, clinic aides, and transportation for clients. It combined a complete array of therapeutic and diagnostic services with preventive medicine.[38] Few of the African American community land projects of the FSA were large enough to justify a clinic. The Mileston Project, in Holmes County, Mississippi, was large enough for a health center and had one. Likewise, the Lakeview Project, which included a portion of Lee County, had one, as did Gee's Bend in Alabama in Wilcox County, which adjoins Lowndes.[39] Other arrangements were made for the health needs of the small projects. The Haywood County Farms Project had a home economist of the project similar to Uralee Haynes in Lowndes County. She gave "quite a lot of advice with regard to sanitation and is rendering every assistance possible in connection with her regular visits," according to Stanley Rice's report for 1939. Haywood County, at this time, did not have a public health department to serve the project or its members.

The members of the Haywood County project were exceedingly grateful for these modest federal health efforts. They took the occasion of a visit by the project's home economist to express their gratitude in a letter addressed to "Dear Friends" at the FSA. The letter is very much the same as those sent from the Sea Islands in 1865 that explained the relationship of land and citizenship for the newly freedpeople. It also described their improvement using the figure of a ladder. But unlike the prescription of individual effort of Booker T. Washington and others, this ladder was supported by the federal government. On the other hand, the letter is very different from those in the Freedmen's Bureau's archives complaining of the poor health and treatment of African American soldiers in the army.

> We the negro tenants of the farm of Haywood County, Stanton, Tenneseee, wish to thank all of the good people for making it possible for us to live so very comfortable. Also for the wonderful instruction that is given us last month by our good supervisor, Mrs. F. B. Buntin, who take us each month by the hand, lead us steep by steep up the ladder which we hope to reach success through the plans she so carefully lay before us, such as the live at home plan, the protection of our health which we need so badly to know.
>
> We farmers did not dream such a great thing would present itself to us, so we the negro tenants of Haywood County are ready to take the plow and hoe in our hands an start cutting our way to success for we hear *your* ringing, clinging sound behind us calling forward. And, we must say for Miss Martha Smith who came through our farm and visited in some of the homes, and after learning what part she plays in our lives we know that she is an ideal woman—"For the mission of an ideal woman is to make the whole world home like." We thank you.

Twenty-six women from the project signed the letter.[40]

The health program of the FSA was among the recommendations of President Franklin D. Roosevelt's Special Committee on Farm Tenancy. The committee took note of "debilitating disease, malnutrition, and general morbidity" among farm tenant families. An attack on the problem of tenancy, according to the special committee, had to include work to improve the general level of health.[41] The program was cut back drastically to make federal funds available for armaments in World War II and then killed in the crossfire of the American Farm Bureau and the FSA. The presidential tenancy committee's report was a special target for the American Farm Bureau. The successor agency of the FSA, the Farmers Home Administration, had no provision for innovation in health care until the time of the Carter administration.[42] Then, as we have seen, loans financed the construction of rural community health centers. These included the Douglas Community Health Center in Haywood County and the clinic on Johns Island. In addition, the FHA provided loans for other construction on Johns Island and in Lee County.

A Health Front in the War on Poverty

By the mid-1970s a cluster of community health centers in the rural South expressed renewed national commitment to address directly the poverty and inequality of African Americans in the rural South. That commitment, like the Freedmen's Bureau and the FSA, was part of a much larger vision. In the halcyon days of the mid-1960s Sargent Shriver, head of the Office of Economic Opportunity (OEO), suggested that 1976, the bicentennial of Declaration of Independence, would be an appropriate date by which to eliminate poverty in America. The conditions of African Americans in the rural South served as measures of the stark conditions of poverty and how well or poorly we were doing as a nation in eradicating them.

The health front on the War on Poverty opened slowly and grudgingly, as people in the OEO became aware of the relation of health to poverty and the surprising lack of imaginative approaches to deal with that relationship. Experience gathered in other programs in the OEO, like Head Start and the Job Corps, indicated to agency heads that health was a problem of the poor. The children in Head Start programs had significant dental problems, for example, and adults who had finished job-training programs could not find work frequently because of some physical impairments.[43] Health was a component of several programs, costing an estimated $60 million of the OEO's $2 billion budget, but the agency was not happy with its fragmented approach. Early grants to hospitals and institutional providers to give health exams to the OEO program participants, such as Job Corps members, carried with them the hope of agency staff that somehow providers would become more sensitive to the needs of the poor. This unrealized hope only added to the dissatisfaction within the OEO about its health program. Paying the health bills of the poor might give them better access, but as long as that access was to an unchanged system, it was not the improvement the staff sought.

It soon became apparent that more needed to be done to deal imaginatively with the volume and nature of health problems of the poor. Early participants in the OEO health programs remember the disappointment of Shriver with proposals from officials of the Public Health Service. In fact, he reacted angrily to the "same old tired set of programs they had been peddling for a number of years."[44] He stalked out of one meeting and began a search for new ideas.

Julius Richmond was the point man in the OEO for new ideas on health care. Richmond was ubiquitous and tireless. He was director of Head Start, dean of the medical school at Syracuse, head of the Department of Pediatrics there, and assistant director of the OEO. He was genial, well-respected within the OEO, and always challenging someone gently. He turned criticism into initiatives and critics into collaborators to improve a situation. In this way, he was a catalyst in the formation of the Office of Health Affairs (OHA). On July 13, 1965, a century and two months after Howard accepted his post with the Freedmen's Bureau, Shriver and Richmond along with Joseph English, a psychiatrist, decided to establish an Office of Health Affairs in the OEO.

English was enthusiastic about the task. He had worked with Peace Corps volunteers and believed that the volunteer physicians he met there would return to the United States ready to change health care for the poor. He envisioned the OHA as a channel for their efforts. These "health care-niks" were excellent medical clinicians who had acquired additional skills in community development and change in the Peace Corps. Enough of them, with this combination of skills, English imagined, could change health care in the United States. But the major initiative of the OEO in health care was to come from nonphysicians on the staff. It would also lean heavily on previous reforms among African Americans in the rural South and the civil rights movement.

As Shriver, Richmond, and English planned, the Research and Demonstration Division (R and D) of the OEO had already started what would become its most important activity in health care, the community health center. One person handled health issues in R and D, Lisbeth Bamberger Schorr. Schorr had worked with the United Auto Workers in Detroit to establish a community health program before going to Washington in 1958 to work with the Social Security Department of the AFL-CIO on health legislation. From 1962 to 1965 her work at the AFL-CIO revolved about the passage of Medicare. She began work at the OEO in January 1965, while continuing her work at the AFL-CIO. After completing her work day at the AFL-CIO, she would go to the OEO and work six or seven more hours. The work days at the OEO, at that time, extended until 11:00 P.M. regularly. In April 1965, with the passage of the Medicare legislation, Schorr came to the OEO and devoted her full-time attention to a number of initiatives that she had underway.

The OEO had a health program in search of a model. Proposals were coming in that made Schorr "absolutely aghast" because of their emphasis on changing poor people and instilling in them a realization of the importance of health through the health education efforts of professionals. The climate at the OEO and R and D was one of action, and so Schorr took what was to her an inadequate proposal from officials in Chicago and made a planning grant to Joyce Lashoff to develop a different and better program in the same city. Schorr, like Alvord of the Freedmen's Bureau's educational program and Alexander in the FSA, depended heavily on the network of people she had developed in her previous work to stimulate ideas for the new federal program. In the spring of 1965 she coordinated a meeting of her contacts and people recommended by others. The results of the meeting were mixed. An idea paper solicited from faculty at Yale University proved to be of little use, but other ideas exchanged at the meeting would eventually develop into the model for which R and D was searching.

At the time of the spring meeting in 1965 Schorr and her boss, Sanford Kravitz, had solicited a proposal from Tufts University. Count Gibson, M.D., head of the Department of Preventive Medicine at Tufts University, and H. Jack Geiger, M.D., who was leaving Harvard to join Gibson at Tufts, had submitted the proposal. Gibson had approached foundations for support to begin a clinic in the rural South without success. He then approached acquaintances in the surgeon general's office who arranged a meeting for Gibson with Schorr that encouraged both of them to follow up in a week's time with another meeting including Kravitz and Geiger. That meeting ended in Kravitz's invitation to the two physicians to abandon their request for a $30,000 planning grant and to take on a commitment to begin a health clinic in Mississippi with a $1 million grant. Gibson and Geiger were flushed with the prospect. Their entire department's budget was $65,000. In the next four months they worked "with a level of intensity, such as I don't expect ever to go through again" until June 25, when Schorr called and exclaimed, "He [Shriver] signed off! He signed off!" The OEO was closer to a model.

The program that the OEO funded was very different from that which Gibson and Geiger initially discussed in late February. Tufts committed to two health centers, not one. One in the urban North, at a housing project at Columbia Point in Boston, and one in the rural South, at a place not yet designated. Gibson was most familiar with Columbia Point and thought Kravitz's invitation was an opportunity to build upon work he had already been doing there. Gibson came to Tufts in 1958, in part, because of the home medical service it conducted. This work was a continuation of the program first started by the Boston Dispensary in 1796, and Columbia Point was one of the sites of the program when Gibson came to Tufts. This progam had been the formative grounds of other health care reformers. Michael M. Davis had directed the program just before becoming head of the Medical Services Division of the Rosenwald Fund in 1928. Gibson expanded the program at Columbia Point to include research that compared care in the home as contrasted with care in a physician's office and established an office in the projects as a base of that work. He had additional plans to expand the services of the program. What was needed, in his estimation, was a well-defined population small enough to study but large enough from which to learn the pattern and sources of illness. Then health services would be defined in relation to the needs of the community, all its needs. Gibson suggested to Geiger, during their flight from Washington to Boston, that they use Kravitz's blank check to underwrite a much expanded program in Columbia Point as well as beginning a program in Mississippi. Gibson's idea had the advantage of getting something done soon. In fact, the Columbia Point health program opened on December 13, 1965, and was a key in disseminating the neighborhood health center idea even as the rural Mississippi site was still in development.

Despite its later start, the rural Mississippi site influenced the community health center movement more than its urban counterpart. Geiger and Gibson hatched their plans in Mississippi in the summer of 1964 when they participated in the Medical Committee for Human Rights (MCHR) work to provide health care assistance to civil rights workers and others. Geiger had helped organize the MCHR and recruited Gibson to do a stint of service in late August 1964. Geiger had preceded him by about a month, and their time in Mississippi overlapped a few days. The MCHR worked in Holmes County, Mississippi, at Mileston to develop a small community health clinic. Mileston had been a site of a large FSA program for 110 African American families and one of the few all–African American projects large enough to warrant a community health center.

Geiger and Gibson collaborated informally after the summer. They worked together to raise funds for the community clinic in Holmes County. The MCHR recruited nurses and a part-time physician to staff the clinic, and the MCHR chapter in Boston raised sufficient funds to purchase a van for the clinic. Gibson and his wife drove the van down to Mississippi in December and met Geiger there. Conversations among them and local leaders, including a physician, Robert Smith, sharpened their understanding of the needs in the rural South, especially the need for institutional change. Geiger and Gibson continued their late-night conversations in Atlanta, where their flight back to Boston was delayed because of fog. Geiger had made plans to go to Nigeria to begin a community health center in association with the University of Ibaden the next year and lamented his lack of a sponsor to do that very same work in the United States. The next morning Gibson offered Tufts to Geiger as a sponsor of his community health work. The two men shook hands and began a formal collaboration that led shortly to the first community health center grant within the OEO.

The two men had important differences. Geiger was steeped in social medicine. In fact, for a time, as a student at Case Western Medical School in 1955, he believed he had invented the field. He thought of it as primarily a different attitude on the part of health care providers, a sensitivity to the background of the patient. Subsequently, he learned much more about social medicine, including its origins. He trained with Sidney Kark, chairman of the Department of Social, Preventive and Family Medicine at the medical school at the University of Natal in South Africa. Kark had begun his work with government support for a demonstration project in research and training, the Institute of Family and Community Health.[45] Geiger spent seven months of 1957 and 1958 with Kark's program in his third and fourth years in medical school. He chose Kark's program because it seemed the only place where someone was actually doing social medicine and not just writing about "bullshit, . . . fuzzy, bleeding heart, tender-loving-care, non-specific kinds . . . of approaches."[46]

What he found was a department where teaching, research, and training revolved about practice at several health centers. The health centers served separate populations in and around Durban, including two communities, Lamotville with about 22,000 people and Merebank, an Indian-Asiatic community of 10,000 people. In addition, one rural clinic in Pholela had served the Zulu-speaking population on a 500-square-mile area of this reserve for about fifteen years by the time Geiger arrived. In these centers, over time, Kark had developed a program of service, training, and research. Geiger worked in the urban and the rural setting and found an important element of the social medicine for which he had been looking.

> They were quantitative places. They had data. Not only did the data inform them, and modify their program, not only did they do research, but they had a coherent program that emerged from a set of principles. That was where I learned about populations. That was where I learned about applied epidemiology. That was, in effect, where I learned about social epidemiology. And that was where I learned about community organization in relation to health care, even though it was subsumed under things like health education and so on, it was quite clear. That was where I learned about paraprofessionals. That's where I learned about the idea

of other kinds of intervention than the classically medical or the classically public health. In terms of the environment and nutrition, I learned those too. That was where I obviously, by the very nature of the scene, learned about cross-cultural factors—didn't learn about them for the first time, but learned about them in terms of real experience.[47]

Geiger learned from Kark to begin with the community and from there to move to the appropriate health or medical intervention, which might involve the skills of others besides the physician, as in the provision of sanitation or the improvement of nutrition. Geiger, perhaps because of his MCHR involvement, went beyond Kark and began to understand community organization as a healing process if it addressed the pathological conditions that promoted illness and morbidity.

Gibson had different training that led to a different approach. He took a clinical approach in medical care and applied it to the community. There were important implications for the physicians' control in each of these positions. Gibson's position represented a radical position, compared with the ordinary physician's focus on an individual patient. But it was conservative compared to Geiger's emphasis on a community process that was not only beyond the physicians' control but necessarily entailed conflict of community residents with physicians and other professionals over control of programs.[48]

These differences were seeds of conflict that would grow later, but in the spring of 1965 they were gestating in the soil of new possibilities and federal support. In retrospect, Geiger recognized that the final proposal that he and Gibson put forward combined an urban project and a rural project of 500 square miles, just like the program of Kark with whom he had studied. Schorr and Kravitz were pleased to have health centers under development in areas of need and with the sponsorship of a prestigious university and medical school. The work of Geiger and Gibson joined a proposal from the Denver Community Action Program that Schorr had reshaped, and the health program of the OEO was underway.

By July 1965 Schorr had precedents. The OEO would be active in its health program and intervene to fashion sponsors and proposals for its program. She depended on and encouraged people like Geiger and Gibson, who were looking for the opportunity to innovate in health care. In September 1965, and in the wake of the riots in Watts, the University of Southern California Medical Schools inquired about a health program it could conduct in Watts. In July 1966 the OEO awarded a grant for a neighborhood health center in Watts and four other urban areas. The program evolved to the point of guidelines, but it remained very informal and confusing. The Community Action Program (CAP) made grants in health care, the R and D program of the OEO made grants for health centers, and by late 1966 the Office of Health Affairs began, but it did not as yet make grants for health centers.

Schorr became acting director for health in CAP and the main conduit for health programs at the OEO without full credit or recognition for her work. Shriver, in particular, overlooked her efforts and initiated studies or program development with others as if the OEO had no one on staff to deal with health. Male physicians within the OEO often had more recognition than Schorr, despite her more extensive experience. Nonetheless, she continued to conduct major initiatives. In June 1966 David Burke, a legislative aide to Senator Ted Kennedy, called Schorr to solicit her reaction to the intentions of Kennedy to introduce health legislation. Kennedy had it in mind to require every participant in an OEO program to have a health examination. Schorr explained to Burke that this was typical of the "fix-up" efforts that the health people in the OEO had firmly rejected by this time and reminiscent of the earliest and unsuccessful grants of the OEO in health care. Schorr recounted this conversation with Richmond the following day. After agreeing with her assessment, Richmond asked her what she had done. When she explained nothing, he exclaimed, "Oh, my God! Get yourself up there right this minute and talk to him about what he should do. If he wants to put in an amendment."

Schorr did that and unexpectedly began a metamorphosis. She explained to Burke the concept of the neighborhood health center and the program at Columbia Point. Kennedy visited Columbia Point and shortly thereafter, Schorr, English, and Burke worked on an amendment to the OEO legislation to appropriate $100 million for neighborhood health centers. The final version of the bill that passed in April 1967 contained $50.8 million for the centers.[49] On the basis of only a few centers, in their planning stage or earliest operational stage, the OEO now undertook a broad program to disseminate them. Some estimates used an analogy to Head Start with 600 to 800 health centers throughout the country.

The speed of passage amazed veteran Washington officials. Schorr had worked on health care legislation for seven years, three years on Medicare, and knew the long history of some legislation. But the neighborhood health center program had a great deal of appeal and moved quickly. It fit the national mood for action and increased public services and opportunities for the poor. It enlisted a new set of physicians in the programs and in the OEO that impressed congressional leaders, including Kennedy, who got along well with Geiger and Gibson. Burke contrasted the lack of notable opposition to this legislation to the opposition to the Teacher Corps, which obviously struck some southern congressional representatives as too similar to the schools of the Freedmen's Bureau and the American Missionary Association. "The Teacher Corps had within it the elements of far more political implications to it. 'Pull these strangers from the North and sending them in to teach our Southern children, etc.' That's different from, 'Who are these doctors from the North coming down to Mound Bayou?' So, I don't recall any great opposition."[50]

There was opposition, of course. Tufts University's effort in Mississippi, for example, was opposed by the governor. The OEO had made the grant to Tufts without the identification of a specific location in Mississippi. In early 1966 Geiger and Gibson selected Mound Bayou. When the governor of Mississippi, Paul Johnson, was informed of their choice, he expressed his opposition to the president of Tufts. Geiger and Gibson's MCHR activities had earned them a place in a dossier in the anti-integrationist office of the governor, the State Sovereignty Commission,[51] and their proposal for a full-fledged health care center would bring protest from the governor, the state health department, and the state medical association. They anticipated that opposition and made clear with Kravitz and Schorr that the funds from the OEO had to come from R and D. Those funds, unlike other OEO grants, were not subject to the veto of a governor. Shriver had already run afoul of state authorities in Mississippi in his efforts to fund the Child Development Group of Mississippi,[52] and Geiger and Gibson did not want to be entangled with the governor in their work.

What Geiger and Gibson did not know was that their work with the MCHR had also found its way into dossiers of the FBI. The FBI investigated the MCHR for possible infiltration by the Communist party but came up with little evidence. FBI investigators listed Geiger as one of eleven "subversives" in the Mississippi project. His attendance, as a University of Chicago student, at a Civil Rights Congress meeting on December 19, 1948, was the evidence of his subversive background. At that meeting, the record explained, Geiger criticized the university policy forcing faculty to take a loyalty oath. Previously, the record noted, Geiger had been a student sponsor of a rally for Henry Wallace during the presidential campaign. Another frail strand of evidence was the support of the MCHR for the Irving W. Winik Health Center in Holmes County, Mississippi. The FBI described Winik as a Communist party member. The investigation reported innuendo about one of the physicians in Mississippi Summer. Comments of a colleague of the physician found their way into FBI dossiers. "I cannot say that I know him to be a member and as a matter of fact, he probably has never been an actual member of the Communist Party. I have no doubt that [name deleted] is completely dedicated in principle to the ideals of the Communist Party and that he is sympathetic with the Soviet Government in Russia."

Based upon the information that they had accumulated by November 1965, agents of the Chicago office of the FBI decided that there was "no clear picture" of Communist infiltration of the MCHR in Chicago and suggested that an investigation was not warranted. FBI director J. Edgar Hoover, however, ordered the office agents to continue their "preliminary investigation." Accordingly, an FBI informant attended Joyce Lashoff's presentation in January, 1966, on the health needs and health care patterns of Chicago's poor. Schorr and the OEO had funded this study. The informant reported some names of people at the January 26, 1966, meeting and that "of the total number in attendance (about 100 people) 15% were negro."[53]

Despite suspicions of the FBI, work continued on the health centers. John Hatch chose Mound Bayou and recommended it to Geiger and Gibson as the site for the southern health center. Hatch was working with the Boston Housing Authority and with the Columbia Point project when he asked to work on the southern project. Geiger and Gibson hired him and sent him to select the project site in Mississippi. Hatch suggested Mound Bayou, which had an important history as an African American community dating back to its origins during the Civil War at Davis Bend, Mississippi. Actually, John Davis, brother of the president of the Confederacy, had instituted several measures of self-government and economic management among the slaves of the plantation. After the war a former slave leader from the Davis Plantation, Ben Montgomery, leased and then purchased land from Davis to begin a colony of freedmen with the approval of the Freedmen's Bureau. Later, frequent flooding discouraged the colonists. Montgomery's heirs, with incentives from a railroad company developing a route between Memphis and New Orleans, settled Mound Bayou along the right of way of the new railroad.[54] The Davis Bend experiment of the Freedmen's Bureau provided the basis for an independent African American community that stood out for the self-esteem of its residents.[55] In 1967, after a brief period of Hatch's planning and a century of history, Mound Bayou would become pivotal in federal efforts in social change once again.

Models and Muddles

The OHA would face additional and more strident opposition in the future, but in 1967 its greatest challenge came from expansion. Schorr left the OEO in January 1967. Those who took her place were flooded with applications. The OHA program was committed to a new actor in health care, the community health center. The OHA staff leaned toward the community end of the spectrum from community to health and placed greater weight on social change than on excellent clinical programs. They did not endorse poor medical care, of course. But if a proposed program did not improve prevailing local standards of care, they might still support it if it did not include exploitation of federal funds by local providers and had some chance of promoting social, political, or economic change.

The other precedent that Schorr established and that remained after her departure was agency action on behalf of the programs. The increase in program size made it impossible to maintain the personal attention that Schorr had devoted to a smaller number of programs proposed by many people whom she knew or came to know extremely well. Nonetheless, the new staff tried to relate to the grantees in ways different from other government agencies. Even in the Nixon years, one staff member recalled, "We were substantial advocates of the grantees in the sense that the feds seldom had been elsewhere."[56]

English and others were also committed to a new style of relating to grantees. Despite the growth of the OHA, he maintained "an eternal struggle against rigidity" to preserve as much flexibility for later grantees as that which the early grantees had enjoyed. He and his successors adopted several specific means to do this. First and foremost, they worked to keep control of the neighborhood health center program in the OHA. This meant fighting off other divisions within the OEO, like CAP, and resisting reorganization within the OEO, like regionalization. Up to its last days the OHA ran its program from a central staff in Washington that maintained a sense of commitment to the original vision of the OEO and that resisted compromises to that vision.

In a sense the OHA staff clung to the mythical and golden glory days of the OEO. The time of the early OEO was different from the times federal agencies ordinarily work in, and many staff members had stories that illustrated that. Schorr recalled calling people late at night to request their help in a distant city the next day to hammer out a proposal and getting their help. English recalled the enthusiastic response he received from Peace Corps physicians to his offer to them of employment. Burke recalled the 89th Congress "would pass a ham sandwich if it had social improvement content." John Frankel, who replaced Schorr at CAP, recalled working twenty-hour days to process the flood of proposals in 1967 as "the most satisfying time— I felt that everything that I had ever done in my life was preparatory to that moment."[57] Members of the OHA found that staff in other government agencies were transferring to the OHA because the neighborhood health center concept, in Kravitz's estimation, was "a vehicle for their dreams and social aspirations and commitments."[58]

The times and the sudden increase in funding fed the unlimited expectations of the OHA. The neighborhood health center had come out of the R and D program of the OEO that was the most innovative section of the early days of the agency. The OHA preserved that early risk-taking element in the War on Poverty. For some, such as John Frankel, the neighborhood health center became the vanguard of the antipoverty effort. "We knew that we were a program that might save the whole concept of the poverty program. And we were committed to a path of making it fly."[59] But by 1967 the War on Poverty was stalled on several fronts. The CAP program faltered, and the OEO funding peaked at about $2 billion. The cost of the war in Vietnam increased and claimed money that might otherwise have been available to the OEO. In contrast to these features of the OEO, the OHA had a large infusion of funds in 1967 and a model that still generated enthusiasm.

The special and important mission of the OHA seemed to warrant unique organizational arrangements to get its job done, including special access and even new relations with Congress. Throughout most of its history the health programs of the OEO enjoyed special appeal to the agency's director and other influential decision makers. English enjoyed direct access to Shriver, and English's successor, Thomas Bryant, had equally direct access to Donald Rumsfeld when he directed the OEO. Don Pugliese joined the OHA in 1967 and was asked by English to represent the community organizing and action side of OHA's work. Pugliese relished the work, especially because it represented new and imaginative demands on institutions and practices. He remembered an exchange between English and Congresswoman Edith Green about the neighborhood health centers that might be apocryphal but summarized well the spirit of the agency and its risk-taking attitude in 1967.

> She [Green] was grilling Joe English on what NHCs [Neighborhood Health Centers] were all about. And she said something like this, "Dr. English, you are sitting

there telling me that you are opening a health center in a poverty area, and you are going to have social service support, community organization support, and comprehensive health, a brand new facility, vehicles to drive people back and forth, nobody has to pay for services if they don't have coverage"—she went right down the line. "Dr. English, you know, I make a congresswoman's salary and I live in a fine suburb, and I can't get that kind of health care."

And Joe gave her a beautiful answer. He looked her in the eye and said: "That's right!" That was the most fantastic piece of congressional hearing that I saw in my life. It was the genius of English.[60]

Several factors limited the enthusiasm and expectations of the OHA staff eventually. There was a lack of imagination and commitment outside of the OHA and in the health care institutions for the OHA's agenda. It occurred to some staff members later that perhaps there were few people in the nation, fewer than thirty, who could conduct successful and innovative neighborhood health centers. Although university faculty supplied good ideas, they could not be depended on to round out the ideas emerging within the OHA and from discussions that the OHA initiated. The 1965 study at Yale, for example, did not satisfactorily combine health care and community change, as the OHA desired. Kravitz later estimated the OHA's big mistake was to think that because much of the progressive thinking on health care and change came from the universities, then the universities themselves would provide leadership and change.[61]

This tide of expectations for institutional change crashed against the rocky coast of institutional self-interest. Hospital sponsors of poverty programs were concerned with costs of existing operations and turned the OHA overtures for change into the same refrains that hospitals were familiar with. One particularly galling example of hospitals' penchant for income before change involved the hospital administration that refused to release telephone operators from work to attend classes so that they could learn to speak Spanish. The OHA staff members assumed that Spanish-speaking operators could better serve the hospital's patients. The hospital administration refused unless the OHA grant would pay for the time of the operators and their replacements. Medical schools expressed little interest in innovation but were much more ready to use OHA funds to finance programs already planned with large overhead costs. Eventually, the OHA staff were "burned" so many times by medical schools that they would not enter into an agreement unless there were two or three young faculty at the school they trusted and who were part of the program.

Schorr's early work elicited the response of one or two faculty members at medical schools or teaching hospitals, like Geiger and Gibson, but it occurred to some later that this was not a portion of the pool of ideas and resources available, but the total supply. Instead of a tide in which participation in the OEO programs lent prestige to physicians and engendered change in the teaching, research, and service of medical schools, it became apparent that the OHA was dealing with a trickle of one or two mavericks on a few campuses. These mavericks pulled their reluctant institutions into programs with the force of personality and perseverance and the lure of large sums of money in the overhead costs attached to service programs for the poor. After some initial attention because of the size of grants involved, these mavericks often found their work drew them further from the mainstream of their institutions. The successful implementation and administration of their programs meant concerns with matters far removed from those of their institutions.

There were comparable problems at the local level as well. Grants made to local boards of health, as in Lowndes County, proved to be the least successful and most criticized programs, as they became little more than funding conduits for local physicians.[62] There were few places with local leadership ready to take on a major administrative task such as conducting a health center with imagination. Such efforts required a sponsoring group to locate residents who were sensitive to the needs of local people, willing to address them, and in possession of appropriate skills or trainable. Additionally, such a group had to recruit medical and administrative professionals. Those with the personal skills and ability to acculturate to communities and clients of great poverty were in short supply. Even when persons could be found, the more effective they were the more likely they would burn out. Most OHA staff expected a local program's administrator to begin to burn out at eighteen to twenty-four months and to leave after three years.

In addition to dealing with the supply of resources and imagination, the OHA painfully sorted out the conflicting agendas of community groups, project sponsors, and itself. English even took the step of working directly with the board of health of Lowndes County to establish a program there. English wanted to gather community development experience in this country. He had acquired some abroad during his work in the Peace Corps. He was approached by Dr. Meadows of Lowndes County after a speech in Montgomery and began working with the doctor and the board of health to begin a community health program. This development was especially opportune because Lister Hill, by now a powerful member of the Senate from Alabama, was anxious to find a poverty program that did not get people in Alabama upset. English was looking for Hill's support just as FSA officials had sought his support thirty years previously.[63] The doctors of Lowndes County were happy with the program English worked out, Hill was happy with the program, and English was happy with Hill's support of the Kennedy Amendment. It turned out to be one of the worst programs the OHA funded, and it improved only when the OHA, under Leon Cooper, intervened, withdrew funding, and insisted on a reorganization based on the lessons of consumer participation that the OHA had learned since the time of English's initiative.[64]

Following familiar professional relations and political opportunities did not yield the combination of community change and medical service that the OHA staff wanted. The combination they sought came from dealing with community groups with which they were less familiar, far less comfortable, and at far greater political risk. There were often painful consequences for the OHA and program sponsors. The transition of control of the Watts community health program to a community organization and from the University of Southern California was an early lesson that conflict was inevitable if community control was taken seriously. It was in the climate of black power that had made its way from Lowndes County to California by this time. At Columbia Point in January 1969 conflict reached the point that the OHA hired a mediator from the American Arbitration Association to chair a meeting of the OHA staff, Tufts University administrators, and the Columbia Point Health Association Board, which Hatch had helped form just three years earlier.[65] Frankel recalled one meeting in his office in which a group from Pittsburgh came in, insisting on a particular physician as their project director. Frankel had information on the man that made it clear that he was not appropriate, and the dispute turned to confrontation.

> They completely surrounded my desk and my conference table, and they stood behind me lining the walls. I finally screamed for Joe English to come down. Joe came and sat down. And I said, "I am chairing this meeting, and I am not going to talk until you guys sit down, because we are going to talk." And they never sat down. Joe took over. We were both terrified and I mean terrified.[66]

Conflict and threat came also when the OHA intervened to establish greater community control in health programs, especially in the rural South. On one occasion word reached the OHA through the FBI that an OHA staff member, Wendy Goepel, was about to be killed in Lowndes County. Frankel and English worked successfully to get her out of the county immediately.[67]

Through this frequently painful experience, the OHA staff acquired lessons they applied later in the program. First, it seemed to them that a balance had to be struck between medical professionals' dominance of health care and the participation of local residents in a process of community change. In striking that balance, they gave preference to the process of community change. A program could neither be just excellent clinical services nor just community action. Pugliese pushed hard on his understanding "that the delivery of health care was an accidental emolument available to the community but what we were really opening was 'community multipurpose centers.' That is, a community organization base that did several goods, and made it possible for people to do things for themselves." He offered this view to counterbalance the physicians on the OHA staff who were satisfied to begin innovative health programs. Health services were the key, but they had to unlock a door to community service and organizing. Pugliese thought that Geiger's work in Mound Bayou came closest to his model.[68]

The second lesson was that the balance that they sought between community change and health services was best achieved by starting with community groups especially incorporated to conduct the health services and working toward medical providers. Working the other way seemed far less effective. Boards of health, hospitals, and medical schools, in that order, seemed impervious to change themselves and unconcerned with change of the economic and political conditions of the programs' participants that had bearing on their health. The preponderance of change that they sought, if any, was behavior modification of the programs' participants. The OHA sought more systemic change and the creation of new programs in the provision of health locally that incorporated problems of housing, environment, food supply, work, income, political participation, and other health-related factors. The OHA had required all programs to have advisory boards and eventually increased the status of these boards to boards of directors. The OHA did this with a great deal of conflict in its program in Watts and Columbia Point. It also fought with the board of health in Lowndes County and ended its support of the program there because the board would not permit its advisory board assume more authority. In Lee County the OHA opposed local doctors and politicians who attempted to block the construction of a clinic building for the OHA-supported program there, which had a board of directors recruited from local African American residents by VISTA volunteers initially.

The OHA had moved from its early view of "maximum participation [of citizens] on our terms" and an illusion that it was conducting a program of redistributive justice. Kravitz finally came to understand the programs as palliatives in themselves but also as the means to develop local leadership from whom change came. As Daniel Zwick explained, the task of the OEO and later the HEW was "to find people within that community who want to do something, and increase their ability to do it." Sometimes that task became very personal, as when "you had to try to support Olly Neal."[69]

The OHA also learned that flexibility was key to the successful implementation of local programs. The OHA was flexible with local grantees and flexible in its internal matters. It interpreted its mandate broadly when necessary, as in the case of the construction of facilities. There was no specific legislative authority for the OHA to grant funds for the construction of new buildings, but the legislation could allow an interpretation to permit such allocations, and the OHA made them. Likewise, the OHA staff intervened to support some institutions it thought were important to the change they sought, like Meharry Medical College.[70]

A final lesson the OHA learned was that the key to maintaining as much flexibility as possible in administration was to maintain control over its own program. Initially, health staff within Head Start and Legal Services fought to be clear of other people in the OEO, in particular, the CAP program. At the same time Schorr depended on the advice of people outside the agency, but decisions on proposals and grants remained within the agency and not with reviewers outside of it. To a degree, the OHA staff continued to feel the need to remain free from the decision-making authority of people who were experts in medical care but yet far behind in their conceptualization of health care and community change. The OHA adopted new forms of accountability to replace the standard mechanism of review by a set of external experts. First, accountability to the grantee was paramount. Second, informal mechanisms of consultation were important. Long after they had left the OHA, both Schorr and Richmond were consulted regularly on new opportunities for and threats to the OHA. The final effort to maintain flexibility and control came with the OHA staff members' resistance to the new federalism of the Nixon administration and the regionalization of programs.

The OHA adjusted much better than expected initially to a change of administrations in 1969. President Nixon's domestic policy advisor, Daniel Patrick Moynihan, was sympathetic to the OHA's efforts. The OHA's programs made converts out of other Nixon administration members who were skeptics. Donald Rumsfeld, Nixon's appointee to direct the OEO, was one such convert after a trip he took to Denver and to one of the OHA's prototype programs. Rumsfeld continued the OHA program and permitted the OHA to begin new centers by transferring financial responsibility for older programs to the HEW. Relieved of this budget pressure, the OHA had "new" money to begin new centers. OHA veterans like Daniel Zwick handled the complex administrative matters involved astutely. Zwick provided important and valuable political advice about these matters to the OHA directors less experienced than he was and transferred community health center programs to the HEW relatively intact.

With these funds, between 1970 and its end in 1973, and in the middle of this transition, the OHA made some of its most important grants, which were based on the lessons it had acquired. Community groups became the primary category of health center sponsors, and many more grants were made in rural southern communities to groups with African American leaders. Leon Cooper became director of the OHA in late 1971 and influenced some of these changes. He was the first African American to head up the OHA, and he rose up through the ranks, having been a physician-administrator in the OHA program in Atlanta. Cooper had studied medicine at Howard. He was far less enamored with the urban centers than others at the OHA had been. For one reason, he was committed to the health centers as social change and not medical change and expected that if "you stick a health center in a Mound Bayou . . . you expect to see some changes, whatever they may be. Far more change than a health center in Brooklyn would bring about."[71] Second, he was deeply impressed with Mound Bayou as a model and the potential of new health centers like it, such as the one starting in the Beaufort-Jasper, South Carolina, area.

The Beaufort-Jasper Comprehensive Health Services had direct lineage from the Sea Island experiment during the Civil War. The center began its work just as Dr. Bailey, the Penn alumni, ended his sixty-five-year medical practice on St. Helena. It approached health comprehensively, as teachers and health aides of Penn School had done previously, and targeted poverty as the source of illness. The result was an array of programs that had precedents on the island in times past. The center introduced a basic, inexpensive home, just as Saxton had done, and began a cooperative bank, also as Saxton had done more than one hundred years earlier. The water supply continued to be a problem that the center addressed. The staff assisted one hundred families of Fiscue Island to begin a food-buying cooperative to alleviate the problems of short supplies and high prices. By the late 1970s the center had five satellites and about 300 people employed in its various programs. Thomas Barnwell, Jr., organized the original proposal for the clinic and served as its first administrator from 1970 to 1978. He had attended Penn School and worked there before the clinic began. His father was also an instructor at Penn. Other health center staff members, such as Emory Campbell who directed health education and action, had also attended Penn School. Campbell eventually became director of the Penn Community Center, as we saw, and Barnwell now serves as the center's board chairman.

The examples of Mound Bayou and Beaufort-Jasper encouraged Cooper, in these last days of the OHA, to make grants to begin the Lee County Cooperative Health Center and the Sea Islands Comprehensive Health Care Program. Lee County would eventually establish a satellite clinic at Lakeview where the FSA had conducted one in the 1930s. In addition, Cooper provoked the reorganization of the Lowndes County program and approved its transfer from the board of health to the citizen and consumer board of directors that Sam Bradley organized.

After the OHA ended, the HEW continued a program to begin community health centers that, although it definitely emphasized health more than community change, incorporated many other aspects of the OHA's neighborhood health center concept. HEW incorporated the lessons of the OHA, especially in regard to community participation and the formation of new nonprofit corporations of community residents to direct the health centers. Some members of the OHA found it "freaky" that the HEW would begin to "out-do" the OEO, in a sense. It appeared to some at the OHA that the rhetoric of the HEW staff suggested they had spent their lives in the OEO. The Rural Health Initiative of the HEW incorporated many of the elements of the community health centers of the OHA and provided grant support to plan and begin the Douglas Community Health Center in Haywood County, Tennessee. In a sense, the OHA members felt that they had captured the HEW. It was their intention to do that. English left the OHA after Nixon's election to take a position at the HEW and to prepare for the inevitable transfer of community health centers from the OHA to the HEW. When Frank Carlucci left the OEO to join the HEW as undersecretary, he took with him respect and admiration for the community health center program.

The influence of the OHA went beyond the HEW and successive agencies. By 1970 poor health and poverty were bonded in reflexive causality. The era of scientific medicine, which Flexner's survey of medical education engendered, brought with it the belief in the efficacy of medical intervention for the improvement of health. But Flexner's influence pushed health care into the realm of the physical sciences, with an emphasis on the chemistry and physics of the body. The social context of a person's health, including the relation of class status to illness, was ignored, as were the financial barriers that poor people faced in accessing scientific medicine. The community health centers placed the illness of poor people back into the context of their conditions of poverty and instituted cost-effective services to treat illness and to prevent it. The scientific revolution of medicine did not improve the health of low-income groups, it only instilled the belief that health improvement was possible. The efficacious means of health improvement for poor people came from outside of organized, scientific medicine and from a combination of sources such as the neglected tradition of social medicine in the United States and abroad; the incessant but modest efforts of health-care reformers like Septima Clark and Modjeska Simkins; the experience and commitment of some African American health professionals and their allies in foundations and federal programs like those in the FSA; and the demand for increased political participation of excluded groups that came from the civil rights movement. The OHA catalyzed the bond of understanding of poverty and health by developing an efficacious model. By 1982 the OHA and HEW had started 827 community health centers, a number that English projected in 1967 but seemed only slightly less improbable than his timeline for eliminating poverty by 1976.[72]

Ten years after submitting the first successful proposal for a neighborhood health center to the OEO, Gibson reflected on the changes that had ensued. "I think in some ways, in the fullness of time, we have reached a special kind of mission here with health centers in the United States that wouldn't have been anticipated a decade ago."[73] Gibson's former cohort at Tufts, Jack Geiger, also reflected on his experience with change in the rural South.

> When we had first organized [the farm co-op at Mound Bayou] and people were working for $4.00 a day cash and $6.00 a day shares, and the first harvest was brought in and people would come in and look at all of the food. And they would look at their share and say, "Gee, that's a lot. Mrs. Jones who lives across the road, she was sick and couldn't work a lot all summer, so why don't you give her half of my shares." And the most mind blowing thing about that was that it was not stated as if it were a big thing.
>
> And when I thought about it, it seemed to me that this was one of the responses that people could make by having lived in a survival culture, at the edge of survival for a substantial period of time. One of the ways that you can go on is that you can decide that you require each other for your mutual survival.[74]

Geiger drew upon a century-long tradition of sharing for mutual survival within the African American community in the rural South. The health centers at Mound Bayou, Beaufort-Jasper, and the four of the narratives were well within a long tradition of protest and change efforts, as well.

PART III

The Politics of Hope

Marybelle Howe confessed to exasperation about questions why people like her acted for change.

> In my generation, you just went ahead and did it. You work, you don't analyze. Sometimes that will get you in trouble, I admit. But if you have good goals, you're not going to get too far off.
>
> It's your generation that asks, "Why?" This kills me. These young people asking these most intimate questions. "What impelled you to do so and so?" Hell, I don't know myself. Why should I try to explain them to you when I never bothered to explain them to me. Esau Jenkins is another example. He wanted to help people. That was all of his philosophy I ever got.

Accordingly, this section does not dissect the motives and psychology of the narrators. It examines the factors that made their change efforts possible and the changes they feel they have made.

As modest as their efforts are in a grand scheme of things, they do constitute a portion of that grand scheme. They especially offer a glimpse of the vitalized democracy that Myrdal saw possible in America. The first chapter of the section describes three vital democratic actors common to change efforts of the 1860s, 1930s, and 1960s in these counties. They are the local community of memory, redemptive organizations, and heroic bureaucracies. The second chapter examines the record of change in these counties to suggest the progress we have made as a nation toward democratic equality and the public expression of our view of human dignity.

CHAPTER 9

Process: Sources of Reform

Three sets of actors recur in the narratives and the histories of change efforts they describe. A community of memory nurtures local leadership through narrative. Redemptive organizations work to transform social, economic, and political arrangements, locally and nationally. Finally, federal agencies, heroic bureaucracies, encourage and support local leaders and redemptive organizations. The narratives and their historical context permit us material to make generalizations about each set of these actors and their contribution to change. Similarly, because we are dealing with events in four places, and not one case study, these generalizations offer insight into social movements in America, as well as local change efforts.

The Community of Memory and Social Change

The stories of the narrators detail specific experiences but also convey a unique interpretation of events and institutions. They express the "truth" of the lived experience of a subordinate group of people. Their "truth" informs listeners about the evil of oppressors and the wrongdoing of employers and officials. They warn about the violence and deceit that members of the dominant community have used and might still use. There are also stories about the heroic resistance of some people in the face of this evil and deceit. The stories suggest a variety of styles of resistance and the wisdom of choosing a time and a means to resist oppression. They support a special sense of virtue for those who share the traditions that make the narrated experiences meaningful. Those people living within these traditions are a community of memory that these stories continue, instruct, and inspire to action.[1]

Evil and Wrongdoing

The stories in our interviews detail violent and corrupt dealings of people in authority toward the members of the community of memory. The perpetrators of violence include deputies and sheriffs who beat and even killed African American men with slight provocation and no accountability. The stories recount violence by mobs led by police officers; they assume that the police were members of mobs or of Ku Klux Klan action and that they might threaten members of the community. The stories suggest that members of the community could get very little protection from law officers. Instead, community members devised alternatives of self-defense to counteract police inaction.

Members of the community received warnings from these stories that they could depend on little justice from white police or court officers. Crimes of blacks against whites were severely punished, often without trial. Even in jail the injustice continued in the form of leased and forced labor. Crimes of whites against African Americans went unpunished and were often explained and excused by the behavior of the members of the community of memory. The injustice could extend to whites who supported African Americans as well. For example, the murderers of both Viola Liuzzo and Jonathan Daniels were acquitted in state courts. In the latter case Daniels was alleged to have drawn a switchblade knife on his murderer. Without police protection, members of the community suffered violent retaliations from whites on trivial matters such as arguments over dogs.

Cheating is a fundamental and enduring element of race relations in these stories. One favorite story of Square Morman illustrates the cheating that went on between the races. Mormon is a partially disabled farmer in Fayette County, Tennessee, who led in civil rights efforts in his county. His story is not in the narratives but exemplifies splendidly the "truth" of narratives within the community of memory. The story involves Mr. Charlie, a white man; Mr. Charlie's cow; and Uncle Tom, an African American man. Uncle Tom is envious of Mr. Charlie and his cow and expresses interest in having one or buying half of Mr. Charlie's. Mr. Charlie eventually agrees to sell Uncle Tom half of the cow. Mr. Charlie explains to Uncle Tom the assets and liabilities of each half. The front half has beautiful eyes, a melodious lowing sound, and requires modest maintenance, food twice a day. The back half passes waste, attracts flies, and requires that someone milk it twice a day and market the milk at considerable effort. Uncle Tom chooses the front half, and Mr. Charlie praises him for driving a hard bargain and making such a good decision in his first business deal. Uncle Tom pays to feed his half, and Mr. Charlie keeps all the revenue from the milk and cream from his half. Uncle Tom realizes, when he is penniless, that he made a very poor deal with Mr. Charlie. He attempts to renegotiate the deal, but Mr. Charlie expresses satisfaction with the existing arrangement and affirms that "a deal's a deal." The story recalls the metaphor of Frederick Douglass that the Freedman's Saving and Trust Company was the black man's cow but the white man's milk.[2]

Community members have many stories of other such "deals." There are stories of electoral processes altered by discarding ballot boxes from heavily African American precincts and changes in the requirements for running for public office just as African American candidates became eligible to do so. Stories of recent electoral irregularities and "long counts" continue to convey suspicion of cheating against African American candidates. The stories of various forms of wrongdoing establish members of the community of memory as a manipulated, subordinate group.

Fear is a common element in the stories from the four communities and directly measures the violence and terror that enforced racial inequality. People with economic and political authority cheated members of the community of memory, and they had little choice but to pretend that they did not recognize the deception or that they accepted it. There were "countless ways one was supposed to fear," as Charles Smith recalled. The intense and pervasive fear within the community of memory also serves as a measure of the heroism of the community members in stories in which they resisted the conditions of violence and terror. Finally, the pervasive fear also measures the changes that the community had to make.

Precedents of Resistance

There is a history of resistance, not always successful, to subordinating violence. Mattic Lee Hocombe Moorer, now seventy years of age, recounted listening, as a child, to the stories of "slavery time people." She still recalls with pride that despite selling her grandmother three times, her various masters "never could make her a slave out of her, never could." Moorer's stories of the civil rights movement in Lowndes County are now part of the community of memory there.

Stories often featured parents who exemplified resistance to inequality and injustice. Sometimes this resistance never reached action but remained in-family expressions of awareness of pay differentials and other discriminatory employment practices. Olly Neal, Jr., could recall, for example, that his mother observed injustice, even if quietly. She would "talk strong" within the family more often than outside of the family or outside of the African American community. Neal recalled,

> She never allowed us to talk back to older whites but that didn't stop her from talking strong. I remember in 1949, my Daddy and Momma bought a blue Chevrolet truck. Momma brought the truck over to what was at that time called Busby Chevrolet, I believe. Now white folks were in the habit of referring to older black men as uncle, and the white man at the Chevrolet place called her auntie. She turned to him and said very calmly, "How is my sister doing?" He said, "What?" And she said, "Well you must be my sister's son because I only have one sister and if I'm your aunt you must be her son!" But I remember one later occasion when I took the truck over to Busby's and they asked me, "This Uncle Olly's car?" And I replied, "Hell no, it's *Mr.* Neal's car!" Of course they went straight and told Momma and Daddy. And when I got home, Momma whipped my tail for doing the same thing she had done. She was just fearful of us getting killed.

Often the stories, such as Jesse Cannon, Jr.'s, story of integrating Haywood County High School, describe enduring pain to make things easier for others to follow. His story also suggests the profound psychological distance that his schoolbus traveled. The community he left and the school he attended were "two different worlds or two different planets." Some of the stories took lessons from past efforts of resistance and applied them to the present. The accounts of the Southern Tenant Farmers Union's origins routinely include the plea for a biracial union made by a man who had seen his efforts to organize African American farm workers through the Progressive Farmers and Household Alliance suppressed in the Elaine Massacre of 1919.

Styles of Resistance

The heroes and heroines of these stories are most often ordinary people like the narrators and listeners of the stories. Their heroism comes from extraordinary action, but not in being extraordinary. Their resistance however, is a lifelong attitude expressed in the extraordinary act. There are common elements that express courage in the stories. A member of the community may look dominant persons in the eye. Jesse Cannon talks about looking Mr. Douglas in the eye. A reporter for the *New York Times* thought it important to explain that Olly Neal "does not lower his eyes when he talks to white men."[3] Bill Jenkins thought that his father's strength had to do with confronting people, eye to eye, and then suggesting collaboration.

Whites didn't like him because he would not bow down to them. He would look them right dead in the eyes and say, "You put your pants on just like I do. You may have some assets but I know I got some too. So what we need to do is see to exchange some ideas and we can get further instead of trying to confront each other."

Modes of sophisticated resistance occur in the stories. Olly Neal's mother's use of a white man's salutation of "auntie" to inquire about her sister, his mother supposedly, exemplifies a subtle resistance that uses the prejudice of whites. The conclusion of Square Morman's story of Mr. Charlie's cow is another. It uses the dominant community's deception as a premise for action. Uncle Tom decides to have his half of the cow for food, takes a two by four, and hits the cow over the head, killing it. When Mr. Charlie clamors to protest the death of "his" cow, Uncle Tom explains that he didn't do anything to Mr. Charlie's half, he just knocked the hell out of his. Similarly, such stories illustrate the intelligence of the community members in using the bias of dominant community members. Bill Saunders's story of an old man who ran a red light in Charleston invoked a world in which everything has a double meaning, one for whites and one for African Americans. It also praised those community members who could pry open the prejudice of dominant community members to extricate themselves from a problem.

> There was an old man. I forget his name but his memory stays with me like the memory of Esau Jenkins. He was smart and he knew how to get things and get things done, even when he didn't have power.
>
> One day, right here in Charleston, this old man ran a red light. Drove right through the intersection on red. And this cop, white cop of course, pulls him over. He tells him to get out of the truck and begins to tell him off and curse him and call him all kinds of names. You know.
>
> Well, the old black man, he just stands there and takes it. Finally the cop says, "Uncle, didn't you see that light was red?" And the old black man, with his hat in his hand—you never spoke to a white person with your hat on—says, "Well, officer, of course I did, sir." And the cop stares at him, amazed. You know. He says, "Then why the hell did you drive right through it."
>
> This time the old black man looks at the cop amazed and says, "Well, officer, sir, I thought green meant go for you and red meant go for us."
>
> The cop didn't know what to do and called him some more names and let him drive off.
>
> If that happened today, a young black man would start cursing the cop back and argue that the light wasn't red and probably end up with a fine and under arrest.

You see, we have to keep alive the wisdom of measuring a situation and getting what we want.

Finally, there are stories of resistance that invoke a higher standard of human dealings than that which is offered. This higher standard shames those who are engaged in deceit. Dr. C. P. Boyd, for example, believes he touched the conscience of the white judge who convicted him for faulty brakes when he extended kindness to him in return. Charles Smith feels the same way about his protest to the other all-white commissioners about their letter that implied his consent to their termination of the health program.

Comparisons Between and Within Communities

Many of the stories of the narrators express disbelief and dismay about the values and attitudes of the dominant community members. Whites acted at times as if African Americans could not be trusted but still delegated food preparation and the raising and nurturing of their children to them. Especially upsetting were the lengths to which dominant community members would go not to share what they had with community of memory members. Stories told of instances of swimming pools and athletic facilities that were formerly all-white but that white officials closed to whites and blacks rather than integrate them. African American parents could not understand why white parents would keep their children from such facilities rather than share them with African American children. These instances of dominant community action were all the more disconcerting because stories in the community of memory, like Mr. Charlie's cow, made clear that blacks and whites had common interests and bonds and could not act separately without mutual injury.[4]

There are also stories of white persons who expressed characteristics different from those of the dominant community. Many of the people who played significant roles in the establishment of the community health centers, especially the professionals, were white. Dan and Janet Blumenthal were among the "white kids" that Olly Neal remembers kindly in Lee County, for example. Linda Lingle and Marybelle Howe on the Sea Islands are other examples. In addition, there were local white people who played modest but important roles. Linda Lingle remembers, for example, a white man from Johns Island who was a member of the National Guard Medical Corps. He would bring medical supplies to the clinic and worked there as well. There were white allies among federal officials in these stories as well.

Kenneth McConnochie, the physician of the reorganized health services in Lowndes County, inspired an award for outstanding staff members. John Doar, of the Justice Department, assisted newly registered voters in Haywood County to win federal injunctions and assert their rights. He was a "God-sent" man, in the terms of Betty Douglas. What seems to distinguish them is their recognition of the ability of members of the community of memory, of the injustices they face, and of the common bond between members of the dominant and subordinate community. They accepted the validity of the tradition of the community of memory, understood the "truth" of their stories, and appreciated the values of the community. Clyde Johnson, for example, a white organizer for the Alabama Sharecroppers Union in Lowndes County, admired the storytelling ability of the people he was organizing. "I would listen to them tell stories of events years before. I was kind of a listener anyway. The fact that I would listen impressed them a lot. They were terrific storytellers."

A great deal of merit is imputed to anyone who has coped in the repressive atmosphere of race relations as the community of memory understands them. Bill Saunders put a specific level of learning on this coping. "Any blacks walking around on the streets of Charleston today that are 40 years old, have at least a masters degree in psychology to be able to survive." Likewise, people are seen as heroic even if stories suggest their fear. Annie Hrabowski, an elderly woman and early supporter of SNCC in Lowndes County, recalls that her father had no fear. But she also tells the story of his panic at her suggestion one day, when she was about six years old and Jim Crow ruled race relations, that they enter the courthouse by the front door. Allowance is made for individual fear because of the climate of terror that each person lived in and had to mediate individually. In more than fifty interviews no member of the community of memory ever referred to another as an "Uncle Tom" or a militant. Rather, community of memory members explained that members of the dominant community use those terms to divide them.

This is not to say that members of the community of memory accept every African American person as equal within it; they do not. There are class differences among African Americans that the narrators felt. African Americans from the rural areas often felt discriminated against by African Americans in the towns of the same county. C. P. Boyd found these class strictures so strong that his grades dropped and in junior year of high school he transferred from Brownsville to another high school in an adjoining county. Class differences strained the boundaries of the community of memory; dependence on and allegiance to whites clearly divided it. Teachers and others whose incomes were not only greater than most other African Americans but dependent on white authorities were a distinct class within the community of memory. There is frequent mention of the African American middle and professional classes and their lack of support for local movements except those that benefited them directly, like voter registration. Likewise, as important as the church was to the local movements, preachers were less important. The church provided African American people a religious faith in justice and righting wrong, but local clergy provided cautious leadership in the pursuit of justice because of their relation to the white community. Differences in skin color are very important, although this was seldom mentioned in the narratives. African American men and women of lighter skin color and with white parents or grandparents often had more advantages. They were more likely to own land or attend better schools. The white community accentuated class differences among African Americans. Lee County narrators recalled that children of certain families were "selected" to attend the previously all-white schools. The narratives express resentment about the stigma of class as well as pride in the accomplishment of the civil rights movement in reducing class differences among African Americans that were based on the subordination imposed on all of them.

Some privileged African Americans reclaimed a clear place in the community of memory by participating in voter-registration drives and other forms of organized action that risked their status. Uralee Haynes, of Lowndes County, and her husband were both school teachers at the time of Selma March. Their employer, the school superintendent, had intimidated them and deterred them from their intention to register to vote after World War II. In light of that, they were slow to lend direct and obvious assistance to the movement in Lowndes County in 1965. They did so before other African American professionals in the community in order to express unity with the African American community. Their actions loosened their ties to the white community, the base of their privilege, and tightened them to the African American community of the county.

Self-Definition and New Definitions of Self

The narrators expressed the pain of discovering the limitations of their existing relationships. Once they participated in organized efforts at change, such as voter registration or the conduct of health services, some of them found that others that they trusted and regarded as friends were opposed to them and their efforts and even wished them harm. Tom Sanderlin in Haywood County recalled that some white people, whom he thought "were my best friends in the world," spoke to him differently after he joined the Haywood County Civic and Welfare League. "They'd ask me what could they do *to* me not what could they do *for* me." Thomas Ishmael, in Lee County, recalled his surprise that after working for white officials' elections, those same people he supported would not support his efforts to organize the clinic. They would not agree to serve on the board and even attempted to organize a board and clinic of their own to block the efforts of which he was a part.

As traditional relations changed and the elements of power and opposition within traditional relations became apparent, new definitions of self emerged. In some cases there are remarkable transitions in the same people in efforts of resistance and change that are two and three decades apart. Jesse Cannon, Sr., for example, began his claim for his farm subsidy check in 1936 with a disclaimer to the white official who disputed his story, "You're a white man and I'm a negro and I can't call you a liar." But thirty years later when another white man was trying to dissuade Cannon and others from registering to vote, he told him, "They register dogs, they register old cars, trucks, why couldn't we be registered?"

Collective expressions of new definitions of self evolve from efforts at change. In Haywood County the residents of the FSA project organized the 8th of August celebration that commemorated the project and served as a homecoming festival for the community. In Lowndes County, Steve Wilson was stymied in his attempts to initiate dental services into the clinic because the Alabama Dental Association would not endorse his application. Wilson awoke one night and said, "Damn, I know what to do." He met with the local chapter of the all-African American National Dental Association and argued convincingly, "You are the area professional society." This insight, which came in a flash, reversed decades of deference to the imposed definition of professional standards and status from the white community.

This new definition of self comes with three realizations about the community of memory. First, there is a great deal of pride in some achievement, such as the conduct of health services. Neal measures the increase in self-esteem among African Americans in Lee County by what people involved in the conduct of the health services went on to do on the school board, on the county commission, and in economic development. Second, there is pride that these achievements represented change, not for just the members of the community of memory, but for poor people of other subordinate groups as well, including poor whites and women. There is pride and affirmation of self that given authority, members of the community of memory showed no desire to replicate racial discrimination or reciprocate for past injustices. Healing, not vengeance, is the virtue that these stories extol. Finally, there is a realization that change is not always dependent on what others will permit or assist you to do. There is the memory of a time, such as 1969, for Olly Neal, when "I just wouldn't abide for anything going on that I could deal with and I tried to deal with the things I couldn't abide."

The Bases of the Community Memory

Economic security and space are two specific mechanisms that permit the continuation and expression of the content of the community of memory. They are implied in the narratives. Economic dependence was a basic element of the fear that is the starting point of most of the stories of heroic resistance. Landowning provided economic security and supported the expression of resistance within the community of memory. African American landowners were free to demonstrate during the day and to work their fields at other times, unlike African American tenant farmers. Likewise, African American landowners were free to house civil rights workers, unlike tenants. In fact, on some occasions when tenants were moved from their rented homes and lands for registering to vote, they moved to the notorious tent cities, which were possible only because other African Americans owned land on which to pitch tents. The relative economic security that landownership imparted was essential to the political expression of resistance to oppressive forms of inequality among the members of the community of memory. As Charles Smith recalls, "Landownership really put leadership in the hands of the people who were determined to get registered to vote and to teach their sisters and brothers the importance of it." Likewise, an economic base within the African American community supported initiatives on behalf of the community. For example, the African American funeral director in Marianna provided the cooperative clinic its first space. African American beauticians were central coordinators of the Citizenship Schools.

All of the communities had schools or centers of training that were important sources of leadership preparation and training. In Haywood County the Douglas School not only replaced dilapidated buildings that served the African American children of tenant farmers but attracted a cadre of talented African Americans as teachers. Assessing the impact of the Douglas School, Tom Rice estimated that "the school brought this community up 100 percent." But it did not do so in isolation. Families in the community supported the school. They were able to do so because the economic base of the Project provided them freedom from the control of landlords that impacted on the schooling of their children and genuine hope for educational and economic opportunity and improvement for their children. These schools were important as space in which the community of memory could express itself and maintain its alternative historical understanding. There were problems with this. The schools of the nineteenth century, especially, dealt with the elite of the African American community and accentuated the class differences among the community of memory. Nevertheless, many of the graduates of these schools, Septima Clark from Avery Institute and Stokely Carmichael from Howard, for example, became important leaders of collective action efforts later.

The African American church was the only organization within the community of memory under the members' control for most of the time since Emancipation. It provided a space for decision making and leadership training. Of course, many African American clergymen were prominent in the civil rights movement, but it was the officers of the local churches who led the first efforts at organizing and voter registration and who made the core of the civil rights movement.[5] Likewise, it was the space of the African American church that housed the Union League meetings, the early schools for the freedpeople, the organizing efforts of African American agricultural workers in Alabama and Arkansas and of the civil rights movement in more recent times. The church provided a space where the community of memory could weave the strands of its traditions and virtues with people of the Old and New Testament. Theology blended with everyday life, and the stories of the Bible and their own stories illustrated the same virtues and traditions of resistance and hopeful expectation for deliverance. Annie Hrabowski told a story of a courthouse door she and her father could not enter. But she also assessed, without specific reference to that incident, that "The Lord has opened the door for us." Jesse Cannon, Sr., judged that "the Lord suffered" that a sheriff was killed before he carried out his threat to kill African Americans who attempted to register to vote. Bob Mants reflected on his work and the people with whom he worked and thought that they related themselves to "the children of Israel in the biblical days."

Redemptive Organizations

Interwoven in the stories of these four communities are numerous organizations, some of which were local and others, national. The various freedmen's relief societies, Union leagues, several northern philanthropies, the NAACP, SNCC, CORE, and the SCLC were national examples of these organizations. These organizations provided assistance in the forms of funds and other resources to local leaders and for local change efforts. Among the local redemptive organizations they assisted are the Penn, Fargo, and Calhoun schools and related organizations like the Calhoun Land Trust; organizations of agricultural workers in the black belt of Alabama and in eastern Arkansas; and political organizations like the local leagues, Progressive Club, Lowndes County Freedom Organization, Concerned Citizens of Lee County, and the Haywood County Civic and Welfare League. The health centers resembled these redemptive organizations and had a similar set of characteristics and purposes.

These national redemptive organizations sustain local efforts, but they neither create nor start them. In fact, the national organizations benefit from their association with local efforts. The NAACP, for example, gained financially and in reputation because of its defense of the members of the Progressive Union of Elaine, Arkansas. James Forman, executive secretary of SNCC from 1961 to 1966, gained formative experiences in Fayette and Haywood counties. He learned especially the interrelatedness of basic problems and the deference national organizations should give to the judgment of local leaders. Five years later Lowndes County gave Forman and SNCC "a new lease on life" by the lessons local leaders imparted. As he listened to Courtland Cox report on the aspirations of the Lowndes County Freedom Organization, the list crystallized for Forman the essence of organizing for SNCC: power, black power.[6]

These organizations are redemptive in the sense that their members interpret their work as redeeming society of some evil. The American Missionary Association extended the separatist, redemptive orientation of Congregationalism to the national sin of caste.[7] The work of the organizations also redeemed them. It provided a social and political purpose to supplement their emphasis on their own members and offered their members a means to leave the mundane and to pursue the noble. Marybelle Howe, for example, supported political change on Johns Island from the association of Church Women United in Charleston.

The changes these organizations propose benefit groups of oppressed and disadvantaged groups but disrupt existing social, economic, and political arrangements. Members of these organizations undertake unique and radical lifestyles to carry out the work of the organization. They may even risk friendships or lose them because of their beliefs. Their work is a call and not entirely a choice, as Bill Saunders said eloquently.

It's not the kind of life you choose. You get caught up in it. But you wouldn't choose to be misunderstood. A preacher near here gave a sermon, "Being Picked Out to be Picked On." That's a heavy subject. To see clearly things ahead of your time carries a heavy price. You're friendless. There's no one you can talk with straight across the board, not even your family. Ten years later, they may see what you are saying but by that time, you've gone on.

To Measure and Transform Society

The transformation that redemptive organizations propose may take different forms and different strategies. The NAACP worked steadily through the courts and less so through the Congress to eliminate laws that restricted the franchise of African Americans. Likewise, the NAACP, the Commission on Interracial Cooperation, and other groups worked to end lynching through public opinion and legislation but understood the relation of their efforts to social transformation. Acquiescence is complicity in a social problem, such as lynching, and the end of a social problem requires that many people end their acquiescence to the conditions of a subordinate group and in the wrong actions of others. Redemptive organizations urge individuals to end their compliant silence and call public agencies and agents to higher standards in the performance of their duties. The National Freedmen's Aid Association criticized Howard's policies of cutting relief rations to the freed people, to his embarrassment. Likewise, the Southern Tenant Farmers Union, and others, prodded the New Deal's agricultural programs to do more for southern agricultural workers. The NAACP criticized and upset the FBI for its investigations of lynchings.[8]

Implicit in this work of transformation is a standard with which to measure society, as well as oneself and public agencies. Norman Thomas lamented an economy in which cotton pickers could not afford to buy cotton underwear. The Haywood County Civic and Welfare League measured the lack of African American voters by the registration of dogs and trucks. These standards and measures are a constant reminder of the change that has to occur to achieve some semblance of fairness, equity, or well-being. John Hulett, for example, proposed that members of the Lowndes County Freedom Organization provide "a model for democracy."[9]

Redemptive organizations begin their transformation of society with demands on their own members. High personal standards and commitment to transcendent organizational goals are apparent in redemptive organizations. The six qualifications of the American Missionary Association, for example, included: missionary spirit, health, energy, culture and common sense, exemplary personal habits, and experience. The work ruled out people with "singularities and idiosyncracies of character" because of its "gravity and earnestness." Likewise, "nowhere is character . . . more important."[10] Both the Fargo and Calhoun schools had exacting standards for their students as well as the participants in their annual conference for local farmers. Some members contribute money and resources from afar. Other members take on the problems of others directly. In some cases their members work with, live, and risk like the people they are supporting in a change effort. Still other redemptive organizations, such as the Union Leagues, STFU, Cotton Pickers League, Progressive Union, Alabama Sharecroppers Union, Citizenship Schools, and others that were repressed before they could attain a name, work to benefit their members directly and in so doing achieve a new standard that will benefit others at the same time, such as $1.00 per hundred weight of cotton or bus service to schools.

The work of redemptive organizations benefits others, directly and primarily. Tom Ishmael and Pitson Brady made a point of their ability to take care of their own health care bills. It was their concern for those who could not that prompted them to work to develop the community health centers. Members of redemptive organizations judge the status and reputation of each other by their contribution to change, not their education, prestige, or position in the organization. Olly Neal fired well-educated African Americans who could not make sacrifices that did not have immediate benefit for themselves directly. Steve Wilson did the same thing. He fired African American professionals in the health center if they did not contribute to the change the center was pursuing. On the other hand, Bill Saunders lamented firing a white man who could make sacrifices merely to make room for an African American man as director. All three men agree that the work of their different organizations was to make the greatest number of people better off rather than to create well-paying positions of authority for a few African Americans. Are the programs reaching those in need? How many are being helped by how much? These are the constant questions a redemptive organization asks itself.

Providing New Examples

The worst cases of need and repression attract redemptive organizations most. The freedmen's relief societies were attracted to the Sea Islands because of the isolated and deplorable conditions of the "contraband" there. The founders of both Calhoun School and Fargo School were likewise attracted to their areas by the severe need. SNCC chose to work in Lowndes County because of its notorious reputation. In all of these cases there was an attitude of making change in a particular place to prove that it could be done anywhere.

After some time and success, the efforts of redemptive organizations provide models for legislation and public programs. The Penn School and the Calhoun Land Trust impacted the FSA. Certainly, the freedmen's relief societies worked hard, and with some success, to influence the policies of Reconstruction. The Medical Committee on Human Rights, Sidney Kark in South Africa, and the Boston Dispensary all contributed to the community health centers of the War on Poverty. In addition to this contribution, redemptive organizations also protest inadequate public policies. The Southern Tenant Farmers Union and the Alabama Sharecroppers Union took the issues on which they were working to Washington to acquire changes in the legislation of the Agricultural Adjustment Administration (AAA) and its administration.

New and unimagined examples of positive human relations occur within redemptive organizations. For example, the redemptive organizations recounted here provided more examples of cooperation between the races and among the socioeconomic classes than American society ordinarily provides. African Americans staffed the early schools of the American Missionary Association and provided educated African American men and women the opportunity to impart education to others. The clinics functioned somewhat similarly in health care. Bill Jenkins used a film about the health center on Mound Bayou to stimulate the imagination of people on Johns Island about what was possible there. Likewise, Olly Neal found important new ideas in Mound Bayou to replicate in Lee County. The Lowndes County Christian Movement provided Uralee Haynes and other African American teachers and professionals an opportunity to work collectively with other African Americans of different socioeconomic classes. Similarly, middle- and upper-class black and white college students from around the country often acquired their first, life-changing experience with collective action through SNCC or events sponsored by the SCLC.[11]

Although redemptive organizations shun accommodationist policies such as those of Booker T. Washington's programs, they differ in the degree of trust and cooperation they extend to other groups. The Union Leagues and several labor organizations were secretive and exclusive because of the danger of violent repression. SNCC became exclusively African American after time to better express the power of African Americans and in so doing

strained its relationship with other civil rights organizations. The other organizations, like all of the health centers and schools, maintained broader alli-
ances. A key difference in the way redemptive organizations relate to others
is their primary focus. If it is political organizing and economic change, they
tend to be more exclusive than if the focus is on providing services.[12]

Redemptive organizations set new and higher standards for a subordinate group. The Haywood County Farms Project was the largest terracing
project in the state, and its African American participants were the first to
have electricity. Residents on the Calhoun Land Trust were the first African Americans in the county to live in painted houses. Within the space of
redemptive organizations, members set examples for one another as well.
C. P. Boyd had an experience of new race relations within his church in Iowa.
Septima Clark observed how Esau Jenkins saw blacks and whites live and
work together at Highlander Folk School in a new way. The impact was profound on Jenkins, as it was on Rosa Parks, whose refusal to yield her place
on a Montgomery, Alabama bus signaled the start of the bus boycott there.
That boycott, of course, became a benchmark of the civil rights movement.

> At Highlander, I found out for the first time in my adult life that this could be
> a unified society, that there was such a thing as people of different races and
> backgrounds meeting together in workshops, and living together in peace and
> harmony. It was a place I was very reluctant to leave. I gained there the strength
> to persevere in my work for freedom, not just for blacks, but for all oppressed
> people.[13]

Part of the new standard are the trust and responsibility given to members of a subordinate group to play new roles in new arrangements. African
Americans, in the events we recounted, established their own schools, land
reforms, and health services, and they conducted them in the face of overwhelming odds. The recent organized efforts to establish health care had
precedents in African American–led efforts to establish schools in the 1860s
and 1870s. In both instances local leadership for new services far exceeded
the ability and resources of government agencies to respond, and in both instances at different times, the action to establish such programs was understood as extremely political because it exceeded what wealthy landowners
were willing to provide. Sometimes, as in the wake of Theo Calloway's
lynching in Lowndes County in 1888, local residents organized to provide
for their basic and fundamental security from violence. That violence came
from those who were supposed to provide protection. The local redemptive organizations are most numerous in the labor movement such as the

Progressive Farmers and Household Union, the Southern Tenant Farmers Union, and the Alabama Sharecroppers Union, to mention a few.

The Progressive Club, the Haywood County Civic and Welfare League, the Concerned Citizens of Lee County, and the Lowndes County Freedom Organization are just some of the local redemptive organizations recounted in the narratives about recent events in these communities. Like the efforts to organize schools for the freedpeople, these organizations generated local enthusiasm and support; one example was the cooking of hamburgers at 3:00 A.M. in Marianna. People in these organizations speak of once-in-a-lifetime experiences of working like a family and of the excitement of "doing good." Not everyone welcomes the new examples and standards of redemptive organizations. Historic accounts and the narratives are punctuated with reprisals, arson, gunshots, and even murder.

Obviously, redemptive organizations do not always live up to their ideal. Hierarchy, racism, and sexism within their organizations often undermine the ideals they pursue. Even so, the extraordinary criticism and controversy these organizational failings engender testify that redemptive organizations have as their goal to surpass existing conventions in setting examples.

Sowing the Seeds of Change

The work of these organizations continues in unforeseen ways even after some of them end. The work of the American Missionary Association, for example, fashioned Hampton Institute, which trained Booker T. Washington, who founded Tuskegee along the lines on which he was trained, and later it supplied teachers to Calhoun Colored School. Floyd Brown embodied the teachings of Tuskegee and imparted them to his students at Fargo, who included E. C. Burnett, who took them to heart and tried his best to pass them on to his students in Lee County, who included Olly Neal, Jr. Sam Bradley, a Tuskegee alumni, echoed Washington in his own philosophy: "Know where you want to go and work towards getting there." Avery Institute also influenced tens of thousands of African American southerners through the work of Septima Clark. The students of the Citizenship Schools that Clark directed influenced thousands of other Americans. In this way a redemptive organization begun in one era may provide a basis for reform in another. The American Missionary Association, for example, provided an administrative home, support, and a staff member, Andrew Young, for Citizenship Schools, one hundred years after its origins. Maria Weston Chapman is a person who bridged the work of redemptive organizations of two eras. A resident of Boston in 1865, she supported Pierce on his proposed work on the Sea Islands. She linked it to her past involvement in abolitionist work. "Our [abolitionist society's] lectures of 30 years' standing do not put the case so squarely and effectually as the rising generation. . . . We have trained to do a preparatory work, and well we have performed it." She felt a duty to sustain Pierce and the guided transition to freedom.[14]

In like manner the activities of one redemptive organization provides models for others in different places and at different times. John Hulett brought with him to Lowndes County his experience with the Alabama Christian Movement, which began after the state of Alabama suppressed the NAACP. He replicated the state organization in the county. The Lowndes County Christian Movement fostered the development of the Lowndes County Freedom Organization, which contributed to the black power movement nationally. Similarly, redemptive organizations may take on new goals of transformation. The Medical Committee for Human Rights, for example, initially supported civil rights workers but later worked, especially in the Chicago area, on the health status and care of people in prison, occupational safety and health, and health care for the poor.

Heroic Bureaucracies

The narratives and their historical context suggest that periodically some agency of the federal government sets out to redress a severe problem of inequality and repression. It does so in a manner that shatters existing practice and the stereotype of ponderous, ineffective, self-defeating bureaucracy. Three such heroic bureaucracies occur in the histories of these communities: the Freedmen's Bureau; the FSA, especially the Resettlement Administration; and the OHA.[15]

A heroic bureaucracy premises its work on the possibility and necessity of social change to undo some injustice or subordination of a specific group of Americans. It explains this injustice as an inefficiency within existing social, economic, and political arrangements. It offers some form of social audit that takes into account all the costs of the injustice and denial of opportunity. Heroic bureaucracies calculate the costs of their program, including the redistribution of wealth and power entailed, as small, given the benefits of the program and the human costs of the injustice. They incorporate in their work hopes for impacts for a set of citizen-clients which include new forms of political leadership and change at the local level. In general, heroic bureaucracies attribute more human dignity and worth to members of subordinate groups and consequently depart radically from the dominant perjorative views of members of these groups. Heroic bureaucracies are experimental, and the most innovative aspects of their program are short-lived. This diminishes the perceived value of their immediate outcomes, which are further diminished by efforts to discredit the agency and its programs. The impacts of the short-lived experiment may be lasting, however, and provide important new beginnings for later change efforts. Put together, these characteristics equal revolutionary new expectations of government action by, for, and with a subordinated group of people.

New Distributions of Benefits

The programs of heroic bureaucracies distribute benefits to a group of people who do not have them ordinarily. The Freedmen's Bureau developed schools for freedpeople. Similarly, the FSA assisted African American landless farmers in the South to purchase land and in some instances provided school buildings and health services. Between 1966 and 1973 the OHA spent $50 million in the establishment of more than one hundred neighborhood health centers. By 1982 there were 827 of them.[16]

The new distribution of the benefits from these agencies are obvious. There were very few schools for African Americans in the South before the Civil War. The Freedmen's Bureau and its immediate predecessors were clearly the main impetus in the formation and conduct of schools during and after the war and in the formation of state-supported schools.[17] The overwhelming majority of African American farmers in the South were little more than debtor peons from Reconstruction to the New Deal. Early programs of the New Deal such as the AAA actually made the condition of the tenant farmer, and especially the African American tenant farmer, worse.[18] The Resettlement Administration was the first public effort to assist African American farmers acquire land since Reconstruction. In terms of the OHA, poor African Americans in the rural South were distinguished by less access to health care, worse health status, and health care of poorer quality.[19]

Extraordinary Events and Extraordinary Responses

The unusual circumstances surrounding heroic bureaucracies permit them to undertake their broad and ambitious missions. The origins of our heroic bureaucracies and the impetus for their programs of democratic equality and enhanced human dignity are, in part, reactions to extraordinary events: Emancipation, economic depression, or a mass movement for civil rights. Political terror and political assassinations also contribute to the extraordinary climate of heroic bureaucracy. Events suspend or dispel what had been regarded as normal and foster deep introspection about national institutions, aspirations, and possibilities. Heroic bureaucrats offer some grand design amid the fragments of a by-gone order of things. Howard likened the end of the Civil War and the "actual, universal fact" of Emancipation to an earthquake and took as his first priority "to put the colored man or woman on a permanent basis on a higher plane." Tugwell thought that the Depression had taught Americans that "the jig is up. The cat is out of the bag. There is no invisible hand. There never was." Members of the OHA staff remember their belief that their success "might save the whole concept of the poverty program."[20]

New alignments of the president, the Congress, and other decision makers are other extraordinary elements of the political climate of heroic bureaucracies. The uniquely enhanced prestige of Lincoln and Kennedy by assassination suspended the ordinary give and take of the executive and the legislative branches for a while. This may mean extraordinary conflict, as it did in the case of the Freedmen's Bureau, or extraordinary cooperation, as in the case of the quick passage of the OHA in a Congress that would pass "a ham sandwich if it had some social improvement content," as one participant of that Congress put it. In addition, heroic bureaucrats enjoy extraordinary access to major decision makers in the early period of their work. Saxton and Howard dealt directly with Secretary of War Stanton; Tugwell had access to Secretary of Agriculture Wallace and FDR; and members of the OHA enjoyed regular access to Sargent Shriver and, through him, Sen. Edward Kennedy.

The unusual initial political circumstances of a heroic bureaucracy change, and these changes jeopardize them. For example, direct and ordinary access to major decision makers generally does not carry over to later heads of heroic bureaucracies. Will Alexander, for example, did not enjoy the access to Wallace that Tugwell did. But unusual events keep the bureaucracies going. Congress moved to protect the Freedmen's Bureau from the president by naming Howard commissioner for life, his own or that of the agency, and reserving the power of appointment to Secretary Stanton.[21] Tugwell's departure from the Resettlement Administration reduced its conflict with others. President Nixon's election in 1968 probably extended the independence of the OHA, a Democratic administration's program, for a longer time.

A Humphrey administration would probably not have tolerated a maverick health program that caused problems with big city and rural southern Democrats.[22] No more than FDR could tolerate AAA policies that split the New Deal alliance with Southern Democrats. Public opinion also changes. The public soon tires of ongoing extraordinary events and the heroic response they require. Klan terror from 1867 to 1872, so shortly after the Civil War, and a Great Society program of the 1960s, which demonstrated that poverty was more difficult to eradicate than we had thought, lessened national resolve to see grand designs for change carried out.

With the change in the winds of public opinion and other changes, a heroic bureaucracy trims its sails. Several years after its euphoric beginnings, it strikes a course of compromised programs, the outcomes of which still leave a lasting wake. The Freedmen's Bureau, for example, limited its program almost exclusively to the development of schools for freedmen after 1868. The Resettlement Administration developed the vast majority of its all-African American, community-oriented programs four years after the New Deal began and after extensive criticism of other New Deal agricultural programs. The OHA made a major commitment to develop community organizations to begin and conduct health centers only in 1970 and after five years of working to get hospitals and medical schools to lead in the neighborhood health center movement.

Agitation, Not Adjustment

Despite some adjustment to their environment, heroic bureaucracies thrive on the constant stimulation of their institutional environment. Normal bureaucracies prefer stable, not turbulent, institutional environments, and heroic bureaucracies also pay heed to their institutional environment. However, organizational survival in a placid environment is a secondary, not a primary consideration. The Freedmen's Bureau's head and key staff members opposed the president's policy on pardons to former Confederates and the restoration of land to them; the FSA continued its program of forming farming communities and services after 1937 legislation instituted an emphasis on individual tenant farmers and land purchase; and the OHA made a larger proportion of grants to community groups to conduct health program and several of its most controversial grants in the Nixon years, especially 1970 to 1972. Decisions to conform to political constraints are most often imposed on the agency externally. Andrew Johnson imposed a policy on the Freedmen's Bureau of restoration of lands to former Confederate owners, even taking them from freedmen by military force. The threat and experience of congressional hearings tempered the conduct of the FSA.[23] And the end of the OHA followed the demise of the OEO and the parceling out of its programs to other agencies.

The longevity and growth of a heroic bureaucracy give its critics the chance, and more reasons, to bring it from its extraordinary origins into the ordinary channels of government. Heroic bureaucracies are particularly susceptible to becoming targets for other actors in the public realm because of their abnormal origins, unusual organization, and rapid growth. In addition, the friction they cause in the new distribution of goods and in their challenge to the existing forms of economic and political power in the communities of their programs makes them "disturbers of the peace" for the "banker-merchant-farmer-lawyer-doctor-governing class."[24] The "minor surrenders of privilege" that Tugwell understood to be the goal of a heroic bureaucracy and the price of the common good[25] become too costly to critics, who end the bureaucracies.

Heroic bureaucracies are also vulnerable to criticism when measured by the administration of normal bureaucracy. The rapid growth of heroic bureaucracies and the rapid turnover of staff hinder administrative capacity. Careful administration is secondary to getting an important and large job done quickly. Heroic bureaucracies often find themselves with vastly expanded budgets and staffs with which to administer a program, the purpose and shape of which are still emerging. The staff of the Freedmen's Bureau went from no staff to almost a thousand people in a year, but at the same time its funding was severely curtailed. From May 1935 to May 1936 the Resettlement Administration grew from a staff of twelve to a staff of 16,386. By 1938 the FSA's budget was $180,150,000, or one-quarter of the budget of the Department of Agriculture.[26] The OHA, after only eight demonstration projects, had almost $50 million appropriated in 1967 and began developing health centers at a rate four times faster than before.[27] Critical scrutiny generally provided sufficient evidence of wrongdoing for those who were looking for it. In general, however, that evidence did not convince disinterested observers of poor administration or inefficiency.

Experiment over Precedent

The extraordinary circumstances of its beginning and continuation explain in part the distinguishing emphasis on experimentation in a heroic bureaucracy. Extraordinary times call for extraordinary measures, which

Howard acknowledged were "quite new . . . and hitherto always contended against by our leading statesmen."[28] FDR demanded "bold, persistent experimentation" on behalf of a nation in need.[29] The members of these heroic bureaucracies interpreted loose mandates as broadly as possible. Both the Freedmen's Bureau and the OHA provided funds for the construction or purchase of facilities without specific authority. The FSA provided an array of services that included the payment of poll taxes and health premiums as part of successfully rehabilitating participants to full status as citizens and guaranteeing the repayment of loans.[30] Eventually, as we have seen in the case of the FSA, this discretion becomes grounds for criticism of "administrative ingenuity."

Heroic bureaucrats view themselves as the vanguard of new government effort, the legacy of a revered president, or the unique expression of a public commitment to the needy and oppressed. People from outside of government find in them unique opportunities to conduct social change. People within government, dissatisfied with their opportunities to conduct social change within normal bureaucracies, transfer to them. As one OHA official put it, "Most of those people found in the OEO neighborhood health center program, a vehicle for their dreams and social aspirations and commitments."[31]

There are problems of sharing the dream of the heroic bureaucracy with everyone in its ranks. In the decentralized efforts of the Freedmen's Bureau and the FSA, Washington officials had frequent complaints about local administrators and the difficulty of infusing them with the same dreams, aspirations, and commitments obvious in Washington. The OHA deliberately held out for centralized administration far longer than other OEO programs in order to protect the unique esprit of the agency and to stamp individual projects with it directly from Washington. However united and radical a heroic bureaucracy might appear to those outside it or opposed to it, there are radical, moderate, and conservative interpretations of its purpose within it. Howard had a very disparate set of assistant commissioners, and President Andrew Johnson required the dismissal of the more radical assistants, such as Saxton, before the end of 1865. Tugwell and Alexander had important differences on farm ownership as a mechanism of change. Tugwell was inclined to interpret the efforts to create self-sufficient farmers from tenant farmers as romantic nostalgia and part of the "historic homesickness" for individual initiative as a solution to all public problems. Alexander came to share some of Tugwell's misgivings but understood that African American tenant farmers required a starting point for broader forms of change and that self-sufficiency for them was not nostalgia but an exodus toward reform and change. Likewise, within the OHA some officials looked to the physicians returning from the Peace Corps to do wonders in changing medicine in American, while others who borrowed from Head Start envisioned a plethora of community-based services under local control with less professional dominance and dependence, and still others looked to community organizing for a model.[32]

Heroic bureaucrats like Schorr, Howard, Tugwell, and Alexander are less inclined to stay in public service long precisely because longevity requires a degree of conformity to bureaucratic purpose that is unacceptable to them. Howard sought to end the Freedmen's Bureau, believing it to be a temporary necessity. He cut its program back to education by 1868 and guided the bureau to its end in 1872. On the other hand, the FSA and the OHA both faded eventually into less distinguishable bureaucratic forms conforming to powerful economic and political groups, sometimes with interests antithetical to their original clients.

Heroic Bureaucracies and the Grass Roots

Subordinate group members find new roles as clients, employees, and decision makers because heroic bureaucracies promote new forms of participation in public life and programs. Each of the agencies we have studied encouraged the formation of groups among the people they served to make decisions about the administration of the program and means to promote general welfare. The Union Leagues had informal support and explicit but limited protection from the Freedmen's Bureau. The neighborhood action groups of the FSA and the boards of the community health centers were new forms of participation based on new perceptions of the citizenship of the people served by the agencies.[33] Needless to say, this formation of new actors engendered opposition to the agency and its program. These new groups represented the agencies' creation of new actors in the political environment and not merely responses to an existing powerful political actor. These new groups represented the hope of heroic bureaucrats that new political actors would defend new reforms.

Community residents and their allies working for change gain general endorsement and strategic support from heroic bureaucracies. Linda Lingle recalled her VISTA days on the Sea Islands. "Back then the federal government seemed like our friend. There were risks that others and I took in being VISTA volunteers then. We had run-ins with the local police but we felt that there was someone we could call." A decade earlier, C. P. Boyd, and others in Haywood County, felt that they had a direct line to the Justice Department. Those calls could take place at odd times, as Olly Neal recounted in his story of calling Governor Bumpers at 2:00 A.M. with Leon Cooper of the OHA at his side. In Lowndes County federal officials expressed their admiration of local African American leaders for their confrontation of the local white elites. An OEO official thought it "beautiful" the way Sam Bradley opposed members of the Lowndes County board of health. In Lee County federal officials informed white local officials, "Gentlemen, you've had your chance," and funded the OEO clinic with an African American group as new sponsor. On Johns Island, the OEO officials held up grants until Bill Saunders's election as representative of his community to the OEO board was accepted.

Developing the skills of people in the programs sufficiently to permit them to carry on the program and other anticipated but unspecified forms of change by themselves is an explicit goal of heroic bureaucracies. This leadership, heroic bureaucrats assume, will spur additional and intended but unspecified change. This was perhaps best expressed by a rural rehabilitation supervisor for the African American community projects of the FSA in Alabama.

> If out of all our work there does not come a sort of group solidarity supported by a new bond of loyalties, and if out of it all there does not arise a leadership which can take over and carry on where our "management" leaves off, our new white houses are destined to become tombstones for a great idea that somebody had and grand humanitarian effort that somebody made.[34]

The agricultural advisor to the farmers of the Haywood County Farms Project is an example of the local-level technical assistance that heroic bureaucracies provide. They also provide for education and other preparation of staff and participants for the programs they are assisting. This assistance is, in part, conducted as compensation for past inequalities.

In the case of the Freedmen's Bureau and the FSA, which were decentralized, there were local agents at the county or multicounty level and with the FSA supervisors and other staff for local projects. Tom Rice indicated a significant change from the tenant farming system he knew to the participation in the Haywood County Farms Project when he talked about his "supervisor" and about how they did not have "bosses" then. The local program of the OHA was administered by men and women hired locally, people

like Olly Neal, Bill Jenkins, Jean Carney, and Steve Wilson. These administrators were much more likely to be African American than the supervisors
of the local programs of previous heroic bureaucracies. The OHA provided
many more opportunities for employment to local people to be served by
the program than the preceding agencies as well.

Neal recalled the support of the OHA and its advocacy on behalf of the
Lee County efforts.

> There's no question that the health concepts for the program were able to be dis-
> cussed and put into practice because there was a federal government out there
> that could be approached and from whom the money for these things could be
> gotten. That's what made Leon Cooper, a black man, and Bill White, a white man,
> so important. Cooper [head of the OHA] kept the underlings at OEO from de-
> stroying us and other centers. OEO brought in its VISTA people and physicians,
> like Arthur Frank, who were very committed to the ideas we were trying to im-
> plement. If we had been dealing then with other officials, we never would have
> arrived at any proof that what we were talking about made sense. They never
> would have let us do it. This gave us an opportunity to develop and prove that
> some of the things would work.

In addition to teaching others, heroic bureaucrats learn. They learn about
their own political and institutional environment and apply those lessons.
The OHA, for example, began with the modest mission of coordinating
health programs within the War on Poverty and evolved from that because
of lessons its staff acquired about the possibilities of something much more
enterprising and relevant to the needs of the poor. Most importantly, however, they learn from the people they serve. They generally come to learn to
trust in new organizations of community members they serve and to distrust
people in established centers of power such as medical schools, boards of
health, extension services, and local political and economic elites. Likewise,
they come to accept the outputs of their programs as limited, however important, and as palliatives, as one OHA officer described its programs. The
greater significance of the program, according to another OHA staff member, is the local leadership that came from OHA's effort "to find people within
that community who want to do something, and increase their ability to do
it." Olly Neal understood that he was dealing with an unusual federal agency
in the OHA. "I don't know if you can say this about many other programs
that the feds create, where the people are so enabled by their creators that
they'll let them tell them where to go."

Local leaders and heroic bureaucrats are united in taking broad approaches in dealing with a problem. This is not to suggest there is agreement about a systematic analysis of the problem. There is not. But there is a rejection of conventional wisdom about the nature of the problem and an affirmation of a need for new understanding. This new understanding involves a cluster of problems to deal with. Howard stated them well and included among the tasks of the Freedmen's Bureau:

> To rehabilitate labor, to establish the actual freedom of the late slave, to secure his testimony in the local courts where they were opened by the whites as they were here and there, to bring freedmen justice in settling past contracts and in making new ones, and to give every facility to the Northern societies for their school work.[35]

Heroic bureaucracies seem to seek out the worst places to begin work. They do choose, even among the worst cases, those that have the greatest prospect for success. But from the Sea Islands experiment forward, heroic bureaucracies have entailed or stimulated local efforts to improve housing, health, political participation, education, capital formation, and employment in places where the need for these efforts was obviously acute.

Remnants for Later Reform

Heroic bureaucracies, like redemptive organizations, have long-lasting impacts, many of which are intended but not specified. For example, Du Bois insisted that without the impact of the Freedmen's Bureau schools, the freedpeople would have been driven back to slavery. The schools, along with the churches, permitted space for leadership and the acquisition of knowledge that was sufficient "to thwart the worst designs of the new slave drivers." Those schools had an impact on the Resettlement Administration in providing them a model of local development. Myrdal noted that the colleges of the Reconstruction era prepared African American social workers and other professionals of the FSA.[36] In this way the outcome of one agency provided an impact that permitted a later agency resources with which to conduct its program and to have new outcomes, which in turn impacted a later agency.

Occasionally, there are reminders that the remnants of reforms of one era serve as a foundation for later reforms. One OHA staff member recalled visiting the health center in San Luis, New Mexico, in what had been an FSA health clinic building.[37] The first OEO neighborhood health center in the rural South was in Mound Bayou, which had its beginnings as an all-African

American incorporated community in the Freedmen's Bureau program at Davis Bend, Mississippi.[38] The site of the community clinic that Geiger and Gibson conducted for the Medical Committee for Human Rights was in Mileston, Mississippi, which was one of the few African American FSA projects large enough to have a health center. The Lee County Cooperative Clinic maintains a satellite clinic in Lakeview Arkansas, where the FSA once instituted a health center as part of its project.

Limits to Heroism

Heroic bureaucracies may be comprehensive in their approach but they are not adequate to their task in scope or duration. The Freedmen's Bureau's schools at no time enrolled more than 10 percent of the freedchildren in the South; the FSA enrolled 1,151 African American farm families in its land-redistribution programs when a thousand times as many needed assistance; community health centers are much more extensive but still do not reach all those in need with the services required. All three bureaucracies met fewer needs of fewer people after cutbacks in their appropriations or the cessation of their operation. Significantly, each of the heroic bureaucracies in this study found themselves with lower appropriations because of the need to fund a war or pay off war debts.

In addition to these limits, heroic bureaucracies curtail their programs and their efforts to fend off criticism of their "paternalism." Howard took satisfaction in reducing the relief rations of the four million refugees and African Americans from about 150,000 a day to half as many by September 1865. This measure warded off charges that the Freedmen's Bureau was too generous.[39] Heroic bureaucrats are entrapped in dispelling the stereotypes and prejudices of their critics about their clients. Consequently, stringent measures were used to prove to others that African Americans will work, are credit worthy, or can administer large programs. Fortunately, even as heroic bureaucracies undergo criticism from the right, they have critics among redemptive organizations who chastise them for falling short of their intentions.

Relatedly, heroic bureaucrats sometimes extol inappropriate models for local conditions. This is part of their attempt to replicate idyllic conditions or institutions in low-income communities. Even as the reformers on the Sea Islands sought to "plant the Northern pine" and to foster a black yeomanry, the "Northern pine" was giving way to factories, and the New England yeoman and his family was being recruited to them as a labor force. Similarly, the FSA created family farm units that were important to foster political change, but they were not economically viable in an age of mechanized agriculture. Finally, the OHA and especially its HEW successor agencies were inclined to conceptualize the health centers as forms of medical care where dedicated health professionals, who were in very short supply for this purpose, could innovate a blend of health care and community organizing. This conceptualization diminished the significant and dynamic role of local people in administrative and ancillary service roles.

Part of the history of each heroic bureaucracy, despite efforts to anticipate its critics, is its critics' disparagement of its outcomes, denial of its impacts, and restoration of the prejudices and biases that the heroic bureaucracy set out to change. The opponents of the heroic bureaucracies generally influence the historical judgment of the agency as well as its demise. In two of the four clinics of this study, intense media coverage of federal dealings with the center's administration and board thoroughly discredited them, although there was little or no substance to the charges made against them. This type of discrediting of local achievements had precedent in President Johnson's "fact finding" effort on the Freedmen's Bureau, which was particularly critical of Saxton. The most frequent charges against a heroic bureaucracy are paternalism and its allegedly mistaken assumption that a group of people need assistance.[40] These criticisms contend that the meritorious among the needy are capable of competing in American society, which has equality of opportunity and which rewards merit. Government programs do not provide but sap initiative. The meritorious, these criticisms continue, do not need government assistance, and those who are not meritorious do not deserve it. A second frequent charge is that a heroic bureaucracy attempts to reach too high a level of service for its clients. Edith Green was incredulous that the community health centers provided services not available to her. The congressional committee investigating the FSA found fault with the agency for attempting to raise the living standards of its clients to those near the highest prevailing in a community.

Shared Hopes and Expectations

In many respects, a heroic bureaucracy does little more than catch up with the efforts of other actors and their change efforts. Its revolutionary expectations are basically lessons they acquire from members of the community of memory and of redemptive organizations about the nature of subordinate groups and their problems. Technically speaking, the Freedmen's Bureau did not begin schools for freedpeople but nurtured them by supporting the efforts of others. It never supported local efforts to the degree that local people undertook them.[41] Similarly, the Resettlement Administration may be seen as the first official action of land acquisition that local African Americans had been attempting since Reconstruction. Likewise, the Medical Committee for Human Rights provided H. Jack Geiger the work in Mileston, Mississippi and the ideas of local leaders. He combined these with experience in South Africa to shape the formation of the first community health centers of the OHA.

The work of the community of memory is less documented than the work of redemptive organizations and heroic bureaucracies. In fact, it is the record of these latter that provide us the best written record of the community of memory. The unwritten stories within the community of memory provide analysis of social problems and goals for social change that most often exceed those of heroic bureaucracies and redemptive organizations. From the time of Saxton forward, the community of memory seems to be the repository of the hope and the harbinger of analysis and aspirations of later redemptive organizations and heroic bureaucracies. Together local leaders, redemptive organizations, and heroic bureaucracies contribute to a process of change. The nature of that change is what we examine next.

CHAPTER 10

Progress: Race, Leadership, and Change

In many ways the community health centers resembled the early schools for the freedpeople as reforms. In both instances a federal agency combined with local leaders to begin a set of services of unprecedented scope and quality. Both the schools and the health centers had integrated staffs who were willing to provide whites and blacks better services than prevailing practice provided. Like the teachers before them, many of the physicians and staff members of the community health centers were regarded as disturbers of the peace. Initially, they were not granted professional recognition by local medical associations, in most instances, and were ostracized. The staffs of the health centers lived with the fear of violent reprisal for their work, just as teachers in the schools had lived with fear one hundred years before them in the same communities. The provision of space for the health centers was opposed, just as space for school houses had been.

The staff of the health centers, no less than those of the bureau schools, were troublemakers because of the "mischief" of greater social equality that their services implied. Blumenthal earned the opposition of the medical association of Lee County because, in the words of one of its members, "He's going to the churches and telling Negroes all they have to do to get what they want is rear up."[1] Actually the staffs, like the teachers before them, were divided about the political nature of their work and the degree of change that was possible or desirable. But whatever their own concerns, their work, like that of the teachers before them, exceeded the preference of local authorities and elites, although it fell short of their worst fears. The staff and board members understood the essence of the local opposition to their efforts as a battle for control of services. This understanding, in the instance of Sara Sauls, led them to turn down an offer of financial support. It was unacceptable because it entailed control over the program by those who had opposed it and who intended that the program be far more limited than what was possible and needed. Du Bois had his fictionalized school principal, who was based on Thorn at Calhoun School, do the very same thing for the very same reason.

The controversies over the health centers and the reprisals and discredit that came in the early 1980s have to do with the success of the centers, not their failures. The centers, no less than the schools, land redistribution, and other earlier changes, exceeded the forms of public service and social capital that existed and that some authorities and elites wanted to keep in limited supply. The schools, and the health centers, were opposed and then limited in their role because they were pockets of subtle and overt resistance to the political and economic subordination of African Americans in the rural South.

Reform, Retreat, and Reaction

Segregated waiting rooms, long waits, demand of proof of payment before services, all these experiences appear frequently in the narratives. Bridges, drawn up to permit luxury boats to pass under them, not only impeded travel to Charleston hospitals but reminded the Reverend Mr. Goodwin of the important and obvious class differences that separated African American residents on Johns Island from health services in Charleston. Jean Carney's all-day unsuccessful wait to gain medical attention for her grandmother reminded her about the caste norms of racial subordination. Less common, but also reported, were incidents of physician incompetence, abuse of patients, and withdrawal of services as retaliation for the political action of a patient. These are the starting places of efforts to improve health care.

Initially and at the height of their operation, the community health centers deliberately remedied these conditions. They provided direct access to several new services such as medical care, pharmacy services, and dental care. They charged according to the ability to pay and did not withhold services because of an inability to pay. The integrated staffs served black and white clients and thereby placed these community health centers in the forefront of integrated efforts in their counties. They provided transportation. They developed new forms of care like speech therapy and alcohol and drug dependence rehabilitation. The centers also included preventive services such as health education and nutrition programs such as Women, Infant and Children's Food Program (WIC) and Meals on Wheels among their services. The innovative forms of medical health care gave community health center patients access to a wide array of integrated services that represented change in the provision of health services not only locally but within the health care system. Several of the community health centers won national awards and commendations from professional organizations and even the federal government.

Evaluations by public health professionals strongly support the contention of those directly involved with the community health center that they were administered well and provided taxpayers with their money's worth of services.[2] Demonstrating the ability to run a million-dollar program well and effectively was part of changing the community's self-perception and one of the centers' purposes for some administrators. Neal's "greatest pride is that no one can say that black folks, in fact, did not run" the Lee County Co-operative Clinic. Because of the community health center, the community residents saw their first African American physicians and dentists, male and female. An African American certified public accountant was found to audit the books in Lee County, as part of the center staff and board's determination to express self-worth through community health center management.

In addition, the centers provided important and new training and employment opportunities for local men and women. They employed as many as one hundred staff, most of whom were local residents. The clinic sponsored some staff members through training to acquire skills they needed for the new positions it was creating. The local economy offered few comparable opportunities. Even major new investments, like the GE plant in Lowndes County or Kiawah Island near Johns Island, did not provide as many skilled jobs for local people. They relied more heavily on people from outside of the county for their skilled workforce. Nor did these developments contribute as much to raise the standard of care and well-being of those who were the least well off in the counties.

The centers were successful locally but were also part of national movements for greater equality that included changes in health care. The change intended in the community health center movement included new forms of health care for the very poor that shifted the locus of care from hospitals to the community and from an exclusive emphasis on illness treatment to a new emphasis on preventing illness and promoting health. The movement envisioned new types of health care providers such as nurse practitioners, new roles for community people in dealing with health care, new training for physicians, and new definitions of health that entailed the economic and social order. Of the reforms in health care attempted in the last quarter-century, the community health centers are among the most successful.[3]

Like the change efforts before them, all four community health centers underwent extensive conflict over control of the community health center but yet continue in some fashion. In the case of Lee County most of the conflict between African American residents and the white political and medical elite occurred before the center began. The center continues relatively intact but with a less comprehensive array of services because of budget cuts. Ironically, the hospital in the county is closed because of the sort of financial problems that have plagued many small hospitals and those serving low-income and uninsured groups. In Lowndes County the unity of the African American community about the health center dissipated after Steve Wilson's departure. The pressures of reduced funding produced fissures in the African American community and protests of one segment of the community over reductions in services, new fee schedules, and personnel changes. The center is presently administered by another health program within the black belt. On the Sea Islands the health center was removed from the control of the board and given to a new board composed of the medical and political elites of Charleston. The original Sea Island board still manages a $3 million program of home health services, a nursing home, a pharmacy, and laboratory services. It also maintains ownership of the building that the clinic occupies and where health services are still provided.

In Haywood County local politicians, at the urging of federal officials, formed a new board to conduct the health program. The new board members dismissed Jean Carney as a condition for continued government funding but eventually, on June 30, 1986, stopped services when federal funds ended. The clinic resumed operation in late 1987 under the administration of a hospital in nearby Fayette County. But leaders of the community health center doubted the commitment of that hospital to the rural poor of Haywood County. The hospital administrator had discharged an indigent patient in a case that made national news because of its apparent callousness. An uninsured twenty-one-year-old diabetic man, admitted to the hospital in a serious condition, had a $9,400 debt at the hospital. The administrator helped him out of his hospital bed and assisted him to the parking lot, where he left him. Friends found the sick man there and took him home, where he died twelve hours later. Official investigations exonerated the hospital from any wrongdoing, but the incident was a flashback to the conditions the health center had set out to change.[4] The hospital stopped services at the Haywood County clinic in 1989. At present, a community organization, JONAH, is participating in efforts to resume services with state funding. JONAH is a predominantly African American organization whose goals are similar to those of the Union Leagues and the Haywood County Civic and Welfare League.

These changes were part of a reaction to reform, and like previous re-actions, this one included discrediting the programs and their leaders. Audits became ordinary occurrences. Federal troops had inspected the confusing titles to land of the freedmen on the Sea Islands, in 1865, and removed those whom they could for violation of the boundaries of the title and other con-ditions. Now federal auditors came in to examine confusing arrangements of indirect costs and regulations with different federal agencies and blamed local leaders and administrators for any shortcomings as much as they could. Publicity about the audits far exceeded the problems that the audits uncov-ered. If one audit proved fruitless, another was begun. In the extreme case of the Sea Island Comprehensive Health Care Corporation on Johns Island, there were forty audits. The result of those audits was payment by the fed-eral government to the corporation of $261,000 for the conduct of services while federal funds were suspended. These audits and the suspicion over the management of the community health centers contrasted sharply with public awards, formal and informal praise, positive publicity, and favorable evaluations that the community health centers had received from agencies and researchers inside and outside of government, just a year or two earlier. The audits suggested incompetence. The rumors of administrators with luxury cars suggested corruption.[5]

Officials of the Reagan administration, especially, reduced the number and changed the nature of the community health centers. Several changes were entailed. First, the broad relation of health care to poverty that was part of the original OEO health program was narrowed. The health centers resembled limited, but still innovative, medical interventions with less em-phasis on preventive health measures after the adjustments of the Nixon and Carter years.[6] In the Reagan years these preventive measures were ended in the federal effort to have the centers emulate "reasonable" criteria of utilization and cost-benefit ratios based on private health care. The Reagan administration also reduced the number of community health centers. In 1982 alone, Reagan administrators defunded 239 out of the 827 community health centers.[7] For those that remained, the private practice of medicine became the explicit emphasis and model for health care for underserved areas and the community health centers.[8] Thus, what had started as a reform of the inadequacies of American health care was itself reformed to conform with the system that it was intended to change. New public forms of health care became more like private forms of health care.

Social Capital

The subordination of rural African Americans required public programs of minimal investment in social capital. Health care, education, and civil rights are all, at root, social capital, the means to produce and reproduce human beings. As capital is the means by which we produce and distribute goods and services, social capital is the investment we make in health, education, housing, communities, and culture to reproduce people.

Social capital is also the root of democratic equality. Conflicts over it are disputes over whether some people will have less of it than others, how much investment in people is appropriate in view of our expectations of them and their economic and social roles, and whether or not different amounts of it are warranted by "natural" differences among sets of human beings. These conflicts ultimately entail a dispute over whether or not some human beings, on the basis of the color of their skin or some other characteristic, are intended for subordinate economic and political roles. Such conflicts engulfed the early education programs for the freedpeople and the struggle over the civil rights of African Americans in the 1860s and 1870s as well as the 1960s and 1970s. These were radically democratic eras because some new policies and practices challenged the legal and social discrimination against a subordinate group of people and its basis in "natural" differences. These policies expanded social capital for subordinate groups and thus provided them new opportunities to meet new expectations of greater equality.

In contrast to these eras, for most of the time since the Civil War, social capital in the rural South came from large landowners to produce, reproduce, and maintain an agricultural workforce.[9] Because the work was relatively unskilled and there was an oversupply of laborers, the landowners spent little social capital to maintain their labor force. Low wages and low social capital investment went hand in hand. New forms or larger amounts of social capital were opposed. Schools of the freedpeople, for example, were burned, terror discouraged political participation, and severe economic reprisals often followed the African Americans' efforts to find better jobs or to organize for better working conditions. Sharecropping was the ordinary economic role for African Americans, and the poor schools, poor housing, poor health, and poor nutrition of agricultural workers were line items in a budget of social capital spent to produce and maintain sharecroppers. When agricultural production changed and there was less demand for labor, African Americans in the rural South migrated in large numbers because there was no work and an absolute paucity of social capital on which to survive. They moved to other areas, largely urban areas of the South and North, where employment opportunities and social capital were better.

In general, investment in social capital still comes from and follows upon the needs of private capital and has as its central purpose the production, reproduction, and maintenance of a labor supply. There are individuals, generally with large amounts of private capital, who maintain that their era's amounts and forms of social capital are sufficient to reproduce people and prepare them for their economic and political roles and that no new public funds need be expended. They trust the market to determine the supply and demand of labor, wages, and, consequently, social capital. Their policies reinforce or increase class differences. Then there are other individuals, generally with small amounts of private capital, who maintain that their era's forms and amounts of social capital are insufficient because they produce, reproduce, and maintain inadequate standards for human life and do not prepare people for expanded and improved economic and political roles. The market is not trusted to determine social capital because it distributes goods and services among people in proportion to their present position. Those with more already tend to get more resources when the market allocates them. Consequently, this group contends that new forms and increased amounts of social capital from public sources are needed to raise people's standard of living and prepare them for new economic and political roles. Their policies are intended to increase upward mobility for those in lower socioeconomic classes.

Generally, the differences in social capital supply, forms, and uses are mediated along a center segment of the continuum from private to public sources. There are times, such as Reconstruction, the New Deal, and the War on Poverty, when public policy shifts temporarily further to the public source end of the continuum of social capital. Government begins to spend more money on new forms of social services to achieve some new form of democratic equality or at least to reduce glaring disparities among groups of Americans. Those policies are subsequently amended, and public policy moves back toward the private end of the continuum. The Nixon and Carter administrations adjusted social capital supply, forms, and uses from the Great Society years in this manner. The Reagan administration shifted to the private source end of the social capital spectrum dramatically.[10]

Social capital includes investment in people, as people, and not only in relation to the needs of an economy or specific economic sector. But ordinarily social capital is spent to reproduce people as a labor force or what some economists call "human capital."[11] When a group of people have a subordinate role in the economy, the social capital invested in them is modest. When people have no role in the economy, social capital may not be invested in them at all. Whenever social capital exceeds the minimum needed to preserve an existing workforce and challenges the private control of social capital, there is conflict. The health centers were controversial precisely because, as new forms and larger amounts of social capital, they departed from the private provision of health care. They were controversial later as the private pattern was imposed on them.

The provision of permanent space for services to the low-wage workers or the unemployed is often the clearest signal for some opponents that social capital has exceeded its limited purpose and triggers their reaction. This is one reason that it is rare that construction costs are included in social programs. The Freedmen's Bureau, the FSA, and the OHA were all exceptions. Howard interpreted the legislation of the Freedmen's Bureau very broadly to permit support of the construction of schools that were often burned. The FSA built homes, schools, and, sometimes, clinics for tenant farmers. The OHA also provided funds for health center buildings.

These construction funds brought controversy. When the OHA provided funds to the all-white board of health in Lowndes County with which to construct a clinic building, there was no protest. But transferring it to a new board organized and controlled by African Americans brought on conflict. Attempts to provide funds to the Lee County Cooperative Clinic group for the construction of its clinic building set off one of the most severe controversies in the OHA and in the antipoverty program in Arkansas. When the community health centers program was transferred to HEW, construction funds were no longer part of the program. When the Sea Island Community Development Corporation found sufficient funds to buy fifty-five acres of land, they found, like others, that their problems escalated. Bill Jenkins pointed out precisely, "As long as we were in those trailers, we had no problems." Permanent space for health services suggests an ongoing investment in the health care of poor people that exceeds the practice of investment needed to reproduce a poor workforce with limited employment possibilities. Poor health came in a package called poverty that included high unemployment, low wages, unskilled work, below-average education, substandard housing, and contaminated environments. Whatever the human costs of these factors, they also produced a surplus of tractor drivers for "Mr. Charlie," to use John Wilson's term for low-wage laborers, and maids and custodians for condominium developments such as Kiawah Island.

The narrators of this study worked on health care but dreamed of improved factors in the re-production and maintenance of people, for example, housing, education, political participation, and most of all improved employment. The health center was only one form of social capital but a new and expanded amount that was available. When other forms were available, these same people developed them as well. In Lee County and Lowndes County the leaders in health care established new avenues to credit and capital through the formation of credit unions. The health centers provided training and work separate from the existing employment patterns of their respective counties and part of a vision of expanded services and employment for local residents. Improved water supply and sanitation were new forms of social capital that three of the centers brought to their communities. Improved housing was a project of two of the centers. Ironically, some of these measures repeated earlier, forgotten efforts. For example, administrators at Beaufort-Jasper introduced a low-cost model home to the area around Penn Center, just as Saxton had done one hundred years before them. Political participation is also social capital or a resource for human development. It was in short supply when men like Tom Ishmael and Sam Bradley worked in support of white officials in order to earn a path to voting for themselves and other African Americans. As long as that path was blocked to exemplary but not white-made black leaders, African American residents of these areas lived in fear of the law and lacked personal security, a basic component of human well-being.

The health centers, as expanded forms of social capital, were political and economic threats. They attracted and invested new forms of social capital apart from existing wage employment opportunities, just as previous reform efforts had attempted to do. This established a flow of social capital investment apart from private capital locally, and forms and amounts of social capital investment greater than those from local and state public sources. Ultimately, the centers' role as social capital explains the ongoing local opposition to them and changes in federal policy toward them.

Social Capital Entrepreneurs

The perspective on the health centers as forms of social capital suggests that their organizers were social capital entrepreneurs. They sought capital to invest in people in excess of traditional, private forms of social capital investment. This increased investment was intended to produce a higher standard of housing, health care, and education that expressed the inherent dignity of local people and that prepared them better for expanded economic and political roles. Health efforts spilled over so easily to housing, water and sewerage, education, and other programs because they were all instances of improved social investment in people. Groups like the Sea Island Community Development Corporation dragged reluctant federal partners into investments they were able but hesitant to make. Bill Runyon, for example, recalled the reluctance of HUD to lend money to build housing on Johns Island. The housing required additional investments for water and sewerage as well. This success hinged on an entrepreneurial ability to identify and attract forms of investment from public agencies in areas they would ordinarily ignore. Private sources of capital also ignored these places unless their development would benefit people outside the area. The development of resort condominiums on the Sea Islands is an example.

Not surprisingly, the narratives point out that race and class distinctions apply even among social capital entrepreneurs. Jim Martin, a white man, was able to obtain a letter from a bank in Charleston promising a loan for the housing project on Johns Island. When Martin left and was replaced with an African American man, the bank tried to renege on the loan. Similarly, Bill Saunders pointed out, "The Penn School survived because you had whites teaching there. There were good schools run by blacks and put out of business by whites. Avery Institute survived because it had white leadership. But other schools in Charleston with black leadership did not survive."

There are examples of social capital entrepreneurship preceding the health centers and related to them. The Freedmen's Bureau provided school buildings, hospitals, and health care. The FSA provided land, school buildings, and clinics. We have some idea that the initiative of the freedpeople of the South far exceeded the capacity of the Freedmen's Bureau to respond in terms of support for education. But lost to our view are the various individuals, like Richard Lynch in Savannah, who saw to it that there were targets for federal funds and that the return on the money spent was substantial.[12] We also know that the FSA created a set of landowners by its social capital. The FSA paid the poll tax of participating farmers as part of its program of change in social capital forms. The clients of the FSA programs led later efforts to expand the political participation of African Americans in the rural South.[13]

Redemptive organizations also played the role of social capital entrepreneurs. The Union Leagues were the first to encourage and improve political participation and to fashion new citizens. Citizenship Schools, SNCC, and various local organizations would work later to improve the status of the newly enfranchised through the ballot box and the power to choose their own public officials. Similarly, various associations of relief for freedpeople provided new schools in cooperation with local organizations of the freedpeople themselves. African American agricultural workers also organized to improve the conditions and wages of work and thus add to the income and security of all families of the area. Other groups organized to provide resources for them in their efforts or to defend them when reprisals occurred.[14] These social capital entrepreneurial organizations sometimes linked distant people with the need for resources in their area. The Lowndes County Freedom Organization acquired financial assistance from the diaspora of former residents, especially those in Detroit, for its economic development efforts. Prior to that, Thorn demonstrated mastery at recruiting resources for the Calhoun Colored School from distant people. She did her best to make them feel some degree of responsibility for the conditions she and the faculty at Calhoun addressed.

Parents provided social capital, especially education. At the time of the Freedmen's Bureau, freedmen and freedwomen sought and provided for education and other services to give their children a better chance in life than they had. Olly Neal, Jr., recounted the extraordinary efforts of his father to build a home in Marianna where the schools were better and to sell a farm close by for a farm far distant because it gave resources to the family to provide for the education of Neal and his brothers. Neal remembers that his father would "always do what he thought was best for his children." Parthenia Kelly explained how political change encouraged her and her daughter to undertake the frightening task of challenging practices of segregated transportation and education. Many narrators explain their actions in terms of parental roles. In the face of their own fear of the possible violent retaliation of others to their efforts to register to vote, some of the people found their courage in their preference for their children's future. As Sam Bradley recalled his reasoning, "I have children and if that's [registering to vote] the last good deed in this life I can do to make it better for them, I'm going to do it." Parthenia Kelly added, "I was really thinking about my children" when she decided to register to vote.

As so many of the narratives suggest, parents became social capital itself, not just its providers. Their example of resistance to the forms of inequality they faced and of acquiring the resources they needed to improve themselves were important means to the narrators to aspire beyond subordination. The number of references to parents in our narratives is striking, especially mothers who taught school and set examples for their children in acquiring their own education. Olly Neal remembered that his mother attended classes over many years to acquire her degree in 1959, "before any of her children." Her efforts required going to school in the summer and regular travel. She took classes offered in Forrest City by Philander Smith College. She would also go to Saturday classes in Fayetteville, which required leaving home about 3:00 A.M. "Whoever had some classes, she would go to them." Examples such as hers suggested the willingness to sacrifice to acquire what was worthwhile.

When the narrators worked to improve health care, they continued roles as social capital entrepreneurs that they and others filled before. They raised scarce resources from varied sources to invest in people that others had ignored and declared surplus. The Douglas Community Health and Recreation Council brought to their part of Haywood County student groups to conduct free physical examinations to local residents, staff and funding to begin and continue health services, and finally a new building for the clinic. This building, like the clinic buildings in the other areas, was the largest social service building in the county. The Lowndes County Health Services Association also played a social capital entreprenuerial role when it restored to the county the equipment that had been removed from the health center. They also brought to the county for the first time funds to supplement the nutrition of infants, pregnant women, and recent mothers in the WIC program. The Reverend Mr. Goodwin raised similar scarce resources from the Washington area for use on Johns Island. Rural Mission not only attracted church funds for the first health care program on Johns Island but the weekend and eventually full-time services of a physician. From these beginnings, the Sea Island Comprehensive Health Care Corporation brought the organization to bring a new building for the clinic, a nursing home, housing development, and sewage treatment facility. The Lee County Cooperative Clinic gathered and provided social capital from the time Sara Sauls went door to door and church to church collecting for the health center. The housing project it constructed and the program of clean water supply it initiated for Lee County and the rural South are other forms of social capital and exemplify the centers' entrepreneurial role.

The Nature of Change

When one examines the succession of change efforts, it is apparent that change in social capital has occurred even if specific reforms have been retracted. Mattie Lee Holcombe Moorer is sure that Lowndes County has been "blessed" with change and has more hope than before because of the

health center. It cares for women and children in a manner far superior
to anything Moorer remembers as past practice. She compares the health
center with her own experience of birthing her first child.

> When my baby birthed in 1931, I could not deliver and my daddy had to ride
> 21 miles to get a doctor. My father kept good horses and they were well trained
> and they would travel, so he speeded. The doctor had a good horse. He got his
> little black satchel while his man, who worked for him, hitched his horse up to the
> buggy and put its harness on. And they came on. When they got here, I was right
> at the point. He had a choice to make, save me or the baby. So then, I never will
> forget, he hardly sterilized the knife and he worked those hours and pulled my
> baby and broke his neck and that was the best he could do. And I don't forget that.
> Maybe that is the reason, I went all the way to help the clinic keep going. I
> donated hours just to sit down and talk with the mothers to get them to come to
> the clinic. . . . They get the type of milk they need. They get everything they
> need, right here in Lowndes County. That's why Lowndes County has hope.

Moorer is part of a generation that remembers, with some resentment,
going without resources and services. She and others remember that African American school children received school books only after they were
outdated and no longer fit for use by the white students. They remember
that schools for African American children were grossly inadequate structures without basic services like electricity. When new buildings did come,
in the late 1940s, this generation understands them as cynical efforts to support spurious claims of local officials that separate schools were equal and
to forestall the federal demands for educational change that came eventually
with *Brown v. Board of Education*.[15] Children, like Earl Rice, were bused
long hours, past schools for whites, to deliver them to their segregated and
second-rate institutions. Moorer remembers selling eggs too valuable for
her to eat. Likewise, Septima Clark remembered farm workers on Johns
Island suffering from malnutrition.

In contrast to these memories, African Americans may now claim a
greater share of the resources they produce, a greater share of public resources, and hold public officials more accountable for denying or withholding basic services. Clark is a particularly poignant example of this. She was
instructed in an institution with limited African American control, Avery Institute; she taught in a white-dominated school system that fired her for her
NAACP membership; but she died in a setting initiated and conducted by an
integrated group with African American leadership and federal support. As
Bill Jenkins observed:

It is wonderful that we were able to care for Ms. Clark before she died. She gave most of her life trying to better the life and livelihood of her fellow people. I was glad she ended up here. She got the best care we could afford. There's a book out now and she's on the cover.[16] They took her picture while she was in the nursing home. It had most of the black women who had made a difference.

John Wilson, as we have seen, linked his and others' new understanding of their rights to public service to their participation in the community health center.

Lee County Cooperative Clinic opened up the eyes of a lot of people. It's been an inspiration for a lot of things we never dreamed of: water, sewers, paved streets. We never thought of things like that except in Marianna. We saw those things as white folks' business. But after LCCC, we were part of it.

The narrators emphasized that achieving a fair portion of resources required protest of existing systems of service distribution in the past. As Septima Clark succinctly judged, "You have to fight to live in America." That fight contested the inadequacy of public services and wage labor for African Americans in the rural South in the past. The protests of the civil rights movement were over insufficient public resources, especially the vote. The origin of the Sea Islands center was in protest to conditions of poverty and hunger. The Lowndes County health center had its origins in protest of the original board's willingness to relinquish the funding for the program rather than to reorganize it. The roles of protest in the achievement of fairer portions are limited beginnings to a political economy of preference. The community leaders of the narratives, and their predecessors, often articulate a vision of the economics they prefer. At its base, this preferred economy provides the opportunity for all people to work at jobs that pay enough to support families in security and perhaps comfort. Achieving a portion of public resources for education, housing, or health care are only steps to move from an economy of the "cotton dollar," as Bob Mants put it, and from jobs as "Mr. Charlie's tractor driver," in the words of John Wilson. The greatest disappointment of Olly Neal was his inability to develop from the health center new forms of work. His disappointment accentuates the ultimate goals of these efforts: to transform the nature of economic activity, to increase employment, to improve the conditions of work, and to increase and improve social capital for these objectives.

In addition to a new economy of portions, a second clear form of change is the reduction of subordination. More services in these communities has meant less petty subordination. One person in Lowndes County, for example, estimates there are no segregated waiting rooms in the physicians' offices in the county because of the health center. If there are, she did not know of them because the physicians she uses have ended the practice of separating patients on the basis of skin color. Extreme forms of the subordination of African Americans, especially unpunished violence toward them and extra-legal violence toward them by those in authority, have also declined. Moorer judged that Lowndes County is "blessed" with John Hulett, who, in her estimation, "is the best high sheriff I have ever known anywhere from Lowndes County. Because he does not kill. He does not shoot. He doesn't beat prisoners up." Moorer's assessment of Hulett suggests that the clearest form of change and progress in race relations is that white mobs and law officials don't kill, injure, or ignore the legal rights of African Americans and their allies as often as before. When such violence does occur, the law is more likely to protect the rights of the injured and to punish perpetrators of violence.

Jesse Cannon knew of three instances over thirty years in which African American men had shot white police officers. He used those incidents as measures of change in the legal protection of African Americans from police. In 1937 Albert Gooden was lynched in the aftermath of the shooting death of a white deputy. There was no evidence that Gooden had killed him and much evidence that the deputy had used excessive violence that started the shooting. Gooden was a moderately successful African American and a target for white resentment. He was taken from police custody and lynched.[17] In 1943 Burton Dodson fled Fayette County for his life in the aftermath of the death of a member of a deputized mob. His trial in 1959 sparked the voter-registration effort in Fayette and Haywood counties. In 1960 Willie Jones was tried and ultimately found not guilty for shooting a sheriff who was out of uniform and threatening him. Cannon reflected on these events and remarked, "We knew something had changed when a black man killed a white policeman and he was not lynched."

There is less violence and more services, in large measure, because there are more African American voters, African American public officials, and white elected officials dependent on African American voters. The narratives convey the fear of disfranchised people of police and the unfair treatment they received. Traffic violations are frequently cited. C. P. Boyd was arrested and fined for faulty brakes. John Hulett sued Alabama over its justice-of-the-peace system all the way to the U.S. Supreme Court because of his conviction on a speeding charge. Linda Lingle recalled that her only fear on Johns Islands was an instance when police stopped her one night and berated her for driving with a "nigger."

The extremes of disfranchisement and disadvantage were cumulative and sinisterly synergistic. Legal and extra-legal obstacles prevented African American men and women from voting, and their absence from the electorate meant that issues affecting them did not find their way into the campaigns of candidates for public office. Since the political campaigns had little bearing on their lives and needs, many disfranchised African Americans showed little concern with the campaigns and politics in general. Their consequent apathy became another reason that the needs of local, African American residents did not become campaign issues. Consequently, the education of African American children suffered, as did other essential services that compromised the living conditions of everyone. The poverty of African Americans and their poor education supported the judgment that most of them, according to conventional wisdom, were not ready to exercise the franchise well. This conclusion validated the wisdom of the legal and extra-legal obstacles to their registration and voting.[18] This was a spiral of disadvantage, according to Myrdal. For Du Bois, it was worse. A disfranchised group, he wrote, "is worse than helpless. It is a menace, not simply to itself, but to every other group in the community . . . it will be ignorant; it will be the plaything of mobs; and it will be insulted by caste restrictions."[19]

There is an upward spiral that comes with increased political participation. The more subordinate groups participate in politics, the less likely it is that repression will continue. As that repression subsides, participation increases. That increased participation includes new roles to find new forms and amounts of public services and social capital. The new participation recounted here includes the health centers, of course, but extends further, from registering African Americans as voters to the election of African American candidates to positions that oversee the allocation of resources for schools and other services. These new positions instituted and preserve the new politics of portions that Jim Crow denied and violence suppressed before.

The new politics of portions has severe limits. African American elected officials are more successful in acquiring new services for the general public than in closing the gap in services between races and socioeconomic groups. People in poverty, African Americans and others who have a lower standard of social capital, acquire new and better services as a consequence of their legislative action to benefit all Americans. Major legislative efforts to address directly the conditions of those in severe need have far less success, and those that address the severe needs of African Americans have almost no success.

This is not a new development. Direct efforts to narrow the gap between the poor and the rich, subordinate and dominant groups, blacks and whites, like the Civil Rights Act of 1990, have run into consistent and similar criticism. The Tennessee legislature rejected the Fifteenth Amendment, in 1870, as "odious class legislation. . . . It singles out the colored race as its special wards and favorites." Similarly, President Andrew Johnson vetoed the Freedmen's Bureau bill in 1865 because a system of support "for one class or color of our people more than another" was not consistent with constitutional principles.[20] The consequence of this form of egalitarianism limits the ability of politically weak minorities to achieve change. Representatives of these groups are more likely to find success in providing new amounts of social capital for everyone than new forms of social capital for those in greatest need. McElwee and his African American colleagues, in Tennessee in the 1880s, were able to acquire major new appropriations for an asylum in west Tennessee to serve the mentally ill. They acquired only modest increases in appropriations for the education of African American teachers. And they were mainly unsuccessful in ending existing discriminatory practices.

C. P. Boyd insists, as do other narrators, that his political preference is not control by African Americans for the benefit of African Americans but a new politics that invests more resources in people who have the fewest resources. "The democratic ideal involves liberty and justice and the ideal of equality. That summarizes my whole philosophy and attitude." His belief sounds remarkably similar to the "American Creed," as Myrdal annunciated it. Charles Smith also disavowed control for the exclusive benefit of African Americans. He summarized a common preference about power and its relation to new forms and amounts of public service. "Whoever happens to be the kind of person who has the best ideas, that idea ought to then be adopted by all people. . . . If we were to develop all of the people and utilize that human resource, together, we could do some of the kinds of things that need to be done." Bill Saunders echoed this sentiment on Johns Island and explained that he seeks only the opportunity for African Americans to compete without social and legal hindrance and impediments. But perhaps Pitson Brady said it most concisely in Lee County. He ran for political office because "we needed representation. . . . We decided we should have a part of what was going on; we didn't want all of it, just a part of it."

A limit to the new politics of portions is the difficulty African American candidates have in acquiring elected public office in order to practice them. A detailed examination of local elections in the black belt revealed that African American candidates often gained a plurality of the votes, as much as 40 percent of the vote. But in the ensuing run-off primary election to determine a majority candidate, they lost to white candidates.[21] This happened in the Charleston area as well, where both Bill Saunders and the Reverend McKinley Washington had pluralities in primary elections for the state senate but lost in run-off elections for the nomination.

African American candidates for elected office have the greatest prospect for success in elections in which African American voters form a large majority and vote as a bloc. These conditions meant victory for the Reverend Mr. Washington, Jean Carney, C. P. Boyd, and other narrators, some of whom served on school boards. They also provided the margins of victory for James Rapier, Samuel McElwee, and other African American politicians of the nineteenth century. They all ran in single-member districts where African Americans were 50 percent or more of the voters. This is indicative of the national pattern in which most African American elected officials represent African American districts. In 1988, 4,400 of the 6,829 African American elected officials were in the South, and the vast majority of them represented single-member, predominantly African American districts. Of course, this is itself an indication of the new politics of portions. But it also illustrates the limits to and the difficulty with such politics. John Hulett and Uralee Haynes won countywide elections in Lowndes County, which is 75 percent African American. Where African American voters do not have an overwhelming majority, African American candidates have smaller prospects for success. Only in 1990 did the first African American candidate for a countywide office in Arkansas win an election. That was for coroner in Lee County. Such a candidate must build a coalition of a solid bloc of African American support and a sizable minority of the white vote. The prospects of success increase if candidates move to win more white votes even at the risk of losing African American support. They do this most successfully if they distance themselves from the politics of protest and the politics of portions that have meant the greatest gain for African Americans of low income. This applies to a more modest degree to white Democratic candidates in the South as well, but African American candidates have more difficulty proving their distance from the politics of portions and the politics of protest.[22]

The changes recounted in the narratives suggest modest progress toward a grand vision of democratic equality and human dignity. Nonetheless, it is clear that public services are distributed more fairly to African Americans and that there is less unpunished violence toward them. There are not enough public services, just more. And there is still too much racial violence, although there is less.

Disturbing Trends

There are also obvious differences in the political participation of African Americans since 1963 when Sam Bradley made plans to register to vote and was told by a white friend that arrangements had been made to kill him for doing so. He has run for political office, unsuccessfully, but other African Americans, including an early SNCC field worker in Lowndes County, became elected officials there. Bill Saunders in Charleston became the head of the county Democratic party. Olly Neal was appointed deputy prosecutor recently and currently serves on a panel to oversee a federal court-ordered reapportionment of state legislative districts. This provides him a new role in the politics of portions. Both C. P. Boyd and Jean Carney are elected public officials in Haywood County. In three of the counties African American leaders, often associated with the community health centers, are on the boards of education or head them up. Despite this success, there is not confidence that the progress made is irreversible or that it does not require constant vigilance to maintain. There are not clear lines demarcating one era from another because of legislation or events. A "new" era contains some elements of the past. Memories about illegal obstacles to political participation in the past support suspicions about current events. C. P. Boyd recounted the outcomes of a recent election in Haywood County with considerable skepticism.

> In 1986, we had the famous Jack Dempsey long-count. People in Shelby County [Memphis] were through counting their election before people in Haywood County counted their votes. The reason, we had a young black man running for sheriff. Personally, I could be wrong, I believe that he won. But something went on. Who knows? They counted the votes in a secret place and he lost by 30 votes.

Other setbacks, including conflicts over the health centers, create ambivalence among the narrators about the amount and nature of change they have seen. Bill Saunders speaks of the hundred-year cycle he sees in American history. He fears that the 1990s may be a decade when the legislation of the 1960s is eliminated and new legal and extra-legal means of discrimination and racial subordination appear.[23] The possibility that this will happen is directly related to his understanding of the acquisition and loss of civil and economic rights for African Americans between 1865 and 1900. Saunders is hopeful that there will not be a recurrence of that earlier time because African Americans have a stronger economic base now than they did then. In addition, an era of renewed subordination would mean losses for women and other ethnic minorities that have made important economic and political gains since the 1960s. These groups, if united, present a more formidable political force than African Americans in the South did in the 1890s. In general, Saunders has guarded confidence in the ability of African Americans to progress through several avenues, all of which require continued political organization.

> I believe that we have enough political power right now to impact state and local government. When I speak of political power, I'm not referring to blacks alone. There is such a beautiful political alliance that blacks could make with women. There are other groups, like poor whites, who share the same problems that blacks suffer from. I feel that blacks are going to have to quit locking ourselves into fighting for things we call black when they really benefit everybody.

John Hulett does not speak of grand cycles, but he understands that, although there has been progress, it is not necessarily permanent.

> There's been some progress. But it's a continual struggle. You have to keep doing it, over and over. Our children have to do it. Our grandchildren have to follow in our footsteps. You have to get the awareness over to them that you can't give up, you can't quit, because things don't go well; you have to keep fighting. That's what we have to keep telling them.
>
> It is possible we could go backward and that bothers me. I hope that the coming generation will not go backward and we can continue to move forward. But I don't think Lowndes County is going back. I definitely don't. Even though we have had our problems and disappointments, I think we are going forward.

Hulett's political success has brought him problems indicative of changed federal attitudes toward the political participation of African Americans in the rural South. Hulett is one of the few African Americans who have won countywide elections in black belt counties such as Lowndes. He was rumored to be in line for a federal indictment in the wake of an extensive investigation into electoral fraud in the black belt after the Democratic primary of September 1984. The Justice Department, which was started in 1866 to enforce the civil rights of the freedpeople, investigated several prominent African American political leaders in the area for violation of the Voting Rights Act of 1965, a law designed to remove impediments to the political participation of people like Hulett. The men and women who worked hard and risked their lives in organizing efforts to acquire this legislation were now investigated under a broad interpretation of its provisions.

The Justice Department acted with a zeal that reflected how high a personal priority of the attorney general the case was. Before anyone brought charges of irregularities, absentee ballots were numbered by state officials "to assist in looking into anticipated irregularities."[24] Three separate U.S. attorneys' offices participated: Mobile, Birmingham, and Montgomery. A major African American political figure in each of the counties was indicted or thought to be in line for indictment. A thousand African American voters in the black belt counties were visited and questioned by the FBI and other federal officials. Some were taken by bus to Mobile to testify who they voted for and who assisted them with their absentee ballot. The intensity of questioning of older people, some in their nineties and who could not have voted for most of their adult lives, brought many of them to the point of doubting that they would vote again.[25]

Despite this massive effort, the Justice Department succeeded in gaining only one conviction in this case. An all-white jury, after twenty-three hours of deliberation over five days, found Spiver Gordon guilty on four counts of vote fraud. One juror explained the decision as a compromise and believed the verdict would be overturned on appeal. In the summer of 1988 Gordon's conviction was overturned.[26] Justice Department officials complained of the difficulty of gaining convictions from juries and indictments from grand juries with African Americans on them in cases such as these.[27] But the investigation served other purposes, and Hank Sanders, the defense attorney in the case, pointed out the historical significance and precedent of the investigation.

> It is difficult for many to fully comprehend the effect of over 1,000 persons being interviewed and interrogated by the FBI, numerous persons being indicted, highly publicized trials and violation of the secrecy of the ballot. Considering all the problems, the violation of the secrecy of the ballot may be the most devastating. Many persons voted only after strong assurances that their ballots were secret and that no one would know how they voted. In poor rural areas, many elderly, uneducated and fearful Blacks are still at the mercy of rich and powerful local whites. The knowledge that their vote is not secret will be extremely discouraging and will undoubtedly chill future participation in the election process.
>
> I see a disturbing trend developing which parallels a devastating development

over 100 years ago. In 1865, Blacks were freed from slavery. A short time thereafter, a constitutional amendment was enacted which guaranteed blacks the right
to vote. Numerous Black officials were elected in the West Alabama Black Belt
and other places throughout the South. Within a few years, there were few Black
elected officials and the right to vote was effectively lost. We refer to this period
as Post Reconstruction.[28]

Sanders might have added that he had ended the "Post Reconstruction"
period personally in a small way. He was the first African American state
senator since Reconstruction and specifically, since 1874, the same year
Rapier lost his election in the black belt. The Alabama legislature gerrymandered Rapier's district, part of which Sanders now represents. Key to
Sanders's election was the reapportionment of Alabama's legislature that
African American leaders had worked successfully to acquire through the
courts.

Another limit to the progress described in the narratives entails the belief
that white Americans treat the rights of African Americans as a gift from
them, something that white people give and African Americans must earn.
Sam Bradley believes, for example, that African American political officials
are judged more exactingly by the standards common to black and white
political officials. There are some startlingly clear examples of this double
standard among the events we have recounted. As federal authorities pored
over expenditures of HUD funds by the Sea Island Development Corporation
to find some wrongdoing, presidentially appointed HUD officials in Washington were plundering the federal treasury. Similarly, the Justice Department
investigated voter fraud in the black belt because the integrity of the electoral process was "one of the highest priorities of the Attorney General."[29]
That same attorney general, at the same time, however, conducted his office
for the financial benefit of friends in a way that "should not be tolerated of
any government employee, especially not the attorney general," according
to the Office of Professional Responsibility within the Justice Department.[30]

This limit of double standards is not new, either. The very first Army
regulations toward African American troops in the Civil War were blind to
color and promised African American troops no special treatment. The result was a diet that made many of them sick and the extra-long and extra-hard
work details that took their lives. Clearly, a unique element of the freedom
of African Americans is the requirement that they use it to disprove preju-
diced views toward them. This was the test of liberty that Pierce offered the
freedpeople on the Sea Islands in 1861. They were to test and disprove the
northern assumption that they were lazy and would not work without being

whipped. This perverted freedom is manifest at the local level in stories such as the one Sam Bradley told about his orientation that tested his resilience to the term "nigger."

Olly Neal, Jr., has internalized this exacting and double standard in a personal style that he calls paranoia.

> Paranoia has something to do with what you know: what's given can be taken away. You know that there are plenty of folk who desire to take it away. Therefore, you don't act like normal people. You run scared all the time. You do a better job of covering your backside than anybody else does.
>
> That simply means that you gained these opportunities but you can't be as free with them as anybody else. I could cite you a number of cases of people who have not gone outside of the normal pattern of conduct though they now stand either convicted or charged with crimes. What they did is, they challenged a certain system and that made it incumbent upon those who were in charge to find a way to grab them.
>
> I've been paranoid for the last 18 years. I still got to be scared. I'm gonna run scared the rest of my life or they are gonna to get me one day. I can't do things like leave my car unlocked. If I saw you on the road, I won't give you a ride. You have to be damn close to me to get into my car or my house. If I let you in, you might leave something behind for the police to find. I know, for example, that in the summer of 1986, there was instituted a major drug investigation. The original target of that investigation was me and a few others. They said we had to be selling drugs, we were too damn independent. Well, you know, that certainly taught me a few things.
>
> I haven't been charged yet and I've been on the forefront for 18 years. I attribute that to my paranoia.[31]

For Neal, African American leaders cannot act "normal," despite their achievements, and need to remain scared that what is seen as "given" by others will be taken away. Bill Saunders echoes these sentiments in his opinion that the continued progress of African American political leaders requires that they stay out of the spotlight and remain unnoticed until they have solidified their positions with a firm base of power. Prejudice robs ordinary African Americans of the right to try something and fail because in that failure may be the "corroboration" of white prejudice. Likewise, the failure of some is more likely to be attributed to the inability of all rather than the inadequate preparation of many African American children in American schools.

But the test of prejudice is more complicated than individual judgments. The real test of prejudice is the ability of a person to maintain values and beliefs despite contrary evidence. Consequently, African Americans cannot disprove the prejudice of others even if given the opportunity. Their achievements corroborate the views of those who always thought them equal but get reinterpreted by those determined to cling to their prejudice of inequality. For example, Fullerton and Steedman found a successful plantation on Edisto Island under the direction of freedpeople. Rather than being seen as a model of what was possible, from which to acquire lessons and to replicate them, this success was contrasted with the lack of success of others. This lack required, seemingly, the complete restoration of former white landlords to control of the economy. Successful African Americans, such as the children in the Avery Institute, are held to be atypical and not representative of the average against whom prejudicial standards, it can be inferred, still apply. Time after time, in the events we recounted when African Americans succeeded too well as farmers in an economy of tenancy or as human service providers in an economy of need, reprisals followed rather than a decline in prejudice. These reprisals included lynchings, trials, and audits. These reprisals came from a few, but the acquiescence of many accompanied them. These reprisals are an extreme form of prejudice that requires the destruction of evidence that challenges it, such as successful reforms and capable reformers.

The community health centers are part of a larger pattern of reform, retreat, and reaction replicated in the Freedmen's Bureau, the FSA, and the OHA. Beginning with the land-redistribution effort on the Sea Islands, the federal government begins reform, retreats from them, and then reacts to eliminate and discredit them. Indeed, if it was not for the wartime prices for cotton and the success of new strawberry crops, farmers in the Haywood County Farms Project might not have had the chance to buy their farms before the FSA was discredited. Closing a clinic here and there, discrediting local leaders in social and political change, and intimidating African American voters and their elected officials are today, no less than a century ago, actions that have a synergism and momentum that retreat and react to recent reforms.

Despite this pattern and its element of discredit, it is also obvious that one partial reform has an impact on later efforts at change. The landownership effort on the Sea Islands left a remnant that assisted in electing the first African American man to public office in the twentieth century in rural South Carolina. Likewise, the land programs of the Resettlement Administration provided an economic base for the civil rights movement in the rural South. The health centers of that program provided a model and in some instances the actual space for the later efforts at community health centers of the OHA. Indeed, the narratives of this book as well as the historical context suggests that the remnant of one political reform is used as building materials for the next. The hope entailed in our limited progress to achieve democratic equality and to express a high standard of human dignity is the courage, imagination, and ability of the ordinary people of this country when they undertake the extraordinary. That courage, imagination, and ability are reflected in the efforts within communities of memory and redemptive organizations at almost all times and in the public programs of heroic bureaucracies occasionally.

Conclusion

By the end of the 1980s the conditions of African Americans in the rural South no longer measured the extremes of inequality and repression in America. Although we found new evidence of hunger and excesses of illness and death among them,[1] they lost their place as measures because other conditions had grown so much worse. The underclass and the homeless, to mention just two other groups, offered new extremes of human need for Americans. But the conditions of poverty and repression of African Americans in the rural South offer parallels, as well as origins, to these more current and publicized problems. The underclass of our inner cities have a direct connection to the subordinate class of agricultural workers in the rural South who migrated to urban areas. Once there, some of the "old" problem of racial inequality became part of the "new" problem of the underclass.[2] The homeless on our streets testify to the capacity of Americans to tolerate the spectacle of severe deprivation and insults on human dignity not unlike our tolerance of lynching for half a century.

Extreme forms of human need like these do not seem to penetrate the American conscience sufficiently to challenge our belief in the adequacies of public services and economic opportunities. If anything, our values and beliefs in low amounts of social capital and private, not public, forms of it are now stronger than before, despite new human evidence of their inadequacy. It is precisely this reaffirmation of private forms of reduced social capital that creates the new social problems that crowd off old ones from the public agenda and awareness. These problems, and others, are the current "American dilemma." We tolerate, accept, and even defend severe human needs. We integrate them with our ideals of equality and human dignity that these needs contradict.

We have these "dilemmas" for the same reasons that Myrdal enumerated earlier. We justify low amounts and limited forms of social capital because of what we "know" about the people who bear their human costs. We place the burden of remedy on those with need. The "American Creed" holds that no group should fall to such low standards of living as homelessness, hunger, chronic poverty, or unemployment. When we find such groups, we impose an assumption that adequate opportunities for education, training, and employment are available. We conclude that the conditions of groups with severe needs are the choice of group members or the consequence of some characteristic, for instance, the "culture" that they have. The values and facts that our dominant majority holds about the needs of groups with severe economic needs protects us from having to improve their condition. It remains difficult for the majority of Americans to accept their responsibility for the condition of low-income minority groups today, just as it was when Myrdal suggested their relation. We still prefer to accept the moral nature of public problems of human need and deprivation as an individual matter and not a social relationship.[3]

Instead of debating and establishing standards of democratic equality and human dignity, we much more often discuss whether our social programs are doing too much. The minimum we set is not a standard high enough to advance the general welfare but a standard low enough to punish people for their alleged lack of effort. We continue to avoid the costs of social capital investments in people for roles beyond the economy. Our shift to private forms of social capital only further minimizes investments in human beings who are not workers. We largely ignore investments in people as parents, citizens, artists, and the other human roles that establish and maintain a creative and democratic society. Like Howard, no administrator or politician wants to be found feeding others who are idle. The result is that in times like the 1980s, we weave "a safety net" and place it so close to the ground that people do not feel it break their fall. The Reagan policies of privitization of social capital created greater numbers of poor, more severe forms of poverty, and greater acceptance of these conditions.

With the increase of social needs such as homelessness, the security of everyone is eroded. Our policies of social capital are not a safety net for a few. In the metaphor of Martin Luther King, Jr., social capital is "an inescapable network of mutuality, . . . a single . . . garment of destiny" that covers us all. The sharecropping system ensnared African Americans and whites together. The disfranchisement of African Americans reduced the degree of political participation of all groups. The social capital policies of the 1980s meant not only less for the poor but a redistribution of wealth from the bottom ranks to the top. In 1989 the lowest 20 percent of American families had 4.6 percent of family income, their lowest share since 1954. On the other hand, the highest 20 percent of families had 44.6 percent of family income, and the highest percent had 17.6 percent. Both of these shares were the highest ever recorded. The middle classes had the lowest share of family income ever recorded.[4]

The social capital entrepreneur understands not only the role of the majority in determining the conditions of subordinate groups but the stake that the majority have in improving them. Olly Neal worries that those in authority may eventually "get him," that he would not be available for later interviews. He explained, "If I am in jail, you are less free" and offered that assessment as a test of my understanding of his work and beliefs.

That is the litmus test of a social capital entrepreneur, such as Neal and the others: to what degree does a policy or program directly improve the conditions of people who are the worst off? They intend to raise the bottom standard as a means of social improvement. It is this standard, and not the excessive wealth of a few, that provides the security of most people in a society. The education of citizens with the lowest income determines the average ability of people to participate in the economy and politics of a society that everyone shares. The economic security of citizens at the bottom of the economic ladder determines how far anyone is from deprivation and need. The adequacy of social capital is the best measure of the risk most people have in bad times. Even as Americans dream of how far they can rise, most must remain mindful of how far they can drop if unemployment, disability, or some other event requires them to depend on the public provision of social benefits. Addressing the needs of those at the bottom of the economic ladder guarantees everyone a higher level of security. Sharecropping instituted a hierarchy of misery in which poor whites could take bitter solace that they were better off than another group of people. The level of living of the poorest African Americans in the rural South did not make poor whites well off, only better off than a poorer group. The meaning of that relative measure depends of course, on that by which we measure. New and larger forms of social capital aimed to remove the most severe needs in society are prerequisites to the democratic equality and human dignity of everyone. Social capital entrepreneurs currently convey the hope of Du Bois that before the end of the century we will accept the "deliberate distribution of property and income by the state on an equitable and logical basis . . . as the state's prime function." It was such a "deliberate distribution" of new forms of social capital, including full political participation, that stirred the imagination of the narrators and of America in the civil rights movement.

In the 1960s African Americans in the rural South inspired the world with their efforts to end political, social, and economic subordination. In the closing days of the 1980s a song they had popularized, "We Shall Overcome," became an anthem of liberty around the world. It could be heard in televised reports from Tiananmen Square, the Berlin Wall, and in South Africa. At the same time however, America was retreating from the social policies that gave these lyrics tangible and explicit meaning. The gains made by African Americans in the rural South were jeopardized or revoked by federal reactions to past social policies. New priorities in federal spending and taxation required those with wealth to do less for those without it and asked those in need to do more for themselves. Supply-side economics made public problems private and private gain a public good. The U.S. Supreme Court constricted interpretations of affirmative action, discrimination, and civil rights.[5] We no longer inspired imaginations about the democratic potential of our society but measured carefully and with some resentment the most we had to do to remove discriminating barriers to subordinate groups. Changes to redress the problems of African Americans in the rural South no longer inspired hope at home but skepticism, if not scorn. We had exported the hope that we discouraged at home.

Inevitably, some social movement will call us to higher standards of democratic equality and human dignity than we have now. That movement will also call upon the government to act not only for the dignity of those in need but to improve the image of ourselves reflected in the human conditions of great need. At that time, reforms like the community health centers and those that preceded them might remind us about the relation of social movements and effective public policies of social capital.

The four community health centers of this study are obviously only minor actors in the dramatic history of Reconstruction, the New Deal, the civil rights movement, and the federal War on Poverty. But they are a part of them. They offered space for new investment in people, the development of people in new roles, and the renewed expression of the hope of freedom that we extend to others around the world with pride. These health centers are places where large movements and broad social commitments converged and touched individual, specific, human lives. They are spaces where people expressed their imaginations and dreams of democratic equality and human dignity. In enough of these places, history is made and acquired. In them we learn the course of reform and from them we acquire and maintain our hope in it.

Epilogue

My final advice to those who are thus moved by injustices and human needs and who think they perceive better possibilities through social organizations, is to go ahead.

Fail as gloriously as some of your predecessors have.

If you do not succeed in bringing about a permanent change, you may have at least stirred some slow consciences so that in time they will give support to action.

And you will have the satisfaction, which is not to be discounted, of having annoyed a good many miscreants who had it coming to them.

—Rexford Tugwell [1]

Notes, Interviews, Index

Notes

Acknowledgments

1. Leon F. Litwack, *Been in the Storm So Long: The Aftermath of Slavery* (New York: Vintage Books, 1979), 449.

Introduction

1. Alice Sardell offers an analysis of the community health centers as a movement to reform American health care that fell short of its goal in *The United States Experiment in Social Medicine: The Community Health Center Program, 1966–1986* (Pittsburgh: University of Pittsburgh Press, 1988). H. Jack Geiger, M.D., stresses the changes that the community health centers brought about in "Community Health Centers: Health Care as an Instrument of Social Change," in *Reforming Medicine: Lessons of the Last Quarter Century*, ed. Victor W. Sidel and Ruth Sidel (New York: Pantheon Books, 1984), 11–32. For favorable assessments of community health centers, see Karen Davis and Cathy Schoen, *Health and the War on Poverty: A Ten Year Appraisal* (Washington, D.C.: Brookings Institute, 1978), 161–202; Cecil G. Sheps et al., "An Evaluation of Subsidized Rural Primary Care Programs: I. A Typology of Practice Organizations," *American Journal of Public Health* 73 (Jan. 1983): 38–39; Lisbeth B. Schorr, *Within Our Reach: Breaking the Cycle of Disadvantage* (New York: Doubleday, 1988), 130–34; Paul Starr, *The Social Transformation of American Medicine: The Rise of a Sovereign Profession and the Making of a Vast Industry* (New York: Basic Books, 1982), 370–74.

2. For more complete accounts of these local civil rights movements see the following. On Citizenship Schools see John Glen, *Highlander: No Ordinary School, 1932–1962* (Lexington: University Press of Kentucky, 1988), 155–73, and Carl Tjerandsen, *Education for Citizenship: A Foundation's Experience* (Santa Cruz, Calif.: Emil Schwarzhaupt Foundation, 1980). No complete account of events in Haywood County is yet available. Registration efforts are discussed often in other accounts of the civil rights movement. For an oral history of events

in neighboring Fayette County at the same time see Robert Hamburger, *Our Portion of Hell* (New York: Links Books, 1973). The events in Lowndes County are recounted in Stokely Carmichael and Charles V. Hamilton, *Black Power: The Politics of Liberation in America* (New York: Random House, 1967). Lee County's events are conveyed by Marvin Schwartz, *In Service to America: A History of VISTA in Arkansas, 1965–1985* (Fayetteville: University of Arkansas Press, 1988).

3. On Reconstruction see these recent works: Eric Foner, *Reconstruction: America's Unfinished Revolution, 1863–1877* (New York: Harper & Row, 1988), and James M. McPherson, *Ordeal by Fire: The Civil War and Reconstruction* (New York: Alfred A. Knopf, 1982). For earlier work that stressed the democratic nature of Reconstruction, see W. E. B. Du Bois, *Black Reconstruction: An Essay Toward a History of the Part Which Black Folk Played in the Attempt to Reconstruct Democracy in America, 1860–1880* (New York: S. A. Russell, 1935), and James S. Allen, *Reconstruction: The Battle for Democracy* (New York: International Publishers, 1937). On the civil rights movement, see Juan Williams, *Eyes on the Prize: America's Civil Rights Years, 1954–1965* (New York: Penguin Books, 1987), and Taylor Branch, *Parting the Waters: American in the King Years, 1954–63* (New York: Touchstone Books, 1988). In addition there are several works that cover race relations in other periods more completely than this study. See J. Morgan Kousser, *The Shaping of Southern Politics: Suffrage Restriction and the Establishment of the One-Party South, 1880–1910* (New Haven, Conn.: Yale University Press, 1974); Steven F. Lawson, *Black Ballots: Voting Rights in the South, 1944–1969* (New York: Columbia University Press, 1976); John B. Kirby, *Black Americans in the Roosevelt Era: Liberalism and Race* (Knoxville: University of Tennessee Press, 1980); and Robert Frederick Hunt, *The Eisenhower Administration and Black Civil Rights* (Knoxville: University of Tennessee Press, 1984).

This book does suggest how local struggles for change extended beyond civil rights and began from common and enduring problems of racial inequality. It also shows how national organizations, far more prominent in social movements for racial equality, borrowed, learned, and otherwise gained from what Clayborne Carson calls "freedom struggles." Other examples of this type of study are William Henry Chafe, *Civilities and Civil Rights: Greensboro, North Carolina and the Black Struggle for Equality* (New York: Oxford University Press, 1980); Robert J. Norrell, *Reaping the Whirlwind: The Civil Rights Movement in Tuskegee* (New York: Alfred A. Knopf, 1985); Jo Anne Gibson Robinson, *The Montgomery Bus Boycott and the Women Who Started It: Memoir of Jo Anne Gibson Robinson*, ed. David Garrow (Knoxville: University of Tennessee Press, 1987); and John Dittmer, "The Politics of the Mississippi Movement," in *The Civil Rights Movement in America*, ed. Charles W. Eagles (Jackson: University Press of Mississippi, 1986), 65–93. For a discussion of the need for studies of this sort see Clayborne Carson, "Civil Rights Reform and the Black Freedom Struggle," in *The Civil Rights Movement in America*, 19–32.

4. Karen Davis and Ray Marshall, *Rural Health Care in the South* (Atlanta: Southern Regional Council, 1975), 25–30. For other early assessments of the political nature of community health centers, see Michael Lipsky and Morris Lounds, "Citizen Participation and Health Care: Problems of Government Induced Participation," *Journal of Health Politics, Policy and Law* 1 (Spring 1976): 85–111; Robert R. Alford, "The Political Economy of Health Care: Dynamics Without Change," *Politics and Society* 2 (Winter 1972): 127–64.

5. For a more complete discussion of the methods of this study and their assumptions, see Yvonna Lincoln and Egon G. Guba, *Naturalistic Inquiry* (Beverly Hills, Calif.: Sage Publications, 1985).

6. Southern Regional Council, *Health Care in the South: A Statistical Profile* (Atlanta: Southern Regional Council, 1974).

7. W. E. B. Du Bois in *The Unfolding Drama: Studies in U.S. History by Herbert Aptheker*, ed. Bettina Aptheker (New York: International Publishers, 1978), 140; Du Bois, *Black Reconstruction*, 383. Because little record of ordinary people is saved, there are major problems in conveying the significance of their actions. The Union Leagues of the Reconstruction era, for example, were instrumental in putting the policies of Congress, especially the vote for black men, into prompt and effective action. Recent scholarship compares the scope of their activity and membership to the civil rights movement. Yet we have little record of them, and that which we do have most often comes from newspapers and observers who were opposed to them. Most scholars of Reconstruction depend very heavily on the work of historians who had a negative view of Reconstruction. They attributed the success of the League movement to the alleged attraction of African Americans to secret ceremonies and to coercion and even death for defection from the League. Walter L. Fleming, *Documentary History of Reconstruction: Political, Military, Social, Religious, Educational and Industrial, 1865 to Present Time*, vol. 2 (Gloucester, Mass.: Peter Smith, 1960), 4, see also 3–29. For an earlier discussion of the Union Leagues see Paul Skeels Pierce, *The Freedmen's Bureau: A Chapter in the History of Reconstruction* (Iowa City: University of Iowa Press, 1904), 161–71. For a recent study, see Michael W. Fitzgerald, *The Union League Movement in the Deep South: Politics and Agricultural Change during Reconstruction* (Baton Rouge: Louisiana State University Press, 1989).

8. This second round of conversations offered new insight and material. One man confessed that his interview had been a pseudo-conversation and that he had given me information that he thought I wanted. He had doubted my stated purpose and background and suspected I was actually from the FBI, whom he did not trust, apparently. Upon receiving and reading the chapter on his community, he came to believe my purpose and requested that I give the project up. He had no qualms about his interview because he had been circumspect and evasive.

But his lifetime's experience led him to believe that a study such as mine could stir up the violence and repression of whites toward black that had been, and evidently remains for him, a constant element of race relations. In general, however, the reactions in each community to drafts of Chapters 1 through 4 were positive and encouraging, and elicited more cooperation. Harry S. Sullivan did a "psychiatric reconnaissance" of southern blacks. Among his findings were "pseudo-conversations" in which people interviewed relayed what they thought the interviewer wanted to hear. There was only one of these among my interviews that I am aware of. I had many checks on the accuracy of the interviews because I interviewed other people about the same events. Charles S. Johnson, *Growing Up in the Black Belt* (Washington, D.C.: American Council on Education, 1941), 328–33.

9. Alasdair MacIntyre, *After Virtue: A Study in Moral Theory*, 2d ed. (Notre Dame, Ind.: University of Notre Dame Press, 1984), 204–25. For a study of an alternative tradition, see John Langston Gwaltney, *Drylongso: A Self-Portrait of Black America* (New York: Random House, 1980).

10. See the Sources section for information on this and other interviews. A prime example of a variation of facts in a single story that illustrates the same truth is the story of Esau Jenkins's reaction to the shooting death of a black man in an argument over a dog. One version of the story occurs in Chapter 4. There are several such incidents, or several versions of the same incident; probably both. The nature of the argument varies from story to story. But the truth remains that black people could be shot in the heat of anger over trivial matters; that white people who did such shooting most often went unpunished; and that it took heroism to protest such conditions. John Egerton, author and commentator on the South, expands on this relation of meaning, facts, and truth as a southern characteristic. He tells the story of a white southerner who, upon completion of a point, swears, "I may not have all the facts just right but that is the absolute truth." John Egerton, "Myth, Media and the Southern Mind: Review," *Southern Changes* 9 (March 1987), 16.

11. MacIntyre, *After Virtue*, 215.

12. The historiography of Reconstruction is illustrative that "facts" are poor arbiters of truth if they do not acknowledge the enacted dramatic narrative of which they are part. Beginning in the mid-1950s scholarly opinion shifted about Reconstruction more completely than perhaps in any field in American history. Michael Les Benedict, *The Impeachment and Trial of Andrew Johnson* (New York: Norton, 1973), 192–202, and Bernard A. Weisberger, "The Dark and Bloody Ground of Reconstruction Historiography," *Journal of Southern History* 25 (Nov. 1959), 427–47. One finds current studies that explain Reconstruction as democratic reforms that did not go far enough rather than as misconceived or misplaced idealism. These current studies differ radically from the scholarship of the past, which emphasized corruption and incompetence in Reconstruction

administrations. For example, Walter L. Fleming, the influential historian of Reconstruction of the early twentieth century, found justification for some repressive measures of Reconstruction in the "roaming and thieving propensities of Negroes." Walter L. Fleming, *The Freedmen's Savings Bank: A Chapter in the Economic History of the Negro Race* (Chapel Hill: University of North Carolina Press, 1927), 13. Likewise, recent studies attribute the failure of Reconstruction in national trends and leaders and not in the inadequacies and personalities of freedpeople and carpetbaggers. Robert G. Morris, *Reading, 'Riting, and Reconstruction: The Education of Freedmen in the South, 1861–1870* (Chicago: University of Chicago Press, 1981), and Foner, *Reconstruction*. It is a fitting historic irony that Foner's study should have received some financial support from the Dunning Fund of Columbia University History Department. William A. Dunning fashioned the dominant historiography of Reconstruction for the first half of the twentieth century.

13. See, for example, Charles Murray, *Losing Ground: American Social Policy 1950–1980* (New York: Basic Books, 1984). For general discussions of the relation of facts, values, the social sciences, and public policy, see Gunnar Myrdal, "A Methodological Note on Valuations and Beliefs" and "A Methodological Note on Facts and Valuations in Social Science" in *An American Dilemma: The Negro Problem and Modern Democracy* (New York: Harper & Brothers, 1944), 1027–34 and 1035–64. Robert N. Bellah, Richard Madsen, William M. Sullivan, Ann Swidler, and Steven M. Tipton, "Social Science as Public Philosophy," in *Habits of the Heart: Individualism and Commitment in American Life* (Berkeley: University of California Press, 1985), 297–307.

14. Myrdal, *An American Dilemma*, 21.

15. Ibid., 5.

16. Ibid., 214.

17. Ibid., 808.

18. Joel Williamson is especially critical of Myrdal's assertions of the hegemony of an American creed. *The Crucible of Race: Black-White Relations in the American South since Emancipation* (New York: Oxford University Press, 1986), 248–49. For information on recent polls on the efficacy of self-effort, see Earl Black and Merle Black, *Politics and Society in the South* (Cambridge: Harvard University Press, 1987), 167.

19. Myrdal, *An American Dilemma*, xliii–xlviiii.

20. James Agee and Walker Evans, *Let Us Now Praise Famous Men* (Boston: Houghton Mifflin, 1969), 188.

21. Du Bois, *Black Reconstruction*, iii.

22. Ibid., 711–29. Myrdal was among those readers of Du Bois's work who accepted his revision of Reconstruction history. Du Bois endorsed and praised Myrdal's work as well. See David W. Southern, *Gunnar Myrdal and Black-White Relations: The Use and Abuse of An American Dilemma, 1944–1969* (Baton Rogue:

Louisiana State University Press, 1987), 212, 90. For a more modest revision of Reconstruction historiography of the time, see Francis B. Simkins, "New Viewpoints of Southern Reconstruction," *Journal of Southern History* 5 (Feb. 1939): 49–61. For a major revisionist study of Reconstruction in the 1930s, see Allen, *Reconstruction*.

23. Myrdal, *An American Dilemma*, xix–xx.
24. Ibid., 716. Robert Bellah and his associate authors also found hope in the midst of a troubling analysis of American political and social life. They offer a vision of a "social ecology," manifest in the civil rights movement, to counter the individualistic and alienating dominant American culture. Bellah et al., *Habits of the Heart*, 286–90.
25. Du Bois, *Black Reconstruction*, 519.

Chapter 1

1. Portions of this chapter first appeared in Richard A. Couto, "A Place to Call Our Own," *Southern Exposure* 9 (Fall 1981): 16–22.
2. Income and demographic measures are taken from Southern Regional Council, *Health Care in the South: A Statistical Profile* (Atlanta: Southern Regional Council, 1974); *Characteristics of the Population: 1970 Census of the Population, Tennessee* (Washington, D.C.: U.S. Government Printing Office, 1973), Tables 124 and 128; and *Characteristics of the Population: 1980 Census of the Population, lation, Tennessee* (Washington, D.C.: U.S. Government Printing Office, 1983), Table 186.
3. In 1989 the health center, under operation by a neighboring county's hospital, closed once again. Local authorities acquired the center building in 1990 and began plans to reopen health services.

   As in other instances, the audit of the Douglas Community Health Center revealed few problems and no wrongdoing. The problems included failure to institute a 5 percent cost-of-living raise for staff from July 1, 1982, to December 31, 1982; payment of $3,934.38 for in-patient care of clinic patients who had been referred by clinic physicians to other providers for this needed and required care the cost of which federal regulations disallowed; and failure to post sick days for one employee. The most serious charges included a conflict of interest in procuring a retirement plan through the husband of the clinic administrator; some possible excess days of maternity leave for the clinic administrator; and the award of a contract for audit without competitive bidding. The audit made no suggestion of fraud or deliberate error. The most severe interpretation of the audit would suggest no more than $8,000 of errors over a three-year period. "Federal Inspector Lists Corrective Measures for Douglas Health Center," *The States—Graphic Brownsville, TN.*, Feb. 12, 1984, p. 1. For an analysis of the Reagan administration crackdown on community health centers, obvious by 1984, see Tom Frieden, "Community Clinics: Providing Care to Those Who Need It," *The Nation* 240 (Oct. 13, 1984): 348–50.

Chapter 2

1. Marvin Schwartz, *In Service to America: A History of VISTA in Arkansas, 1965–1985* (Fayetteville: University of Arkansas Press, 1988), 243.

2. Income and demographic measures are taken from Southern Regional Council, *Health Care in the South: A Statistical Profile* (Atlanta: Southern Regional Council: 1974); *Characteristics of the Population: 1970 Census of the Population, Arkansas* (Washington, D.C.: U.S. Government Printing Office, 1973), Tables 124 and 128; and *Characteristics of the Population: 1980 Census of the Population, Arkansas* (Washington, D.C.: U.S. Government Printing Office, 1983), Table 186.

3. Dan Blumenthal, "Building a Base for Reform," *Southern Exposure* 6 (Summer 1978): 83–89. See also Dan Blumenthal, "Out-OEO-ing OEO: Institutional Innovation in the Public Health Service" (Honors thesis, Department of Government, Harvard University, 1970).

4. CBS broadcast an investigative report on America's health care in 1970 on two successive nights during prime time. Events in Marianna were part of that report. Daniel Schorr, *Don't Get Sick in America* (Nashville: Aurora Publishers, 1970), 34–44.

5. *Wall Street Journal* coverage of the school boycott portrays Judge Adams's combative attitude. "Asked if using a fire hose on the children, particularly in the near-freezing temperature, wasn't bad strategy, the judge replied, 'We had no choice. It was too windy to use tear gas.'" "Black vs. White: A Boycott Devastates Little Southern Town Bypassed by the 60s," *Wall Street Journal*, February 14, 1972, p. 6.

6. This project expanded statewide and then nationally. It is currently carried on by the Virginia Water Project, which still lends technical assistance to rural low-income communities and their leaders' efforts to acquire a safe and reliable supply of water.

7. The film, "The New Healers," compares health innovation in Tanzania and Lee County. It was produced by WGBH and broadcast as part of the *Nova* series in 1977.

Chapter 3

1. Income and demographic measures are taken from Southern Regional Council, *Health Care in the South: A Statistical Profile*, (Atlanta: Southern Regional Council, 1974); *Characteristics of the Population: 1970 Census of the Population,*

Alabama (Washington, D.C.: U.S. Government Printing Office, 1973), Tables 124 and 128; and *Characteristics of the Population: 1980 Census of the Population, Alabama* (Washington, D.C.: U.S. Government Printing Office, 1983), Table 186.

2. Kenneth M. McConnochie, M.D., "Health Care as a Weapon in the War on Poverty: The Case of Lowndes County, Alabama" (manuscript photocopy, 1979).

Chapter 4

1. Income and demographic measures are taken from *1980 Census of Population and Housing: Census Tracts for Charleston and North Charleston, South Carolina* (Washington, D.C.: U.S. Government Printing Office, 1983).
2. David J. Garrow, *Bearing the Cross: Martin Luther King, Jr. and the Southern Christian Leadership Conference* (New York: Vintage Books, 1988), 565.
3. Herbert Kohl, "Letter," *New York Review of Books*, Jan. 19, 1984, p. 51.
4. The poverty of African Americans on the Sea Islands came to the nation's attention once again in the late 1960s. The Field Foundation sponsored a survey of hunger and poverty in America. A physician in the Beaufort area assisted the survey and presented evidence of illness and hunger there. For a portion of the publicity around these events, see Robert Coles and Harry Huge, "Strom Thurmond Country: The Way It Is in South Carolina," *New Republic* 159 (Nov. 30, 1968): 17–21 and Jack Bass, "Letter," *New Republic* 160 (Jan. 11, 1969): 33.

   See also "Witnesses Report on Negro Starvation in Georgia and South Carolina," *New York Times*, Nov. 10, 1967, p. 18. The report of the Citizens Crusade Against Hunger earned modest mention in the *New York Times*, April 26, 1968, p. 22. Senator Fritz Hollings converted to the crusade against hunger. "Hunger: An Undeveloped Country," *Time*, Feb. 28, 1969, p. 25. For another account of the study on hunger, see Robert Coles, *Still Hungry in America* (New York: World Publishing, 1969).

   As in many other cases, reprisals visited the physicians who attracted national attention to the problems of the Sea Islands. " 'Hunger Doctor' in South Carolina Is Fined $500 for Improper Drug Records," *New York Times*, August 30, 1970, p. 43.
5. Cecil G. Sheps, M.D., also wrote to Ophie Franklin to express his deep distress and that of his colleagues over rumored budget reductions. He explained that he and his colleagues surveyed 627 community health programs in the country, gathered detailed data on 194, and studied 40 of them intensively. The Sea Island Comprehensive Health Care Services was one of those studied intensively and was, in the estimation of the team, "one of the most impressive and effective in the country." He added, "Your program is clearly making a striking

and vital improvement in the health and lives of the people of the Islands." Letter of Cecil M. Sheps, M.D., to Ophie Franklin, July 13, 1982.

6. "Summary of Compliance and Financial Management Problems at Sea Island Comprehensive Health Care Corporation and Franklin C. Fetter Family Health Center," U.S. General Accounting Office, Human Resources Division (April 23, 1982).

Chapter 5

1. *Autobiography of Oliver Otis Howard: Major General United States Army*, vol. 2 (New York: Baker & Taylor, 1908), 167–69; Edward Pierce, "The Contrabands at Fortress Monroe," *Atlantic Monthly* 14 (Nov. 1861): 627–30; Paul Skeels Pierce, *The Freedmen's Bureau: A Chapter in the History of Reconstruction* (Iowa City: University of Iowa Press, 1904), 38.

2. Edward Magdol, *A Right to the Land: Essays on the Freedmen's Community* (Westport, Conn.: Greenwood Press, 1977), 77; Theodore Rosengarten, *Tombee: Portrait of a Cotton Planter* (New York: William Morrow, 1986), 259.

3. Howard recounted this exchange on topics, including the meaning of slavery and freedom. He wrote later, "It would have been wise if our statesmen could have received, digested, and acted upon the answers these men gave their questions." *Autobiography of Oliver Otis Howard*, 189; Willie L. Rose, *Rehearsal for Reconstruction: The Port Royal Experiment* (New York: Oxford University Press, 1984), 325; LaWanda Cox, "The Promise of Land for the Freedmen," *Mississippi Valley Historical Review* 45 (Dec. 1958): 429–30.

4. Rosengarten, *Tombee*, 258.

5. Rose, *Rehearsal for Reconstruction*, 29, 31.

6. Saxton was a native of Massachusetts, an abolitionist, and certainly beyond his contemporaries in understanding the aspirations of the freedpeople. His brother, Samuel Willard Saxton, about whom we know more, suggests some of the family background that influenced Saxton. Samuel Saxton lived for two years at Brook Farm, the New England experiment that combined work, classical education, and radical equality. Emerson called it "a French Revolution in small." Samuel served his brother as an aide-de-camp on the Sea Islands. *National Encyclopedia of American Biography*, 4: 219; Thomas H. Johnson, *Oxford Companion of American History* (New York: Oxford University Press, 1966), 111.

7. Rose, *Rehearsal for Reconstruction*, 283.

8. Ibid., 294.

9. Ibid., 295. Rose recalls poignantly examining these preemption claims. "Today packet after packet of these musty little papers may be found among the records of the tax commission, brittle and dry as the broken hopes to which they are the mute witnesses" (287).

10. Ibid., 329.

11. Saxton later recounted this discussion with Stanton before a congressional committee looking into the impeachment of President Johnson. U.S. House of Representatives, *Reports of the Committee Investigating Impeachment*, Serial no. 1314, 40th Cong., 1st sess., 1867, p. 116.

12. Claude F. Oubre, *Forty Acres and a Mule: The Freedmen's Bureau and Black Landownership* (Baton Rouge: Louisiana State University Press, 1978), 46; Julie Saville, "A Measure of Freedom: From Slave to Wage Laborer, South Carolina, 1860–1868" (Ph.D. diss., Yale University, 1986).

13. Rose, *Rehearsal for Reconstruction*, 338.

14. Martin Abbott, *The Freedmen's Bureau in South Carolina: 1865–1872* (Chapel Hill: University of North Carolina Press, 1967), 54–55, 59.

15. Rose, *Rehearsal for Reconstruction*, 351.

16. Abbott, *The Freedmen's Bureau in South Carolina*, 55–56.

17. Rose, *Rehearsal for Reconstruction*, 353–54; see also *Autobiography of Oliver Otis Howard*, 229–34; W. E. B. Du Bois, *Black Reconstruction: An Essay Toward a History of the Part Which Black Folk Played in the Attempt to Reconstruct Democracy in America, 1860–1880* (New York: S. A. Russell, 1935), 602–603; Leon F. Litwack, *Been in the Storm So Long: The Aftermath of Slavery* (New York: Vintage Books, 1979), 405–407.

18. Litwack, *Been in the Storm So Long*, 406.

19. Mary Ames, *From a New England Woman's Diary in Dixie in 1865* (Springfield, Mass.: The Plimpton Press, 1906), 99–103.

20. Saville, "A Measure of Freedom," 32.

21. See both Oubre, *Forty Acres and a Mule*, 53–54 and Saville, "A Measure of Freedom," 34. At least six freedmen played a prominent role in organizing protest and writing to Washington officials. They include Henry Bram, F. C. Desvanny, F. Sampson, Ishmael Moultrie, R. Tolbert, and Ned Murray. Magdol, *A Right to the Land*, 162.

22. Rose, *Rehearsal for Reconstruction*, 355; Abbott, *The Freedmen's Bureau in South Carolina*, 59; Margdol, *A Right to the Land*, 158–59. Myrdal pointed out that land as property obviously stood in another category of property than humans in the estimation of northern legislators. Slave property was primarily southern, and the federal government took it without offering compensation. Landed property, however, was common to the North and the South and attracted only spurious legislative attempts at confiscation. Emancipation had far fewer implications for property rights in the North than land redistribution would have had. Gunnar Myrdal, *An American Dilemma: The Negro Problem and Modern Democracy* (New York: Harper & Brothers, 1944), 226.

23. James S. Allen, *Reconstruction: The Battle for Democracy* (New York: International Publishers, 1937), 53; Peter Kolchin, *First Freedom: The Response of Alabama's Blacks to Emancipation and Reconstruction* (Westport, Conn.: Greenwood Press, 1972), 67–68. As late as 1885, it was evident to sympathetic white

observers that African American workers maintained their strong preference for landownership. Kolchin, *First Freedom*, 325.

24. Joel Williamson, *After Slavery: The Negro in South Carolina during Reconstruction, 1861–1877* (Chapel Hill: University of North Carolina Press, 1965), 82–83.

25. George R. Bentley, *A History of the Freedmen's Bureau* (New York: Octagon Books, 1974), 99.

26. "The Sea Islands: Letter from Gov. Orr," *New York Times*, Feb. 5, 1866.

27. Litwack, *Been in the Storm So Long*, 406–407; Julie Saville, "A Measure of Freedom," 17–21.

28. Allen, *Reconstruction*, 62.

29. Rose, *Rehearsal for Reconstruction*, 356.

30. A valid claim had to meet several criteria. First, the settler had to be occupying the land and cultivating crops by Oct. 17, 1865, the day that General Howard visited Edisto Island. Second, the land claimed had to be in complete accord with the boundaries stated in the possessory title. This meant the exact acreage and the right location. This latter requirement was very confusing. Land division on St. Helena was done by straight lines without regard for the history or past land divisions. This made the division on the island largely unintelligible to most people. Familiar landmarks like Edgar Fripps's house at Seaside became "Section 5 Town 2, South; Range 1 East." Saville, "A Measure of Freedom," 17–21, 38. Rosengarten, *Tombee*, 266.

31. Williamson, *After Slavery*, 84.

32. Ibid., 31–32.

33. Allen, *Reconstruction*, 64–65; Frances B. Simkins and Robert H. Woody, *South Carolina during Reconstruction* (Chapel Hill: University of North Carolina Press, 1932), 229; Edwin D. Hoffman, "From Slavery to Self-Reliance: The Record of Achievement of the Freedmen of the Sea Island Region," *Journal of Negro History* 41 (Jan. 1956): 32–34.

34. General James B. Steedman and General Joseph Fullerton, "The Bureau: General Steedman's Report for South Carolina, Florida and the Sea Islands," *The* [Charleston] *Courier*, June 16, 1866.

35. Abbott, *The Freedmen's Bureau in South Carolina*, 28; Pierce, *The Freedmen's Bureau*, 64–66.

36. Steedman and Fullerton, "Report for South Carolina, Florida and the Sea Islands," 3.

37. Ibid.

38. Carl R. Osthaus, *Freedmen, Philanthropy, and Fraud: A History of the Freedmen's Savings Bank* (Chicago: University of Illinois Press, 1976), 3; Walter L. Fleming, *The Freedmen's Savings Bank: A Chapter in the Economic History of the Negro Race* (Chapel Hill: University of North Carolina Press, 1927), 1.

39. Douglass in Osthaus, *Freedmen, Philanthropy and Fraud*, 1. See also Du Bois, *Black Reconstruction*, 600.

40. Hoffman, "From Slavery to Self-Reliance," 37; "The Sea Islands of South Carolina: Their Peaceful and Prosperous Condition" (Charleston, S.C.: The News & Courier Book Press, 1880), 5, 10, 13. This extensive report mentions a cooperative of African American farmers operating on Edisto Island. This could be the same farm that Fullerton and Steedmen learned of fifteen years earlier. Allen, *Reconstruction*, 65.

41. Du Bois, *Black Reconstruction*, 603.

42. Eric Foner, *Reconstruction: America's Unfinished Revolution, 1863–1877* (New York: Harper & Row, 1988), 161–68; Lester C. Lamon, *Blacks in Tennessee, 1791–1970* (Knoxville: University of Tennessee Press, 1981), 40; Litwack, *Been in the Storm So Long*, 408.

43. Abbott, *The Freedmen's Bureau in South Carolina*, 117. Du Bois equated the vagrancy and apprenticeship provisions of the Black Codes with slavery. The justice system that enforced these laws was, in Du Bois's estimation, a deliberate attempt at "social degradation and private profit." "Making every allowance for the excitement and turmoil of war, and the mentality of a defeated people, the Black Codes were infamous pieces of legislation." Du Bois, *Black Reconstruction*, 167.

44. Litwack, *Been in the Storm So Long*, 415.

45. Alrutheus A. Taylor, *The Negro in Tennessee, 1865–1880* (Washington, D.C.: Associated Publishers, 1947), 42. Laws dealing with vagrants, contract, and debt brought freedpeople, especially young men, into court and eventually into jails. A freedperson who left the employment of a landowner while in debt ran the risk of arrest. Other freedpeople who left with their debt paid and in search of other work ran the risk of arrest as vagrants during the time of travel. African American workers were free, in theory, to move from one work place to another to find better terms for their labor. But should they be found in transit without money or employment, they were subject to arrest and jail terms for vagrancy. Du Bois, *Black Reconstruction*, 166–80. In some places, like Lowndes County, landlords made agreements not to hire African Americans from any place within ten miles of their plantation. This made the freedom of laborers to travel and relocate even more theoretical. Litwack, *Been in the Storm So Long*, 415. Prisoners provided the state with revenue. They were leased out for their labor. By 1877, between 500 to 600 prisoners in Tennessee were leased to coal mines, railroads, and private farms. The revenue from their leases was "a handsome profit," according to the superintendent of prisons. Convict labor subsidized the rebuilding of the railroad after the war and the industrialization of Tennessee. In 1884 the Tennessee Coal, Iron and Railway Company leased all of the main prison population of Nashville. See Lamon, *Blacks in Tennessee*, 39; Randall G. Sheldon, "From Slave to Caste Society: The Penal Changes in Tennessee, 1830–1915," *Tennessee Historical Quarterly* 38 (Winter 1979): 467. Similar changes occurred in other southern states. The convict labor system in South Carolina, for example, began in 1873. By 1877 and "Redemption" it was a

large-scale operation rocking with abuse and public scandal. Between September 1877 and April 1879, the state leased 258 convicts to the Greenwood and Augusta Railroad. More than half of them died while working for the railroad or within ten days of returning to prison. The public investigation into this contract and condition brought about some reform measures, but the system continued. George B. Tindall, *South Carolina Negroes, 1877–1900* (Baton Rouge: Louisiana State University Press, 1966), 260–76.

46. Myrdal found this the case in the 1930s as well. *An American Dilemma*, 240–42.
47. Litwack, *Been in the Storm So Long*, 396.
48. Ibid., 423.
49. Ibid., 421.
50. Ibid.
51. Herman C. Nixon, *Forty Acres and Steel Mules* (Chapel Hill: University of North Carolina Press, 1938), 21.
52. Charles S. Johnson, Edwin R. Embree, and W. W. Alexander, *The Collapse of Cotton Tenancy: Summary of Field Studies and Statistical Surveys 1933–1935* (Chapel Hill: University of North Carolina Press, 1935), 13.
53. Norman Thomas, *The Plight of the Share-Cropper* (New York: League for Industrial Democracy, 1934), 23.
54. Ibid., 24.
55. Ibid.
56. Bureau of Labor Statistics, *Report No. 836 Labor Unionism in American Agriculture* (Washington, D.C.: Government Printing Office, 1945), 393.
57. Charles S. Johnson, *Growing Up in the Black Belt* (Washington, D.C.: American Council on Education, 1941), 6–7, 74; T. J. Woofter, Jr., *Black Yeomanry: Life on St. Helena Island* (New York: Henry Holt, 1930), 10.
58. Myrdal, *An American Dilemma*, 230, 240–42. Nate Shaw, a member of the Alabama Sharecroppers Union, estimated metaphorically, "Nigger got caught in the spokes of the wheel anyway it rolled." Theodore Rosengarten, *All God's Dangers: The Life of Nate Shaw* (New York: Vintage Books, 1974), 337.
59. Guy Carawan and Candie Carawan, *Ain't You Got a Right to the Tree of Life? The People of Johns Island, South Carolina* (New York: Simon and Schuster, 1966), 162.
60. Roberts gave his affidavit to members of the International Legal Defense Fund. His and others' affidavits may be found in the archives of the NAACP. Affidavit of Henry Roberts, NAACP Administration Files, Record Group II, Box C-348, Montgomery Lynchings 1927–36, Library of Congress, Washington, D.C.
61. John Beecher, "The Share Croppers' Union in Alabama," *Social Forces* 13 (Oct. 1934): 128; Bureau of Labor Statistics, *Labor Unionism in American Agriculture*, 289–95; F. Ray Marshall, *Labor in the South* (Cambridge: Harvard University Press, 1967), 156; Albert Jackson, "On The Alabama Front," *The Nation* 141 (Sept. 18, 1935): 329.
62. Clyde Johnson, "Rural Revolt in the Southeast: History of the Share Croppers

Union," paper prepared for the History Conference, The Citadel, Charleston, S.C., April 1979. Johnson was organizer for the Alabama Sharecroppers Union. The local sheriff, R. E. Woodruff, continued a particularly violent reprisal that turned Lowndes County into a "miniature Civil War." Bureau of Labor Statistics, *Labor Unionism in American Agriculture*, 299. The sheriff and a posse of about thirty-five landlords and deputies conducted nightriding raids, breaking into homes, kidnapping individuals, and beating them. Twenty African American men and women were reported beaten and six killed. Three unidentified bodies were reclaimed from the swamps of the county. Annie May Meriwether, wife of an organizer, described her beating and the terror of the reprisal.

> The mob entered the house and someone pointed to me and said, "There's one of the sons of bitches we're looking for." They asked me where Jim Press [her husband] was. I told them I didn't know, he had left early in the morning. They started tearing up the place looking for leaflets. They found the leaflets under the mattress. They said, "Here they are. Yes, you're one of the leaders in the meetings around here. You're the one we're looking for. Tell what you know about the meeting. I already know you know but I want to hear what kind of damned lie you're going to tell." Vaughn Ryles was doing the biggest of the talking. . . .
>
> Vaughn Ryles started doubling the rope and told me to pull off all my clothes. He said, "Lay down across the chair, I want naked meat this morning."
>
> I lay down across the chair and Ralph McGuire held my head for Ryles to beat me. He beat me about 20 minutes. He was beating me from my hips on down, and he hit me across the head.
>
> They said, "Now see if you can tell us what you know."
>
> I said, "I joined the Union but I didn't go back to any more meetings."
>
> They said, "Is that all you know about it?"
>
> I said, "Yes Sir."
>
> They were all cussing. Ryles said, "If that's all you know, lay back across the chair."
>
> I lay back down on the chair and they beat me for about 15 minutes more. They beat me over the same place. They let me up and I still didn't know anything for them. . . .
>
> Then Vaughn Ryles put a loop in the rope and told me to come over and when he put the rope around my neck that I would know. . . .
>
> Then he threw the rope over the rafters and then he and Ralph McGuire drew me up about 2 feet from the floor. My sister-in-law said they kept me there for 15 or 20 minutes and then let me down. I was unconscious. She said I laid there about 10 minutes and then I got up. Then Ryles said, "See if you can tell what you know." He said, "If you don't the limb will get you next time."
>
> Then I told him I joined the Union but I never did attend. I said, "They elected me Captain but I know you wouldn't like for it to be here and I wouldn't take any part in it."

Vaughn Ryles said, "If you had said that to start with I would never have beat you." Then he said, "Put on your clothes and go over to your house. Both of you." Then he saw my little girl and said to her, "What in Hell do you know about it." But she didn't say anything.

They marched us on ahead of them and said, "We might stop before we get there but you all better go on back." So we went on to the house. They had my husband hid. I passed right by where he was but I didn't know he was there. They stopped at my sister's house and got [him]. . . . They walked him about a mile and a half and set him out back of a cow barn in the hot sun from about 11:30 till about a half before sun-down that evening.

When I saw the mob leaving I told my sister-in-law, "I'm not going to stay here [her home]. They might kill me, but they will kill me trying to get away from here. I'm going to see where Jim Press is." Then we got out and took to the woods and stayed there until about a half-hour before sun-down. Then I heard guns firing about 75 or 100 times. There were other hands in the wood and when I got to where they were they told me about my husband being shot. They were lynching him then. . . .

Saturday morning I left for Birmingham. I left my little girl with my aunt and then my mother came and got her. She is 7 years old.

Affidavit of Annie May Meriwether, NAACP Administration File, Record Group II, Box C-348, Montgomery Lynchings, 1927–36, Library of Congress.

The police report of Jim Press Meriwether's death differed substantially from the account of his wife. In their account, Meriwether was in custody and on the way to the Hayneville jail. Supposedly, when he and his guards reached a point where he had hidden a shotgun, Meriwether "jerked free and grabbed the shot gun." Because he was coming out of the ditch with the shotgun in his hands, sheriff deputies had no alternative but to shoot him. Meriwether was executed in a manner similar to Ben Patterson forty-four years before in Lee County. What had changed in the rural South was the felt need to concoct an alibi for the mob's murderous action. Bureau of Labor Statistics, *Labor Unionism in American Agriculture*, 299. Albert Jackson, "On the Alabama Front," *The Nation* 141 (Sept. 18, 1935): 329.

63. William F. Holmes, "The Arkansas Cotton Pickers Strike of 1891 and the Demise of the Colored Farmers' Alliance," *Arkansas Historical Quarterly* 32 (Summer 1973): 109–10. See also Floyd J. Miller, "Black Protest and White Leadership: A Note on the Colored Farmers' Alliance," *Phylon* 33 (June 1972); and Jack Abramowitz, "The Negro in the Populist Movement," *Journal of Negro History* 38 (July 1953).

64. Holmes, "The Arkansas Cotton Pickers Strike of 1891," 112–13.

65. Ibid., 117; Philip S. Foner and Ronald L. Lewis, eds., *The Black Workers: A Documentary History from Colonial Times to the Present*, vol. 3, *The Black Workers during the Era of the Knights of Labor* (Philadelphia: Temple Univer-

sity Press, 1978), 348–64. A repression of organized Colored Alliance farmers took place earlier, William F. Holmes, "The LeFlore County Massacre and the Demise of the Colored Farmers' Alliance," *Phylon* 34 (Sept. 1973): 267–74.

66. O. A. Rogers, "The Elaine Race Riots of 1919," *Arkansas Historical Quarterly* 19 (1960): 142–50. The specific demands of the Progressive Union were reminiscent of those of the freedpeople in the months immediately after the Civil War. Saw mill workers in Melwood refused to allow women within their families pick cotton or to work for the white landlords at any price. The union demanded higher wages for cotton pickers, and some refused to work at the wages offered. In addition, the union members made plans to buy land in Melwood to give them better access and more control of the means of work and income.

67. Mary W. Ovington, *The Walls Came Tumbling Down* (New York: Arno Press and the New York Times, 1969), 155; Rogers, "The Elaine Race Riots," 146–47.

68. Walter F. White, *Rope and Faggot* (New York: Arno Press and the New York Times, 1929), 103, and " 'Massacring Whites' in Arkansas," *The Nation* 109 (Dec. 6, 1919): 715–16; Rogers, "The Elaine Race Riots," 147–48.

69. Rogers, "The Elaine Race Riots," 149.

70. Ibid., 150; Robert L. Zangrando, *The NAACP Crusade against Lynching, 1909–1950* (Philadelphia: Temple University Press, 1980), 85; White, *Rope and Faggot*, 103; Ovington, *The Walls Came Tumbling Down*, 158–60.

71. For the best account of the trials and the legal issues involved in this case, see Richard C. Cortner, *A Mob Intent on Death: The NAACP and the Arkansas Riot Case* (Middletown, Conn.: Wesleyan University Press, 1988).

72. Cortner, *A Mob Intent on Death*, 179–80.

73. Donald H. Grubbs, *Cry from the Cotton: The Southern Tenant Farmers' Union and the New Deal* (Chapel Hill: University of North Carolina Press, 1971), 88. For an account of the efforts of STFU to lobby Washington officials, see H. L. Mitchell and J. R. Butler, "The Cropper Learns His Fate," *The Nation* 141 (Sept. 18 1935), 328.

74. Howard Kester, *Revolt among the Sharecroppers* (New York: Covici Friede, 1936), 56; H. L. Mitchell, *Mean Things Happening in This Land: The Life and Times of H. L. Mitchell, Co-founder of the Southern Tenant Farmers' Union* (Montclair, N.J.: Allanheld, Osmun, 1979), 40.

75. Grubbs, *Cry from the Cotton*, 92, 117; Bureau of Labor Statistics, *Labor Unionism in American Agriculture*, 310.

76. The STFU had already affected Washington politics in 1935, although not in the manner it intended. From mid-January to Feb. 6, 1935, staff of the legal section of the AAA clashed with the administrator of their agency over a policy the STFU proposed. The staff wanted Section 7 of the AAA Act interpreted to permit tenant farmers and sharecroppers to remain on their plantations despite any change in their employment status caused by crop reductions. Landlords, such as those the STFU confronted, interpreted the provision to mean the same number of tenants but not the same tenants. This interpretation permitted them to

evict STFU members and replace them with docile tenants. Secretary of Agriculture Henry Wallace bowed to expediency in this instance. The legal staff's broad interpretation would have angered the planters and their congressmen and senators, whose support FDR needed desperately. Wallace's choice had implications for the New Deal alliance, and he chose to preserve it. He sided with the AAA administrator and acquiesced in the firing of the nine legal staff members. Wallace supported new reform initiatives in general, however, and two months later the Resettlement Administration began within the Department of Agriculture with Rexford Tugwell in charge. The new agency gave the reformers in AAA hope and some vindication. For information on the controversy within the AAA, see Sidney Baldwin, *Poverty and Politics: The Rise and Decline of the Farm Security Administration* (Chapel Hill: University of North Carolina Press, 1968): 52ff.; Bureau of Labor Statistics, *Labor Unionism in American Agriculture*, 300; Mitchell and Butler, "The Cropper Learns His Fate," 328.

77. Bureau of Labor Statistics, *Labor Unionism in American Agriculture*, 310; Kester, *Revolt among the Sharecroppers*, 91.

78. Johnson, Embree, and Alexander, *Collapse of Cotton Tenancy*, 64–66.

79. Lester M. Salamon, "The Time Dimension in Policy Evaluation: The Case of the New Deal Land Reform Experiments," *Public Policy* 27 (Sept. 1979): 182–83.

80. Press Release, U.S. Department of Agriculture, Farm Security Administration, Information Division, Oct. 1942. This and other material on the Haywood County Farms Project can be found in the Farm Security Administration Archives, Record Group 96, AD TN 27, 2–21, National Archives.

81. Justification Alabama Farm Tenant Security Project, Box 17, FSA Files, Record Group 96 RR-AL 27, March 31, 1937, National Archives. There were early and unsuccessful negotiations between officials of the Resettlement Administration and individuals in Lowndes County to begin a full-fledged land-redistribution program there. The work was intended to continue plans made at Tuskegee with the Rosenwald Fund that were canceled with the onset of the Depression. These records may be found in FSA Files, Record Group 96, AL-15, Box 38, National Archives.

82. *House Committee Investigating the Activities of the Farm Security Administration*, 78th Cong., 2d sess., May 9, 1944, Report 492, pp. 2–11, 23.

83. Ibid., 7.

84. Ibid., 86–88.

85. Baldwin, *Poverty and Politics*, 401–402.

86. Pamela Browning, "Black Farming: The Erosion of a Scarce Resource," *Perspectives* 15 (Winter-Spring 1983): 40–50.
U.S. Commission on Civil Rights, *The Decline of Black Farming in America* (Washington, D.C.: Government Printing Office, 1982). Guy Gugliotta, "The Hard Row of Black Farmers," *The Washington Post National Weekly Edition* (Sept. 17–23, 1990): 10–11.
The policies of the FHA eventually elicited a protest in west Tennessee.

"Black Farmers Still Sitting in at FMHA Units," *The* (Nashville) *Tennessean* (March 15, 1981): 1.

87. Nixon, *Forty Acres and Steel Mules*.

Chapter 6

1. *Autobiography of Oliver Otis Howard: Major General United States Army*, vol. 2 (New York: Baker & Taylor, 1908), 98.

2. Willie C. Rose, *Rehearsal for Reconstruction: The Port Royal Experiment* (New York: Oxford University Press, 1984), 43, 76–78. Joe M. Richardson, *Christian Reconstruction: The American Missionary Association and Southern Blacks, 1861–1890* (Athens: University of Georgia Press, 1986), 17.

3. Richardson, *Christian Reconstruction*, 4.

4. Martin Abbott, *The Freedmen's Bureau in South Carolina: 1865–1872* (Chapel Hill: University of North Carolina Press, 1967), 134.

5. Henry Lee Swint, "Notes and Documents: Reports from Educational Agents of the Freedmen's Bureau in Tennessee, 1865–1870," *Tennessee Historical Quarterly* 1 (Winter 1942): 51–80, and (Spring 1942): 152–70.

6. Kenneth B. White, "The Alabama Freedmen's Bureau and Black Education: The Myth of Opportunity," *Alabama Review* 34 (April 1981): 107–24.

7. Swint, "Notes and Documents," 169.

8. George R. Bentley, *A History of the Freedmen's Bureau* (New York: Octagon Books, 1974), 172–73, 184.

9. Peter Kolchin, *First Freedom: The Responses of Alabama's Blacks to Emancipation and Reconstruction* (Westport, Conn.: Greenwood Press, 1972), 180.

10. James M. McPherson, *Ordeal by Fire: The Civil War and Reconstruction* (New York: Alfred A. Knopf, 1982), 3; Bentley, *History of the Freedmen's Bureau*, 183.

11. Kolchin, *First Freedom*, 180.

12. Ibid., 179; Paul Skeels Pierce, *The Freedmen's Bureau: A Chapter in the History of Reconstruction* (Iowa City: University of Iowa Press, 1904), 83–86.

13. Swint, "Notes and Documents," 75–76.

14. Kolchin, *First Freedom*, 148.

15. Pierce, *The Freedmen's Bureau*, 100–101.

16. Bentley, *History of the Freedmen's Bureau*, 171; McPherson, *Ordeal by Fire*, 574.

17. Ronald E. Butchart, *Northern Schools, Southern Blacks, and Reconstruction* (Westport, Conn.: Greenwood Press, 1980), 9; McPherson, *Ordeal by Fire*, 574.

18. Richardson, *Christian Reconstruction*, 105.

19. Ibid., 200; A. Knighton Stanley, *The Children Is Crying: Congregationalism among Black People* (New York: Pilgrim Press, 1979), 42.

20. Richardson, *Christian Reconstruction*, 72.

21. Herbert G. Gutman, "Schools for Freedom: The Post-Emancipation Origins of Afro-American Education," in *Power and Culture: Essays on the American Work-*

ing Class, ed. Ira Berlin (New York: Pantheon Books 1987), 263; Richardson, *Christian Reconstruction*, 123. In addition to all this assistance, ordinary freedpeople played central roles in the school movement as well. Older, better trained students assisted younger, beginning students informally and assisted teachers formally, and in some cases for pay. Richardson, *Christian Reconstruction*, 189. African American residents of an area would organize resources, including assistance from the Freedmen's Bureau, to begin a school just as the first African American landowners did on the Sea Islands in 1863. In 1865, for example, freedpeople living near Helena, Ark., contacted the Freedmen's Bureau to request that it establish a method to tax them for the support of schools for their children. This began the AMA normal, or teacher training, school there. Leon F. Litwack, *Been in the Storm So Long: The Aftermath of Slavery* (New York: Vintage Books, 1979), 499.

22. The AMA had the longest history of the freedmen's relief organizations. That explains, in part, its capacity to do so much so quickly. Three missionary associations combined with the Amistad Committee in 1846 to form the AMA. The Amistad Committee had formed in 1839 to organize assistance for slaves who had rebelled on board a Spanish ship and sailed the ship to northern Long Island, eventually. The issue whether or not to return them to Spanish authorities went before the U.S. Supreme Court. The Court refused to return them, and the men returned to Sierra Leone in 1841. Organizers and officers of the American Antislavery Society, founded in 1833, became officers of the AMA. This background gave the AMA a strong abolitionist tradition, a cadre of leadership and support, and the resources of three missionary associations. Stanley, *The Children Is Crying*, 20; Frederick L. Brownlee, *New Day Ascending* (New York: Pilgrim Press, 1946), 21; Augustus Field Beard, *A Crusade of Brotherhood: A History of the American Missionary Association* (Boston: Penguin Press, 1909), 15–31.

23. Richardson, *Christian Reconstruction*, 83.

24. Stanley, *The Children Is Crying*, 20.

25. Ibid., 52; Kolchin, *First Freedom*, 144.

26. Richardson, *Christian Reconstruction*, 4, 9, 200, 193–95.

27. Stanley, *The Children Is Crying*, 75.

28. Swint, "Notes and Documents," 152–53.

29. W. E. B. Du Bois, *Black Reconstruction: An Essay Toward a History of the Part Which Black Folk Played in the Attempt to Reconstruct Democracy in America, 1860–1880* (New York: S. A. Russell, 1935), 642.

30. Gutman, "Schools for Freedom," 266.

31. Richardson, *Christian Reconstruction*, 209.

32. Earle H. West, "The Harris Brothers: Black Northern Teachers in the Reconstruction South," *Journal of Negro Education* 48 (Spring 1979): 126–38; Kolchin, *First Freedom*, 154–62.

33. Richardson, *Christian Reconstruction*, 208, 237–55.
34. Stanley, *The Children Is Crying*, 76–77.
35. Du Bois, *Black Reconstruction*, 648.
36. Sandra E. Small, "The Yankee Schoolmarm in Freedmen's Schools: An Analysis of Attitudes," *Journal of Southern History* 45 (Aug. 1979): 398; Swint, "Notes and Documents," 58, 62.
37. Kolchin, *First Freedom*, 175–76.
38. Gutman, "Schools for Freedom," 270.
39. Swint, "Notes and Documents," 59–60.
40. Kolchin, *First Freedom*, 150.
41. Letter of J. L. Poston to F. S. Palmer, April 26, 1867, Letters and Papers of the Bureau of Refugees, Freedmen and Abandoned Lands, Vol. 75, p. 2, Manuscript Division of the Tennessee State Archives; Lester C. Lamon, *Blacks in Tennessee, 1791–1970* (Knoxville: University of Tennessee Press, 1981), 39; *Autobiography of Oliver Otis Howard*, 377–78.
42. Swint, "Notes and Documents," 64.
43. Ibid., 158.
44. *Autobiography of Oliver Otis Howard*, 376.
45. Du Bois, *Black Reconstruction*, 647.
46. White, "The Alabama Freedmen's Bureau and Black Education," 107–24.
47. Small, "The Yankee Schoolmarm in Freedmen's Schools," 391–93, 402, 381.
48. White, "The Alabama Freedmen's Bureau and Black Education," 122.
49. Swint, "Notes and Documents," 64.
50. Ibid., 164.
51. Ibid., 68.
52. Kolchin illustrates this well by explaining the ease with which freedchildren were separated from their parents after Emancipation through apprenticeships on the basis of the belief that African American parents were children themselves and incapable of affection and parental responsibility. *First Freedom*, 114–23.
53. Bentley, *History of the Freedmen's Bureau*, 183.
54. Loren Schweninger, "James T. Rapier of Alabama and the Noble Cause of Reconstruction," in *Southern Black Leaders of the Reconstruction Era*, ed. Howard N. Rabinowitz (Urbana: University of Illinois Press, 1982), 79–99.
55. William J. Simmons, D.D., *Men of Mark: Eminent, Progressive and Rising* (Cleveland, Ohio: Geo. M. Rewell, 1887), 503–505; Joseph H. Cartwright, "Black Legislators in Tennessee in the 1800's: A Case Study in Black Political Leadership," *Tennessee Historical Quarterly* 32 (Fall 1973): 274–81.
56. Glenn N. Sisk, "Negro Education in the Alabama Black Belt, 1875–1900," *Journal of Negro Education* 22 (Spring 1953): 129; Horace M. Bond, *Negro Education in Alabama: A Study in Cotton and Steel* (Washington, D.C.: Associated Publishers, 1939), 148–56.
57. Bond, *Negro Education in Alabama*, 252–53.

58. Gunnar Myrdal, *An American Dilemma: The Negro Problem and Modern Democracy* (New York: Harper & Brothers, 1944), 951, 902 note b.

59. Ibid., 903.

60. Stanley H. Rice, "A Proposal to Annex RR-TN 23, Haywood Farms, to RR-TN 27, Tennessee Tenant Security Farms Project, 21 January 1938," FSA Files, Record Group 96, AD TN 27, 702-01, National Archives.

61. T. J. Woofter, Jr., *Black Yeomanry: Life on St. Helena Island* (New York: Henry Holt, 1930), 11, 22, 244. Eventually, it became apparent to African American observers that the Sea Islands were a demonstration of the length of time it took white people to recognize the ability of African Americans to succeed at education, work, and other matters if given the opportunity. Edwin D. Hoffman, "From Slavery to Self-Reliance: The Record of Achievement of the Freedmen of the Sea Island Region," *Journal of Negro History* 4 (Jan. 1956): 41. For the many connections of Will Alexander to studies on race relations and efforts of change, see Wilma Dykeman and James Stokely, *Seeds of Southern Change: The Life of Will Alexander* (Chicago: University of Chicago Press, 1962).

62. Donald Spivey, *Schooling for the New Slavery: Black Industrial Education, 1868–1915* (Westport, Conn.: Greenwood Press, 1978), 7.

63. Rose, *Rehearsal for Reconstruction*, 356. See also R. S. Holland, ed., *Letters and Diary of Laura M. Towne: 1866–1871* (Cambridge, Mass.: Riverside Press, 1912).

64. Du Bois criticized the content and dominance of Washington's educational views. W. E. B. Du Bois, *The Souls of Black Folk* (rpt.: Millwood, N.Y.: Kraus-Thomson Organization, 1973), 41–59.

65. Clement Richardson Ellis, ed., *National Encyclopedia of the Colored Race* (Montgomery: National Publishing, 1919), 28.

66. *The Booker T. Washington Papers, Volume 3, 1889–95* (Urbana: University of Illinois, 1974), 161–62, 163–64, 481–84.

67. Robert G. Sherer, *Subordination or Liberation* (University, Ala.: University of Alabama Press, 1977), 68–69.

68. Letter provided by Rose Ellis, Fort Deposit, Ala. For a history of the school, see Rose Herlong Ellis, "The Calhoun School, Miss Charlotte Thorn's 'Lighthouse on the Hill' in Lowndes County, Alabama," *Alabama Review* 37 (July 1984): 183–201.

69. William L. McDavid, "Calhoun Land Trust: A Study of Rural Resettlement in Lowndes County, Alabama" (master's thesis, Fisk University, 1943), 52, 44, 72.

70. Ibid., 57.

71. In 1915 the school had twelve white teachers and fifteen African American teachers. Sisk, "Negro Education in the Alabama Black Belt, 1875–1900," 134.

72. W. E. B. Du Bois, *Dusk of Dawn: An Essay toward an Autobiography of a Race Concept* (rpt.: Millwood, N.Y.: Kraus-Thomson Organization, 1975), 86.

73. Du Bois, *The Quest of the Silver Fleece: A Novel* (New York: Negro Universities

Press, 1911), 178–79. Du Bois undoubtedly utilized some of his own teaching experience in this novel. He drew upon that experience and the fortunes of his students to reflect on the nature of progress. Du Bois, *The Souls of Black Folk*, 60–74.

74. McDavid, "Calhoun Land Trust," 73.
75. Floyd Brown, *He Built a School* (Fargo, Ark.: Fargo Agricultural School Museum, n.d.), 39.
76. Ibid., 57.
77. Small, "The Yankee Schoolmarm in Freedmen's Schools," 393.
78. Sisk, "Negro Education in the Alabama Black Belt, 1875–1900," 129–30.
79. Du Bois, *Black Reconstruction*, 123.
80. Ginna Rae McNeil, *Groundwork: Charles Hamilton Houston and the Struggle for Civil Rights* (Philadelphia: University of Pennsylvania Press, 1983), 63–152. Pauli Murray, *The Autobiography of a Black Activist, Feminist, Lawyer, Priest, and Poet* (Knoxville: University of Tennessee Press, 1987), 180–231.
81. Cynthia Griggs Fleming, "A Survey of the Beginnings of Tennessee's Black Colleges and Universities, 1865–1920," *Tennessee Historical Quarterly* 39 (Summer 1980): 195–209.
82. Du Bois, *Black Reconstruction*, 667.
83. Myrdal, *An American Dilemma*, 881.
84. Ibid., 546.

Chapter 7

1. Claude F. Oubre, *Forty Acres and a Mule: The Freedmen's Bureau and Black Landownership* (Baton Rouge: Louisiana State University Press, 1978), 53–60; Willie L. Rose, *Rehearsal for Reconstruction: The Port Royal Experiment* (New York: Oxford University Press, 1984), 351–56; *Autobiography of Oliver Otis Howard: Major General United States Army*, vol. 2 (New York: Baker & Taylor, 1908), 238–40; and Joel Williamson, *After Slavery: The Negro in South Carolina during Reconstruction, 1861–1877* (Chapel Hill: University of North Carolina Press, 1965), 81–85.
2. Julie Saville, "A Measure of Freedom: From Slave to Wage Laborer, South Carolina, 1860–1868" (Ph.D. diss., Yale University, 1986), 28–29.
3. General James B. Steedman and General Joseph Fullerton, "The Bureau: General Steedman's Report for South Carolina, Florida and the Sea Islands," *The* [Charleston] *Courier*, June 16, 1866.
4. James S. Allen, *Reconstruction: The Battle for Democracy* (New York: International Publishers, 1937), 60; Leon F. Litwack, *Been in the Storm So Long: The Aftermath of Slavery* (New York: Vintage Books, 1979), 270.
5. George C. Rable, *But There Was No Peace: The Role of Violence in the Politics of Reconstruction* (Athens: University of Georgia Press, 1984), 25–39.

6. W. E. B. Du Bois, *Black Reconstruction: An Essay Toward a History of the Part Which Black Folk Played in the Attempt to Reconstruct Democracy in America, 1860–1880* (New York: S. A. Russell, 1935), 325–80.

7. Allen W. Trelease, *White Terror: The Ku Klux Klan Conspiracy and Southern Reconstruction* (Westport, Conn.: Greenwood Press, 1971), xxiv.

8. Alrutheus A. Taylor, *The Negro in Tennessee, 1865–1880* (Washington, D.C.: Associated Publishers, 1947), 57–58. Du Bois, *Black Reconstruction*, 289–91.

9. U.S. House of Representatives, *Reports of the Committee Investigating Impeachment*, Serial No. 1314, 40th Cong., 1st sess., 1867, p. 116.

10. *Trial of Andrew Johnson, President of the United States, Before the Senate of the United States, on Impeachment by the House of Representatives for High Crimes and Misdemeanors*, 40th Cong., 2d sess., 1868, vol. 3, p. 247ff. See also John R. Labovitz, *Presidential Impeachment* (New Haven, Conn.: Yale University Press, 1978), 49–56.

11. Everette Swinney, *Suppressing the Ku Klux Klan: The Enforcement of the Reconstruction Amendments, 1870–1877* (New York: Garland, 1987), 21.

12. Ibid., 57.

13. Ibid., 71–72.

14. Ibid., 104.

15. Du Bois, *Black Reconstruction*, 186.

16. Taylor, *The Negro in Tennessee*, 2–3.

17. Ibid., 23–24; Trelease, *White Terror*, 6–7.

18. Allen, *Reconstruction*, 93–94; Eric Foner, *Reconstruction: America's Unfinished Revolution, 1863–1877* (New York: Harper & Row, 1988), 283–85.

19. Stephen Powers, *Afoot and Alone: A Walk from Sea to Sea by the Southern Route* (Hartford, Conn.: Columbia Book, 1872), 67; Michael W. Fitzgerald, *The Union League Movement in the Deep South: Politics and Agricultural Change during Reconstruction* (Baton Rouge: Louisiana State University Press, 1989), 61.

20. Fitzgerald, *The Union League Movement in the Deep South*, 115; and Walter L. Fleming, *Documentary History of Reconstruction: Political, Military, Social, Religious, Educational and Industrial, 1865 to Present Time*, vol. 2 (Gloucester, Mass.: Peter Smith, 1960), 13–16.

21. Allen, *Reconstruction*, 94.

22. Wayne F. Binning, "The Tennessee Republicans in Decline, 1869–1876," *Tennessee Historical Quarterly* 39 (Winter 1980): 471; Walter J. Fraser, Jr., "Black Reconstructionists in Tennessee," *Tennessee Historical Quarterly* 34 (Winter 1975): 365; Fitzgerald, *The Union League Movement in the Deep South*.

23. Allen, *Reconstruction*, 66, 95–99; Fleming, *Documentary History of Reconstruction*, vol. 2, 8–11, 22–29; Fitzgerald, *The Union League Movement in the Deep South*.

24. Selected Records of the Tennessee Field Office of the Bureau of Refugees, Freedmen, and Abandoned Lands, Manuscript Division of the Tennessee State Archives, Roll 17, vol. 136, p. 31, Letter of F. S. Palmer to W. H. Bower, June 10,

1867; "Riot: The Fruit of Radicalism Blossoming in Brownsville," *Memphis Daily Appeal*, May 15, 1867.

25. Paul David Philips, "A History of the Freedmen's Bureau in Tennessee" (Ph.D. diss., Vanderbilt University, 1964), 300, 308; Rable, *But There Was No Peace*, 85; Swinney, *Suppressing the Ku Klux Klan*, 171–72; Taylor, *The Negro in Tennessee*, 55.

26. Taylor, *The Negro in Tennessee*, 55; Thomas B. Alexander, *Political Reconstruction in Tennessee* (New York: Russel and Russel, 1950), 160.

27. Alexander, *Political Reconstruction in Tennessee*, 161.

28. Stanley F. Horn, *Invisible Empire: The Story of the Ku Klux Klan, 1866–1871* (Cos Cobb, Conn.: John E. Edwards, 1969), 397.

29. Taylor, *The Negro in Tennessee*, 93–94; Trelease, *White Terror*, 21.

30. For biographical information on Forrest, see Robert S. Henry, *"First with the Most" Forrest* (New York: Bobbs-Merrill, 1944); Horn, *Invisible Empire*; Andrew Lytle, *Bedford Forrest and His Critter Company* (New York: McDowell, Obolensky, 1960). Forrest traveled throughout the South developing railroads after the war. His work in eastern Arkansas won the affection of residents there, who named the seat of St. Francis County, Forrest City.

Other prominent former Confederates also expressed objection to the state governments of the time. Edmund Pettus, a former confederate general, testified to a congressional committee about Klan activity in Alabama. He claimed little knowledge of the Ku Klux Klan and assumed its members to be from a lesser class of whites. His opposition to the Klan, on class grounds, was undoubtedly an important reason for the lack of Klan influence in the black belt of Alabama. It was widely believed that Pettus was the prominent, unnamed Selma resident who founded the Knights of the White Camellia, which had many more members than the local Klan, used fewer disguises and less violence, but worked just as determinedly to change an unwanted political system. Pettus gave the committee riveting testimony on the thoughts and feelings of white leaders in the black belt on congressional reconstruction. "The local government of the State of Alabama is imposed on the people of this particular locality without their consent. They have never consented, either to the form of government, or to the selection of those who hold offices. In other words, our government has been manufactured by Federal authority and without the consent of the people."

Pettus asserted that the disfranchisement of 5,000 to 10,000 white men was "a simple act of tyranny" that was intended to enable "one particular party to control the government." These disfranchised men were not the disguised terrorists whom Congress sought to curb, but the most qualified and experienced leaders in the South, who were excluded from public roles. This exclusion was detrimental to the South and violated the battlefield understanding that men like himself had with Union army leaders like Grant and Sherman. The battlefield terms were straightforward. If the Confederates dropped their weapons, returned home, and acted as peaceable citizens of the United States, they "shall not be disturbed by the authority of the United States." If the terms of surrender meant anything, Pettus explained to the committee, they meant the freedom to enjoy the rights of property and person guaranteed by the laws of the land generally, including the right to run for and to hold public office. Pettus recognized the right of the conqueror over the conquered but considered it bad faith "to make a promise to men with arms in their hands and violate it as soon as they had surrendered those arms."

Pettus reported a divided opinion among whites about the freedmen's suffrage. He suggested that people like himself "were in a new condition of things and opinion was being molded by circumstances." Sentiment was generally against suffrage, and those in favor of it generally supported some form of qualification test, of property, education, or both, for freedmen. U. S. Congressional Joint Select Committee, *Klan Hearings, Testimony Taken on Condition of Affairs in the Late Insurrectionary States, Alabama, Vol. 1, Report 22, Part 3*, 42d Cong., 2d sess. (1872), 382–92.

Civic leaders in Selma later honored Pettus and named a bridge in the city after him. That bridge was the scene of Bloody Sunday and the start of the Selma March in 1965.

31. Horn, *Invisible Empire*, 413. There were an estimated 40,000 freedmen eligible to vote in the 1867 election, the same number that Bedford used to estimate the armed men he could put in the field.

32. Ibid., 411–15.

33. Selected Records of the Tennessee Field Office of the Bureau of Refugees, Freedmen, and Abandoned Lands, Manuscript Division of the Tennessee State Archives, Roll 17, vol. 137, p. 381, Letter of F. S. Palmer to W. H. Bower, Aug. 10, 1868; vol. 138, p. 39, Letter of F. S. Palmer to W. H. Bower, Oct. 13, 1868; p. 134, Letter of F. S. Palmer to W. H. Bower, Dec. 21, 1868; p. 78, Letter of F. S. Palmer to J. S. Porter, Nov. 11, 1868.

34. Taylor, *The Negro in Tennessee*, 73.

35. Ibid., 100.

36. Trelease, *White Terror*, 152–53.

37. Ibid., 349–61.

38. Swinney, *Suppressing the Ku Klux Klan*, 206–37; Eric Foner, *Nothing but Freedom: Emancipation and Its Legacy* (Baton Rouge: Louisiana State University Press, 1983), 89–110.

39. For discussions of comparable events in the three other states see Rable, *But There Was No Peace*. For additional accounts in areas of this study see Foner, *Nothing but Freedom*, 89–110; Loren Schweninger, "Black Citizenship and the Republican Party in Reconstruction Alabama," *Alabama Review* 29 (April 1976): 83–103; Schweninger, "James T. Rapier of Alabama and the Noble Cause of Reconstruction," in *Southern Black Leaders of the Reconstruction Era*, ed.

Howard N. Rabinowitz (Urbana: University of Illinois Press, 1982), 86–89; Peter Kolchin, *First Freedom: The Responses of Alabama's Blacks to Emancipation and Reconstruction* (Westport, Conn.: Greenwood Press, 1972), 229–65. Kolchin mentions an insurrection of freedmen and a separate government established in Perote in the black belt in 1867 that federal troops quelled (273). Kolchin also discusses the Alabama black belt Leagues and their leaders. He offers important distinctions among the African American economic and political elites of the time that parallel later differences between Booker T. Washington and W. E. B. Du Bois (308). Fitzgerald traces the radical nature of the Leagues to their economic goals of protecting the rights of African American rural agricultural workers. Fitzgerald, *The Union League Movement in the Deep South.*

40. Alrutheus A. Taylor, *The Negro in South Carolina during the Reconstruction* (New York: Russel and Russel, 1924), 232–60. Foner, *Nothing but Freedom*, 74–110, and *Reconstruction*, 570–87.

41. W. E. B. Du Bois, ed., *The Atlanta University Publications, No. 16, The Common School and the Negro American. 1912* (rpt.: New York: Arno Press, 1968), 116; Walter L. Fleming, *Civil War and Reconstruction in Alabama* (Spartanburg, S.C.: Reprint Co., 1978), 806. It is possible that Rapier had influence even long after his rapid demise from political power. In his last years he devoted himself to encouraging the migration of African Americans from the South to Kansas, termed the exoduster movement. He worked with groups in Tennessee and died in poverty after giving his wealth to support these efforts. Elisha Scott, a prominent African American Kansas lawyer, came from an exoduster family from Tennessee. He and his sons played a large role in the school desegregation suit. Richard Kluger, *Simple Justice: The History of Brown v. Board of Education and Black America's Struggle for Equality* (New York: Alfred A. Knopf, 1976), 384–95. Schweninger, "James T. Rapier," 91–92.

42. Taylor, *The Negro in Tennessee*, 103; Swinney, *Suppressing the Ku Klux Klan*, 288. Tindall offers a later instance of the violent suppression of African American political participation. In Phoenix, S.C., in 1898, the white Republican candidate for Congress encouraged African American political participation and began gathering affidavits from African American men about interference with their efforts to vote. A riot broke out during which a Democrat died. Eight African American men were lynched on November 9 and 10, and many more, a number impossible to determine, lost their lives in the retaliation. The losing Republican candidate, his brother, and his father were charged with inciting a riot, but the charges were dropped. George B. Tindall, *South Carolina Negroes, 1877–1900* (Baton Rouge: Louisiana State University Press, 1966), 256–58.

43. William J. Simmons, D.D., *Men of Mark: Eminent, Progressive and Rising* (Cleveland, Ohio: Geo. M. Rewell, 1887) 503–505; Joseph H. Cartwright, "Black Legislators in Tennessee in the 1800's: A Case Study in Black Political Leadership," *Tennessee Historical Quarterly* 32 (Fall 1973): 274–81.

44. Joseph H. Cartwright, *The Triumph of Jim Crow* (Knoxville: University of Tennessee Press, 1976), 116.

45. J. Morgan Kousser, *The Shaping of Southern Politics: Suffrage Restriction and the Establishment of the One-Party South, 1880–1910* (New Haven, Conn.: Yale University Press, 1974), 92.

46. Carl H. Moneyhon, "Black Politics in Arkansas during the Gilded Age, 1876–1900," *Arkansas Historical Quarterly* 44 (Autumn 1985): 222–45.

47. Ibid.; and Kousser, *The Shaping of Southern Politics*, 123–30.

48. Moneyhon, "Black Politics in Arkansas," 241. Myrdal offered a description of the caste order of race that coincides with Moneyhon's analysis. Myrdal also offered a brilliant analysis of caste and class. Gunnar Myrdal, *An American Dilemma: The Negro Problem and Modern Democracy* (New York: Harper & Brothers, 1944), 60–61, 689–705.

49. Kousser, *The Shaping of Southern Politics*, 134.

50. Ibid., 130–38.

51. Ibid., 169.

52. Fleming, *Civil War and Reconstruction in Alabama*, 806.

53. Fitzgerald, *The Union League Movement in the Deep South*, 241–42.

54. Steven F. Lawson, *Black Ballots: Voting Rights in the South, 1944–1969* (New York: Columbia University Press, 1976), 7–9; Jack Abramowitz, "The Negro in the Populist Movement," *Journal of Negro History* 38 (July 1953); Dewey W. Grantham, *Southern Progressivism: The Reconciliation of Progress and Tradition* (Knoxville: University of Tennessee Press, 1983), 123–25.

55. Swinney, *Suppressing the Ku Klux Klan*, 328–30.

56. Kousser, *The Shaping of Southern Politics*, 228; Nancy J. Weiss, "The Negro and the New Freedom," in *The Segregation Era, 1863–1954*, ed. Allen Weinstein and F. O. Gatell (New York: Oxford University Press, 1970) 129–42; Allen, *Reconstruction*, 91.

57. Myrdal, *An American Dilemma*, 564.

58. Simmons, *Men of Mark*, 502–505. For a discussion of the major effort to acquire antilynching legislation, see Robert L. Zangrando, *The NAACP Crusade against Lynching, 1909–1950* (Philadelphia: Temple University Press, 1980).

59. "Lynched at Hayneville: Theo Calloway Disposed of by a Very Quiet Mob," *Montgomery Advertiser* (March 30, 1888): 1, and "An Incendiary Sheet on the Lowndes Lynching," *Montgomery Advertiser* (April 8, 1888): 1.

60. "The Lowndes Lynching: Correspondence between the Governor and the Sheriff," *Montgomery Advertiser* (April 5, 1888): 1. For other coverage of this exchange, see "Seay vs. Brinson," *Montgomery Advertiser* (April 7, 1888): 2; "The Lowndes Convention," *Montgomery Advertiser* (April 23, 1888): 2.

61. The first report from the county cited evidence that the danger was overstated. Rather than finding a real danger in the existence of 100 or more armed African Americans organized for violent reprisal, the report found "far more reason-

able" the story that "the [white] people of Sandy Ridge had worked themselves up to an unnecessarily high pitch over the rumors which have been going the rounds. . . ." "Blood in Lowndes: A Red Sequel to a Red Deed," *Montgomery Advertiser* (May 5, 1888): 1. "Peace in Lowndes: The Situation at Sandy Ridge Not So Serious," *Montgomery Advertiser* (May 6, 1888): 1; "The Lowndes Trouble: The Ring-Leaders Have Surrendered," *Montgomery Advertiser* (May 7, 1888): 1.

62. "Letohatchie: All is Quiet—The Troops Save Sandy Ridge," *Montgomery Advertiser* (May 9, 1888): 2. The *New York Times* reported the story as a foiled plot to kill whites. "Negroes of Lowndes County (Ala.) Plot to Murder Whites," *New York Times* (May 10, 1888): 6.

63. Ida B. Wells-Barnett, *On Lynchings: Southern Horrors, A Red Record, Mob Rule in New Orleans* (rpt.: New York: Arno Press and the New York Times, 1969), 8–15.

64. Williamson suggests that by 1893 lynch mobs were conducting themselves as if their members had gone to school to study the procedures for their deeds. Joel Williamson, *The Crucible of Race: Black-White Relations in the American South since Emancipation* (New York: Oxford University Press, 1984), 184.

65. Ibid., 183–88. For a particularly appalling and barbaric lynching by burning at the stake that was widely publicized and gathered media coverage, see William Pickens, "The American Congo—Burning of Henry Lowry," *The Nation*, 122 (March 23, 1921), 426–28. See also Walter F. White, *Rope and Faggot* (rpt.: New York: Arno Press and the New York Times, 1929). The burning of an African American boy at the stake seared an impression into H. L. Mitchell's memory. Mitchell begins his account of the Southern Tenant Farmers' Union with the description of the lynching of Ligon Scott in Dyersburg, Tenn., on Dec. 2, 1917. Scott was only a few years older than Mitchell at the time. H. L. Mitchell, *Mean Things Happening in This Land: The Life and Times of H. L. Mitchell, Co-Founder of the Southern Tenant Farmers' Union* (Montclair, N.J.: Allanheld, Osmun, 1979).

66. Philip S. Foner and Ronald L. Lewis, eds., *The Black Worker: A Documentary History from Colonial Times to the Present*, Vol. 3, *The Black Workers during the Era of the Knights of Labor* (Philadelphia: Temple University Press, 1978), 348–64.

67. James R. McGovern, *Anatomy of a Lynching: The Killing of Claude Neal* (Baton Rouge: Louisiana State University, 1982), 11. Those instances of criminal convictions and actual jail sentences given to the white lynchers of African American victims indicate a boundary for caste subordination. White southerners did recognize excess in subordination. In one case in west Tennessee in 1911, for example, four white young men ambushed and killed an African American farmer bringing his cotton crop to market. They hung his two daughters who were with him and burned the cotton crop. They were brought to trial and sentenced. Two of them served prison sentences for their crime, and two were hung in a legal

execution. Lynchings by a small number of white men of lower class and with no ostensible reason exceeded the norms of subordinating African Americans and could bring criminal charges and prosecution. National Association for the Advancement of Colored People, *Thirty Years of Lynching, 1898–1918* (New York: National Association for the Advancement of Colored People, 1919), 20.

68. Tindall, *South Carolina Negroes, 1877–1900*, 240–44.

69. Myrdal, *An American Dilemma*, 562–64; Williamson, *The Crucible of Race*, 188–89.

70. White allies of the NAACP's efforts, the Commission on Interracial Cooperation, in 1930 assessed the costs paid by American society by the continuation of lynching. These included divisions within the African American community and the moral and political corruption of the white community. African Americans disavowed knowledge of lynching victims whenever possible, just as whites attributed lynching to parties unknown, outsiders, or people from the lower classes. Local African American leaders were quiet about lynchings because of their dependence on the white community. Even church leaders and preachers were "compromised into letting things take their course." Among whites, citizenship was debased and law and government crucified. There was a "tendency to translate barbarism into virtues." African Americans lost faith in their white neighbors. The commission judged that lynching was an expression of a basic lack of respect for human beings and for organized society. These factors were prices that all southerners as well as all Americans, white and black, paid for lynchings. Southern Commission on the Study of Lynching, *Lynchings and What They Mean* (Atlanta: Commission on Interracial Cooperation, 1931).

Charles Johnson, the distinguished Fisk sociologist, corroborated that African Americans distinguished among lynchings. Some were quiet affairs that African Americans accepted with resignation as "private" matters and as "justifiable punishment for the indiscretion of some irresponsible Negro." Other lynchings were mob outbursts that left deep scars of "horror, fear and dismay." Charles S. Johnson, *Growing Up in the Black Belt* (Washington, D.C.: American Council on Education, 1941), 317.

71. Donald L. Grant, *The Anti-Lynching Movement, 1838–1932* (San Francisco: R and E Research Associates, 1975), 51; C. Vann Woodward, *The Strange Career of Jim Crow*, 2d ed., rev. (New York: Oxford University Press, 1966), 72–74.

72. White, *Rope and Faggot*, 112.

73. Before the work of the NAACP, Tuskegee University Library maintained records and reported annually on lynchings. I am grateful to Daniel T. Williams, Tuskegee University archivist, for providing me with information on the lynchings of Will and Jess Powell.

There are numerous other instances of lynchings to reestablish the subordinate place of African American men. In Montgomery, in 1919, a set of lynchings of former soldiers spilled over into mob violence against wealth and professional African Americans, causing some of them to flee the city for their lives. NAACP Adm. Files, Group II, Box C 34, Montgomery Lynching, 1927–36, Library of Congress. The Elaine Riots also targeted successful African American men in addition to agricultural workers. Dr. A. E. Johnson, a prominent dentist in Helena, Ark., who was well known in the South, was killed. He and his three brothers, one of whom was a physician, were arrested while squirrel hunting during the time of the suppression in and around Elaine. Evidently, Johnson feared for his life and that of his three brothers. He fought with one of his captors, who died from an ensuing gunshot, probably from his own weapon. The other "deputies" immediately shot Johnson and his brothers to death. A subsequent search of Johnson's house and office yielded rifles and ammunition, not unusual for a hunter. This discovery led to the charge that Johnson had planned an armed insurrection of African Americans and that the gunfight at the Hoop Spur Church had been an unplanned and premature expression of the plot. NAACP Adm. Files, Group I, Marianna, Ark. Lynching, 1919, Library of Congress; Richard C. Cortner, *A Mob Intent on Death: The NAACP and the Arkansas Riot Case* (Middletown, Conn.: Wesleyan University Press, 1988).

74. Myrdal, *An American Dilemma*, 560; Robert L. Zangrando, *The NAACP Crusade against Lynching, 1909–1950* (Philadelphia: Temple University Press, 1980), 11.

75. Southern Commission on the Study of Lynching, *Lynchings and What They Mean* (Atlanta: The Commission, 1931), 10–12; Jessie D. Ames, *The Changing Character of Lynching: Review of Lynching, 1931–1941* (Atlanta: Commission on Interracial Cooperation, 1942), 8.

76. NAACP Adm. Files, Group II, Box C 34, Lynching—Hayneville, Library of Congress.

77. NAACP Adm. Files, Group I, Box G 198, Brownsville Branch; Group II, Box A 393, Tennessee Lynching—Williams, Library of Congress.

78. Myrdal, *An American Dilemma*, 566.

79. Zangrando, *The NAACP Crusade against Lynching, 1909–1950*.

80. Lawson, *Black Ballots*, 17–19; Cortner, *A Mob Intent on Death*, 146.

81. Lawson, *Black Ballots*, 23–54. For a discussion of the changes in Howard University's Law School, see Richard Kluger, *Simple Justice: The History of Brown v. Board of Education and Black America's Struggle for Equality* (New York: Alfred A. Knopf, 1976), 126–31, and Ginna Rae McNeil, *Groundwork: Charles Hamilton Houston and the Struggle for Civil Rights* (Philadelphia: University of Pennsylvania Press, 1983).

82. Lawson, *Black Ballots*, 70.

83. Ibid., 47.

84. Ibid., 56.

85. Thomas Burke, "We Told Washington: The Cotton Pickers Visit the Government," *The Nation* 141 (Dec. 4, 1935): 649–50.

86. Doug McAdam, *Political Process and the Development of Black Insurgency 1930–1970* (Chicago: University of Chicago Press, 1972), 81; Oscar Glantz, "The Negro Voter in Northern Industrial Cities," *Western Political Quarterly* 13 (Dec. 1960): 999–1010; Thomas R. Brooks, *Walls Come Tumbling Down: A History of the Civil Rights Movement, 1940–70* (Englewood Cliffs, N.J.: Prentice-Hall, 1974), 121.

87. Alexander Heard in the course of his work with V. O. Key on politics in the South came to the conclusion that the growing African American vote outside of the South meant that no party could afford to bruise the political feelings of African Americans and that racial discrimination no longer had a place in national politics. *A Two Party South?* (Chapel Hill: University of North Carolina Press, 1952), 233.

88. Guy Carawan and Candie Carawan, *Ain't You Got a Right to the Tree of Life?: The People of Johns Island, South Carolina* (New York: Simon and Schuster, 1966), 167; Juanita Jackson, Sabra Slaughter, and J. Herman Blake, "The Sea Islands as a Cultural Resource," *Black Scholar* 5 (March 1974): 37.

89. Carawan and Carawan, *Ain't You Got a Right to the Tree of Life?* 163–64.

90. John Glen, *Highlander: No Ordinary School, 1932–62* (Lexington: University Press of Kentucky, 1988), 158–66; Carl Tjerandsen, *Education for Citizenship: A Foundation's Experience* (Santa Cruz: Emil Schwarzhaupt Foundation, 1980), 153. The voter-registration work of the Citizenship Schools had urban precedents that Ralph J. Bunche documented in his work for Myrdal. Ralph J. Bunche, *The Political Status of the Negro in the Age of FDR*, ed. Dewey Grantham (Chicago: University of Chicago Press, 1973), 253–327. For other assessments of preceding registration efforts among African Americans in the South, urban areas primarily, see Harvey Lee Moon, *Balance of Power: The Negro Vote* (Garden City, N.Y.: Doubleday, 1949), 174–96, and Luther P. Jackson, "Race and Suffrage in the South Since 1940," *New South* 3 (June–July 1948): 1–26.

91. Glen, *Highlander*, 170.

92. Ibid., 168; Aldon D. Morris, *The Origins of the Civil Rights Movement: Black Communities Organizing for Change* (New York: Free Press, 1984), 153.

93. Tjerandsen, *Education for Citizenship*, 196, 186.

94. Glen, *Highlander*, 169; Tjerandsen, *Education for Citizenship*, 186. For an oral history of the civil rights movement in neighboring Fayette County, see Robert Hamburger, *Our Portion of Hell* (New York: Links Books, 1973).

95. Mingo Scott, Jr., *The Negro in Tennessee Politics and Governmental Affairs, 1865–1965* (Nashville: Rich Printing, 1964), 90–94, 186–89. Bunche offers information on leagues and civic associations in other parts of the South, in urban areas primarily. Bunche, *The Political Status of the Negro in the Age of FDR*, passim.

96. James Forman, *The Making of Black Revolutionaries: A Personal Account* (New York: Macmillan, 1972); see esp. "Georgia Mae Hard Times," 116–30; "Forgetting the People," 130–37; and "Diary of Fayette," 137–45.

97. Charles V. Hamilton, *The Bench and the Ballot: Southern Federal Judges and Black Voters* (New York: Oxford University Press, 1973), 30, 182, 186–87, 191–92; Lawson, *Black Ballots*, 269. The Presidential Commission on Civil Rights conducted hearings in Macon County, Ala., in 1958 that assisted voter registration efforts in Tuskegee. One witness at the hearing offered a statement very similar to those of the narrators in Chapters 1 to 4 about his desire to vote. Horace Guice also shared a similar background to them. He became a landowner through the FSA in 1942 and used his economic independence to reach for political rights.

> I have come up to the other requirements to make myself a citizen. I would like to be a registered voter. . . . It's like I want to become part of the government activity and so forth. . . . I have never been arrested and always has been a law-abiding citizen; to the best of my opinion has no mental deficiency, and my mind couldn't fall on nothing but only, since I came up to these other requirements, that I was just a Negro. That's all.

Robert J. Norrell, *Reaping the Whirlwind: The Civil Rights Movement in Tuskegee* (New York: Alfred A. Knopf, 1985), 113–14.

98. For information on the trials in Hayneville, see Jack Mendelsohn, *The Martyrs: Sixteen Who Gave Their Lives for Racial Justice* (New York: Harper & Row, 1966).

99. David J. Garrow, *Bearing the Cross: Martin Luther King, Jr. and the Southern Christian Leadership Conference* (New York: Vintage Books, 1988), 394; Mendelsohn, *The Martyrs*, 203.

100. Mendelsohn, *The Martyrs*, 209. Wilkins's attorney, Matthew Hobson Murphy, Jr.—self-appointed chief counsel of the United Klans of America—demonstrated in the courtroom the low level of white American bigotry and the environment of the newly registered voters. His concluding remarks disparaged LeRoy Moton, Liuzzo's African American companion in the car, Liuzzo herself, and tapped every prejudice he assumed the all-white, all-male jury shared, as he spoke to them, "one white man to another."

> You know what the nigger [Moton] said on the stand. No. Yeah. No. Yeah. Like a ten-year-old boy. He should have been saying Yes, sir and No, sir before that honorable white judge. But the buck hasn't got the sense, the morals or the decency. . . .
>
> I said now look, boy. Look down at your feet. Niggers only understand this kind of talk. How many feets away was that car? So he looked down at his feet and said about twenty-five feet away. . . . He said he passed out for twenty-five to thirty minutes. . . . What's he doing down there all that time? In that car alone with that woman. . . .
>
> . . . Then the nigger ran up the road and a truck came by and he stopped it. There was a rabbi in that truck. A rabbi. Of course, he stopped and put the nigger

> in the back. And there they were—rabbi with a nigger . . . white woman, nigger man, nigger woman—all in there, feet to feet. . . .

Mendelsohn, *The Martyrs*, 192.

101. Clayborne Carson, *In Struggle: SNCC and the Black Awakening of the 1960's* (Cambridge, Mass.: Harvard University Press, 1981), 162–63; Andrew Kopkind, "Lowndes County, Alabama: The Great Fear Is Gone," *Ramparts* 13 (April 1975): 9–10.

102. Margaret Long, "Black Power in the Black Belt," *The Progressive* 30 (Oct. 1966): 22.

103. Stokely Carmichael and Charles V. Hamilton, *Black Power: The Politics of Liberation in America* (New York: Random House, 1967), 114.

104. Ibid., 118–20.

105. Carson, *In Struggle*, 300.

106. Forman, *The Making of Black Revolutionaries*, 443–44, 116–45. "About 100 Negroes Meet in Frogmore," *New York Times*, Jan. 20, 1968, p. 40.

Chapter 8

1. Willie L. Rose, *Rehearsal for Reconstruction: The Port Royal Experiment* (New York: Oxford University Press, 1984), 39–40.

2. Mason Crum, *Gullah: Negro Life in the Carolina Sea Islands* (New York: Negro Universities Press, 1968), 253, 269. The fundamental violent assumption of the subjugation of one human being over another, which is the premise of slavery, expressed itself occasionally in forms of violence that rendered physical and mental injury. Amy Chapman recalled an incident from her slavery in Alabama in an unusually graphic account of discipline that, though infrequent, occurred with enough regularity to impose a discipline of fear.

> One day I seed ole Unker Tip Toe all bent over a-comin' down de road an' I ax him whut ail him an' he say: "I's been in de stocks an' been beat till de blood come. Den ole Massa 'ninted my flesh wid red pepper an' turpentine an' I's been moot dead but I somewhat better now." Uncle Tip Toe belonded to de meanes' ol' marster around here.

Rawick, *The American Slave: A Composite Autobiography, Volume 6, Alabama and Indiana Narratives* (Westport, Conn.: Greenwood Press, 1972), 64–65.

3. Ira Berlin, Joseph P. Reidy, and Lesley S. Rowland, eds., *The Black Military Experience* (New York: Cambridge University Press, 1982), 637–39; 648–52. See also Herbert Aptheker, "Negro Casualties in the Civil War," *Journal of Negro History* 32 (Jan. 1947): 10–80.

4. Berlin et al., *The Black Military Experience*, 634–36.

5. Ibid., 633.

6. Ibid., 645.

7. Ibid., 640–41.

8. Ibid., 654–55.

9. R. S. Holland, ed., *Letters and Diary of Laura M. Towne: 1866–1871* (Cambridge, Mass.: Riverside Press, 1912), 153–54. Towns were crowded with refugees as well. Laura Towne's first impressions of Beaufort were of "streets full of the oddest negro children—dirty and ragged, but about the same as so many Irish in intelligence, I think." Holland, *Letters and Diary of Laura M. Towne*, 6.

10. Carl H. Moneyhon, "First Freedom 1860–1900," in *Persistence of the Spirit: The Black Experience in Arkansas*, ed. Tom Baskett, Jr. (Little Rock: Arkansas Endowment for the Humanities, 1986), 18–19; Gaines M. Foster, "The Limitations of Federal Health Care for Freedmen, 1862–1868," *Journal of Southern History* 158 (Aug. 1982): 356.

11. Joel Williamson, *After Slavery: The Negro in South Carolina during Reconstruction, 1861–1877* (Chapel Hill: University of North Carolina Press, 1965), 319.

12. *Autobiography of Oliver Otis Howard: Major General United States Army*, vol. 2 (New York: Baker & Taylor, 1908), 259–60; Gunnar Myrdal, *An American Dilemma: The Negro Problem and Modern Democracy* (New York: Harper & Brothers, 1944), 161–62.

13. W. E. B. Du Bois, *Black Reconstruction: An Essay Toward a History of the Part Which Black Folk Played in the Attempt to Reconstruct Democracy in America, 1860–1880* (New York: S. A. Russell, 1935), 226; Paul Skeels Pierce, *The Freedmen's Bureau: A Chapter in the History of Reconstruction* (Iowa City: University of Iowa Press, 1904), 87–94. John Cox and La Wanda Cox, "General O. O. Howard and the 'Misrepresented Bureau'," *Journal of Southern History* 19 (Nov. 1953): 427–56.

14. *Autobiography of Oliver Otis Howard*, 214, 350–51.

15. Ibid., 203.

16. Ibid., 361.

17. Pierce, *The Freedmen's Bureau*, 87–94.

18. Ibid., 127.

19. Du Bois, *Black Reconstruction*, 229–30.

20. Pierce, *The Freedmen's Bureau*, 113, 127.

21. Todd L. Savitt, "Politics in Medicine: The Georgia Freedmen's Bureau and the Organization of Health Care, 1865–1866," *Civil War History* 28 (1982): 45–64; Foster, "The Limitations of Federal Health Care for Freedmen," 362. For an account of one of the physicians on the Sea Islands, see Gerald Schwartz, ed., *A Woman Doctor's Civil War: Esther Hills' Diary* (Columbia, S.C.: University of South Carolina Press, 1984). The abolitionist teachers provided a great deal of health care, especially on the Sea Islands. They also criticized the inadequate efforts of others. Elizabeth Botume recalled her efforts to vaccinate her students against smallpox. Elizabeth H. Botume, *First Days amongst the Contrabands:*

The American Negro, His History and Literature (rpt.: New York: Arno Press, 1968), 44–45. She also related her intolerance for the attitude and performance of a doctor whom the federal government provided. He

> was exasperatingly indifferent. He might have been a brother of a "bureau offi-cer," who was sent down especially to take care of the contrabands, and who wished all the negroes could be put upon a ship, and floated out to sea and sunk. It would be better for them and the world. When we expressed our surprise that he could speak so of human beings, he exclaimed, "Human beings! They are only animals, and not half as valuable as cattle."
>
> When the doctor came, I went from room to room and talked with the poor sick people, whose entire dependence was upon us. Finally, I could endure his apathy and indifference no longer.
>
> "Leave me the medicines, and I will take care of these people as well as I can," I said.
>
> "Oh! we only give Dover's Powders and quinine, and any one can deal them out," was his reply. In time, I added castor oil and painkiller to my stock, and then my medical stores were complete.
>
> I could not, however, excuse the doctor, a man in government employ, drawing a good salary with no heart in his work. Beaufort was reported to be a depot for officials whom the government did not know what to do with.

Botume, *First Days amongst the Contrabands*, 117–18.
22. Martin Abbott, *The Freedmen's Bureau in South Carolina: 1865–1872* (Chapel Hill: University of North Carolina Press, 1967), 139. For a very short time Sax-ton formed a staff of six physicians who provided health care independently of the plantation superintendents on the Sea Islands. But this direct provision of health care was exceptional, as was so much of Saxton's work.
23. Laura J. Webster, "The Operation of the Freedmen's Bureau in South Carolina," 153. *Smith College Studies in History* 1 (Jan. and April 1916): 65–163. William-son, *After Slavery*, 320; Foster, "The Limitations of Federal Health Care for Freedmen," 354, 371.
24. W. E. B. Du Bois, ed. *Atlanta University Publications, No. 11, The Health and Physique of the Negro Americans, 1906* (rpt.: New York: Arno Press, 1968), 98.
25. Ibid., 95–100.
26. E. Richard Brown, *Rockefeller Medicine Men: Capitalism and Medical Care in America* (Berkeley: University of California Press, 1979), 115–16.
27. Ibid., 44–46.
28. Ibid., 148.
29. Edward H. Beardsley, *A History of Neglect: Health Care for Blacks and Mill Workers in the Twentieth-Century South* (Knoxville: University of Tennessee Press, 1987), 78. Some improvement in the health of African Americans came as a consequence of migration to urban areas, where housing, education, nutri-

tion, employment, and wages may still have been substandard but were higher than those they left in the rural South. Family size decreased among the urban migrants, and this contributed to improved health and increased resources. How much improvement occurred is hard to determine because records on the health status of African Americans in the rural South were not kept at all or were poorly kept. The health problems of African Americans became better known beginning in the early twentieth century because of their migration to urban areas where officials kept better records. Beardsley, *A History of Neglect*, 27, 129.

30. Carter G. Woodson, *The Rural Negro* (Washington, D.C.: Association for the Study of Negro Life and History, 1930), 1–18. There were other general consequences for medicine as well. Flexner offered a scientific model of health care that would push health care into the realm of the physical sciences, with an emphasis on the chemistry and physics of the body. The social context of a person's health, including the relation of class status to illness, received far less attention than the science of illness and intervention. By the 1920s studies of African Americans in the rural South, such as Woodson's, had sections on health in which physician-patient ratios and hospital bed-population ratios were more prominent than data on the economy or education in explaining health status. The use of these measures indicate the success of Flexner's report in changing attitudes about the relation of health to medical care.

Moreover, the scientific aura of medicine instilled the political views of physicians with increased legitimacy as the informed views of trained scientists. The histories physicians wrote and their views on the health care of African Americans in particular were infused with some of the most virulent class bias and racism of their times and did little to recommend physicians as reflective interpreters of their times. Richard H. Harrison, *Medicine in America: Historical Essays* (Baltimore: Johns Hopkins University, 1966), 284. Myrdal found a relation of the biological sciences and medicine not to the American creed of equality and opportunity but to "conservative and even reactionary ideologies." The scientific basis of these ideologies contributed, in Myrdal's estimation, to a tendency to accept biological causation, to reject social explanations except when "under the duress of a siege of irresistible evidence," and to a "do-nothing policy" in political matters. Myrdal, *An American Dilemma*, 91.

In addition to this consequence for the conceptualization of race and health, the Flexner report presented very practical problems for the medical training of African Americans. There were few places where his recommended training could be conducted after medical school. In the 1920s there were 183 hospitals with 6,500 hospital beds for African American patients in the entire United States. Many were small and many operated as an annex to the white hospitals, with African American patients shuttled back and forth for services and convalescence. The National Hospital Association and National Medical Association approved only seven of these hospitals for internships. These thirty-five internships could not serve the one hundred or more African American medical students completing their studies annually. Woodson, *The Rural Negro*, 12–32. Beardsley, *A History of Neglect*, 37.

31. Theodore Rosengarten, *All God's Dangers: The Life of Nate Shaw* (New York: Vintage Books, 1974), 314.

32. John Beecher, "The Share Cropper's Union in Alabama," *Social Forces* 13 (Oct. 1934): 131.

33. T. J. Woofter, Jr., *Black Yeomanry: Life on St. Helena Island* (New York: Henry Holt, 1930), 103–13.

34. Beardsley, *A History of Neglect*, 103, 108–12. In addition, African American physicians in the North worked to improve health care and medical training in the South. Some did this directly by spending time in providing services and training in the South as well as indirectly by using foundation contacts to funnel money and ideas into the South for medical services and change. Beardsley, *A History of Neglect*, 86–87.

35. Correspondence of James E. Heizer, Press Release, Oct. 14, 1938, FSA Files, Record Group 96, Box 1, National Archives.

36. Frederick D. Mott and Milton I. Roemer, *Rural Health and Medical Care* (New York: McGraw-Hill, 1948), 393–96, 409.

37. Correspondence of James S. Heizer, Will W. Alexander to George S. Mitchell, FSA Files, Record Group 96, Box 1, National Archives.

38. Mott and Roemer, *Rural Health and Medical Care*, 402. Even where opposition was mute and the FSA acquired the cooperation of local doctors, problems remained. The program represented improved access but not improved care. The quality of care, generally low in rural areas, did not improve simply because people had better access to it. Even with improved access, the amount of care was less than other Americans received. Financially, the program had problems as well. There was a low level of participation; 30 percent of all persons eligible participated. Those who did not participate tended to be those at higher risk for illness and with disproportionate need for care. The people with low risk stayed in the program for short periods, whereas the high-risk clients stayed much longer. The premiums were low in recognition of the low income of the eligible families. Physicians sometimes cut back the volume of services without a change in their premiums. This brought their income from the FSA programs in line with their regular charges. In addition to these problems, the clients of the program had little to say in the management and implementation of the plans. In general, FSA officials negotiated the plans with local medical associations.

39. Matilda Ann Wade, "Community Nursing—FSA Style," *Public Health Nursing* 34 (Feb. 1942): 82–88; E. C. Burnett, interview by author, Marianna and Fargo, Ark., Oct. 30, 1987.

40. Letter to "Dear Friends" from Lucille Boyd et al., FSA Files, Record Group 96, RP TN-27, 103–84, National Archives.

41. U. S. House of Representatives, *Committee Investigation of the Activities of the FSA*, 78th Cong., 2d sess., May 9, 1944, Report 492, p. 85.

42. Shortly after the war, a program to increase hospitals and hospital beds, one sponsor of which was Sen. Lister Hill from Alabama, offered some hope to meet rural health care needs. The cost of the Hill-Burton bill or the National Hospital Survey and Construction Act, came to an estimated $3.3 billion, or the cost of American participation in World War II for sixteen days in the spring of 1945. By the late 1960s the supply of hospital beds in low-income states reached the levels of those in high-income states, and the Hill-Burton program played a large part in the change.

    However, the Hill-Burton Act had several shortcomings in terms of the needs of rural African American southern communities. Hospital sponsors had to provide matching funds and demonstrate that the hospital would be financially self-sufficient. This requirement made poor communities, often with greatest need, least eligible for the program. Funds went disproportionately to middle-income communities. A provision of the bill required that hospitals provide "a reasonable volume of hospital services to persons unable to pay," but this provision went unenforced because no regulations were issued for twenty years. In addition, the bill prohibited racial discrimination except where separate but equal facilities were available. And until 1963 many Hill-Burton hospitals refused to treat African Americans. Then the U.S. Supreme Court ruled that separate but equal was no more constitutional in its application to hospitals than it was to schools. The Civil Rights Act of 1964 began the desegregation of hospitals, which was the most rapid and is still the most thorough desegregation of any set of institutions in American society. Mott and Roemer, *Rural Health and Medical Care*, 509; Paul Starr, *The Social Transformation of American Medicine: The Rise of a Sovereign Profession and the Making of a Vast Industry* (New York: Basic Books, 1982), 348–51; Beardsley, *A History of Neglect*, 263.

43. Lisbeth Bamberger Schorr, telephone interview by Thomas May, Oct. 16, 1975, and Nov. 16, 1977; Joseph English, M.D., interview by Peter K. New, New York, N.Y., Oct. 13, 1975, Dec. 15, 1975, telephone interview by author, Dec. 3, 1987; Lisbeth Bamberger and Joseph English, "Background, Context and Significant Issues in Neighborhood Health Center Programs," in *Neighborhood Health Centers*, ed. Robert M. Hollister, Bernard M. Kramer, and Seymour S. Bellin (Lexington, Mass.: Lexington Books, 1974), 45.

44. Joseph English, M.D., interview by Peter K. New, New York, N.Y., no date.

45. Sidney L. Kark, M.D., "Family and Community Practice in the Medical Curriculum: A Clinical Teaching Program in Social Medicine," *Journal of Medical Education* 34 (Sept. 1959): 901–10. Sidney L. Kark and Guy W. Steuart, *A Practice of Social Medicine: A South African Team's Experience in Different African Communities* (Edinburgh: E. and S. Livingstone, 1962), vi; H. Jack Geiger, M.D., interview by Peter K. New, Stony Brook, N.Y., June 26, 1974. This in-

stitute affiliated with the medical faculty at the University of Natal with support of a grant from the Rockefeller Foundation. It was the Rockefeller Foundation that sponsored Geiger's travel to South Africa as a student and proposed, in 1964, to sponsor his work in Nigeria, which was in many ways a replication of Kark's model.

46. Geiger, interview.

47. Ibid.

48. H. Jack Geiger, M.D., "Community Control and Community Conflict," in *Neighborhood Health Centers*, ed. Hollister et al., 133–42.

49. Isabel Marcus, *Dollars for Reform: The OEO Neighborhood Health Centers* (Lexington, Mass.: Lexington Books, 1981), 63.

50. David Burke, interview by Peter K. New, n.p., Aug. 12, 1976.

51. Count Gibson, M.D., interview with Peter K. New, Stanford, Calif., March 7, 1974.

52. Polly Greenberg, *The Devil Has Slippery Shoes: A Biased Biography of the Child Development Group of Mississippi* (London: Macmillan, 1969).

53. FBI files on the Medical Committee on Human Rights, Box 43, Special Collections, The University Library, University of Illinois at Chicago.

54. Claude F. Oubre, *Forty Acres and a Mule: The Freedmen's Bureau and Black Landownership* (Baton Rouge: Louisiana State University Press, 1978), 168–69; William L. McDavid, "Calhoun Land Trust: A Study of Rural Resettlement in Lowndes County, Alabama" (Master's thesis, Fisk University, 1943), 12–17.

55. Charles S. Johnson, *Growing Up in the Black Belt* (Washington, D.C.: American Council on Education, 1941), 250.

56. Daniel I. Zwick, interview by Thomas May, place not given, May 13, 1975.

57. John Frankel, M.D., interview by Thomas May, place not given, Jan. 23, 1975.

58. Sanford Kravitz, interview by Peter K. New, no place given, Oct. 9, 1975.

59. Frankel interview.

60. Dan Pugliese, interview by Thomas May and Peter K. New, place not given, April 11, 1975.

61. Kravitz interview.

62. Marcus, *Dollars for Reform*. Richard A. Couto, *Poverty, Politics and Health Care: An Appalachian Experience* (New York: Praeger, 1974).

63. For the efforts of the Resettlement Administration in Lowndes County, see FSA Files, Record Group 96, AL-15, Box 38, National Archives.

64. Philip D. Carter, "Agonies of Change in Lowndes County," *Washington Post*, Aug. 16, 1971.

65. Gibson interview.

66. Frankel interview.

67. Ibid.

68. Pugliese interview.

69. Zwick interview.

70. The OHA recruited Les Falk, M.D., to the community health program at Meharry. Falk at the time served at the innovative health centers of the United Mine Workers of America near Pittsburgh. His experience in this program as well as the regard of the OHA staff had for him as an "old FSA-type" made him valuable enough to them to relocate him and match him with new initiatives like those with which he had worked before.

71. Leon Cooper, M.D., interview by Thomas May, place not given, May 12, 1975.

72. Alice Sardell, "Neighborhood Health Centers and Community Based Care: Federal Policy from 1965–1982," *Journal of Public Health Policy* 4 (Dec. 1983): 497.

73. Gibson interview.

74. Geiger interview.

Chapter 9

1. For discussions of the community of memory, tradition, and virtue, see Robert N. Bellah et al., *Habits of the Heart: Individualism and Commitment in American Life* (Berkeley: University of California Press, 1985). They base their discussion on Alasdair MacIntyre, *After Virtue: A Study in Moral Theory*, 2d ed. (Notre Dame, Ind.: University of Notre Dame Press, 1984), esp. 204–25.

2. Carl R. Osthaus, *Freedom, Philanthropy and Fraud: A History of the Freedmen's Savings Bank* (Chicago: University of Illinois Press, 1976), 1.

3. Roy Reed, "Widespread Racial Violence Persists in Eastern Arkansas Farming Area," *New York Times*, Oct. 10, 1971.

4. These stories capture the rhetoric of Martin Luther King, Jr., that African Americans and whites are "caught in an inescapable network of mutuality, bound together in a single garment of destiny." The phrase occurs often; see, e.g., "Letter from a Birmingham Jail," Martin Luther King, Jr., *Why We Can't Wait* (New York: New American Library, 1964), 77.

5. Stokely Carmichael and Charles V. Hamilton, *Black Power: The Politics of Liberation in America* (New York: Random House, 1967).

6. James Forman, *The Making of Black Revolutionaries: A Personal Account* (New York: Macmillan, 1972), 116–45, 443–44.

7. A. Knighton Stanley, *The Children Is Crying: Congregationalism among Black People* (New York: Pilgrim Press, 1979), 7–18. I base this discussion of redemptive organizations on James Q. Wilson, *Political Organizations* (New York: Basic Books, 1973), 30–46. For an early analysis of SNCC as a redemptive organization, see Emily Schottenfield Stoper, "The Student Nonviolent Coordinating Committee: Rise and Fall of a Redemptive Organization," *Journal of Black Studies* 8 (Sept. 1977): 13–34.

8. Thurgood Marshall traveled across the South investigating the lynchings of African Americans for the NAACP. In some cases, including Elbert William's

lynching in Haywood County in 1940, he quickly gained names of the lynch mob and affidavits about the lynching. In contrast he found that FBI agents seemed unable to do the same in case after case. In the Elbert Williams case, Marshall chided the FBI for conducting its investigation in the company of Sheriff Tip Hunter, whom eyewitnesses identified as the leader of the mobs that abducted Williams and other NAACP leaders. By 1947 Marshall wrote to NAACP secretary Walter White, "I have . . . no faith in either Mr. Hoover or his investigators and there is no use in saying I do." Marshall wrote directly to Attorney General Clark with his criticism of Hoover, as well. Hoover responded by claiming that Marshall was untruthful and declined White's request that he meet with Marshall. Marshall to Berge, Jan. 30, 1942, J. E. Hoover to Walter White, Jan. 13, and Jan. 28, 1947, NAACP Adm. Files, Group II A Lynching 1940–47, Library of Congress.

9. Carmichael and Hamilton, *Black Power*, 114.

10. Stanley, *The Children Is Crying*, 143–44.

11. For the influence of movement work on its participants, see Doug McAdam, "The Biographical Consequences of Activism," *American Sociological Review* 54 (Oct. 1989): 744–60, and Fitzhugh Mullan, *White Coal, Clenched Fist: The Political Education of an American Physician* (New York: Macmillan, 1976). Of course, this experience does not provide new and different values of the participants; it develops those that they bring to change efforts. See Richard A. Couto, *Streams of Idealism and Health Care Innovation* (New York: Teachers College Press, 1984), 22–53.

12. For a discussion relevant to different forms of redemptive organization and the manner in which they differ in staffing, resources, and external relations, see John D. McCarthy and Mayer N. Zald, "Resource Mobilization and Social Movements: A Partial Theory," *American Journal of Sociology* 82 (1977): 1212–1241.

13. Rosa Parks quoted in Myles Horton, with Judith Kohl and Herbert Kohl, *The Long Haul: An Autobiography* (New York: Doubleday, 1990), 149–50. For similar testimony to Highlander as a space, see Carl Tjerandsen, *Education for Citizenship: A Foundation's Experience* (Santa Cruz: Emil Schwarzhaupt Foundation, 1980), 208. Some observers marveled at the ability of Myles Horton, Highlander's director, to get whites and blacks at the same table to eat. When asked how he did it, Horton enumerated three steps: "Prepare the food; set the table; ring the dinner bell."

14. Willie L. Rose, *Rehearsal for Reconstruction: The Port Royal Experiment* (New York: Oxford University Press, 1984), 39; Ida B. Wells-Barnett's remarkable career also spans several organized efforts to curb lynching. Alfreda M. Duster, *Crusade for Justice: The Autobiography of Ida B. Wells* (Chicago: University of Chicago Press, 1970).

15. Accounts of these bureaucracies include assessments of their heroic natures. Du Bois was an early, lonely, articulate voice in his assessment that the Freedmen's

Bureau was "the most extraordinary and far-reaching institution of social uplift that America has ever attempted." W. E. B. Du Bois, *Black Reconstruction: An Essay Toward a History of the Part Which Black Folk Played in the Attempt to Reconstruct Democracy in America, 1860–1880* (New York: S. A. Russell, 1935), 219; see also Du Bois, "The Freedmen's Bureau," *Atlantic Monthly* 87 (March 1901): 354–65. Myrdal distinguished the FSA for its conduct of the large portion of its work where the need was, the rural South, and the unprecedented participation of African American farmers and professionals in the conduct of a public program. Gunnar Myrdal, *An American Dilemma: The Negro Problem and Modern Democracy* (New York: Harper & Brothers, 1944), 273–78. Stanley Baldwin described the FSA as "heroic" precisely because of its effort "to secure social justice and political power for a neglected class of Americans." Sidney Baldwin, *Poverty and Politics: The Rise and Decline of the Farm Security Administration* (Chapel Hill: University of North Carolina, 1968), 4. Isabel Marcus used the term "heroic bureaucracy" to describe the OHA because of its efforts to demonstrate new public programs and policies. Isabel Marcus, *Dollars for Reform: The OEO Neighborhood Health Centers* (Lexington, Mass.: Lexington Books, 1981), 129.

16. Alice Sardell, "Neighborhood Health Centers and Community Based Care: Federal Policy from 1965–1982," *Journal of Public Health Policy* 4 (Dec. 1983): 497.

17. *Autobiography of Oliver Otis Howard: Major General United States Army*, vol. 2 (New York: Baker & Taylor, 1908), 369. Pierce suggests that the Freedmen's Bureau contributed more to the establishment public schools of the South than its critics credit it and less than its supporters assert. Paul Skeels Pierce, *The Freedmen's Bureau: A Chapter in the History of Reconstruction* (Iowa City: University of Iowa Press, 1904), 83–86.

18. Baldwin, *Poverty and Politics*, 130–31; Donald H. Grubbs, *Cry From the Cotton: The Southern Tenant Farmers' Union and the New Deal* (Chapel Hill: University of North Carolina Press, 1971).

19. Karen Davis and Ray Marshall, *Rural Health Care in the South* (Atlanta: Southern Regional Council, 1975).

20. *Autobiography of Oliver Otis Howard*, 251, 363. Rexford G. Tugwell, "Design for Government," *Political Science Quarterly* 48 (Sept. 1933): 330. Frankel interview.

21. *Autobiography of Oliver Otis Howard*, 359.

22. Zwick, Frankel, and Bryant interviews.

23. Baldwin, *Poverty and Politics*, 335–46.

24. Ibid., 120, 279.

25. Rexford G. Tugwell, "Grass Did Not Grow," *Fortune* 14 (Oct. 1936): 116.

26. Baldwin, *Poverty and Politics*, 103, 236.

27. Lisbeth Bamberger and Joseph English, "Background, Context and Significant Issues in Neighborhood Health Center Programs," in *Neighborhood Health Cen-*

ters, ed. Robert M. Hollister, Bernard M. Kramer, and Seymour S. Bellin (Lexington, Mass.: Lexington Books, 1974).

28. *Autobiography of Oliver Otis Howard*, 203.

29. Baldwin, *Poverty and Politics*, 47.

30. Ibid., 350.

31. Wilma Dykeman and James Stokely, *Seeds of Southern Change: The Life of Will Alexander* (Chicago: University of Chicago Press, 1962), 212, Kravitz interview.

32. Pugliese interview.

33. George R. Bentley, *A History of the Freedmen's Bureau* (New York: Octagon Books, 1974), 187–88; Baldwin, *Poverty and Politics*, 207–208; H. Jack Geiger, "Community Health Centers: Health Care as an Instrument of Social Change," in *Reforming Medicine: Lessons of the Last Quarter Century*, ed. Victor W. Sidel and Ruth Sidel (New York: Pantheon Books, 1984), 11–32.

34. Baldwin, *Poverty and Politics*, 283. Lester M. Salamon, "The Time Dimension in Policy Evaluation: The Case of the New Deal Land-Reform Experiments," *Public Policy* 27 (Spring 1979): 150. Bentley, *History of the Freedmen's Bureau*, 15.

35. *Autobiography of Oliver Otis Howard*, 225.

36. Du Bois, *Black Reconstruction*, 667. Myrdal, *An American Dilemma*, 326.

37. Frankel interview.

38. Claude F. Oubre, *Forty Acres and a Mule: The Freedmen's Bureau and Black Landownership* (Baton Rouge: Louisiana State University Press, 1978), 169. Geiger traces a host of influences of the community health centers in "Community Health Centers."

39. *Autobiography of Oliver Otis Howard*, 214. Martin Abbott, *The Freedmen's Bureau in South Carolina: 1865–1872* (Chapel Hill: University of North Carolina Press, 1967), 28.

40. Heroic bureaucracies do run a grave risk of paternalism. Ordinary agents of heroic bureaucracies may foster dependence in those with whom they work. Even the best agents run the risk of another form of paternalism that disregards the resources within the community of memory and the members' ideas for change. Saxton, for example, ignored the efforts of freedpeople to pool their money to purchase land collectively at Beaufort in 1863. Rose, *Rehearsal for Reconstruction*, 272–96. Alexander remarked, ironically, on the satisfaction of a participant of an FSA cooperative project who thought the program was just fine and would permit him to acquire land "of his own" some day. Dykeman and Stokely, *Seeds of Southern Change*, 220. OHA staff members lamented justifiably about their failure to achieve institutional change of medical schools and health care providers with whom they were inclined initially to work. On the other hand, only gradually did they come to understand that establishing community control over programs entailed conflict with professionals and institutions. Fortunately, heroic bureaucracies have the capacity to learn and gain respect for local resources and plans. Kravitz interview.

41. Bentley, *History of the Freedmen's Bureau*, 176, 184; Herbert G. Gutman, "Schools for Freedom: The Post-Emancipation Origins of Afro-American Education," in *Power and Culture: Essays on the American Working Class*, ed. Ira Berlin (New York: Pantheon Books, 1987), 260–97.

Chapter 10

1. Marvin Schwartz, *In Service to America: A History of VISTA in Arkansas, 1965–1985* (Fayetteville: University of Arkansas Press, 1988), 239.
2. Karen Davis and Ray Marshall, *Rural Health Care in the South* (Atlanta: Southern Regional Council, 1975); Karen Davis and Cathy Schoen, *Health and the War on Poverty: A Ten Year Appraisal* (Washington, D.C.: Brookings Institute, 1978); Cecil G. Sheps et al., "An Evaluation of Subsidized Rural Primary Care Programs: I. A Typology of Practice Organizations," *American Journal of Public Health* 73 (Jan. 1983), 38–49. For literature on the difficulty of administering community health centers, see Warren R. Paap, "Consumer-Based Boards of Health Centers: Structural Problems in Achieving Effective Control," *American Journal of Public Health* 68 (June 1978); Robert R. Alford, "The Political Economy of Health Care: Dynamics Without Change," *Politics and Society* 2 (Winter 1972), 127–64; Michael Lipsky and Morris Lounds, "Citizen Participation and Health Care: Problems of Government Induced Participation," *Journal of Health Politics, Policy and Law* 1 (Spring 1976): 85–111; John Hatch and Eugenia Eng, "Community Participation and Control: Or Control of Community Participation," in *Reforming Medicine: Lessons of the Last Quarter Century*, ed. Victor W. Sidel and Ruth Sidel (New York: Pantheon Books, 1984), 223–244.
3. Davis and Schoen, *Health and the War on Poverty*, 161–202; H. Jack Geiger, "Community Health Centers: Health Care as an Instrument of Social Change," in *Reforming Medicine*, ed. Sidel and Sidel, 13, 273; Alice Sardell, *The United States Experiment in Social Medicine: The Community Health Center Program, 1966–1986* (Pittsburgh: University of Pittsburgh Press, 1988); Alice Sardell, "Neighborhood Health Centers and Community Based Care: Federal Policy from 1965–1982," *Journal of Public Health Policy* 4 (Dec. 1983).
4. Clare Ansberry, "Dumping the Poor: Despite Federal Law Hospitals Still Reject Sick Who Can't Pay," *Wall Street Journal*, Nov. 29, 1988, p. 1.
5. See note 5 in Chapter 4. The audits did find fault of a modest degree and on highly technical matters that offered ample room for honest differences of interpretations and mistakes. No charges of fraud or wrongdoing were ever brought against the board members or administrators. "Summary of Compliance and Financial Management Problems at Sea Island Comprehensive Health Care Corporation and Franklin C. Fetter Family Health Center," U.S. General Accounting Office, Human Resources Division (April 23, 1982); letter of Cecil M. Sheps, M.D. to Ophie Franklin, July 13, 1982.

6. Isabel Marcus, *Dollars for Reform: The OEO Neighborhood Health Centers* (Lexington, Mass.: Lexington Books, 1981); and Sardell, "Neighborhood Health Centers."
7. Sardell, "Neighborhood Health Centers," 497.
8. Fitzhugh Mullan, "The National Health Service Corps and Health Care Innovations: Beyond Poorhouse Medicine," in *Reforming Medicine*, ed. Sidel and Sidel, 176–200.
9. Myrdal included an account of the common rationale for the deliberate withholding of land as one form of social capital after the Civil War. He cites a story of Josephus Daniels.

> When I was eighteen I recall asking an old Confederate, "What was so bad about the promise to give every Negro head of a family forty acres and a mule? Wouldn't that have been better help than to turn the ignorant ex-slave without a dollar over to the mercy of Republican politicians, white and black, who made political slaves of them? And if each Negro had been given a piece of land, for which Uncle Sam would pay the Southern owner, wouldn't it have been better for the white man and the Negro?"
>
> The old man looked at me as if I were a curious individual to be raising such an unheard-of question. "No," he said emphatically, "for it would have made the Negro 'uppity,' and, besides, they don't know enough to farm without direction, and smart white men and Negroes would have gotten the land away from them, and they'd have been worse off than ever. . . . The real reason," pursued the old man, "why it wouldn't do, is that we are having a hard time now keeping the nigger in his place, and if he were a landowner he'd think he was bigger man than old Grant, and there would be no living with him in the Black District. . . . Who'd work the land if the niggers had farms of their own?"

Gunnar Myrdal, *An American Dilemma: The Negro Problem and Modern Democracy* (New York: Harper & Brothers, 1944), 226–27.

10. The Reagan years demonstrated the abhorrence of American conservatism for social capital per se and not merely as a budget buster. Those years were not fiscally conservative in any sense. We accumulated huge deficits as we cut back social programs. The reduction in social spending was not part of an aversion to government spending but to the public provision of social capital. For a radical statement of the preference for private control of social capital see Charles Murray, *Losing Ground: American Social Policy 1950–1980* (New York: Basic Books, 1984), 227–36.

   The location of a General Electric plant in Lowndes County offers some lessons in the provision of social capital from private sources. The plant offers risks to the environment of the county, its basic social capital. The plant will manufacture Lexan plastic pellets that will be transported to other plants for the manufacture of strong plastic products such as motorcycle visors. The manufacturing process involves several toxic chemicals that can injure human tissue and adversely affect the nervous system and other organs. These chemicals eventually form waste by-products that must be disposed of. The plant will have a storage capacity of 8,800 gallons for these toxic materials, which it will transport for permanent disposal elsewhere. The other waste will be treated and discharged into the Alabama River. In addition to the risk it poses to the water supply of the county, the plant will draw from aquifers in the county.

This private capital investment offers risk to the existing social capital of the county. In exchange, it promises jobs. But as Mants pointed out, few residents of Lowndes County will acquire any of the 250 new jobs. The plant did not have to invest in social capital to develop a workforce because there is a surplus of qualified labor willing to migrate or commute from outside the county for the jobs.

The tax package offered the plant by the state includes exemption from local taxes, which depletes social capital revenues to a poor county in a poor state. GE did provide $25,000 to the school system and $25,000 to the clinic. Eventually, it made a $1 million, five-year contribution to the school system to develop its math and science curriculum. As generous as this seems, it also exemplifies the preference of private capital sources to specify the amount and form of social capital it will provide and to avoid contributing to public revenues for social capital. Increasingly, states with areas of high unemployment and low income have engaged in a bidding war to provide social capital to private investors and to forgo requests from them for social capital investments in the people and environment of the location. Pamela G. Hollie, "Why Business is Barging into the Classroom," *New York Times*, July 12, 1987, p. F6. Peter Goldberg, "How Altruistic Are Corporate Efforts to Reform the Schools?" *Chronicle of Philanthropy*, Feb. 20, 1990, p. 29.

For the costs in social capital of "successful" economic development see Carter Garber, "Saturn: Tomorrow's Jobs, Yesterday's Myths," in *Communities in Economic Crisis: Appalachian and the South*, ed. John Gaventa, Barbara Smith, and Alex Willingham (Philadelphia: Temple University Press, 1990): 175–89. For the disinvestment in rural African American communities by environmental destruction, see Robert D. Bullard, "Environmentalism, Economic Blackmail, and Civil Rights: Competing Agendas within the Black Community," *Communities in Economic Crisis*, ed. Gaventa et al., 190–99.

11. Robert E. Reich, *The Next American Frontier* (New York: Times Books, 1983), 229–82. Reich is critical of social capital investments such as GE's contribution to Lowndes County's schools. Such contributions mask the massive disinvestment in social capital, including schools, that corporate tax cutting and leniency represent. Goldberg, "How Altruistic Are Corporate Efforts to Reform the Schools?" 30. For a broad survey of recent economic analyses and their relation to human capital, see Steve Fisher, "National Economic Renewal Programs and Their Implications for Economic Development in Appalachia and the

South," in *Communities in Economic Crisis*, ed. Gaventa et al. For a discussion of social capital, see James O'Connor, *The Fiscal Crisis of the State* (New York: St. Martin's Press, 1973), 97–104, 124–44.

12. Herbert G. Gutman, "Schools for Freedom: The Post-Emancipation Origins of Afro-American Education," in *Power and Culture: Essays on the American Working Class*, ed. Ira Berlin (New York: Pantheon Books, 1987).

13. Lester M. Salamon, "The Time Dimension in Policy Evaluation: The Case of the New Deal Land Reform Experiments," *Public Policy* 27 (Sept. 1979): 131–83.

14. Pauli Murray's participation in the lawsuit to end the all-white, all-male juries in Lowndes County was funded by the American Civil Liberties Union. Pauli Murray, *The Autobiography of a Black Activist, Feminist, Lawyer, Priest, and Poet* (Knoxville: University of Tennessee Press, 1987), 363–64. The Citizen's Defense Fund Commission, prominent African American men and women in Arkansas, raised more money than the NAACP for the defense of the Elaine defendants and were the first to contact the extraordinary Scipio Africanus Jones, who defended them. Richard C. Cortner, *A Mob Intent on Death: The NAACP and the Arkansas Riot Case* (Middletown, Conn.: Wesleyan University Press, 1988), 50.

15. For the most complete discussion of this court case see Richard Kluger, *Simple Justice: The History of Brown v. Board of Education and Black America's Struggle for Equality* (New York: Alfred A. Knopf, 1976). For connections of this case to events recounted here, see note 41 in Chapter 7.

16. Brian Lanker, *I Dreamed a World: Portraits of Black Women Who Changed America* (New York: Stewart, Tabori, and Chang, 1989).

17. For a brief account of the Gooden lynching, see Jessie Daniel Ames, *The Changing Nature of Lynching: Review of Lynching 1931–41* (Atlanta: Council on Interracial Cooperation, 1942), 48.

18. Myrdal, *An American Dilemma*, 483.

19. Du Bois in ibid., 512.

20. Alrutheus A. Taylor, *The Negro in Tennessee, 1865–1880* (Washington, D.C.: Associated Publishers, 1947), 73. Martin Abbott, *The Freedmen's Bureau in South Carolina: 1865–1872* (Chapel Hill: University of North Carolina Press, 1967), 134.

21. This report is part of congressional testimony about Albert Turner, former head of the SCLC in Alabama, a close associate of Martin Luther King, Jr., and head of the Civic League in Perry County, and others who faced 142 charges of tampering with absentee ballots. John Hulett was also under investigation, although never charged with the same crime. There is much that is uncertain about the charges and the investigation. What is certain is that the number of African American absentee voters increased dramatically in Perry County and elsewhere in the black belt. It is also certain that this increase contributed to the election of African American candidates. From 1966 to 1976 African Ameri-

can absentee votes for African American candidates in Perry County increased gradually from 0 to 84. In 1976 they jumped to 442, in 1978 to 892, and in 1982 absentee votes for African American candidates reached a record 1,097. In 1982 African American candidates for local and state offices—not federal—drew between 21 and 34 percent of their vote from absentee voters. Hank Sanders, Turner's attorney, in his own race for the Alabama Senate, had 28 percent of his votes from absentee voters, and Turner, in the race for probate judge, had 32 percent of his votes from them.

Turner and Sanders charged that the federal investigation started not because of fraud but because African Americans began winning elections. Previously, they charged, African American candidates would win at the polls only to lose in the count of the absentee ballots. They suggested that the charges and investigation were aimed at reducing African American voter participation and to assist Jeremiah Denton win re-election to the U.S. Senate in 1986. Denton, a white conservative, was the first Republican senator from Alabama since Reconstruction and gained election on the coat-tails of Ronald Reagan in 1980. His election success was crucial to Republicans' maintaining their majority in the Senate. Denton lost to Richard C. Shelby in 1986.

Turner explained that the stakes were high, given Alabama's political tradition. That tradition deferred to representatives and senators with regard to legislation specific to their counties. African American legislators, like Sanders, were moving to change elections in their counties to single-district elections rather than a general vote. This would guarantee that predominately African American districts elected African American representatives and would increase the number of African American elected officials in local government. This in turn could change patterns of taxing and spending. House Committee on the Judiciary, *Civil Rights Implications of Federal Voting Fraud Prosecutions*, Serial 55, Hearing before the Subcommittee on Civil and Constitutional Rights, 99th Cong., 1st sess.; Diane McWhorter, "Celebrity Time Down South," *The Nation* 242 (1, Feb. 1986): 111–14.

22. The algebra of electoral success seems to follow the following equations. If African American voters are less than 25 percent of the electorate, African American candidates have a great deal of trouble winning an election because of the cohesion of white voters against African American candidates or, more precisely, against politics of portions and protest. In elections where African American voters are between 25 and 50 percent of the electorate, most general elections in the South and some urban areas, candidates, white or black, increase their chances of winning if they maintain a cohesive bloc of African American voters 90–95 percent and win 35–40 percent of the white vote. See Earl Black and Merle Black, *Politics and Society in the South* (Cambridge: Harvard University Press, 1987), 140–44. For an account of efforts to achieve new legislative districting that reflects more equitably African American voting strength in Arkansas, see Dan Fleshler, "Making Votes Count in Arkansas—

Challenge to Plantation-Style Politics," *Southern Changes* 12 (August 1990): 14–15. For a cautious assessment that fairer portions of elected offices do not mean new levels of social capital and a politics of preference, see Steve Suitts, "Politics and the Beloved Community: Arkansas Has the Opportunity to Learn from the Experiences of Other Southern States," *Southern Changes* 12 (August 1990): 13–16.

Peyton McCrary, Jerome Gray, Edward Still, and Huey Perry made a particularly cogent and empirical analysis of the changes in the nature of districts and electoral success of African-Americans. "The Impact of the Voting Rights Act in Alabama," paper presented at the annual meeting of the American Political Science Association, Aug. 31, 1989. See also the book review by Huey Perry that offers an assessment of African American political participation in the South. *Journal of Politics* 51 (Nov. 1989): 1012–16.

The model for African American electoral success probably includes voter turnout as well as cohesion among those who do vote. Nevertheless, the point remains that Democratic candidates in the South, white or African American, have more prospect for success by staying no further to the left of their Republican opponents than they have to and as far away from the politics of portions and protest as they can. See Thomas Edsall, "The Democrats Confront a No-Growth Southern Strategy," *Washington Post National Weekly Edition*, July 3, 1989, pp. 13–14, and Susan Anderson, "Eyes on the Prizes, Not the People," *The Nation* 249 (Oct. 16, 1989): 405, 422–25.

Jesse Jackson attempted to nail a plank of protest of run-off primary elections into the Democratic national convention platform in 1984 precisely because of experiences of African American political candidates of victory by plurality and defeat by run-off. Such a measure would give African American voters much more influence and enhance the prospects of African American candidates for electoral success. It was an instance of the politics of protest and portions that factionalized the party, including African American delegates and some state delegations like South Carolina, as the narratives recounted.

For a criticism of single-member districts as the means of acquiring larger numbers of African American elected officials, see Abigail M. Thernstrom, *Whose Votes Count? Affirmative Action and Minority Voting Rights* (Cambridge: Harvard University Press, 1987). Laughlin McDonald wrote a particularly stinging review of the book because it overlooked the history of civil rights. *Southern Changes* 11 (Nov. 1989): 21–23.

23. Our discussion occurred in the summer of 1989 and after several decisions that indicated a majority on the court that favored restrictive interpretations of existing laws and the examination of long-standing precedent that expanded civil rights. Linda Greenhouse, "New Course: A Changed Court Revises Rules on Civil Rights," *New York Times*, June 18, 1989, "The Week in Review Section," p. 1.

24. House Committee, *Civil Rights*, 187.

25. Allen Tullos, "Crackdown in the Black Belt," *Southern Changes* 6 (March–April 1985).

26. Howard Kurtz, "Strike Two for the Justice Department in Ballot-Stuffing Cases," *Washington Post National Weekly Edition*, Sept. 23, 1985, p. 15.

27. McWhorter, "Celebrity Time Down South," 111. Kurtz, "Strike Two," 15.

28. House Committee, *Civil Rights*, 31–32. See also, Jill Zuckman, "HUD Scandal," *Congressional Quarterly Weekly Report* 48 (May 12, 1990): 1481 and Charles H. Moore and Patricia A. Hoban-Moore, "Some Lessons From Reagan's HUD: Housing Policy and Public Service," *PS* 23 (March 1990): 13–18.

29. Ibid., 187.

30. Ruth Marcus, "The Justice Department Renders a Verdict on Ed Meese," *Washington Post National Weekly Edition*, Jan. 23, 1989, p. 31. Howard Kurtz, "Meese Has Met Every One of His Minority Hiring Goals: None," *Washington Post National Weekly Edition*, Dec. 15, 1986, p. 32. For a general treatment of the Reagan administration and civil rights, see Norman C. Amaker, *Civil Rights and the Reagan Administration* (Washington, D.C.: Urban Institute Press, 1988).

31. Neal contrasts his style of paranoia with the forthright protest of a client that he represents. His client, Walter White, sought a promotion in the Soil Conservation Office, a federal agency. His supervisors transferred him to Forrest City and gave him responsibility for programs with African American farmers, a position that took him out of line for promotion. White eventually documented a pattern of racial discrimination in the Soil Conservation Office that included efforts to keep African American farmers off of locally elected boards. His charges set off a major investigation. White was eventually promoted, the Soil Conservation Office promised to improve training and employment opportunities for African Americans, and top officials in the agency were transferred from Arkansas. One month after the investigation concluded and White received his settlement, an arsonist burned his house. A year later local police charged White with the crime. Ward Sinclair, "Walter White Charged Racism; Then an Arsonist Struck," *Washington Post National Weekly Edition*, Nov. 3, 1986, p. 28. For a journalistic account on Neal's efforts and reputation see, Judith M. Gallman, "Olly's Law," *Arkansas Times* 17 (Oct. 1990): 34–37, 75–79.

   Neal and a lawyer associate came under suspicion for involvement with a crack cocaine ring in Detroit that had Lee County connections. Neal cited this suspicion as evidence of the justification for his paranoia and the vulnerability of any prominent, political African American. For an account of the Detroit–Lee County crack ring, see William M. Adler, "Nothing to Lose: How an Arkansas Teenager Became a Self-Made Millionaire—With Hard Work, Savvy and Crack Cocaine," *Southern Exposure* 18 (Winter 1990): 22–27.

Conclusion

1. J. Larry Brown, *Living Hungry in America* (New York: Macmillan, 1987), 38–67. The federal government documented disparities in the health status among American minorities and between them and white Americans. It offered a precise estimate of 58,942 minority deaths due to higher mortality rates among them. The report does not specify measures for rural southern African Americans but documents what was widely believed about the poor health status and its relation to poverty. *Report of the Secretary's Task Force on Black and Minority Health* (Washington, D.C.: U.S. Department of Health and Human Services, 1985). For a study that examines the relation between poverty and the health of African Americans see Mac W. Otten, Jr., Steven M. Teutsch, David F. Williamson, James S. Marks, "The Effect of Known Risk Factors on the Excess Mortality of Black Adults in the United States," *Journal of the American Medical Association* 263 (Feb. 9, 1990): 845–50. For other data on the status of African Americans, see Center on Budget and Policy Priorities, *Still Far from the Dream: Recent Developments in Black Income, Employment and Poverty* (Washington, D.C.: Center on Budget and Policy Priorities, 1988). The report indicates that African American family income in the Midwest is below that of the South. This suggests that the industrial decline in the Midwest has impacted African Americans there severely. This is the area to which most African Americans migrated when the agricultural economy of the South changed and set off a migration to the area. There is evidence of a return migration to the South for economic reasons. The Center's analysis does not distinguish rural from urban areas, however, but it is safe to assume that the economic position of African Americans in urban areas of the South is superior to those in rural areas. See Center on Budget and Policy Priorities, *Laboring for Less: Working but Poor in Rural America* (Washington, D.C.: Center on Budget and Policy Priorities, 1989).

2. Part of the "new" problem of the underclass is the "old" problem of racial discrimination. More particularly, part of the new problem of the underclass is our previous unwillingness and inability to deal adequately with earlier problems of inequality and injustice. Sharecropping for this underclass was as much an economic subordination as the unemployment of the inner city for the new underclass. The rural southern underclass migrated to urban areas. From Haywood, Lee, and Lowndes counties, for example, the African American population decreased by 25,000 from 1940 to 1970. This decline was part of the massive migration of African Americans from the rural South that took place during these years. Nicholas Lemann looks to the rural South directly for an origin of the urban underclass, "The Origins of the Underclass," *Atlantic* 257 (June 1986): 31–61; (July 1986): 54–68. William Julius Wilson points to the effects of historic discrimination that incorporates sharecropping rather than sharecropping itself

as the shaping influence of the African American underclass, *The Truly Disad-vantaged: The Inner City, the Underclass and Public Policy* (Chicago: University of Chicago Press, 1987), 55, 141.

3. Gunnar Myrdal, *An American Dilemma: The Negro Problem and Modern Democracy* (New York: Harper & Brothers, 1944), xliii. Bellah and his colleagues, like Myrdal, comment on the efforts that Americans make to preserve an ideology of individual effort despite the glaring contradiction of racial inequality. Bellah and his colleagues explain the assertions of the efficacy of individual effort as a white majority defense *of* American beliefs. Robert N. Bellah, Richard Madsen, William M. Sullivan, Ann Swidler, and Steven M. Tipton, *Habits of the Heart: Individualism and Commitment in American Life* (Berkeley, Calif.: University of California Press, 1985), 206. But Myrdal explains racial prejudice as a defense of the white majority *from* American beliefs. Myrdal, *An American Dilemma*, 89. The point remains that the enduring inequality of African Americans presents a profound problem for the nation. It violates the dominant sense of upward mobility between borderless socioeconomic positions through which people may pass on the basis of their merit and individual effort.

4. Center on Budget and Policy Priorities, *Rich-Poor Income Gap Hits 40-Year High as Poverty Rate Stalls* (Washington, D.C.: Center on Budget and Policy Priorities, 1990), 2. This new degree of inequality has sparked conservative concern. See Kevin Phillips, *The Politics of Rich and Poor: Wealth and the American Electorate in the Reagan Aftermath* (New York: Random House, 1990). The pattern for more than a century has been that when the economy declines, the economic position of African Americans plummets. The most recent experience suggests that an economic recovery based on high unemployment and deficit defense spending is not a tide that lifts all boats. It leaves the boats of African Americans moored to unemployment, low-wage work, and poverty. There is certainly progress from a century ago. But recent policies and their consequences suggest that as a nation we can acquiesce to the enduring and increased poverty of African Americans just as we did as a nation a century ago. For example, there is evidence that incarceration is a current policy to deal with the large number of African American unemployed men. For example, The Sentencing Project recently reported that 1 in every 4 African American men between 20 and 29 years is under the control of the criminal justice system. *Young Black Men and the Criminal Justice System: A Growing National Problem* (Washington, D.C.: The Sentencing Project, 1990).

The severe economic disadvantage of many African Americans is evident in the economic recovery of the Reagan years. Unemployment among black men and women remains two to three times the rate of whites. Unemployment ranged from a high of almost 20 percent in 1983 to a low of 12 percent in 1988. This latter figure is the lowest rate of unemployment for blacks in two decades, but it is not entirely good news. Wages for black workers are lower, after adjusting for inflation, than during the 1970s and are a smaller portion of the wages of whites. In 1987 the median income for black families was $18,098, or 56 percent of the family income of whites. This is the lowest ratio since the mid-1960s. Poverty increased among black people in 1987 by 2 percent, bringing the rate to almost a third of all black people. White poverty rates fell during the same year by 0.5 percent to 10.5 percent. The Reagan years meant a wider gap between rich and poor blacks also. This gap accentuated class differences among African Americans that the civil rights movement had reduced. The top 20 percent of black income earners increased their income on the average by $3,000 while the bottom twenty lost $1,185 in income. Poverty rates among blacks are highest not in the South but in the Midwest, where black people migrated because of the mechanization of agriculture in the South and where deindustrialization has had its most severe impact (*Still Far from the Dream*).

Mydal asserted that in every society women and children are two groups that are suppressed, and drew parallels between their position and that of African Americans; *An American Dilemma*, 1073–78.

5. Linda Greenhouse, "New Course: A Changed Court Revises Rules on Civil Rights," *New York Times*, June 18, 1989, p. 1. Julius S. Chambers, "The Court and the Black Community," *Southern Changes* 11 (Dec. 1989): 8–13.

Epilogue

1. Rexford G. Tugwell, "The Resettlement Idea," *Agricultural History* 33 (Oct. 1959), 159–64, quoted in Sidney Baldwin, *Poverty and Politics: The Rise and Decline of the Farm Security System* (Chapel Hill: The University of North Carolina Press, 1968), 418–19.

Interviews

Boyd, D. Ed., Currie P. Interview by author. Dancyville, Tennessee, December 17, 1987.

Bradley, William (Sam). Interviews by author. Letohatchee, Alabama, April 17, 1984; Hayneville, Alabama, August 9, 1985.

Brady, Pitson. Interviews by author. Marianna, Arkansas, August 2, 1984; July 23, 1985.

Broadway, Mildred. Interviews by author, Marianna, Arkansas, July 31, 1984; July 24, 1985.

Bryant, M.D., Thomas E. Interview by Thomas May. Washington, D.C., May 14, 1975.

Burke, David. Interview by Peter K. New. Place not given, August 12, 1976.

Burnett, E. C. Interview by author. Marianna and Fargo, Arkansas, October 30, 1987.

Bursey, Cleola. Interviews by author. Marianna, Arkansas, July 31, 1984; July 24, 1985.

Campbell, Emory. Interview by author. Frogmore, South Carolina, May 22, 1987.

Cannon, Jr., M.D., Jessie. Interview by author. Stanton, Tennessee, March 14, 1978.

Cannon, Sr., Jessie. Interviews by author. Stanton, Tennessee, March 13, 1978; December 18, 1987.

Carney, Jean. Interviews by author. Stanton, Tennessee, March 14, 1978; Brownsville, Tennessee, December 18, 1987; Ripley, Tennessee, August 4, 1988.

Clark, Septima. Interview by author. Charleston, South Carolina, July 27, 1984.

Cooper, M.D., Leon. Interview by Thomas May. Place not given, May 12, 1975.

Davis, Casher. Interview by author. Niles, Michigan, September 30, 1987.

Davis, Nann. Interview by author. Niles, Michigan, September 30, 1987.

Dobbins, Eliza. Interviews by author. Marianna, Arkansas, July 31, 1984; July 24, 1985.

Douglas, Betty. Interview by author. Stanton, Tennessee, December 18, 1987.

Egeberg, M.D., Roger O. Interview by Peter K. New. Place not given, June 11, 1977.

English, M.D., Joseph. Interviews by Peter K. New. New York, New York, October 13, 1975; December 15, 1975. Interview by author. Telephone interview, December 3, 1987.

Fields, Frances. Interviews by author, Marianna, Arkansas, July 31, 1984; July 24, 1985.

Frankel, M.D., John. Interview by Thomas May. Place not given, January 23, 1975.

Franklin, Ophie. Interview by author. Johns Island, South Carolina, July 26, 1984.

Geiger, M.D., H. Jack. Interview by Peter K. New. Stoney Brook, New York, June 26, 1974.

Gibson, M.D., Count. Interview by Peter K. New. Stanford, California, March 7, 1974.

Goodwin, Rev. Willis. Interview by author. Johns Island, South Carolina, July 27, 1984.

Gordon, M.D., Jeoffrey. Interview by Thomas May. San Diego, California, January 6, 1976.

Green, Annie. Interviews by author. Marianna, Arkansas, July 31, 1984; July 24, 1985.

Haynes, Uralee A. Interview by author. Hayneville, Arkansas, April 16, 1984.

Hoendel, Ann. Interview by Peter K. New. Place not given, March 4, 1976.

Howe, Maybelle. Interview by author. Charleston, South Carolina, July 27, 1984.

Hrabowski, Annie. Interview by author. Fort Deposit, Alabama, August 10, 1985.

Hulett, John. Interviews by author. Hayneville, Alabama, April 16, 1985; March 2, 1988.

Jenkins, Abraham (Bill). Interview by author. Johns Island, South Carolina, July 26, 1984.

Johnson, Clyde. Interview by author. Telephone interview, June 18, 1988.

Joseph, M.D., Stephen C. Interview by Thomas May and Peter K. New. Place not given, June 17, 1974.

Kelly, Parthenia. Interview by author. Hayneville, Alabama, April 15, 1985.

Kramer, Bernard. Interview by Peter K. New and Thomas May. Place not given, July 2, 1976.

Kravitz, Sanford. Interview by Peter K. New. Place not given, October 9, 1975.

Lingle, Linda. Interview by author. Charleston, South Carolina, July 28, 1984.

McKinley, Rev. Washington. Interview by author. Edisto Island, South Carolina, July 28, 1984.

Mants, Robert. Interview by author. Hayneville, Alabama, April 15, 1985.

Moorer, Mattie Lee Holcombe. Interview by author. Hayneville, Alabama, August 9, 1985.

Morganfield, Alice. Interviews by author. Marianna, Arkansas, July 31, 1984; July 24, 1985.

Morman, Square. Interviews by author. Rossville, Tennessee, July 24, 1985; August 13, 1986. See also, "Sick for Justice," *Southern Exposure* 6 (Summer 1978): 73–76.

Mouton, Lillie. Interviews by author. Marianna, Arkansas, July 31, 1984; July 24, 1985.

Neal, Jr., Olly. Interviews by author. Marianna, Arkansas, July 31, 1984; July 24, 1985; Fargo, Arkansas, October 30, 1987.

New, Gloria. Interviews by author. Marianna, Arkansas, July 31, 1984; July 24, 1985.

Pugliese, Don. Interview by Thomas May and Peter K. New. Place not given, April 11, 1975.

Ramey, Theresa. Interviews by author. Marianna, Arkansas, August 2, 1984; July 23, 1985.

Rice, Earl. Interviews by author. Stanton, Tennessee, March 13, 1978; Brownsville, Tennessee, December 17, 1987; Ripley, Tennessee, August 4, 1988.

Rice, Tom. Interview by author. Stanton, Tennessee, March 13, 1978.

Runyon, William. Interview by author. Charleston, South Carolina, July 27, 1984.

Sanderlin, Tom. Interview by author. Stanton, Tennessee, March 12, 1978.

Sauls, Sara. Interviews by author. Aubrey, Arkansas, August 1, 1984; July 23, 1985.

Saunders, William. Interviews by author. Charleston, South Carolina, July 28, 1984; Johns Island, South Carolina, May 24, 1986.

Scherl, M.D., Donald J. Interview by Thomas May. Place not given, July 1, 1976.

Schorr, Lisbeth Bamberger. Interview by Thomas May. Telephone interviews, October 16, 1975, and November 16, 1977.

Smith, Charles. Interview by author. Hayneville, Alabama, March 3, 1988.

Smith, Mary. Interview by author. Hayneville, Alabama, April 15, 1984.

Trice, Trenton. Interviews by author. Moro, Arkansas, August 1, 1984; July 24, 1985.

Wilson, John. Interview by author. Marianna, Arkansas, July 31, 1984.

Wilson, Steve. Interview by author. Eutaw, Alabama, August 8, 1985.

Zwick, Daniel I. Interview by Thomas May. Place not given, May 13, 1975.